Cortical Visual Impairment

Advanced Principles

Christine Roman-Lantzy, Editor

APHPress

American Printing House for the Blind

Printed in the United States of America.

Library of Congress Cataloging-in-Publication Data

Names: Roman-Lantzy, Christine, 1951– editor.
Title: Cortical visual impairment: advanced principles / Christine Roman-Lantzy, editor.
Description: Louisville, KY : APH Press, American Printing House for the Blind, [2018] | Includes
    bibliographical references and index.
Identifiers: LCCN 2018039467 (print) | LCCN 2018046548 (ebook) | ISBN 9781616480080 (epub) |
    ISBN 9781616480097 (mobi) | ISBN 9781616480103 (pdf) | ISBN 9781616480073 (pbk. : alk. paper)
Subjects: LCSH: Children with visual disabilities—Education. | Children with visual
    disabilities—Rehabilitation. | People with visual disabilities—Education. | People with
    visual disabilities—Rehabilitation.
Classification: LCC HV1626 (ebook) | LCC HV1626 .C655 2018 (print) | DDC 362.4/1—dc23
LC record available at https://lccn.loc.gov/2018039467

www.aph.org

Contents

Foreword   *v*

Acknowledgments   *ix*

About the Contributors   *xi*

Introduction   *1*
  Christine Roman-Lantzy

CHAPTER 1   Phase III Cortical Visual Impairment   *10*
  Christine Roman-Lantzy

CHAPTER 2   A Path to Literacy for Students Who Have CVI   *38*
  Christine Roman-Lantzy

CHAPTER 3   Children with CVI and Complex Communication Needs   *59*
  Sarah Blackstone and Christine Roman-Lantzy

CHAPTER 4   The 'What's the Complexity?' Framework   *93*
  Matthew Tietjen

CHAPTER 5   CVI and the Development of Social Skills   *161*
  Christine Roman-Lantzy

CHAPTER 6   CVI and Orientation and Mobility   *181*
  Alisha Waugh and Christine Roman-Lantzy

CHAPTER 7   CVI and Deafblindness: Considerations for the CVI Range Assessment   *227*
  Tracy Evans Luiselli and Christine Roman-Lantzy

Index   *259*

Foreword

Do the best you can until you know better.
Then when you know better, do better.

—Maya Angelou

During February of 1989, a unique little life entered this world—a baby boy named Jamie.

Jamie had hazel eyes, blond hair, a gentle disposition, and a smile that charmed everyone. He also had a rare neuromuscular disease that interfered with autonomic (or automatic) body functions, so he relied on a ventilator and oxygen for breathing support via a tracheostomy tube in his neck. Additional equipment and routines—such as feeding tubes and central intravenous lines, occupational and speech therapy—were also a part of his daily life.

While many aspects of his hour-to-hour and month-by-month existence were atypical, in many ways Jamie was like any other young child, taking in all sorts of information through different senses and learning about things that matter. By the time he was 18 months old, some of the things that mattered to Jamie included playing hide-and-seek and "boo!" games, reading books and pointing out the ABCs and 123s, watching *Sesame Street*, and eating cookies.

At that time, I (Jeni) was Jamie's very proud mommy. I was also a professional, pursuing master's and doctoral degrees—first in child psychology and then in early childhood special education. As a parent and as a professional, the dreams I was building for my son's future were filled with many hopes.

And at that time, I (Sandy) was more like a sister than a close friend to Jeni, and virtually a family member to her children. I was a single parent raising three children. I, too, was a professional, with a master's degree in early childhood special education and pursuing a doctoral degree in the same field. As a family friend, I was not Jamie's early intervention provider, but I did offer my knowledge and skills to improve his development and to support Jeni in her dreams for her son.

As parents and as professionals, we (Sandy and Jeni) both loved witnessing Jamie defying medical odds and watching his unique personality develop and be expressed as he grew, hour-to-hour and month-by-month. But by the time Jamie was 21 months old, everything that mattered—to Jamie, and to Jamie's family, friends, and providers—suddenly changed. Jamie developed sepsis, a severe blood infection, which resulted in several cardiac arrests. The rounds of CPR and high-tech hospital medicines kept his body from dying each time his heart stopped. But nothing was available to prevent his brain from swelling significantly with each event. Somewhere in the moments of a Saturday night becoming another Sunday morning, Jamie transitioned from an engaging and charismatic toddler who had been dancing through life despite medical complications, into a child with severe brain damage and a devastating prognosis.

As Jamie began to stabilize medically, we began discussing hopes and visions for Jamie's future again, but we were told that all previous dreams for him were no longer reasonable. We were advised to replace purposeful dreams with practical lists of limitations, and to embrace lowered but more realistic expectations. Professionals explained that

vi   Foreword

while Jamie's muscles still worked, he no longer had any purposeful movement because the functional connection between brain and body was gone. He would not walk or talk again. He would not eat or drink again. He would not play hide-and-seek or "boo!" games or enjoy cookies again.

Even worse, professionals also explained that while Jamie's eyes still worked, he no longer had any purposeful vision because the functional connection between the brain and eyes was also gone. The term "cortical blindness" was delivered as a new diagnosis, and it was recommended that we treat him as if he had no vision at all. We were even told that "vision was the least of things that should matter" to us, and that he was no longer capable of "appreciating" his vision.

Back then, both of us already had years of experience both as parents of children with special needs and as professionals in education. We knew how to balance professional input and opinion with parental instinct and preference. But neither of us had heard of cortical blindness before. And neither of us had any way of knowing an important truth: that vision was something that should have, or could have, mattered immensely to Jamie.

We had no way of knowing that a more fitting diagnosis for Jamie would have been cortical visual impairment (CVI). We did not know that CVI was the leading cause of visual impairment for children in the United States and that the visual experiences and intervention needs of this population were typically misunderstood. We had no way of knowing that whether children do or do not have concurrent ocular conditions, in reality, children with CVI have unique visual responses—to people, to the environment, and to a wide array of things that matter. We did not know that there are "phases" of CVI, or that with proper assessment and educational strategies, children *can* learn to use their vision more effectively and progressively resolve some of the common characteristics of this condition.

We did the best we could for Jamie with what we knew at the time, and through insights we gained by chance or with trial and error across time. We accepted that he was defined as a child who was considered blind, but we placed him in front of the television when *Sesame Street* was on, and we still read books to him and described the letters and numbers and colors and connections that were on each page and that were in the room around him. And even though it was clear that he did, indeed, have severe brain damage and would not be fulfilling any of those early-on purposeful dreams for his future, every once in a while (despite being told it was imagination or wishful thinking), it seemed that there was some type of visual response from him, or at least a hint of some visual connection with him.

Nearly two years after the sepsis insult that led to such brain damage and "blindness," it was time for Jamie's one-time-per-year vision services, as designated on his IEP. The teacher of students with visual impairments showed up with a new item—a piece of equipment called a light box. What happened next was a shock to everyone. As she dragged different color strips of luminescent paper across the backlight of the box, Jamie would respond in very clear and consistent ways. He repeatedly winced at the red and yellow strips. But he attended to and laughed out loud at the green and blue strips—again and again and again, until his time with this magical piece of equipment was over.

A few weeks later, during November of 1992, a unique little life left this world. Jamie passed away.

In the 25 years since Jamie died, much has changed. We both completed our doctoral programs in early childhood special education. Jeni specialized in trauma and resilience, family support, and grief and loss resulting from life-threatening conditions or the death of a child. Sandy specialized in vision—specifically, cortical visual impairment, with a dissertation that established statistical reliability for the CVI Range, the assessment tool created by Dr. Christine Roman-Lantzy. This tool can accurately assess functional vision in children with CVI, and it can be the foundation for determining appropriate intervention strategies for children with CVI.

Currently, both of us are faculty associates at the University of Maryland and we both work for Connections Beyond Sight and Sound (CBSS), the Maryland and DC Deaf-Blind Project. Through our work with CBSS we have completed extensive training with Dr. Roman-Lantzy. The knowledge base about CVI continues to grow and improve. We continue to learn more about CVI and about the connection between the eyes and the brain, and learn from the families who have shared their experiences with us. As available information increases, there is a concurrent responsibility for us to continue learning, and to improve our understanding and our skills; in short, to do better.

As we continue working with families and teachers of children with CVI in their homes, schools, and communities, we continue to benefit from new insights and lessons. Sometimes parents or the educational team are highly motivated to learn more and support a child. Sometimes the family or team is less informed and less motivated to learn about CVI. In both situations, though, each child matters and each child deserves our best. It is our professional responsibility to give each child a chance and to support families in building dreams for their children.

Across years of working directly with children with CVI, I (Sandy) have never seen a child with no visual responses, nor a child who does not make progress. For a small number of children, the progress is limited, but it is there. For most children, the progress is amazing. CVI intervention is the link that connects the child to his or her world. Targeted intervention based on solid CVI principles allows the child access to educational programs and communication. Children without speech are able to access symbols that offer choices and provide control in their lives. Children in academic-focused programs learn to read and do math. When children can use vision to get information and make sense of their world, they are excited, their stress decreases, and progress happens. Vision matters, for all children, including children with CVI.

Knowing the things we have both learned within the past quarter century would not have changed the fact that Jamie experienced severe brain damage. Nor would this knowledge have altered the reality that his life would be cut short by medical complications. But understanding CVI, and

being aware of ongoing advancements in assessment and intervention could have, and would have, opened a window of opportunity for Jamie to make more effective use of the vision he *did* have. Perhaps he could have made small choices in his daily routines. Perhaps he could have explored or interacted with his world again. Perhaps he could have simply had more reasons to smile and laugh. We could not have changed the *quantity* of his hours and months in this life, but perhaps we could have positively affected the *quality* of those moments—and that matters.

Our job, as parents and as professionals, is to do our best, to strive for the best, and to expect the best. The definition of *competence* for an educator includes being aware of current advances, knowledge, and research that guides best practice in assessment and intervention. Being a competent professional also necessitates being a lifelong student, always seeking new knowledge and improved understanding, even with familiar issues and with conditions in which we are already well-trained or experienced. And as good professionals, it matters that we set high expectations—for children, for families, for our peers, and for ourselves. We must keep doing the work, staying up-to-date on the newest information about CVI. That is the purpose of this book. We owe it to all our children with CVI to continue learning, and to explore and use the valuable insights and information contained in these pages.

Jennifer Stepanek, PhD
Education and Technical Assistance Specialist
Connections Beyond Sight and Sound
Research Associate, Special Education

Sandra Newcomb, PhD
Technical Assistance and Education Specialist
Connections Beyond Sight and Sound
Senior Faculty Specialist

Department of Counseling, Higher Education,
and Special Education
College of Education
University of Maryland
College Park, Maryland

Acknowledgments

I sincerely thank AFB Press for their support and publication of my materials. I never cease to be surprised by those who contact me from the far corners of the world regarding the publication of my original book, *Cortical Visual Impairment: An Approach to Assessment and Intervention.* Thank you for taking a risk on me and for asking me to document my approach to education for children with CVI. I believe we have made a difference.

I must extend a most sincere thank you to the other authors in this text. It is a dream come true for me to have been able to learn from you and then to synthesize our joint efforts into new approaches that reflect the specialized needs of individuals with CVI. You have enriched my thinking and, indeed, my life. Tracy Evans Luiselli, you and I have forged a path for children with complex needs and CVI for so long. You have invited me to provide training since 1999; I have literally seen your children grow up across the span of time we have been working together in New England. You are the embodiment of what it means to be dedicated to children with complex needs. Even when other professionals balked at you for continually including CVI as a training priority, you were undaunted. Matthew Tietjen, your work in CVI is a product of Tracy Evans Luiselli's CVI Leadership project, and boy have you embraced it. You are a leader. You have broadened my original work into some new and very important concepts. I am honored to have your work in this text. You, my friend, are a rare and wonderful gift to our field and I know we will all watch you continue to move the effort forward in the future. Sarah Blackstone has been a guru in the field of AAC for a long time. Hers is a name that I use when I want to show off about the important people I know. But much more than that, Sarah, you are one of the most generous, child-centered people I have met. You are an intelligent, innovative, and elegant woman. What a privilege to have your critical contributions in *Cortical Visual Impairment: Advanced Principles.* Alisha Waugh, thank you for your work on the O&M chapter. You provide such a unique perspective drawn from your backgrounds as a physical therapist, an O&M specialist, and most importantly, as a mother of a child with CVI. I have had the honor of working with your son and now professionally collaborating with you. It is not a coincidence, of course. Once your son was identified as having CVI, you launched into your quest to immerse yourself in CVI like you were preparing for the "CVI Olympics." Thank you for using your knowledge with families and providers that reaches far beyond the boundaries of your own life.

I would also like to acknowledge the families of children with CVI who have continually asked the questions that obligate me to try harder and dig deeper. I am profoundly in awe of all of you, who have enriched my life beyond words. And though I never thought I'd live long enough to witness it, you have found your collective voice and I believe the most lasting advocacy changes are on the horizon. You are my true north.

As always, I thank my family for being my inspiration. When I encounter a family who has a child with CVI, an uncontrollable thought always occurs to me. I imagine for just a moment what it would be like to be in the shoes of those parents who are so vulnerable in their need to depend on sound advice. I picture my own son and daughter in the circumstance of the family before me. And in that moment, I know that my obligation is clear. There is no doubt that what I want for my children, a full and happy life, is no different than the desires of families I have met all over the world.

And of course, thank you Alan Lantzy for being my champion. Everything I do professionally wears your imprint. And personally . . . well, that's a love story.

—*Christine Roman-Lantzy*

About the Contributors

Christine Roman-Lantzy, PhD, is Director of the Pediatric VIEW (Vision Information and Evaluation at West Penn Hospital) Program at Western Pennsylvania Hospital in Pittsburgh, and a private consultant for Cortical Visual Impairment (CVI) Resources. A teacher of students with visual impairments, certified orientation and mobility specialist, and infant development specialist, Dr. Roman-Lantzy has worked extensively in public schools and neonatal ICUs and NICU follow-up programs, where she collaborated with families, therapists, and physicians. She is the recipient of the 2008 C. Warren Bledsoe Award from the Association for Education and Rehabilitation of the Blind and Visually Impaired for the first edition of *Cortical Visual Impairment: An Approach to Assessment and Intervention,* the first textbook to describe an educational methodology for evaluating the functional vision of students with CVI and offer a framework for intervention. Dr. Roman-Lantzy is also coauthor of the second edition of the *Preschool Orientation and Mobility Screening* and has contributed journal articles and book chapters on orientation and mobility, children with multiple disabilities, and visual assessment for infants and has presented lectures and workshops on CVI and consulted with organizations and educational teams across the United States and around the world. Together with the Perkins School for the Blind, she launched the Perkins-Roman CVI Range Endorsement, providing an opportunity for professionals to demonstrate expertise in the CVI Range framework. Since first working with children with CVI in the mid-1970s, Dr. Roman-Lantzy has assessed thousands of children with CVI and other visual impairments in a variety of settings and continues to be devoted to supporting families affected by CVI.

Matthew Tietjen, MEd, is a certified teacher of students with visual impairments and an education consultant for the Bureau of Education and Services for the Blind (BESB) in Connecticut (Department of Rehabilitation Services). After completing his master of education in the University of Massachusetts Boston's Vision Studies program, Matt began an intensive period of training with Dr. Christine Roman-Lantzy, culminating in his completion of the two-year CVI Leadership Institute (New England Consortium of Deafblind Projects) and a Perkins-Roman CVI Endorsement. As a member of BESB's Special Services unit, Matt has been fortunate to specialize in CVI and is passionate about supporting children with CVI and their families. Matt currently serves as chair of Connecticut's CVI Committee, a group of colleagues who are dedicated to CVI advocacy and professional development at the state and national level. Matt presents nationally on CVI and is a proud member of the Pediatric Cortical Visual Impairment Society (PCVI). Matt spent several years developing the 'What's the Complexity?' Framework and is grateful for the encouragement and support of so many mentors, colleagues, and family members, including: Christine Roman-Lantzy; Amanda Lueck, for her valuable feedback on the early drafts; Peg Palmer; Catherine Summ; Yvonne Locke; Mary Johns; Ellen Mazel; Lotfi Merabet; Mary Zatta; Robin Sitten; Mary-Anne Roberto; Margie, Gary, Katie, Liam, and Sean Tietjen; his colleagues at BESB; and his students and their families—from whom he has learned so much.

Sarah W. Blackstone, PhD, CCC-SLP, is past president and fellow of the International Society for Augmentative and Alternative Communication (ISAAC) and a founder and current board member of USSAAC (US Chapter). She currently serves on the Advisory Council for the National Institute of Deafness and Other Communication Disorders at the National Institutes of Health and is on the Board of Directors of The Bridge School, Central Coast Children's Foundation, and the Community Emergency Response Volunteers of the Monterey Peninsula. Her employment history includes Augmentative Communication Inc., where she wrote and published *Augmentative Communication News* and *Alternatively Speaking*; project director, the Rehabilitation Engineering Research Center (RERC) on Communication Enhancement; chief, Speech-Language Pathology, Kennedy Institute/Johns Hopkins Department of Rehabilitation Medicine; project director, American Speech-Language Hearing Association; and AAC team facilitator, Berkeley Unified School District. Her publications include *Social Networks: A Communication Inventory for Individuals with Complex Communication Needs and their Communication Partners* (2012); *Patient Provider Communication Roles for Speech-Language Pathologists and Other Health Care Professionals* (2015), and multiple chapters and peer-reviewed articles. Blackstone's current professional interests include addressing the needs of children with cortical visual impairment who require AAC, developing the emotional competencies in children who rely on AAC, and ensuring the needs of people with disabilities are not forgotten before, during, or after natural or man-made disasters.

Tracy Evans Luiselli, MEd, PhD, project director for the New England Consortium for Deafblind Technical Assistance (NEC), has extensive experience in providing professional development for service providers working with children who are deafblind. Along with her foundational knowledge and clinical experience in the fields of deafblindness, visual impairment, and severe disabilities, she has over twenty years of experience in the development and implementation of innovative training models in the areas of cortical vision impairment and deafblindness. Along with training service providers across the New England region, Dr. Evans Luiselli is keenly aware of the challenges facing families of children with cortical vision impairment and additional disabilities. Having worked with many families in supporting their learning and understanding of their child's complex needs, she has a core belief that "parents are their child's best teacher," and that they must have the knowledge and skills necessary for effective advocacy and for making informed decisions about their child's learning and sensory needs.

Alisha Waugh is a certified orientation and nobility specialist, physical therapist, Perkins-Roman CVI Range endorsed specialist, and parent of a son with CVI, in Phase III. She is president of Fundamentals First, a company that provides itinerant O&M and PT services to early intervention and school-age students, as well as CVI-specialized consultation for families, schools and providers. She started www.whattodoaboutcvi.com to be an online resource and support for families and providers. Founder of the CVI Academy, a not-for-profit organization, her mission is to promote academic and social success for students with CVI by providing resources and access to appropriate educational supports that meet their unique visual needs so they may acquire the greatest level of independence possible. She and her husband, Cullen, serve on the board and are active in the Pediatric Cortical Visual Impairment Society. They live in Wadsworth, Ohio, with their three children, Behlen, Griffen, and Jocelyn.

Introduction

Christine Roman-Lantzy

Cortical Visual Impairment: An Approach to Assessment and Intervention, published in 2007, provided information about the principles and methods used to evaluate functional vision and to design instructional supports for individuals who have cortical visual impairment (CVI). The centerpiece of that 2007 text was the CVI Range, an assessment tool used to determine the degree of effect of CVI, measured on a continuum from 0 to 10. The scores obtained on the CVI Range are used to guide the design of the interventions and adaptations. These interventions provide visual access to materials and environments in learning settings for children from infancy through the span of their school career.

Since the publication of that earlier book, it has become clear that there is a demand for content that is beyond the scope of the original text. This realization has resulted in two actions: the revision of the original book and the development of a second, more in-depth text.

The second edition of *Cortical Visual Impairment: An Approach to Assessment and Intervention,* published in 2018, is an updated and expanded version of the original, intended to provide the author's current thinking and fine-tuned concepts throughout the chapters. The current volume, *Cortical Visual Impairment: Advanced Principles,* is based on the premise that the reader has previous experience with the basic content found in the earlier book. The content goes beyond the fundamentals and dives more deeply into topics that are extensions of the original concepts, reflecting the author's additional learning since the publication of the earlier, foundational work.

The intent of this book is to use multiple perspectives to provide a more in-depth look at CVI from a variety of points of view. The work of educating individuals with CVI is not solely the responsibility of the teacher of students with visual impairments but is the mandate of an entire community. For this reason, this text includes the input of skilled members of the diverse educational community.

In This Book

Each of the chapters in this book is written to show how educational and other professionals, as well as parents, can provide support for the broader needs of individuals with CVI, beyond improvement of vision, in areas such as literacy, communication, education, social development, and independent travel. Individuals with CVI also constitute a diverse population, so chapters address those with additional needs, such as complex communication challenges or deafblindness. Christine Roman-Lantzy is an author or coauthor of all the chapters, except Chapter 4, dealing with the complexity of learning environments for students with CVI; Matthew Tietjen is its sole author.

Chapter 1, "Phase III Cortical Visual Impairment," contains information that was not addressed in depth in the earlier publication. Frankly, when the original text was published, the author had had few encounters with professionals or parents whose children scored above 7 out of 10 on the CVI Range. After that book was released, however, and as more people became aware of the specialized approaches to functional vision assessment and to the subsequent interventions, more and more children were identified as being in Phase III. The Phase III chapter in *Advanced Principles* addresses the essential elements of teaching children in this final phase of CVI whose needs may appear subtle but who require consistent specialized support and instruction.

Chapter 2, "A Path to Literacy for Students Who Have CVI," discusses the impact of the CVI characteristics on the fundamentals of reading and other forms of literacy. It describes a means of developing literacy for the unique population of children with CVI by specifically addressing the CVI characteristics. The groundwork for literacy begins in Phase II and becomes more refined in Phase III, so there is some overlap between this chapter and Chapter 1, especially in addressing the concepts of *salient features* of objects and images and *comparative thought.*

Educational teams often rely on the teacher of students with visual impairments to adapt materials or provide consultation for access to resources outside their specialty of vision. For example, it is common for speech therapists to ask teachers of students with visual impairments to help select materials for children with complex communica-

tion needs. When it comes to children with more complex communication needs, however, it is important to have the expertise of other professionals. Chapter 3, "Children with CVI and Complex Communication Needs," is coauthored by Sarah Blackstone, a leader in the field of augmentative and alternative communication who has developed a special interest in the needs of students with CVI, and Christine Roman-Lantzy. It offers some solutions to familiar questions such as, "How do we select a communication device for a child with CVI?" and "Is this student with CVI able to use the same communication symbols we use with other students?" This chapter demonstrates how professionals can leave their communication and vision "silos" to integrate, rather than compartmentalize, professional knowledge.

Chapter 4, "The 'What's the Complexity?' Framework," was written by Matthew Tietjen, a teacher of students with visual impairments who has developed a method for considering key factors that are crucial for students with CVI to be able to perform and sustain visual tasks associated with the classroom. The approach includes analysis of the student's CVI Range score, the complexity of the environment, and the visual demands of the task. The goal is to achieve balance in these three elements so that the child can use functional vision across the span of the learning day. Matthew Tietjen also includes an inventory of two-dimensional images as an additional resource for educators.

"CVI and the Development of Social Skills" is addressed in Chapter 5. The impact of the CVI characteristics results in unique barriers to social skill development in individuals with CVI. This chapter describes the obstacles to developing social skills that are associated with CVI and provides suggestions to support increased opportunities for successful social encounters.

Chapter 6 addresses the specialized aspects of orientation and mobility (O&M) for individuals with CVI. "CVI and Orientation and Mobility" is coauthored by Alisha Waugh and Christine Roman-Lantzy. Alisha Waugh brings several areas of expertise to the chapter as both an O&M specialist and a pediatric physical therapist, as well as being the parent of a child who has CVI. This chapter combines content from the essential principles of O&M used with individuals who have ocular forms of visual impairment together with the adaptations necessary for those who have CVI. The adaptations center on the characteristics of CVI, as measured by the CVI Range scores, and the potential impact they have on a child's ability to become oriented in space and to move safely and efficiently. The chapter provides detailed guidelines for addressing each CVI characteristic in each phase of CVI during O&M instruction, as well as numerous specific examples.

The final chapter in *Advanced Principles,* "CVI and Deafblindness: Considerations for the CVI Range Assessment," examines the identification and assessment of individuals who have CVI plus hearing loss and qualify as deafblind due to their dual sensory impairments. Tracy Evans Luiselli is the coauthor of this chapter, along with Christine Roman-Lantzy. Tracy Evans Luiselli has extensive experience in deafblindness as the director of the New England Consortium for Deafblind Technical Assistance and Training for over 17 years. Because the causes of CVI overlap with many of the causes of hearing impairment, the incidence of CVI is significant in the population of individuals identified as deafblind. This chapter focuses on considerations and strategies for addressing the distinct needs of this challenging population as well as administering the CVI Range.

Terminology and a Brief Overview

As already noted, *Advanced Principles* is an extension of the foundational book, *Cortical Visual Impairment: An Approach to Assessment and Intervention,* and, therefore, it does not include an extensive review of the materials covered in the original text. However, definitions of some of the main terms and concepts that are explained in the earlier work are provided here as a review and quick reference for the reader. A more in-depth explanation of each of these terms can be found in the full text.

- **The CVI Range**: A functional vision assessment based on the visual and behavioral traits associated with CVI. The CVI Range is used to determine the degree of effect of CVI on a 0 to 10 continuum: a score of 0 represents little to no functional vision, and a score of 10 represents functional vision that is typical of individuals of the same age. Data is collected from parent interviews, observations of the individual, and direct assessment methods. A copy of the CVI Range is included at the end of this Introduction for readers' convenience.

- **Phases of CVI**: The CVI Range 0 to 10 scale is further divided into three broad phases. Phase I represents a CVI Range score of 0–3, Phase II is a score from above 3 up to 7, and Phase III is defined by a score from above 7 up to 10. Each phase has a distinct set of associated visual and behavioral responses and an overarching goal. The goals for each phase are:
  - *Phase I:* To facilitate and build increasingly stable visual responses.
  - *Phase II:* To facilitate the use of vision in meaningful, functional routines or activities.
  - *Phase III:* To refine the use of functional vision, primarily centered on the use of ventral stream vision.

- **Dorsal stream**: Commonly known as the "where" system of visual processing that governs visual attention to movement, light, form, and color. (This term is explained in more detail in Chapter 1.)

- **Ventral stream**: Commonly known as the "what" system of visual processing that governs visual attention and interpretation of detail. (This term is explained in more detail in Chapter 1.)

- **CVI characteristics**: Ten visual and behavioral traits that are used to describe the functional vision of individuals with CVI. These characteristics include: color preference, need for movement, visual latency, visual field preferences, difficulties with visual complexity, need for light, difficulty with distance viewing, atypical visual reflexes, difficulty with visual novelty, and absence of visually directed reach. The impact of the characteristics is assessed using the CVI Range, and interventions or accommodations are implemented based on the assessed level of 9 of the 10 characteristics (visual reflex differences are not used for intervention purposes).

- **The CVI Progress Chart**: A form used to monitor progress in functional vision after completion of the CVI Range assessment. The CVI Progress Chart is also used to integrate the confounding variables of ocular impairment and CVI when both exist.

- **CVI Schedule**: A form used to design CVI accommodations across natural daily routines.

It is also important to note that a variety of terms are used throughout this book to describe the professional who takes a lead role in supporting students with CVI. Although it is critical that all students with CVI have a teacher of students with visual impairments, it is not always the case that this teacher has the greatest expertise in support-ing the student's specialized needs. Professionals from many disciplines attend workshops or instructional sessions that the author conducts. Expertise in CVI is further substantiated by the types of applicants in the Perkins-Roman CVI Range Endorsement offered by the Perkins School for the Blind, through which professionals can demonstrate their ability to support individuals with CVI in a highly skilled way. Individuals with this endorsement come from the fields of speech-language therapy, physical therapy, occupational therapy, education, and special education, as well as from orientation and mobility and teaching students with visual impairments. Therefore, terminology used to describe the professional who provides CVI services will include CVI instructor, CVI provider, CVI educator, clinician, orientation and mobility specialist, and teacher of students with visual impairments.

Health and Education Crisis

At the Perkins School for the Blind CVI Symposium in April 2017, Dr. Lotfi Merabet referred to CVI as a public health crisis, and it is likely an educational crisis as well. For many, however, CVI continues to be a confusing diagnosis, and there are students who are receiving inadequate support from initial diagnosis all the way through to educational programming. It is hoped that the material in this book will provide parents, educators, therapists, and even medical providers with perspectives that provide solutions to some of the misunderstanding and confusion surround CVI and that ultimately, individuals with CVI can achieve their potential.

The CVI Range

Christine Roman-Lantzy

Student/child's name: _____   Age/Birthdate: _____

Evaluator(s): _____   Evaluation date: _____

This assessment protocol is intended for multiple evaluations over a period of time:

a. Initial assessment (red)

b. Second assessment (blue)

c. Third assessment (green)

Further assessments will require a new form.

Totals	Evaluation #1 (red)	Evaluation #2 (blue)	Evaluation #3 (green)
1. Score for Rating I			
2. Score for Rating II			

No functional vision

Typical or near-typical visual functioning

0	1	2	3	4	5	6	7	8	9	10

Phase I	Phase II	Phase III
Primarily dorsal stream visual function	Dorsal and beginning ventral stream visual function	Refinement of ventral stream visual function

The CVI Range: Across–CVI Characteristics Assessment Method
Rating I

Rate the following statements as related to the student/child's visual behaviors by marking the appropriate column to indicate the methods used to support the scores:

O = Information obtained through observation of the student/child

I = Information obtained through interview regarding the student/child

D = Information obtained through direct contact with the student/child

In the remaining columns, rate each statement with one of the following descriptors:

R   Represents a visual behavior that is resolving or approaching typical behavior

+   Describes current functioning of student/child

+/− Partially describes the student/child; emerging

−   Does not apply to student/child

(continued on next page)

(continued)

CVI Range 1–2: Student functions with minimal visual response

O	I	D	R	+	+/–	–	
							May localize, but no appropriate fixations on objects or faces
							Consistently attentive to lights or perhaps ceiling fans
							Prolonged periods of latency in visual tasks
							Responds only in strictly controlled environments
							Objects viewed are a single color
							Objects viewed have movement and/or shiny or reflective properties
							Visually attends in near space only
							No blink in response to touch or visual threat
							No regard of the human face

CVI Range 3–4: Student functions with more consistent visual response

O	I	D	R	+	+/–	–	
							Visually fixates when the environment is controlled
							Less attracted to lights; can be redirected
							Latency slightly decreases after periods of consistent viewing
							May look at novel objects if they share characteristics of familiar objects
							Blinks in response to touch and/or visual threat, but the responses may be latent and/or inconsistent
							Has a "favorite" color
							Shows strong visual field preferences
							May notice moving objects at 2 to 3 feet
							Look and touch completed as separate events

CVI Range 5–6: Student uses vision for functional tasks

O	I	D	R	+	+/−	−	
							Objects viewed may have two to three colors
							Light is no longer a distractor
							Latency present only when the student is tired, stressed, or overstimulated
							Movement continues to be an important factor for visual attention
							Student tolerates low levels of background noise
							Blink response to touch is consistently present
							Blink response to visual threat is intermittently present
							Visual attention now extends beyond near space, up to 4 to 6 feet
							May regard familiar faces when voices do not compete

CVI Range 7–8: Student demonstrates visual curiosity

O	I	D	R	+	+/−	−	
							Selection of toys or objects is less restricted; requires one to two sessions of "warm-up"
							Competing auditory stimuli tolerated during periods of viewing; the student may now maintain visual attention on objects that produce music
							Blink response to visual threat consistently present
							Latency rarely present
							Visual attention extends to 10 feet with targets that produce movement
							Movement not required for attention at near distance
							Smiles at/regards familiar and new faces
							May enjoy regarding self in mirror
							Most high-contrast colors and/or familiar patterns regarded and interpreted
							Simple books, picture cards, or symbols regarded and interpreted

(continued on next page)

(continued)

CVI Range 9–10: Student spontaneously uses vision for most functional activities at a level approaching near typical

O	I	D	R	+	+/−	−	
							Selection of toys or objects not restricted to the familiar; visually curious in new settings
							Only the most complex environments affect visual response
							Latency never present
							No color or pattern preferences
							Visual attention and interpretation of the environment extends beyond 20 feet
							Views and interprets information from non-backlit two-dimensional materials and simple images
							Uses vision to imitate actions
							Demonstrates memory of visual events
							Displays typical visual-social responses
							Visual fields unrestricted
							Look and reach completed as a single action
							Views and interprets information from non-backlit two-dimensional images presented on complex, visually dense backgrounds

The CVI Range: Within–CVI Characteristics Assessment Method

Determine the level of CVI present in the 10 categories below and add to obtain total score. Rate the following CVI categories as related to the student/child's visual behaviors by circling the appropriate number (the CVI Progress Chart may be useful as a scoring guide):

0 Full effect of the characteristic is present

.25 Behavior on this characteristic has begun to change or improve

.5 The characteristic is affecting visual functioning approximately half the time

.75 Occasional effect of the characteristic; response is nearly like that of individuals the same age

1 Resolving, approaching typical, or response is the same as others of the same age

1. **Color preference** Comments:	0	.25	.5	.75	1
2. **Need for movement** Comments:	0	.25	.5	.75	1
3. **Visual latency** Comments:	0	.25	.5	.75	1
4. **Visual field preferences** Comments:	0	.25	.5	.75	1
5. **Difficulties with visual complexity** Comments:	0	.25	.5	.75	1
6. **Need for light** Comments:	0	.25	.5	.75	1
7. **Difficulty with distance viewing** Comments:	0	.25	.5	.75	1
8. **Atypical visual reflexes** Comments:	0	.25	.5	.75	1
9. **Difficulty with visual novelty** Comments:	0	.25	.5	.75	1
10. **Absence of visually guided reach** Comments:	0	.25	.5	.75	1

CHAPTER

1

Phase III Cortical Visual Impairment

Christine Roman-Lantzy

Author's Note

I have had the opportunity to provide hundreds of instructional sessions devoted to the CVI Range assessment and program planning for students who have cortical visual impairment (CVI). From these opportunities, I have learned a great deal that has refined my work and helped me make it more accessible to others. One observation is that professionals attain skills in conducting the CVI Range, interpreting the results, and planning interventions in a distinct order. Skills are most readily acquired first in Phase I, followed by Phase II, and the skills that pertain to both assessment and intervention for Phase III CVI are reported to be the most difficult to master. At first, I did not understand this problem. However, I eventually realized that the pattern of systematic understanding and skills that flow from Phase I to Phase III mirror my own learning curve.

Cortical visual impairment (CVI) is a condition in which vision is likely to improve over time, especially when trained educators work with students to facilitate improvement in their functional vision. Typically, students will progress through three stages of CVI, as represented by their scores on the CVI Range (see the Introduction) and the ongoing improvement of their behavior on the CVI characteristics (as summarized in the Introduction). CVI Range scores that are above 7 place a student in Phase III. Students who have reached Phase III have gained considerable visual functioning but are still affected by the behavioral characteristics of CVI, and intervention with these students is aimed at the refinement of their behavior on these characteristics.

The considerations associated with Phase III CVI are distinct from those in other phases of CVI. Professionals who work with individuals in Phase III often report being particularly challenged by their specialized needs. Teachers of students with visual impairments and other professionals who use the CVI Range tend to demonstrate competence in assessment and program planning in a particular order; that is, it is easiest to understand and implement the needs of individuals who are in Phase I, more complex for those in Phase II, and most challenging with students in Phase III. Understanding Phase III CVI can be difficult. It can also be easy to misunderstand the behavior of individuals in Phase III. Some of the challenges to understanding individuals in Phase III are explained in Sidebar 1.1.

Challenges to Understandings Individuals in Phase III CVI

The following are some of the reasons why CVI educators find working with individuals in Phase III CVI particularly challenging and why these individuals' behavior is often misinterpreted:

- *The individual with CVI does not "look visually impaired."* Certain behaviors displayed in the earlier stages of CVI, such as attraction to light, latency, inability to visually discriminate the human face, difficulty with distance viewing, and difficulty with novelty, may all have improved or become nearly typical by Phase III. This is not to suggest that the individual has resolved these CVI characteristics; rather, that the behaviors have become less obvious, especially compared to the same behaviors on these CVI characteristics demonstrated in Phase I or early Phase II.

- *The individual with CVI likely uses vision for functional tasks throughout the day, and therefore seems visually efficient.* The individual with CVI may be able to interpret two-dimensional materials and environments if the materials are familiar, presented on a backlit surface, or have few internal details. But it is critical to recognize that just because an individual is looking toward a target, it cannot be assumed that he or she is discriminating aspects of the image or understanding what is being seen. One of the major goals in Phase III CVI is to help mediate the individual's understanding and generalization of salient visual features and to help him or her mentally store this information across visual or cognitive schemes; in other words, to help support the development and interpretation of concepts.

- *The individual with CVI avoids obstacles and never gets disoriented in school or home.* It is important to acknowledge that dorsal stream vision (described later in this chapter), the type of vision involved in guiding actions and recognizing where objects are in space, has been operational for individuals with CVI since Phase I. Moving around obstacles, attraction to light, and attention to large environmental forms are well embedded skills by Phase III. Thus, individuals with CVI who are in Phase III may move freely throughout familiar spaces, rarely, if ever, colliding with unintended targets. They may give the appearance of being able to navigate a familiar environment in ways that suggest precise awareness of the visual features of the setting.

   In fact, many educators and parents of individuals with CVI have discovered that these individuals actually have little knowledge of the specific elements of the environment. Rather, they are using a combination of memory and dorsal stream attention to move through the space. This becomes most evident when the same individual with CVI is taken to an unfamiliar or complex environment. Parents and educators report that the individual behaves very differently, often clinging to the adult or demonstrating reluctance or refusal to participate. Individuals in Phase III CVI frequently continue to have visual field issues, especially in the lower visual field (Roman-Lantzy & Lantzy, 2002–2017). The individual's ability to become oriented in a novel or complex environment is a critical concern. Inability to benefit from incidental learning at distances beyond 10 feet can severely reduce the individual's competence outside of highly familiar environments.

   These types of misunderstandings of individuals' behavior in Phase III CVI also lead to misinterpretations of the services they need and what they're capable of, such as the following misconceptions:

- *Now that the student is in Phase III CVI, contact hours with the student and the classroom staff can be reduced or eliminated.* Given the unique needs of a student in Phase III CVI, the CVI Range results, and the findings of the educational team's assessment, the teacher of students with visual impairments or other CVI instructor will need to continue assuming a lead role in coaching

(continued on next page)

the student's educational or home team. In fact, due to the need for CVI Phase III supports to be put in place across the span of the student's day, it is likely that the teacher of students with visual impairment or other CVI instructor will be required to be a consultant, a collaborator, and a direct instructor on behalf of the student with Phase III CVI. A teacher of students with visual impairments, orientation and mobility (O&M) specialist, or other instructor trained in CVI will be expected to consider adaptations across all areas of the curriculum for most students with CVI. That does not mean the CVI instructor will necessarily be the instructor having the greatest contact with a student. Implementation of a CVI schedule (discussed at the end of this chapter) will help create a blueprint of how and where during the day the CVI adaptations are applied to the student's curriculum.

There may in fact be a direct relationship between the CVI phase and the degree of support needed from the CVI specialist, because students in Phase III CVI require the greatest degree of adaptation and specialized instruction throughout the day, as compared to a lesser degree of support in Phases I and II. This is not to suggest that students with CVI in the earlier phases have fewer needs, but rather that the variety and breadth of the adaptations are more narrowly focused.

■ *It isn't possible for students with multiple and complex needs to achieve Phase III.* Progress across the CVI Range into Phase III is not restricted to a particular group of students. The spectrum of students who score in Phase III on the CVI Range include those who will perform academically at age or grade level as well as those who may utilize their visual abilities to participate in a functional or life-skills curriculum. Expected improvements in visual function cannot be associated with a specific level of cognitive function. In addition, it is important to avoid making assumptions about students' cognitive function when they have experienced a substantial lack of access to visual information. Such deprivation has a profound impact on cognition and learning. Many parents and educators have been both surprised and impressed by the abilities a student with CVI demonstrates once he or she has an opportunity to visually access and interpret the visual world.

For professionals, working with individuals in Phase III CVI is different, more challenging, and involves more aspects of the individual's entire day than in the other phases. However, the basic principles used for Phases I and II continue to hold true, and the key is to remain focused on the descriptions of the CVI characteristics in both assessment and instruction. Practitioners will hopefully find the changes in the children and students they work with to be powerful motivators and gratifying rewards.

This chapter will first provide an overview of Phase III CVI and describe how each of the CVI characteristics is manifested in Phase III. Then, the key elements of instruction during Phase

III, including salient visual features, comparative thought, and mediated learning, will be defined and illustrated.

Overview of Phase III CVI

Phase III represents the highest degree of improvement of the CVI characteristics and the greatest degree of functional vision. CVI Range scores that are above 7 place an individual into Phase III.

To best understand the three phases of CVI, it is necessary to briefly describe the two-stream model of visual processing. In a now widely accepted theory, Goodale and Milner (1992) posited that two separate systems of visual processing operate in the brain to recognize and respond to different types of information at both the unconscious and conscious levels. The so-called *dorsal stream* of visual processing automatically directs human attention to the presence of light, form, and movement. This system is sometimes called the "where" system, because it is involved in guiding actions and recognizing where objects are in space. The *ventral stream*, commonly known as the "what" system of visual processing, occurs with conscious awareness and is associated with attention to details that include visual identification and recognition.

Based on extensive clinical experience and data collected from over 400 individuals with CVI (Roman-Lantzy & Lantzy, 2002–2017), it is this author's belief that individuals with CVI have improvements in functional vision that progress from a primary reliance on dorsal stream vision found in Phase I and early Phase II to improvements in ventral stream function more commonly found in mid–Phase II through Phase III.

In Phase III, the individual with CVI generally has very useful, perhaps even normal, dorsal stream, or "where," visual function. However, Phase III CVI is marked by the individual's continued need to refine ventral stream vision. Ventral stream vision, or the "what" system, is associated with the development of the ability to discriminate details, the ability to interpret complex arrays, the ability to discriminate the features of human faces, and the ability to identify a detail at distance.

Individuals in Phase III CVI have attained significant levels of functional vision, but it is critical to recognize that they are still affected by an underdeveloped ventral visual stream. Although improvements in visual functioning are expected to occur across the span of the CVI Range, in Phase III the progress may slow, and even though an individual's functional vision has significantly improved, aspects of the characteristics of CVI remain active even well into Phase III. CVI is a condition that affects the functional vision of an individual for life. The concept of a cure or complete resolution of CVI is generally unfounded.

Typically, individuals who are in Phase III CVI continue to demonstrate the behaviors associated with the CVI visual and behavioral characteristics, but some are not readily identified as having a visual impairment, as noted at the beginning of this chapter. If, for example, an individual in Phase III is generally able to move without unintended contact with objects in the environment and is able to use more visually complex communication materials—or perhaps even read—some professionals may fail to recognize the remaining aspects of the challenges in Phase III. These challenges can include

- inability to visually discriminate, recognize, or identify novel materials or environments;
- inability to detect targets at distances beyond 10–15 feet away;
- visual field differences, especially lower field function;
- inability to discriminate facial features;
- occasional latency;
- need for detailed targets to be paired with light;
- need for color to be used to highlight materials or environments; and
- inability to use a visually directed reach when targets are presented against a complex array.

The difficulties associated with the CVI characteristics in Phase III can potentially affect the individual in activities such as learning, social competence, safety, and self-esteem, as discussed in chapters throughout this book. It is critical to continue to use the CVI Range in Phase III to measure and monitor the degree to which the characteristics are affecting an individual's behavior and to create adaptations and interventions to address his or her needs. Sidebar 1.2 can be used as a quick reference for the behaviors associated with the 10 CVI characteristics that can be expected in Phase III. CVI characteristics in Phase III are discussed in more detail later in this chapter.

Typical Behaviors of CVI Characteristics in Phase III

The following constitute typical behaviors of CVI characteristics for an individual who scored .75 on the CVI Range, Rating II:

Color preference

- Color highlighting of materials or environment is occasionally necessary.

Need for movement

- Movement is occasionally necessary to elicit visual attention.

- Unintended movement at distances up to 20 feet away may be distracting.

Visual latency

- Latency occurs rarely but may be more sustained if the individual with CVI is fatigued or stressed.

Visual field preferences

- Lower visual field function may be atypical.

Difficulties with visual complexity

Complexity of patterns on the surface of objects

- Visual fixations (and object recognition or identification) can take place on objects or images that have four or more colors or patterns on the surface.

- Two-dimensional images without backlighting are now accessible.

Complexity of visual array

- Visual fixations occur on three-dimensional targets against highly patterned backgrounds.

- Two-dimensional target images are detected against a background of up to 20 additional elements.

Complexity of the sensory environment

- Visual attention or the ability to locate a single target may be compromised when the individual is in a novel setting with multiple, competing sensory inputs.

Complexity of human faces

- Eye-to-eye contact is possible with most people.

- Less attention may be given to the faces of new or unfamiliar people.

- Typical responses are displayed to the individual's mirror image.

Need for light

- Attention on primary sources of light occurs only when the individual is tired, stressed, overstimulated, or ill.

- Backlighting supports visual discrimination, recognition, or identification of two-dimensional materials (a single image or an array of images).

Difficulty with distance viewing

- The individual visually locates and fixates on a specific target in a familiar or novel setting at distances up to 10 feet.

- Visual attention on large moving targets at distances as great as 15–20 feet may be demonstrated.

SIDEBAR **1.2** *(continued)*

Atypical visual reflexes

- Blink-to-touch reflex at the bridge of the nose is consistently present.

- Blink response to visual threat reflex is still intermittent or latent.

Difficulty with visual novelty

- New objects or images are visually discriminated, recognized, or identified based on salient, defining features.

- Visual curiosity is displayed in most new environments.

Absence of visually guided reach (visual motor response)

- Look and reach occur as a single action more than 75 percent of the time.

- Look, look away, reach response occurs primarily when materials are highly novel or highly complex.

Progressing to Phase III CVI

Children with CVI generally begin their visual habilitation (if they have congenital CVI) or rehabilitation (for acquired CVI) through use of their dorsal stream of vision. Phase I CVI, a CVI Range score of 0–3, is associated with use of dorsal stream vision. In other words, individuals in Phase I visually attend to movement, light, or form—low acuity vision associated with the "where" or dorsal stream of visual processing. The individual in Phase I CVI does not look directly at a target, but rather, turns in the direction of the movement, light, or form. Parents often describe this as "looking through," rather than at, the target. The individual perceives the presence of the object but is unable to access its internal details or salient visual features.

In Phase II CVI, the individual scores from above 3 up to 7 on the CVI Range. In early Phase II, the individual with CVI demonstrates a fixation response that is observable as eye-to-object contact. Eye-to-object fixation is associated with the ability to access the ventral stream. Ventral stream vision provides access to internal details and complex arrays and allows for the recognition and identification of patterns (Milner & Goodale, 2006, 2008). Ventral stream vision is the "acuity" part of visual processing. In Phase II CVI, the individual can now not only recognize the presence of a target, but also can begin to recognize what the target is.

In Phase III CVI, the individual scores above 7 on the CVI Range, up to, but never reaching, a score of 10, or typical vision. The goal of instruction in Phase III is to continue the refinement of ventral stream functional vision. This process is associated with the ability to discriminate, recognize, and identify objects and images with greater degrees of complexity. The ongoing development of functional vision from Phase I through Phase III is not associated simply with the passage of time or the increasing age of the child. Rather, improvements to vision occur through the use of the eyes paired with meaningful, rewarding activities that occur throughout the day (Roman-Lantzy & Lantzy, 2010). If keeping the eyes open and random exposure to the environment were the criteria for progression in functional vision, children with CVI would resolve their visual impairment without intervention. But this is not the case. It appears as though a facilitated, intentional approach is necessary for improvements that enable a child to progress to Phase III (Roman-Lantzy & Lantzy, 2002–2017).

It is important to understand that increases in functional vision for a child with Phase III CVI need to be linked to opportunities that help the child learn. In other words, CVI instruction is not a therapy or a set of exercises. Rather, it is an intentional approach to help the child with CVI make meaning of what he or she sees. Increases in scores on the CVI Range are hollow without the increased use of functional vision being intertwined with increased knowledge of the surrounding world. Thus, instruction includes activities designed to help the child access information that supports cognition, language, and overall learning.

For example, if an individual can visually discriminate the differences among photographs of familiar objects, it may be possible for the same individual to discriminate the details that differentiate an array of images in order to be able to use a communication device. Or, if an individual who can sort a variety of three-dimensional animal figures into matching categories (e.g., "find all the dogs"), he or she may be able to use that ability to discriminate the differences between letters or words that are visually similar. It is critical for educators to recognize that the true potential of an individual's ability to learn is only revealed over time as the individual gains access to the visual details that support understanding of materials, environments, and people in his or her world.

The increasing levels of functional vision as measured by the CVI Range are not just numbers on a line. They are meant to provide guidelines for intervention in a precise way. If the CVI instructor is highly intentional and links the improvements to a greater understanding of information and the world at large, it is possible to discover the true cognitive abilities of the individual. Instruction, then, can be a win-win proposition, in which the ability to use increasingly refined vision correlates with increasingly refined learning.

Figures 1.1 and 1.2 provide a representation of the interconnected relationship of the CVI characteristics in Phase III. It is important to consider the characteristics as having a synergistic effect on one another rather than as individual elements to be addressed one by one. Each characteristic has a continuous impact on the other characteristics and, thus, on the individual's functioning. Of course, this is true for all phases of CVI, but the effects can be somewhat obscured in an individual who appears to function as a visual learner.

CVI Characteristics in Phase III

This section provides more in-depth explanations of the effects of the CVI characteristics during Phase III, with particular emphasis on the CVI characteristic of visual complexity.

Color

By Phase III, the individual with CVI no longer demonstrates a preference for a single, specific color. However, the use of vibrant, highly saturated, or intense color can be an important support for students with CVI who are in Phase III. Color is used to help initiate and increase attention to particular elements used in two-dimensional materials and in the three-dimensional world. Color outlining and highlighting of salient visual features is a common application of color in Phase III. Color can be used to tightly outline the shape of a number, word, symbol, or communication icon to facilitate attention to the defining elements of the image (as discussed in more detail later in this chapter). O&M specialists can incorporate the use of color with environmental features into lessons to improve orientation in space.

Movement

Individuals in Phase III may occasionally still need movement to increase attention to a target, especially if the target has internal details or is novel. Movement may be employed as a "reorganizer" or "reset" when individuals with CVI seem unable to locate or attend to a target, as described in the following example:

Jasper, a 6-year-old boy with CVI, is in a regular education class and receives daily support from a teacher of students with visual impairments, Mr. Gonzales. Mr. Gonzales generally works directly with Jasper during mathematics lessons, which are a challenge for Jasper. He seems less attentive during math as compared to other subjects. Mr. Gonzales adapts much of Jasper's

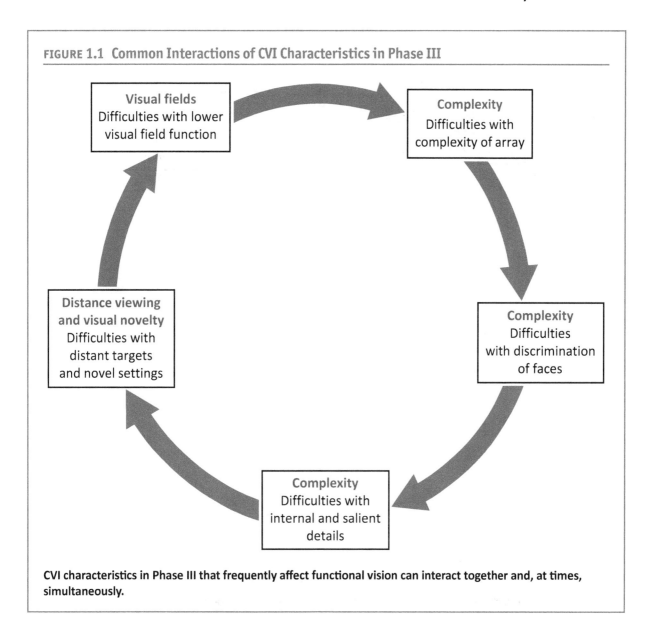

FIGURE 1.1 Common Interactions of CVI Characteristics in Phase III

Visual fields
Difficulties with lower
visual field function

Complexity
Difficulties with
complexity of array

Complexity
Difficulties
with discrimination
of faces

Complexity
Difficulties with
internal and salient
details

**Distance viewing
and visual novelty**
Difficulties with
distant targets
and novel settings

CVI characteristics in Phase III that frequently affect functional vision can interact together and, at times, simultaneously.

math materials by adding color highlighting on the addition or subtraction symbols, elevating the work surface, using color manipulatives on a light box, and reducing the number of math problems on each page.

In today's "mental math" lesson, Jasper is asked to look at a simple addition problem placed on a light box and to provide the sum verbally. After responding to four problems, Jasper begins to look out at the classroom and no longer looks at the visual display on the light box. Mr. Gonzales begins to rhythmically move the strip of paper containing the math problem, without prompting Jasper verbally. After a few seconds, Jasper visually reengages with the math problem.

In this example, the teacher of students with visual impairments intentionally uses movement to help redirect Jasper's visual attention to the lesson. Some software or applications available for use with computers or tablet devices can be used as an effective method to incorporate movement into instruction. For example, some individuals with CVI

FIGURE 1.2 Subtle Interactions of CVI Characteristics in Phase III

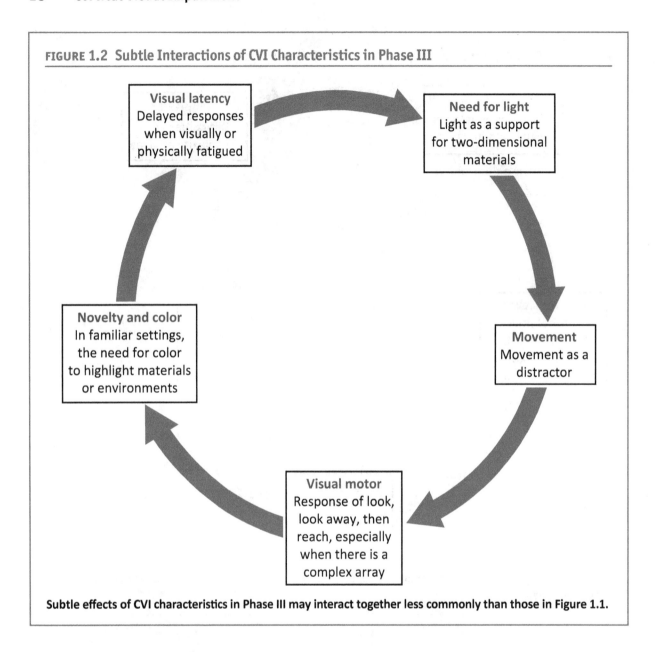

Subtle effects of CVI characteristics in Phase III may interact together less commonly than those in Figure 1.1.

may be proficient with electronic games, even though material presented in a static format, such as two-dimensional illustrations, is much more challenging.

Movement can be a support in Phase III CVI, but in some circumstances, it can also be a distraction. Individuals with CVI who are in Phase III may be unable to suppress their need to visually attend to unintended sources of movement. The individual may be overly attracted, almost captivated, by the movement of people, traffic, images on a video display, a flag, classroom decorations, or the branches

of a tree outside a window. Unlike individuals in Phases I and II, the individual in Phase III is now able to use increased distance viewing abilities to attend to targets at distances beyond 10 feet; therefore, actions that were once ignored may now be perceived. The moving elements of the setting may become more of a visual "compulsion" than the stationary elements. The following scenario illustrates a common impact of movement on learning:

Gracie is a 5-year-old with CVI and expressive language difficulties. She is learning to use a communication device that has a 20-picture display on a backlit system. Gracie's speech therapist reports that Gracie is demonstrating significant gains in the use of her device while working one-on-one in the speech therapist's office. However, Gracie rarely attempts to express her wants or needs using the device while in the classroom.

Gracie sits in the middle section of her special education classroom. There are eight additional students and between three and five adults present throughout the day. The classroom activity is constantly changing as the individual students and adults engage in therapeutic and educational activities. Gracie has been described as distractible and more interested in the people in class than in the materials used for instruction.

It can be helpful to position students with CVI such as Gracie with their back to the areas of greatest random movement in the classroom. Awareness of the effects of movement on some individuals with Phase III CVI may help explain the seemingly inconsistent visual responses that are sometimes observed.

Latency

Visual latency in CVI is a delay in response between the time a target is presented and the time when the individual initiates visual attention. Latency is readily recognizable in individuals who are in Phase I and early Phase II CVI. In Phase III, visual latency occurs less frequently and the periods of latency are often of shorter duration. Latency is most frequently associated with the individual being physically or visually fatigued, hungry, or stressed. Visual latency is likely to increase after a seizure. Since not all adults who work with students at school will be able to recognize visual latency, teachers and therapists need to consult about latency with those who best know the individual with CVI. It is also important to consider patterns or activities that contribute to visual latency in order to provide additional supports, visual breaks,

or additional time to complete a response or to change the routine. It is possible that increases in visual latency can also be associated with other changes in behavior. Parents and educators have reported that when a child with CVI is particularly visually stressed, they noted increased periods of visual latency along with off-task or even disruptive behavior.

Visual Fields

In a seminal article that described the critical differences between ocular and cortical forms of visual impairment, Jan and Groenveld (1993) wrote that visual field defects are almost always present in individuals who have CVI. As a result of these differences in Phases I and II CVI, visual attention is possible only in very limited portions of the visual field. In Phase III, however, these distinct field preferences may have improved, with broader use of the right, left, and superior fields. If preferences remain, the student may turn his or her head or reposition materials to better align the target to a preferred field of view.

It is common for individuals in Phase III CVI to perform best when materials are positioned off midline, especially if the student has strabismus or an eye-teaming difficulty. But the greatest peripheral field of difficulty by far is the inferior, or lower visual field. The data collected by the Pediatric VIEW Program at Western Pennsylvania Hospital from 2010 to 2016 indicates that 85 percent of the over 400 individuals with CVI seen there (Roman-Lantzy & Lantzy, 2002–2017) have atypical responses to materials and environmental features occurring in their extreme lower field of view. Because of the safety issues related to lower field dysfunction, O&M specialists are critical members of the educational team for individuals with CVI. (See Chapter 6 for an in-depth discussion of CVI and O&M.) Use of a mobility cane should be considered for individuals with CVI who move independently but have lower field difficulties.

Light

Individuals in Phase III CVI do not demonstrate light-gazing tendencies. However, they may continue to have an atypical relationship with light. Some individuals with CVI may fail to close their eyes defensively when a bright light is presented at eye level. Others in Phase III may show more subtle responses associated with the CVI characteristic of need for light. It is common for those in Phase III to demonstrate a preference for materials that are paired with light or that have backlit features. For example, individuals in Phase III who may be able to slowly read a paragraph of print on paper will generally be able to read more fluently and from a more typical distance when the passage is presented on a backlit tablet device or a computer screen.

The following example is typical of the response to light of individuals in Phase III:

Will is an 8-year-old boy who is in Phase III CVI. He has been receiving speech and language services since he was in early intervention and continues to use the same laminated paper communication symbols he started with as a preschooler. Will has made slow progress, and the speech therapist believes he is primarily making communication choices randomly or perhaps by color cues. Will's speech therapist asked Will's teacher whether Will is perhaps too cognitively affected to use the communication system designed for him. Will's teacher of students with visual impairments noted his sustained attention on activities using a backlit tablet and suggested that the same communication images be integrated into a program on the tablet. Will tripled recognition of the images within eight weeks after this approach was tried and was even able to visually discriminate images that were visually similar.

The accompanying photo depicts a boy who is in Phase III CVI. He is working on a highly detailed task presented on a computer screen. If this same task was presented on paper without backlighting, he would likely be unable to complete the activity independently. It is also important to note the adaptations in his workspace. The use of a simple background—with the desk covered in black ma-

Christine Roman-Lantzy

A boy in Phase III CVI benefits from the backlit display of a computer screen as well as the visually non-complex background in his workspace.

terial and a black screen behind the computer—as well as an option for task lighting are used to reduce visual fatigue and to support potential difficulties with visual complexity. Note too, the boy's head tilt and the position of the computer screen away from the boy's midline, as discussed in the section on visual fields.

Distance Viewing

The CVI characteristic of difficulty with distance viewing is closely associated with another CVI characteristic, difficulties with visual complexity—in particular, complexity of array. The further away a target is, the more likely it is to blend into the surrounding background visual information. Conversely, objects viewed at near fill more of the viewing display compared to the same targets viewed at greater distances. This is illustrated in the accompanying photographs of a yellow water bottle placed on a bookshelf. In the first image, showing the bottle as seen from a distance of approximately 8–10 inches from the viewer's face, the array contains the bottle and almost no additional objects. In the next image, the same yellow water bottle is viewed from a distance of 3 feet and is seen in an array of 9 additional objects. In the final image, the yellow water bottle is viewed from 5 feet away, and it is embedded in a much more complex array of approximately 60 additional objects.

Christine Roman-Lantzy

A yellow water bottle viewed from a distance of 8–10 inches, 3 feet, and 5 feet shows how the visual complexity of the array containing the bottle increases with distance.

Thus, for individuals with CVI who have a distinct difficulty with complexity of array, even familiar objects may be lost when they are positioned outside the range of their distance-viewing ability. This phenomenon may also help explain how individuals with CVI can have a normal visual exam or 20/20 visual acuity and still not be able to locate targets beyond a specific distance. (The CVI characteristic of difficulties with visual complexity is discussed in more detail later in this section.)

In Phase III CVI, the ability to locate a target at a consistent distance can extend from 10 feet to beyond 20 feet. It is critical to define distance viewing in a specific manner, namely, the greatest distance at which the individual can *always* locate a target across environments. Parents and educators may report that the individual with CVI sees targets that are hundreds of feet away without difficulty, but it is imperative to dig deeper into this response. The following questions can elicit factors that contribute to reports of an individual's occasional ability to see a target at a distance that is atypical for him or her:

- Is the distant target highly familiar, such as a family member or a favorite tablet?

- It the distant target lighted, such as a restaurant sign or computer screen?

- Is the distant target brightly colored, such as a traffic sign or exit sign?

- Is the distant target visually simple, such as a single-color ball or store logo?

- Does the distant target have movement, such as a flag, a balloon, or images on a television?

Like all the CVI characteristics, difficulty with distance viewing improves—along with the CVI Range scores—as individuals move into Phase III, but they often remain a challenge.

Visual Reflexes

Two reflexes are monitored as part of the CVI Range: the visual blink reflex, or blink to touch at the bridge of the nose, and the visual threat reflex, in which an individual blinks when a hand is moved quickly toward the face. These responses are often atypical in earlier stages of CVI, but in Phase III, the blink-to-touch reflex is almost always present and the visual threat reflex is either present, present with latency, or intermittently present. These reflex responses are assessed and monitored and are part of the CVI Range protocol but are not used for intervention or program-planning purposes.

Novelty

Imagine that someone presents you with a disassembled 500-piece puzzle but does not show you the picture of the completed puzzle on the cover of the box. You can *see* all the fragments, but you cannot join the individual pieces of information into a cohesive whole. Now imagine that there is a puzzle made from an image of a favorite object—an Elmo doll, for example. You have a much better chance of being able to see the target as a whole figure due to the deeply embedded image of Elmo

stored in your memory. You may notice Elmo's definitive red color and parts of his black-and-white "googly" eyes. In the first scenario, the array is not only complex, it is novel. In the second scenario, the salient and familiar features of Elmo helped guide you to a conclusion. This brief example helps to explain some of the challenges faced by individuals with CVI who are in Phase III. They may appear to prefer sameness over novel objects, experiences, and environments because of the effect of the CVI characteristic of difficulty with visual novelty.

In Phases I and II, children with CVI may demonstrate a counterintuitive response to novel objects, materials, and environments. Unlike their peers without CVI, they may show little interest in new or novel targets, preferring to attend to targets with which they are familiar. By Phase III, the individual with CVI may engage with novel materials and even demonstrate visual curiosity in new settings. However, the CVI characteristic of difficulty with visual novelty continues to interfere with functional vision. Those in Phase III CVI may have difficulty recognizing unfamiliar forms of targets they have learned to recognize. Many individuals are unable to generalize visual information of a familiar target to a novel or unfamiliar one. For example, a child with CVI may be able to consistently point to a picture of a dog in a familiar storybook but be unable to locate the image of a dog in an unfamiliar picture. Or, an individual who uses a picture display on a communication device may be able to activate a button with an image of a spoon that signifies EAT but be unable to identify a spoon next to a bowl at the lunch table. It is common for individuals in Phase III CVI to be unable to sort through a bin of animal figures to locate the visually varied versions of a particular animal. The difficulty lies in the likelihood that the individual has not visually identified or learned the key salient visual features of the particular target items—the distinct visual features that distinguish objects, images, environments, and people from one another. Salient features will be more fully explained in the context of the CVI characteristic of difficulties with visual complexity.

Difficulty with visual novelty also affects the ability of the individual in Phase III to safely become oriented in new environments. Even though improved distance viewing provides greater access to the elements of the new setting, the individual may not know how to isolate the key elements or interpret them if they are not identical to the features of familiar settings. This difficulty can be confusing to adults who may assume that the individual with CVI who appears oriented in familiar environments is able to generalize the information appropriately to new settings.

Visual Motor Response

In Phase III, the absence of visually guided reach has partially resolved, and the individual with CVI is often able to look and reach as a single, integrated action when the background or array is simple, when the work surface is paired with light, or when the target has movement properties. However, the classic CVI visual motor response of look, look away, and reach continues to be present when materials are highly novel, densely arranged, or when the sensory environment contains multiple, competing sources of input. Visual or physical fatigue can also contribute to the presence of the CVI characteristic of visual motor response.

Visual Complexity

The CVI characteristic of difficulties with visual complexity is one of the most prominent characteristics affecting the individual in Phase III. The ability to process visual complexity is associated with the development and refinement of ventral stream vision. Ventral stream vision processes details of images in the brain and enables an individual to develop visual acuity. Examples of ventral stream visual function include the ability to discriminate faces and details in pictures and to identify embedded details at a distance. In Phase III CVI, the characteristic of difficulties with visual complexity can be categorized into two important components: (1) the ability to discriminate targets from arrays that increase in background complexity, and (2) the ability to identify salient visual fea-

tures. (Salient features are discussed later in this chapter.)

Visual arrays that increase in background complexity are challenging for individuals with CVI when the target images or objects are crowded and have little open space between them. Crowded arrays may be perceived as a kaleidoscope of meaningless color and pattern from which no single target image emerges. Complex arrays that typically challenge individuals in Phase III CVI might include the symbol display on a communication device, maps or charts, illustrations in books, and crowded indoor and outdoor environments.

The following scenario provides an example of behavior associated with complexity of array:

Joaquin was diagnosed with CVI in infancy. He is now 10 years old, and his CVI Range scores are 7–7.5. Joaquin attends public school and participates in both regular education and special education programming. Joaquin uses his power wheelchair to move independently throughout the school building and rarely misses a turn to get to a classroom or the school office. Joaquin almost never bumps into another student. He appears to be happy in his indoor school environment. However, Joaquin generally asks to stay inside during recess and becomes highly anxious on days when the entire school gathers in the auditorium for an assembly. Joaquin asks to stay home from school on days when his class ventures off on field trip excursions. When Joaquin does go outdoors during recess, he generally stays close to an adult or remains stationary near the entrance of the play yard.

Joaquin's reluctance to participate in certain activities may be associated with difficulties related to complexity of the background array. It is common for individuals in Phase III CVI to become overwhelmed in environments that have visually complex, visually crowded surroundings. Environments that contain visually confusing arrays and moving or novel targets can result in individuals with CVI feeling unable to establish visual landmarks

Christine Roman-Lantzy

Environmental features in complex arrays can be taught by isolating an object from the background in a two-dimensional image (left). However, they must also be taught in the natural environment (right).

that orient them to their setting. Students with CVI may demonstrate reluctance or even fear when asked to function in visually and sensorially complex settings.

Complexity of array can impact learning in specific ways. Two-dimensional materials that have numerous, closely aligned details are frequently a challenge to individuals who are in Phase III CVI. Unfamiliar illustrations, photographs, charts, maps, or other densely configured details on a page may be perceived as an array of color and pattern from which no individual target or detail can be isolated or identified. Just as in a hidden pictures puzzle, backgrounds that are too complex seem to create a kind of camouflage of meaningless imagery. It is critical to assess the individual's ability to discriminate, recognize, and identify targets presented in complex arrays in both two-dimensional materials and in the three-dimensional environment.

Educational materials must be adapted for students with CVI to adjust the degree of complexity of array. Typoscopes (cards with a window cut out in them), line markers, or other simple methods for controlling the background on printed materials are readily available or can be easily constructed. It is critical to recognize the individual's threshold for

complexity and to modify materials accordingly. Adults may misinterpret the behavior of an individual in Phase III CVI who is able to find a target image in a familiar picture or scene but fails to locate it when presented with novel materials. Some individuals with CVI are very skilled at memorizing the visual arrangement of a page or display. They may be oriented to the correct image by its color or basic shape, or even by its location. This is an important factor to remember for instruction and further rationale for regular reevaluation using the CVI Range.

The following scenario demonstrates the difficulty that may be associated with increased complexity of array of a visual display.

Francesca, a 7-year-old who was diagnosed with CVI after a childhood head injury, uses an augmentative communication device that has 12 images on a backlit display. She uses the device to make simple requests, although she is frequently prompted to do so by an adult. Francesca is consistently successful when asked if she wants her favorite snack, cheese puffs. The image on the display is a single-colored, orange, elongated shape that represents a cheese puff, positioned in the lower right-hand corner of the 3 × 4–inch display. When Francesca touches the icon, the voice output makes the request for a cheese puff.

Francesca's speech therapist recently added four additional icons to the display. Now there is another orange image to the left of the cheese puff image. There is also a new three-color symbol above the cheese puff symbol. Francesca's recent success rate in correctly locating any of the symbols in the lower-right quadrant of the device has fallen from 90 percent to 30 percent. Instructors have also noticed that Francesca's behavior has changed since the new icons have been introduced: She has become avoidant with regard to her communication device and occasionally bites her own hand.

Part of a Phase III CVI Range assessment includes a thorough evaluation of the degree of complexity of an array. It is critical to determine the number of elements that can be included in a visual array for a student and then provide adaptations or supports accordingly.

Sometimes practitioners can become confused by the fact that a student with CVI may be looking toward or even directly at a complex array, but is unable to distinguish a particular target. It is critical to recognize that not all looking behavior can be equated with understanding or interpreting what is seen. In fact, it is vital for education professionals to carefully determine whether a student's visual attention is accompanied by the ability to discriminate, recognize, and identify what the student with CVI is looking at. For example, a person who reads only English may be exposed to a page of Arabic symbols, but being able to interpret what the symbols mean is an entirely different thing. The person can gaze intently at the page of novel symbols for an extended period of time but fail to gather any meaning from the experience. This is similar to what happens to Andrew:

Andrew's parents enjoy taking the family to the local zoo. Andrew, who is 8 years old, has been to the zoo every year since he was 3. Most of the animals are in natural habitat environments that have rock formations, trees, ponds, or other features that are typical of the species. Andrew's parents believe that Andrew's visual attention is nearly equal to that of his siblings. Andrew looks toward each display intently and gets excited when his siblings vocalize the sound made by each animal. However, when asked about the experience, Andrew is unable to answer any questions about the animals except the sounds they make.

Andrew's experience reminds us that although individuals with CVI may direct their visual attention toward a target, they may not be able to isolate individual elements from the background viewing array.

Some adults with congenital CVI have described the visual world as a kaleidoscope of meaningless color and pattern where no individual element can be isolated or understood. Images that can be interpreted are those that are previously learned and have been understood and committed to memory. How, then, can the mystery of novel visual information be solved? Individuals with CVI need explicit instruction to learn how to interpret visual information. Three important strategies to use in Phase III CVI are making use of salient visual features, comparative thought, and mediated learning.

Interventions for Phase III CVI

Accessing and Interpreting Salient Features

One key to interpreting new images or information lies in the ability to learn the defining or salient visual features. Salient visual features are distinct visual elements that provide a framework for discrimination, recognition, and identification of a visual target. These abilities can be defined as follows:

- **Visual discrimination:** The ability to visually differentiate one target from another; this ability is also the essence of the ability to develop comparative thought.

- **Visual recognition:** The ability to visually recognize a target when a language label is provided.
- **Visual identification:** The ability to look at a target, retrieve the key visual elements, match it to a stored visual scheme (a mental representation of a visual image, object, or environment), and then produce the label or name of the object or symbol.

(A general description of salient features will be provided in this chapter, and salient features will be revisited as applied to literacy in Chapter 2, along with these visual skills and their development.)

Instruction in identification of salient features requires analysis of visual details and can facilitate increased use of ventral stream vision, while also providing a cognitive framework for comparative thought (discussed later in this chapter) and the expansion of visual schemes.

Opportunities for Accessing Information

Individuals with congenital CVI are exposed to visual stimuli, but are unable to benefit from information from the visual world without adaptations that help isolate and provide meaning to what they see. In other words, their visual representations or schemes reflect only the information they can access—things that are a particular color, are familiar, that may be paired with movement and light, and that are offered without additional sensory input. Accessible visual targets are initially limited to items that are within arms' reach and that are presented against a simple background. Clearly, these requirements significantly reduce the quantity and quality of information that represents the visual world. The diminished bank of visual information that these individuals understand and remember is reduced to a tiny fraction of the visual information that is gathered and understood by typically developing children. The visual schemes,

or mental representations of the world, of a child with CVI are reduced to a set of familiar, nearby objects, and thus the visual representations of the world are likely to be fragmented.

The following scenario illustrates the differences in the opportunities for incidental learning experienced by a child with typical vision compared to one who has CVI:

Roberto and Rebecca are twins who were born at 24 weeks' gestation. Rebecca had a fairly normal neonatal course, but had retinopathy of prematurity that did not progress beyond Stage I. She also developed chronic lung disease and was discharged from the neonatal intensive unit on supplemental oxygen. By the time Rebecca reached her second birthday, however, her medical and developmental status was within expected limits.

Roberto's neonatal experiences were more worrisome. He was identified as having bilateral grade IV intraventricular hemorrhages. He also had posthemorrhagic hydrocephalus and periventricular leukomalacia. By Roberto's second birthday, he was diagnosed with cerebral palsy, expressive language difficulties, and CVI.

The results of assessment by Roberto's early intervention team revealed significant global delays. However, the twins' parents believed that Roberto's assessed skills were not representative of his capacity to learn. It frustrated them when they tried to explain to the assessment team that Roberto produced vocal and behavioral cues that were well understood by family members. They told the team that they knew what each of his vocalizations meant, even though they were not expressed in words. Roberto's parents also reported that their son was more content when he was busy or engaged in a learning task and that they thought some of his verbal and behavioral cues sometimes signified frustration. They further explained that Roberto seemed to understand much of the family conversations; in fact, he and his twin sister seemed to find many of the same family conversations amusing. Roberto's early intervention evaluation team was not able to use this information in its formal evaluation, and Roberto was officially identified as having significant cognitive delays.

On a family outing to the beach that occurred the week after the evaluation, Roberto and Rebecca's parents noted some significant differences in their children's experiences. While the twins were having lunch, Rebecca was visually scanning the scene. She watched some children down the beach who were playing catch with a multicolored beach ball. Then she was distracted by a flock of seagulls that were moving in unison above the water. Suddenly one bird swooped to the water's surface and plucked a fish from below the surface. Rebecca's mother noticed her daughter's visual attention on the birds and commented, "Rebecca, it looks like the birds are having their lunch, too." Next, Rebecca saw children lined up at an ice cream truck. She pointed to a child carrying ice cream as she walked past their beach umbrella. The twins' father told her, "Yes, I see the children with ice cream. Maybe we can get some later." Throughout these events, Roberto kept his head down, primarily attending to his yellow sippy cup and the food on the dish that was propped in his lap.

Both Rebecca and Roberto were present for the same set of events, but their experiences were vastly different. Rebecca's vision provided her with access to vast and rich information about her environment. Rebecca was able to gather information incidentally about nature, people, food, and social behavior. Some of the information was available within feet of her position, other information occurred at distances beyond 100 feet. In addition, Rebecca's ability to point to an object or event created an opportunity for *joint attention*, in which adults noticed what Rebecca pointed to and then verbally expanded upon the event Rebecca had indicated through her pointing. Joint attention was initiated by a novel or interesting visual stimulus. Roberto's experience was limited to the numerous and competing environmental sounds and to the object in his lap. Roberto was not able to demonstrate visual curiosity by scanning the beach scene, and he was unable to see the children play ball, watch the birds fly, or observe the interactions at the ice cream truck. Unlike his sister, Roberto was not able to indicate a desire to imitate the actions or experiences of others by using joint attention.

Joint attention is the shared focus of two individuals on an object. It is achieved when one individual alerts another to an object by means of eye gazing, pointing, or other verbal or nonverbal indications. An individual looks at the other person, points to an object, and then returns his or her gaze to the other (Akhtar & Gernsbacher, 2007). Scaife and Bruner (1975) described children's ability to follow eye gaze; they found that most 8- to 10-month-olds were able to follow a line of regard, and that all 11- to 14-month-olds did so. Their research showed that it was possible for an adult to bring certain objects in the environment to an infant's attention using eye gaze. Subsequent research (Bruner, Caudill, & Ninio, 1977) demonstrated that joint attention involves two important skills: following eye gaze and identifying intention. Joint attention is important for many aspects of language and learning, including comprehension, word production, and word learning. Instances of joint attention provide children with information about their environment and allow individuals to establish referents from spoken language. Socioemotional development and the ability to take part in normal relationships are also influenced by joint attention abilities (Moore & Dunham, 1995).

According to Scaife and Bruner (1975), joint attention provides an avenue through which even very young children can elicit rich information from their environment. Since infancy, Rebecca has benefitted from a vast array of information available by means of her intact visual system. By contrast, Roberto has been deprived of an equal opportunity to access the same information. As a result of his CVI, Roberto has had fewer and more fragmented visual experiences than his sister. He does not indicate an interest in an object, person, or event by directing his vision to it. Roberto may listen to sounds in his surroundings or reach out toward something within arm's reach, but he often is unable to associate a word or previous experience with the sound or feel of the object. Roberto's ability to recognize an object, person, or event is limited to those that are highly familiar. Novel objects or events slip away as another random, often misinterpreted sensory experience.

It is critical to consider the likelihood that children with CVI have underdeveloped representations of the world. Children like Roberto do not have access to the quantity or quality of visual information necessary for the formation and development of visual schemes. Visual schemes are the mental images that represent a scene, an experience, or a concept and are based on face-to-face or imagined experiences. For example, if a group of adults is asked to describe a lakeside scene, it is likely they will use a number of common descriptors. If you ask the same individuals to draw the lakeside scene, the drawings may all show a body of water, but the additional details will include elements that have been formed from personal points of view. The details that form the scenario or scheme are drawn from an individual's perspective and are reinforced and expanded through increasing numbers of experiences. How do children with CVI form and develop even the simplest visual representations of their world when they are in Phase I or Phase II?

In addition to the impediments to interacting with and learning from their environment that exist for children with CVI, there are a number of potential obstacles to having their cognitive, language, visual, and learning needs recognized by the adults around them. Unlike individuals who have ocular forms of visual impairment, those with CVI may not be readily identified as having a visual impairment, since it is caused by changes in the brain, not in the eyes. The typical appearance of the eyes and probable reports of a normal eye exam are among the reasons that parents and pro-

viders may not immediately identify a child as visually impaired in the traditional sense. In addition, the likelihood of individuals with CVI having additional disabilities places them at risk for having even fewer opportunities to move, discover, and learn from their environment.

The role of the teacher of students with visual impairments or other CVI educator with students in this situation, then, is to identify and provide the content they are missing, its salient features, and the "rules" for identification of information not only in familiar settings but in novel settings as well.

Instruction in Salient Features

Instruction in salient features begins with familiar objects. Essentially, the CVI educator provides two to three visual elements of the target or object that are central to identifying it. The descriptors selected should include key visual features that are always or nearly always true of the object. For example, the salient features of a cat may be that it is an animal that has triangle-shaped ears and whiskers. An elephant may be described as an animal that has a large body, big floppy ears, and a trunk. Salient visual features do not include the function, sound, or feel of a target object or event. "Says meow" is not a salient visual feature of a cat. Salient features for individuals with CVI are the keys that unlock the rules for visual identification alone.

Salient features are initially used to describe the familiar three-dimensional objects presented in Phase I and Phase II, but they can also be used into Phase III with novel materials, objects, symbols, and environments. Table 1.1 presents an example of how the salient features of numerals would be described to a particular student. The numerals are outlined in red, the student's favorite color, to visually highlight their salient features. Comparative language (discussed in the next section) to describe each numeral is also suggested. In the example, the descriptors and comparative language phrase are chosen in accordance with the student's favorite or preferred experiences. (See Chapter 2 for a discussion of using salient features to teach literacy.)

TABLE 1.1

Dictionary of Salient Features of Numerals

Note: Numerals are grouped according to their salient features:

Open Circles = 2, 3, 5   Closed Circles = 0, 6, 8, 9   Lines and Corners = 1, 4, 7

Initially, teach novel numerals whose salient features differ; for example, teach 1 and 8 together at first. Then teach numerals in groupings of salient features, such as 3 and 8.

Numeral	Description of Sample Salient Features	Sample Comparative Language	Grouping by Salient Feature
1	A long line down	Like a vertical drumstick	Lines and Corners
2	▪ Curve at the top ▪ Diagonal line to a . . . ▪ Short horizontal line at the bottom	Like a sideways swan	Open Circles
3	▪ A little curve at top joins . . . ▪ A larger curve at the bottom	Like a sideways heart missing its point	Open Circles
4	▪ A long vertical line down ▪ A short diagonal line from the top of the line to the left ▪ A short horizontal line across so it makes a triangle in it Suggestions for describing the common version of the numeral 4 written with an open top: ▪ Long vertical line down ▪ Short vertical line down on the left parallel to long line stop then starts ▪ Short horizontal line across	Like a triangle flag on a pole Like an upside down chair	Lines and Corners
5	▪ Short horizontal line on top ▪ Short vertical line on the left . . . ▪ To a big curve at the bottom	Like an *S* with two straight lines	Open Circles
6	▪ Diagonal line down ▪ Circle on the bottom	Like a hand holding a ball	Closed Circles
7	▪ A short horizontal line across at the top ▪ A long diagonal line to bottom left	Like a slide	Lines and Corners
8	▪ A circle on top touches . . . ▪ A circle on bottom	Like a snowman	Closed Circles
9	▪ A circle on top ▪ A short diagonal line (middle right to bottom left)	Like an ice cream cone missing a side	Closed Circles
0	An oval	Like an egg	Closed Circles

Source: Based on the concepts of Dr. Christine Roman-Lantzy, in consultation and collaboration with the student's parent, Iriss Shimony. Yvonne Locke and Marguerite Tancraitor, teachers of students with visual impairments, along with Daniela Bogen, the student's sibling, significantly revised an earlier draft by the student's educational team, including Jonathan Hooper, teacher of students with visual impairments.

Comparative Thought

Comparative thought is the ability to consider two or more pieces of information, and perceive the similarities and differences. Along with emphasizing salient visual features, encouraging the development of comparative thought is another important feature of teaching individuals who are in Phase III CVI. Comparative thought is the cognitive expression of visual discrimination, in which two or more targets or classes of targets are evaluated in terms of a shared trait or set of shared traits, helping an individual to distinguish one feature of an object or image from another. Comparative language is the use of specific language that helps indicate or teach the similarities and differences in two or more targets. Seeing and comparing similarities and differences in the environment is one of the ways that children with typical vision learn about and organize their understanding of the world around them. To take a simple example, if a young child calls a doughnut a Cheerio, an adult would provide comparative language to indicate that, in fact, a Cheerio and a doughnut are both round objects that have a hole in the center. The adult could further explain the differences by stating that the Cheerio is small and crunchy when chewed and the doughnut is much bigger and soft to chew.

The rudiments of comparative thought may exist even before birth and have been demonstrated with a neonate's auditory preferences. When presented with recordings of female voices, including their mother's, newborn infants demonstrate a preference for their mother's voice over all others (DeCasper & Fifer, 1980). Studies of infant's visual behavior (Dobson & Teller, 1978; Fantz, 1963; Fantz, Fagan, & Miranda, 1975; Hubel & Wiesel, 1962) provide evidence that newborns also have visual preferences, reinforcing the notion that vision supports the development of comparative thought.

The development of vision in typically developing infants provides the foundation for them to cultivate the closely related functions of distinguishing salient visual features and comparative thought. Vision evolves steadily during gestation, but in ways that are difficult to study. At the time of birth, however, vision is focused from 8 to 12 inches, the distance from a mother's face when feeding at the breast (von Hofsten et al., 2014). Although testing eyesight in the womb has not been feasible, some information has been learned from testing premature babies. Even premature infants have emerging visual abilities (Graven & Browne, 2008). Full-term newborns have additional visual skills that include visual acuity, contrast sensitivity, refraction, accommodation, spatial vision, binocular function, distance and depth perception, color vision, and sensitivity to flicker and motion patterns (Atkinson & Braddick, 1983). Their eyes search the environment day and night, demonstrating curiosity and basic form perception without needing extensive practice (Slater, Mattock, Brown, Burnham, & Young, 1991). In utero, eyelids remain closed until about the 26th week. However, the fetus is sensitive to light, responding with heart rate acceleration to projections of light on the abdomen (Salapatek & Cohen, 1987).

The sensory information that is so readily available to typically developing newborns allows them to tune into the world around them and to build repertoires of experiences based on information that feeds their cognition, language, and social learning. Children who are born with CVI do not have an incidental way to gain visual information; they must have the information provided directly and intentionally by a person who understands the impact of CVI on human development. Children who have congenital CVI have experienced a form of visual deprivation. Individuals with CVI may "see," but be incapable of interpreting the information that exists beyond arm's reach. Their ability to compare sets of information is profoundly hindered by the inability to build an adequate "data bank" of visual information.

Imagine the stored visual information in the brain as a computer's search engine. Within the search engine there are millions of stored individual bits of information. In the computer's memory, the stored bits of data are organized into categories that can be accessed through key words or phrases. When the key words are entered, a search is launched and content that is associated with the key words is retrieved. The "folders" of information are linked by many ideas. In the human brain, visual schemes and visual memory constitute a powerful search engine. But the folders of visual information in humans are not built automatically. They must be expanded through experience that is meaningful and that is linked to language and cognition. We cannot retrieve data that has not been reliably entered and processed into the brain. If the storage mechanism has been deprived of data, the folders of visual information are devoid of content. How can comparative thought develop if there is so little information to compare? How can cognition be judged in an individual who has been unable to access incidental and direct forms of visual learning?

Venn diagrams, such as the ones in Figure 1.3, can be used to help think about salient features and of ideas, images, objects, environments, and experiences, and to consider them in terms of similarities and differences (comparative thought). Two or more elements are represented by the main circles. The parts that do not overlap are the differences. The intersections between the circles are the shared similarities. The Venn diagram can provide a framework for CVI educators to consult when teaching salient features and supporting comparative thought.

Individuals with CVI first must be taught to visually isolate the salient information that defines each of the individual circles before they can learn to use comparative thought. Only when the defining elements are discriminated and identified can two or more pieces of information be compared and similarities considered. That capacity for discrimination and identification requires ventral stream vision that supports the ability to isolate details in increasingly complex and detailed arrays. This ability begins in Phase II but is much more developed in Phase III. Individuals in Phase II and Phase III CVI have to be taught "what to look for," that is, the visual elements that define the target.

Mediated Learning and CVI

Mediated learning theory presents a model that can be linked to the concepts described in this chapter and to the role of the CVI educator. Reuven Feuerstein, a cognitive theorist and a developmental psychologist who created mediated learning theory (Feuerstein, Feuerstein, Falik, & Rand, 2002), studied groups of children he considered culturally deprived. Some children had been in concentration camps, others were immigrants, and some were unable to benefit from the offerings of a culture for other reasons. All the groups had depressed performances on traditional learning tasks, and Feuerstein believed there were important methods to help enhance the learning of these deprived groups.

Feuerstein described two categories of learning: direct learning experiences and mediated learning experiences. In direct learning, the individual is simply exposed to an experience. In mediated learning, a *mediator* transforms the stimuli or experience. The mediator is generally a parent, teacher, or other person in the life of the learner. The mediator is a highly intentioned person who

> selects, enhances, focuses, and otherwise organizes the world of stimuli for the learner, according to a clear intention and goals for the learner's enhanced and effective functioning. The mediator selects stimuli that are most appropriate to his/her intentions, and then frames, and schedules them; their appearance or disappearance is arranged to structure the learner's exposure according to clearly identified and explicit goals. (Feuerstein et al., 2002)

In the mediated learning experience, the learner is provided information that facilitates the development of information that is interrelated and that transcends the direct experience alone. The mediator must also enter into a shared relationship, one in which he or she attempts to consider the experience through the viewpoint of the learner. In other words, the mediator has the objective of recognizing the potential risks to learning and then customizing the experience by providing the necessary missing pieces to otherwise fragmented learning.

FIGURE 1.3 Examples of Venn Diagrams Used to Illustrate Salient Features and Comparative Thought

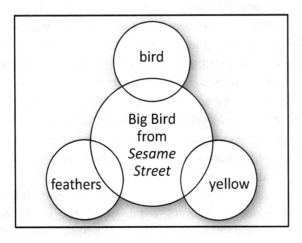

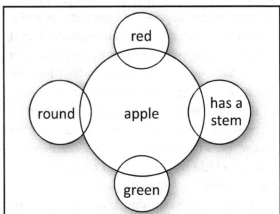

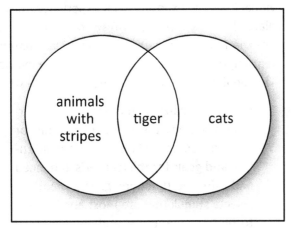

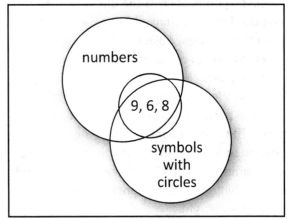

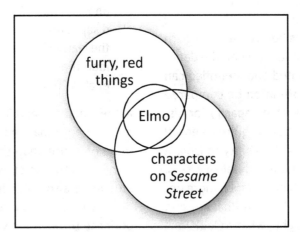

These examples show how salient visual features and comparative language can be illustrated through Venn diagrams.

Individuals who have CVI require a mediator. They are unable to gather all the puzzle pieces that eventually form a whole or complete representation of an object or image. The mediator—in this case, a person who understands CVI—can anticipate the risks for fragmented learning and then provide the strategies and methods not only to help the individual with CVI "complete the puzzle," but also to create a framework for approaches to solving future puzzles. For example, when completing a 1,000-piece jigsaw puzzle, there are a number of strategies that support the completion of the "big picture." Pieces may be arranged into color groupings, border pieces may be identified by the presence of a single straight edge, and sets can be formed from matching internal details. Other strategies may include identifying the shape of the puzzle piece or matching individual pieces to the picture of the completed puzzle image on the box cover. These strategies are not learned to construct a single puzzle, but are acquired strategies that can be applied across all puzzle-solving experiences. The strategies transcend the single moment and can be used and refined in future opportunities.

Individuals with CVI may have countless direct learning experiences. However, it cannot be assumed that unmediated exposure alone will provide the salient information necessary for rich, meaningful concept development. The following example may help illustrate this issue:

Jim is a 5-year-old boy who has cerebral palsy and CVI. He attends a kindergarten program at his neighborhood school. In the spring, Jim's class participated in an outing to a zoo. The children spent four hours visiting the animal exhibits, and then during their lunch break, watched a movie about animals in the wild.

At the zoo, Jim moved slowly and frequently tripped on cracks in the pavement. He fell down a single step that led into the pavilion where the movie was shown. He asked to hold onto the hand of one of the adults who accompanied the children.

When the children returned to their school classroom, they were full of stories about the monkeys climbing on the structures in their habitat, the elephants swaying as they walked, and the giraffe reaching his long neck up to eat leaves from the top of the tree. Many agreed that they liked the monkeys, elephants, and giraffes in the movie but thought seeing them in person was even better. Several children went to the toy shelf and engaged in pretend play using toy zoo animals. When Jim was asked what he liked about the zoo trip, he stated that the bus ride to the zoo was much longer than the ride to school each day. He also remarked that the ice cream treat after lunch was his favorite part.

This scenario provides an example of how different Jim's zoo experience was compared to the experience of his peers without CVI. Jim was present with the other children and had a series of direct experiences, but it is unlikely that he had mediated experiences. Repeat trips to the zoo are not the solution. Exposure alone will not deepen or broaden Jim's representations of this experience. Jim requires a mediator who frames, organizes, and explains the experience. The other children demonstrated comparative thought by discussing their in-person experiences, the movie version of the animals, and the toy animal models. Jim may have gathered little or none of the same visual information. And unlike a child who has an ocular form of visual impairment, Jim's normal eye appearance and his Phase III CVI send confusing signals to the adults around him, who failed to realize that Jim's experience of the zoo trip was limited to his physical presence and random, concrete experiences. Jim did not have the benefit of the visual richness of the day at the zoo. Therefore, Jim's ability to compare classes of information is restricted. If the class trip was intended to provide an enriching and novel experience, Jim was not enriched.

The following scenario provides a contrasting version of what the trip might have been like for Jim, one in which an adult provided a mediated experience that supported his learning of salient visual features and comparative thought.

Jim is a 5-year-old boy who has cerebral palsy and CVI. He attends a kindergarten program at his neighborhood school. In the spring, Jim's class participated in an outing to a zoo. Before the class trip, Ms. Chen, Jim's teacher of students with visual impairments, prepared Jim for the trip. Ms. Chen showed Jim simple photographic images of zoo animals on a backlit tablet device. They looked at various versions of the animals and Ms. Chen described each animal's most visually unique features. For example, she told Jim that a zebra is the same shape and size as many horses. Zebras also have a mane along their long necks just like a horse. But the very special thing about a zebra is that it has black-and-white stripes. Ms. Chen noticed Jim's surprise that there could be a striped horse. Jim asked if people put a saddle on a zebra and ride it like a horse. Ms. Chen told Jim that although it seems like people might ride a zebra, unlike a horse, a zebra is a wild animal that lives outdoors in a warm climate. She explained that even though there are wild horses, most horses live near people and could be in a barn part of the day. Next, Ms. Chen showed Jim a set of realistic zoo animal figures. She suggested that Jim try to sort the animals into groups of the same animal. Jim was encouraged to inspect the objects in ways he preferred—both looking at and touching the figures. The animal figures varied in size and position, and some of the animals shared common traits. Jim was reminded of the defining, salient features that distinguished zebras, elephants, giraffes, bears, monkeys, tigers, lions, and hippopotamuses.

Ms. Chen accompanied the class on the day of the trip to the zoo. She brought the backlit tablet device, and on the bus ride from the school to the zoo she and Jim reviewed the information about the animals and looked at familiar and new images of the animals. Some of the images were embedded in somewhat complex backgrounds, and Jim often had difficulty finding the animal in the new and more complex images. This alerted Ms. Chen that Jim's issues with distance viewing and complexity of array might result in Jim having difficulty seeing the animals in the zoo exhibits.

Ms. Chen made sure that Jim used his long cane in a constant-contact method as he moved independently with his group of classmates. At each exhibit, she and Jim talked about the animals. Ms. Chen used the tablet to take a photograph at each animal display and enlarged the animal in the image so that Jim would be able to see the salient visual features of the animal. Jim was delighted to match the sounds of the animal that he heard in person with the backlit and simplified image on the tablet.

When Jim and his class returned to the school, Jim stated that the giraffe was his favorite part of the field trip. He liked the long neck and brown patches on the animal. Jim further explained that he knew that a goose, a horse, and a zebra all have long necks, but the giraffe's neck was the longest of all.

How do these two versions of the trip to the zoo vary? In the first scenario, Jim's experiences are primarily direct and unmediated, with little opportunity for new learning. Jim is unable to gain new information incidentally or to prompt others to explain the novel setting or the animals at the zoo. In the second scenario, the teacher of students with visual impairments, who was knowledgeable about CVI, provided a mediated learning experience for Jim. Jim was better able to understand the defining features of each of the animals as well as compare them.

Although there is no blueprint for providing a mediated experience, there are methods that can help CVI educators become more intentional in their approach. These are some of the methods the teacher of students with visual impairments used in working with Jim:

- **Knowledge of Jim's visual impairment:** The teacher of students with visual impairments had comprehensive knowledge of Jim's CVI Range scores and the implications of his Phase III visual and learning needs, particularly in regard to specific CVI characteristics:
  - **Visual novelty and salient features:** The teacher highlighted the defining features of the animal figures on the backlit tablet device.
  - **Distance viewing:** The teacher used the backlit tablet device to photograph and enlarge the animals that were too far away for Jim to locate them.
  - **Complexity of array:** The teacher used the backlit tablet device to enlarge the animal images and reduce the complexity of the background array.
  - **Light:** The teacher used the backlit tablet device to help enhance the salient visual features of the animals and the zoo environment.
  - **Visual fields:** The teacher made sure that Jim used his long cane to help with his lower visual field difficulties.
- **Intentionality:** The teacher purposefully planned to provide direct instruction prior to the experience. She also selected devices and materials that would provide access to the visual elements. Methods were planned to help Jim transcend the specific information provided during instruction to achieve broader concept development.
- **Reciprocity:** The teacher considered the experience from Jim's point of view and in light of his visual challenges.

- **Use of comparative language and thought:** The teacher did not simply correct Jim's mistaken notions about the animals. Rather, she drew a comparison between Jim's perception and the correct information. (Jim asked if people put a saddle on a zebra to ride it like a horse. The teacher told Jim that it seems like people might ride a zebra, but unlike a horse, a zebra is a wild animal that lives outdoors in a warm climate. She clarified that even though there are wild horses, most horses live near people and could be in a barn part of the day.)

The teacher of students with visual impairments acted as Jim's mediator, transforming a direct experience into a rich, meaningful, mediated experience.

CVI Schedule

Interventions for Phase III CVI can be described in a planning form known as a CVI Schedule (Roman-Lantzy, 2018), used to implement supports associated with the CVI characteristics across routines of the day. The CVI Schedule provides detailed information about the adaptations, accommodations, or special teaching methods used to promote visual access to materials and environments. Figure 1.4 provides an example for a student whose CVI Range scores are in early Phase III.

Conclusion

Working with students in Phase III CVI is both rewarding and challenging. Individuals who score above 7 on the CVI Range have a significant degree of functional vision. It is critical, however, that parents and educators continue to advocate for and provide educational support to these individuals. The effects of the CVI characteristics may appear to be more subtle than they were in Phases I and II, but there is no doubt that they continue to have a powerful impact on individuals with CVI.

FIGURE 1.4 Sample Morning Routine CVI Schedule

Daily CVI Schedule

Student's name: _Sam Smith_   Age: _7 years_

CVI Range score: _7_   CVI phase: _III_

Time and Activity	CVI Characteristics That Can Be Addressed	CVI Adaptations for This Activity
7:30 a.m.: Breakfast	Color, complexity, novelty	■ Use a blue suction bowl and a placemat with no more than a four-color pattern
8:40 a.m.: Walk to classroom from car (in walker)	Color, movement, visual fields, complexity, distance viewing	■ Use a map on a tablet device of the route from the door of the building to the classroom ■ Have Sam pause to match salient environmental feature with matching feature on the map ■ Put bright blue paint on posts outside classroom, in the hallway
9:00 a.m.: Morning circle with class on mat	Visual fields, complexity of environment/array, distance viewing	■ Position Sam's blue-painted corner chair at the front of the morning meeting area ■ Present materials used for group activities on a low-complexity background and off midline in Sam's preferred field of view ■ Use a slant board to display objects presented at near ■ Photograph images using the tablet device and adapt them to reduce complexity
9:30 a.m.: Literacy activity—reading	Color, complexity of environment (desk area), novelty	■ Highlight salient features of images or symbols in a vibrant color ■ Remove items from the desk to make it less visually complex ■ Use a slant board to assist with lower field function ■ Incorporate comparative language when introducing numbers, letters, and sight words
10:30 a.m.: Physical education	Color, movement, visual fields, complexity of sensory environment, distance viewing	■ Position Sam for best use of his peripheral fields ■ Use a vibrant-colored ball for floor games ■ Incorporate use of movement (e.g., adult wiggles the ball, Sam kicks the ball)
11:15 a.m.: Restroom	Color, visual fields, complexity, novelty (at start of school year)	■ Place shiny strip on outside of restroom door ■ Use a vibrant-colored soap dispenser or color adaptations on faucets, stall doors, or other features

REFERENCES

Akhtar, N., & Gernsbacher, M. A. (2007). Joint attention and vocabulary development: A critical look. *Language and Linguistics Compass, 1*(3), 195–207.

Atkinson, J., & Braddick, O. (1983). Assessment of visual acuity in infancy and early childhood. *Acta Ophthalmologica, 61*(S157), 18–26.

Bruner, J., Caudill, E., & Ninio, A. (1977). Language and experience. In R. S. Peters (Ed.), *John Dewey reconsidered* (pp. 12–22). London, UK: Routledge & Kegan Paul.

DeCasper, A. J., & Fifer, W. P. (1980). Of human bonding: Newborns prefer their mothers' voices. *Science, 208*(4448), 1174–1176.

Dobson, V., & Teller, D. Y. (1978). Visual acuity in human infants: A review and comparison of behavioral and electrophysiological studies. *Vision Research, 18*(11), 1469–1483.

Fantz, R. L. (1963). Pattern vision in newborn infants. *Science, 140*(3564), 296–297.

Fantz, R. L., Fagan, J. F., & Miranda, S. B. (1975). Early visual selectivity: As a function of pattern variables, previous exposure, age from birth and conception, and expected cognitive deficit. In L. B. Cohen & P. Salapatek (Eds.), *Infant perception: From sensation to cognition: Vol. I. Basic visual processes* (pp. 249–345). New York, NY: Academic Press.

Feuerstein, R., Feuerstein, R. S., Falik, L. H., & Rand, Y. (2002). *The dynamic assessment of cognitive modifiability: The learning propensity assessment device: Theory, instruments and techniques.* Jerusalem, Israel: International Center for the Enhancement of Learning Potential.

Goodale, M. A., & Milner, A. D. (1992). Separate visual pathways for perception and action. *Trends in Neuroscience, 15*(1), 20–25.

Graven, S. N., & Browne, J. V. (2008). Visual development in the human fetus, infant, and young child. *Newborn and Infant Nursing Reviews, 8*(4), 194–201.

Hubel, D. H., & Wiesel, T. N. (1962). Receptive fields, binocular interaction and functional architecture in the cat's visual cortex. *The Journal of Physiology, 160,* 106–154.

Jan, J. E., & Groenveld, M. (1993). Visual behaviors and adaptations associated with cortical and ocular impairment in children. *Journal of Visual Impairment & Blindness, 87*(4), 101–105.

Milner, A. D., & Goodale, M. A. (2006). *The visual brain in action* (2nd ed.). Oxford, UK: Oxford University Press.

Milner, A. D., & Goodale, M. A. (2008). Two visual systems re-viewed. *Neuropsychologia, 46*(3), 774–785.

Moore, C., & Dunham, P. J. (Eds.). (1995). *Joint attention: Its origins and role in development.* Hillsdale, NJ: Lawrence Erlbaum Associates.

Roman-Lantzy, C. (2018). *Cortical visual impairment: An approach to assessment and intervention* (2nd ed.). New York, NY: AFB Press.

Roman-Lantzy, C. A., & Lantzy, A. (2002–2017). Pediatric VIEW data bank (unpublished data). Pittsburgh, PA: Western Pennsylvania Hospital.

Roman-Lantzy, C. A., & Lantzy, A. (2010). Outcomes and opportunities: A study of children with cortical visual impairment. *Journal of Visual Impairment & Blindness, 104*(10), 649–653.

Salapatek, P., & Cohen, L. (Eds.). (1987). *Handbook of infant perception.* Orlando, FL: Academic Press.

Scaife, M., & Bruner, J. S. (1975). The capacity for joint visual attention in the infant. *Nature, 253,* 265–266.

Slater, A., Mattock, A., Brown, E., Burnham, D., & Young, A. (1991). Visual processing of stimulus compounds in newborn infants. *Perception, 20*(1), 29–33.

von Hofsten, O., von Hofsten, C., Sulutvedt, U., Laeng, B., Brennen, T., & Magnussen, S. (2014). Simulating newborn face perception. *Journal of Vision, 14*(13), 1143–1152.

2

A Path to Literacy for Students Who Have CVI

Christine Roman-Lantzy

Author's Note

In the early years of my work with children with cortical visual impairment (CVI), I could not have imagined teaching print reading as a viable approach to literacy. I was impressed if the student with CVI could identify images in books. However, as I improved my understanding of how individuals with CVI learn, I began to question why I hadn't considered teaching reading. I pursued input from experts in reading, language, and cognition. It became clearer and clearer to me that the failure to access literacy lay not with the children with CVI but with my inability to teach them properly.

I now know that some children with CVI will achieve the prerequisites for reading and ultimately become competent readers, while others will follow a different path. But I cannot foresee ahead of time which individuals with CVI will read, so I believe that all children must be provided a path to literacy. Some will use symbol systems that are not word based. Others will learn a discrete set of words that can be used for short passages or functional reading. Still others will become skilled readers who will ultimately read fluently, with comprehension and pleasure.

I have also learned that there is no eye report, no neurological history, no MRI, or degree of cerebral palsy that seems to be correlated with being able to learn to read. I do know that all individuals with CVI are more capable than they can demonstrate in Phase I CVI, when there is so little access to the visual world. So I encourage my colleagues to take the risk of believing that your students with CVI are capable of literacy no matter what form it ultimately takes. It is the most fun you will ever have as an educator, and it is extraordinary for the student.

Baseline visual acuity at diagnosis cannot be used to predict final visual performance. The degree of damage demonstrated on brain imaging studies cannot be used to predict final visual performance. (Lehman, 2013)

A Specialized Approach to Literacy

Access to literacy for individuals who are blind or visually impaired has been a concern since at least the 19th century, when Louis Braille developed and refined a system of tactile reading. The concept of literacy for individuals who have visual impairments has continued to be refined for those whose primary access to literacy is tactile or adapted visual media. However, no approach has been developed that is dedicated to the unique needs of children whose visual impairment is defined by the 10 visual and behavioral characteristics associated with CVI.

The foundational principle of this book is to support the needs of children with CVI by using specialized methods, materials, and environments specifically designed in accordance with the CVI characteristics. Therefore, this chapter offers a means to literacy for the specific population of children with CVI, not other forms of visual impairment. It is also critical to recognize that children with CVI are, in many ways, a heterogeneous population. There are individuals with CVI who are cognitively intact, with moderate needs, as well as those with profound needs. Therefore, an approach intended for use with a "special needs" population will never address the needs of the many children with CVI who do not have cognitive challenges. The only way to target learners with CVI is to implement an approach that is centered on the one thing all individuals with CVI have in common: the CVI characteristics.

It will be obvious to vision educators that this chapter does not include the use of a learning media assessment (LMA; Koenig & Holbrook, 1995). The LMA is generally conducted by a teacher of

students with visual impairments as a method of collecting information about sensory preferences, learning settings, and intervention materials and methods for individuals who have ocular causes of visual impairment. The goal is to determine a primary and secondary method for accessing literacy based on the ways in which students with visual impairment interact with materials, or, to "examine the efficiency with which student gathers information from various sensory channels" and "the literacy media the student will use for reading and writing" (Koenig & Holbrook, 1995). A student's primary learning medium is a system in which the individual can both read and write and is either visual or tactile. Secondary learning media can be visual, tactile, or auditory. The LMA is used in conjunction with the functional visual assessment (FVA) to best describe the student's sensory strengths and, ultimately, to synthesize the information into educational recommendations.

These methodologies are designed for individuals who have ocular forms of visual impairment. The ocular FVA and LMA are not used to address the CVI characteristics or the overarching expectation of improving functional vision that are hallmarks of CVI. For example, children who are in Phase I CVI are able to use vision functionally only under strict conditions. Their visual responses are infrequent and inconsistent. It is not unusual for parents of children in Phase I to describe their children as being auditory and tactile learners for both learning and leisure. Because the child in Phase I CVI is just beginning to use functional vision, the results of an LMA for such a child are likely to indicate that his or her primary learning medium would be tactile, with auditory as a secondary method. Following this conclusion, the individual with CVI would be offered tactile pre-braille learning activities without emphasis on the visual supports that lead to improved vision in Phases II and III. Figure 2.1 shows how the use of visual, tactile, and auditory senses changes for children with CVI as they progress through the three phases.

Simply stated, using the LMA presents an innate risk of launching a child with CVI on a trajectory

---

FIGURE 2.1 Learning Modalities by Phase

Phase I	Phase II	Phase III
Tactile and Auditory		
Vision		
Vision: Visual behavior is just emerging.	**Vision:** Integrating vision with function.	**Vision:** Most reliable way to interact with the world.
Visual goal: Build visual behavior.	**Visual goal:** Increase opportunities to use vision; teach salient features.	**Visual goal:** Increase stability of functional vision; handle increasingly complex visual demands.
Tactile and auditory: Most reliable way to interact with the world.	**Tactile and auditory:** Used often to supplement visual tasks and substitute when necessary.	**Tactile and auditory:** Used occasionally to supplement visual tasks and substitute when necessary—mostly to avoid visual fatigue.

© 2018, Roman-Lantzy and Tietjen.

---

that deemphasizes vision and emphasizes tactile and auditory learning. A new approach is necessary for evaluating sensory competence in which visual, tactile, and auditory skills are all expected to reach similar levels. Just as the CVI Range is used to assess the functional vision of individuals with CVI, so, too, there is a need to develop a specialized way to evaluate the changing use of sensory systems as a child's vision progresses across the phases of CVI.

Definitions of Literacy

In order to consider literacy for students with CVI, it is useful to look at the broader definitions of literacy for all students. Literacy has long been broadly defined as "the ability to identify, understand, interpret, create, communicate and compute, using printed and written materials associated with varying contexts" (UNESCO Education Sector, 2004, p. 13). A widely quoted definition of literacy is, "the ability to use available symbol systems that are fundamental to learning and teaching—for the purposes of comprehending and composing—for

the purposes of making and communicating meaning and knowledge" (Stock, 2012).

Other authors have also pondered the complexity of applying definitions of literacy, whether traditional or evolving, to individuals with disabilities. While most authors in this area have recognized literacy as "interactive, constructive, strategic, and meaning-based" (Steelman, Pierce, & Koppenhaver, 1994), they also typically maintain the notion that comprehension and use of *written* text is central to literacy. Steelman, Pierce, and Koppenhaver's definition is a good example: "To be literate is to be able to gather and to construct meaning using written language" (p. 201).

Discussing individuals with cognitive impairments, Beukelman and Mirenda (1998) stated,

Because of these individuals' cognitive limitations, educators may not consider literacy learning as an educational goal. Thus, individuals with cognitive impairments are at risk of being held to reduced expectations and lacking exposure to literacy materials, both at home and at school. If educators believe that reading does not begin until individuals possess certain prerequisite skills, and if educators think of literacy as an "all or none" ability, they will not consider the potential for varying degrees of literacy learning by individuals with cognitive impairments. In truth, individuals with cognitive impairments can and should engage in the same emergent literacy activities as their peers without disabilities (e.g., listening repeatedly to stories, having access to writing tools). We cannot overemphasize the importance of intensive exposure to literacy materials in the early years. (p. 361)

Teaching literacy skills to individuals with CVI requires an approach that is founded on the essential principles of literacy but may vary from approaches used for individuals who have ocular forms of visual impairment. Individuals with CVI may be best able to access literacy when materials and methods are adapted in accordance with the CVI characteristics at the level of a current CVI Range score. The information in this chapter emphasizes an approach that is designed to support literacy only in the population of individuals with CVI as opposed to a broader population of individuals with all forms of visual impairment.

Prerequisites for Introducing Symbols

To consider the use of symbols, including letters and words, with individuals who have CVI, they first need to have the following prerequisites: (1) the use of ventral stream visual processing, including the presence of a visual fixation (a minimum CVI Range score of 4), and (2) a repertoire of "known," or familiar, readily recognizable target objects.

As described in Chapter 1, ventral stream vision is commonly known as the "what" system of visual processing and is associated with the ability to discriminate detail, in contrast with the dorsal stream or "where" system (Milner & Goodale,

2006, 2008). It is sometimes considered the "acuity" part of visual processing because it enables detailed vision. The ventral system is activated when a person demonstrates eye-to-target contact—that is, a visual fixation.

Visual fixation is the establishment of the visual gaze on a single location. Without this ability, an individual is unable to activate the parts of the eye and the brain that transmit and stimulate attention to visual details. This prerequisite is generally represented by a score of at least 4 on the CVI Range, which places the individual in early Phase II CVI. Once an individual with CVI has progressed to early Phase II, he or she is now able to discriminate distinct objects and will generally demonstrate eye-to-object contact while doing so. The ability to perceive detail, the hallmark of ventral stream vision, is evident when the individual is able to advance past visual attention that is limited to movement, light, and color. Individuals with ventral stream visual ability can look directly at a target, rather than simply looking in the direction of the form, color, or lighted properties of the target. The individual may tilt his or her head or use a specialized posture while looking, but it is easy to observe that he or she is no longer just localizing on a target, but is now demonstrating visual fixation. Through this eye-to-object contact, the details of an object or image can begin to be seen. As the individual progresses through Phase II to Phase III, the ability to discriminate even more refined detail increases. Therefore, the ability to perceive and discriminate details associated with symbols used for literacy also increases.

The second prerequisite for the use of symbols is for the individual to have a set of objects that are well known and readily recognized. These objects can serve as the target items for beginning instruction in the use of salient features (see Chapter 1). To accommodate for the confounding presence of novelty, it is important for the individual with CVI to have a foundation of visual experience with the items used to teach salient features. These items can be objects that are part of the individual's routines and that have meaning to the individual. For example, a set of objects used to teach salient features can include a toothbrush, a cup, a favorite character from a familiar book, or a toy. If the individual is familiar with animals or shapes, these types of items can also be used as a platform for teaching attention to visual details.

Sidebar 2.1 provides an overview of the progression of interventions and supports used to teach literacy skills for individuals with CVI that is described in detail throughout this chapter. It begins with the use of objects and moves to two-dimensional materials, the incorporation of salient visual features, the incorporation of comparative thought, and the use of symbolic systems. Due to space limitations, many,

but not all, suggested activities in Sidebar 2.1 are described further throughout this chapter.

Figure 2.2 provides a graphic overview of the basic foundational skills for literacy discussed in the next section. Whether the learner with CVI is using objects or two-dimensional images as initial targets, the skills taught are discrimination, recognition, and identification of salient visual features. The use of known objects or two-dimensional materials always precedes the use of novel materials. The familiar target helps establish recognition and interpretation of salient features prior to the introduction of more generalized versions of the target object or image.

SIDEBAR 2.1

Progression of Interventions to Support Literacy for Individuals with CVI

1. Objects are presented in isolation with appropriate use of language to build toward identification of salient features.

    a. *"This is your red spoon. A spoon has a long handle and a hollow part for scooping food."*

2. Additional versions of the object are presented to promote generalization of the target object. Language input provides salient features (see Sample Script for Phase I, Figure 3.3, Chapter 3).

    a. *"These are all spoons. Some are silver and shiny, others have color, but all of them have a long handle and a hollow part for scooping."*

        i. Discrimination: *"Show me an object (spoon) like the one I am holding."*

        ii. Recognition: *"Look at these objects and find the spoon."*

        iii. Identification: *"What is this called?"*

3. Objects are paired with exact photo image.

    a. Object + image on light box

    b. Object + image on tablet

    c. Object + image in black background book

4. Salient features are taught.

    a. Definitions of salient features are embedded into instruction or routines in the classroom or at home.

        i. Salient features are descriptions of two or three defining visual details that are true of the target all or almost all of the time.

    b. A reference or catalog for salient features is provided, such as a booklet, notebook, or electronic file, with sections for meaningful objects used across the day, for example:

        i. Mealtime objects

        ii. Self-help objects

      iii. Play and leisure objects

      iv. School items

      v. Environments

      vi. Animals

      vii. Symbols

c. Sorting activities are used to reinforce salient features and to build comparative thought.

      i. Practice sorting classes or groups of the same name but varying representations of target items, such as:

         ■ Birds

         ■ Cups

         ■ Balls

         ■ Cats

      ii. Practice sorting two-dimensional representations of the same classes or groups.

d. Symbols, including words, are introduced.

      i. Phonemic awareness of letters and sounds

      ii. Visual descriptions of letters or symbols incorporating salient features

      iii. Discrimination: "Show me one like_____"

      iv. Recognition: "Show me the _____"

      v. Identification: "What is this called?"

      vi. Selection of pairs of high-motivation personal words that are visually discrepant (e.g., *go* and *baseball*)

         (1) Teaching salient features of the sight word

         (2) Color highlighting and outlining of the word pairs to create precise word shapes

         (3) Mixed approaches

            (a) Matching printed words to the empty color outline shape of the word

            (b) Sorting words into groups of "same" words

            (c) Matching the color word outline to the print word

            (d) Matching the print word to the color word outline

         (4) Using comparative language throughout to help refine the similarities and differences of objects, images, or environments

      vii. Books—hardcopy or on a backlit device (tablet or light box)

         (1) "Writing" using words learned or being learned (e.g., teacher- and student-made stories generated from the student's interests and experiences that incorporate the learned sight words)

         (2) Placing one or two words into word shapes in an age-appropriate book in the context of a phrase or sentence

      viii. Word wall, personal word catalog, or inventory

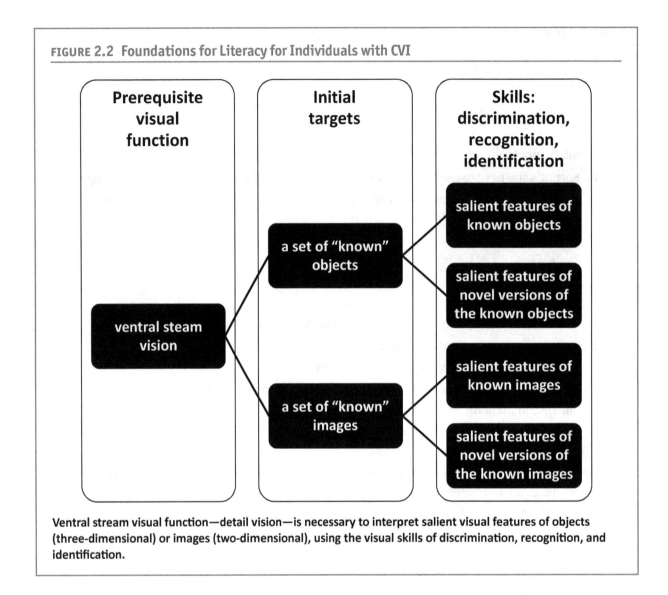

FIGURE 2.2 Foundations for Literacy for Individuals with CVI

Prerequisite visual function

Initial targets

Skills: discrimination, recognition, identification

ventral steam vision

a set of "known" objects

a set of "known" images

salient features of known objects

salient features of novel versions of the known objects

salient features of known images

salient features of novel versions of the known images

Ventral stream visual function—detail vision—is necessary to interpret salient visual features of objects (three-dimensional) or images (two-dimensional), using the visual skills of discrimination, recognition, and identification.

Visual Discrimination, Recognition, and Identification

As noted in Chapter 1, there are three skills or abilities that allow students with CVI to distinguish salient features and help them to visually attend to novel objects and images: visual discrimination, recognition, and identification. These abilities provide the foundation for literacy by enabling students to identify literacy symbols and shapes as well. Visual discrimination, visual recognition, and visual identification are different aspects of learning and are associated with different instructional supports.

At the most basic level, *visual discrimination* is the ability to perceive the visual similarities and differences in targets. It is a basis for the cognitive task of comparative thought, in which two or more targets or classes of targets are evaluated in terms of a shared trait or set of shared traits (see Chapter 1). Visual discrimination can initially be taught through matching or sorting activities.

Long before instruction in salient features is initiated, simple sorting tasks should be introduced. Individuals with CVI may not perceive the key details of even the most familiar items without direct instruction and practice. Visual discrimination tasks are intended to help individuals learn key visual features without introducing the additional elements of the object's name, color, or shape. In discrimination tasks the goal is for the individual to decide which objects share visual traits, rather than attempting to derive a correct language label. The individual does not have to speak at all during visual discrimination tasks. Color is integral to the task because perception of color is a CVI characteristic that is associated with visual attention, but recognizing or naming colors is not required.

The following procedures are examples of methods for introducing simple visual discrimination tasks:

- Collect two sets of objects such as blocks, spoons, or pegs. The sets of objects should be identical in shape with a single color per set, such as one set of red blocks and another set of yellow blocks. The containers used for sorting must be identical and, ideally, transparent, with a wide opening for easy visual inspection.
- Introduce the items to the child with CVI: For example: "I have blocks. Some are red and some are yellow. Let's play with the blocks and put them into containers. I'll put all the red blocks in one container and all the yellow blocks in the other container."
- Place the sets of objects into their respective containers. Remove a single object from either of the two containers and place it between them. Then ask the child to replace it in the container with the matching objects: "There's a block on the table. Can you show me where it belongs?"
- Remove a single object from each one of the sets of objects and place them between the two containers. Then ask the child to replace them with the matching set of objects: "There are

blocks on the table. Can you show me where they belong?"
- Remove increasingly greater numbers of objects from both containers and place them between the two containers. Then ask the child to replace them with the matching set of objects: "There are many blocks on the table. Can you show me where they belong?"
- Remove all objects except one from both containers and place the objects between the two containers. Then ask the child to replace this large set (up to six matching items per container) with the matching one in each container: "There are many blocks on the table. Can you show me where they belong?"

Visual discrimination tasks can be attempted with either objects or two-dimensional materials. If an individual is able to visually discriminate items, the next tasks may include recognition and, finally, identification of a target.

Visual recognition of an object or image includes the use of the language label associated with the target. In this part of the process, the individual is asked to locate a specific item named. In discrimination tasks, the individual with CVI is asked to *"show me one like this"* without labeling the object. In recognition tasks, the individual with CVI is asked to *"show me the block"* from an array of objects that includes a block.

Visual identification activities are the next level and are the most difficult of the three learning tasks, with the individual with CVI being asked, "What is this?" Thus, in addition to being able to (1) discriminate the visual similarities, and (2) recognize a name and locate an object that matches the spoken label, in visual identification, the individual must also (3) produce the label. It is important for adults to be aware of the type of task they are requiring of the individual.

Children with CVI who have motor challenges, expressive language challenges, or cognitive delays can participate in these discrimination, recognition, or identification activities with support from therapists on their educational team. The following vignette illustrates the importance of intentional use of methods that evaluate an individual's ability to discriminate, recognize, and identify targets.

The preschool teacher was becoming frustrated with Louisa's inconsistent ability to learn colors. An occupational therapist who worked in Louisa's classroom happened to listen in on a lesson about color. The therapist listened as the preschool teacher presented various single-color objects to Louisa. The preschool teacher asked Louisa, "What color is this ball?" "Show me the red book," and "I have two pegs and have given you a third one. When I hold up one color, you see if you have one that looks the same as mine." Louisa correctly responded to the requests to match items by color but was incorrect or failed to answer when the response required Louisa to verbalize the name of the color.

After listening to the lesson on colors, the occupational therapist spoke to the preschool teacher about the lesson. She suggested that the teacher was getting inconsistent responses because the questions being asked of Louisa required distinctly different skills. The occupational therapist pointed out that Louisa could in fact discriminate colors and even recognize colors when named. However, when asked to retrieve the color name from memory, she had more difficulty. Therefore, Louisa had difficulty with color naming but was in fact able to see the differences in color and associate a color name with a correct color object. The preschool teacher realized that he no longer needs to work on color matching but should consult with the speech-language pathologist to help Louisa with word retrieval.

The implementation of specific strategies is correlated with a student's responses. Thus, Louisa is better able to demonstrate her knowledge of colors when the task was adjusted to her abilities.

Beginning Instruction in Salient Visual Features

Initiation of instruction in salient visual features does not require full competence in discrimination, recognition, and identification. Discrimination and recognition skills may be acquired throughout the process of learning salient features. However, in order to assess whether a salient feature has been acquired, the instructor should implement methods associated with discrimination and, later, recognition. This is a way for the instructor to determine whether the information has been perceived (discrimination) and if the individual with CVI can associate a name with the feature, image, or object (recognition). Identification of targets is desired, but not mandatory. Just as Louisa's knowledge of color is not dependent on her ability to say the names of the colors, so, too, salient features can be learned even without the ability of the individual to verbalize them.

Definitions and descriptions of salient features are provided in Chapter 1. The method for teaching salient features includes a verbal description of the defining or salient features, as well as a method for visually highlighting these elements. For example, an instructor may present a toothbrush to the child with CVI and state, "This is your toothbrush. It has a long, thin handle and short rows of bristles at one end." The object should be offered in the child's best field of vision, and, if necessary, the instructor should move the object slightly to elicit visual attention. The object is not placed in the child's hand because the goal is visual recognition of the target, not tactile recognition. The visual adaptation might be showing the child a toothbrush that has a bright pink handle and yellow bristles, or other colors depending on the child's color preferences, to draw visual attention to the targeted salient features. If an image is used, fluorescent or vibrant color highlighting can be used to draw an outline around each of the salient features.

As an individual progresses to higher CVI Range scores, his or her ability to perceive detail improves. Color highlighting of the salient features helps draw visual attention to smaller details and to more complex targets. Attention to these details may facilitate increased functional acuity. It is critical to recognize, however, that even if an individual with CVI looks directly at a target or at the salient features, it cannot be assumed that the individual is interpreting what he or she is seeing. Direct instruction that includes intentional language labels must accompany presentation of the object or image. It is critical that adults who support students with CVI provide language descriptions that define the target features and then help the student generalize these key features to new versions of the initial target. For example, if a student with CVI learns that the salient features of an elephant are a nose-like trunk and huge, flapping ears, the adult providing these descriptions must be certain that the student can discriminate and recognize these salient features across a range of representations of elephants.

Adults who support students with CVI provide salient features to promote the development of a framework for thinking about novel visual information. It is hoped that ultimately, the student will develop a metacognitive or internalized strategy. That is, the student with CVI will "think about his or her thinking" by visually examining the salient features and then matching the salient features of a new image to one that is in cognitive and visual memory. Salient features are the stored content that can be compared to new learning as a kind of learning scaffold that supports the student's ability to discriminate and recognize targets that are similar but not identical to the original representation. This process of comparing new objects or images to stored information may also help reduce rigidity in thinking because the student with CVI will be able to perceive how a new version of a known object is not completely novel, but rather, corresponds to a known image or object.

As salient features are being learned, the individual with CVI is also attending to outline or form

and interior visual details. The outline of a target provides broad information about the target—it is a way to begin to discriminate and recognize the target. The internal details provide the refined visual aspects that distinguish targets in subtle ways. For example, the outline or form of a horse may be described as a large animal with a long neck, an elongated face, and a long hairy tail. The internal details may include two brown eyes, a mane, and a white spot on its face.

Once the student develops the skill to recognize objects based on the internal salient features of symbols used for literacy, the educational team will make decisions regarding the mode of literacy; that is, whether the student will use functional symbols and images or letters and words. Figure 2.3 provides considerations for literacy for academic and functional curriculum learners. Both start with the foundational skill of identifying salient features. A *functional curriculum* teaches learners who do not follow an academic curriculum to access everyday words or other symbols. For example, many students who are in special education classrooms may not achieve fluent skills in reading or mathematics but are expected to recognize and use everyday math as well as frequently occurring or community-based words. These can include words used to create a shopping list or math that is associated with paying for a meal at a local restaurant. The remainder of this chapter will focus on the use of words for literacy, but the principles can apply to other literacy materials as well.

Introducing Words

Methods of Teaching Reading

There are numerous methods of teaching reading. The strategies proposed here draw from phonics, sight words, the language experience approach, and the context support method (Griggs, 2000). Children who are taught to read phonetically learn the names of the letters and the sounds that they make. They are taught to "sound out" a word letter by letter and then to combine the sounds into a single word. In the sight-word method of learning reading, children learn to recognize whole

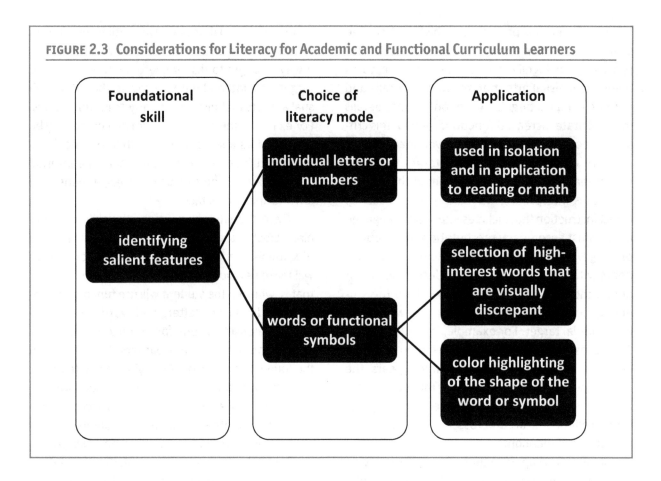

FIGURE 2.3 Considerations for Literacy for Academic and Functional Curriculum Learners

words or sentences rather than individual sounds. The child is asked to look at a word, listen to the adult say the word, and then repeat the word. Flashcards with individual words written on them are frequently used to reinforce learning the sight words, and images that represent the sight word often accompany the word on the flashcard.

The language experience method uses the student's own words to help him or her read. It also incorporates pictures drawn by the student to reinforce and broaden vocabulary. For example, if a student states that his or her mother was watering the flowers, the phrase "mother was watering the flowers" is written on a page, and the student is encouraged to draw a picture of the experience. The language experience approach supports students' concept development and vocabulary growth while offering many opportunities for meaningful reading and writing activities through personal experiences and spoken language.

Another method is the context support method, in which reading materials are selected based on the interests of the child. The child is presented with short phrases to read based on words being learned, while the adult reads a longer passage based on the same content.

Other approaches to teaching reading, such as Orton-Gillingham, are designed for struggling readers. The Orton-Gillingham method (Gillingham & Stillman, 1997) is a highly structured approach that breaks down the elements of reading and spelling into smaller skills. It is a multisensory approach that uses different sensory modalities to teach and reinforce reading.

All the traditional methods used to teach literacy skills assume that the child has normal vision. How then can children with CVI develop the skills necessary for literacy? While there are discussions and methods of teaching reading to individuals who are blind or visually impaired as a result of ocular issues (see, for example, *Building on Patterns* [American Printing House for the Blind, 2010]; Cushman, 2016; Kamei-Hannan & Ricci, 2015; Swenson, 2016; Wormsley, 2016), there is no specific curriculum for teaching reading to individuals with CVI. The impact of the CVI characteristics affects the learner in ways that are different from an individual who is blind or has low vision due to ocular damage. The CVI characteristics have their own impact on access to literacy.

The following are examples of common adaptations used to address the unique literacy needs of individuals with CVI, based on the CVI characteristics:

- **Color:** Color highlighting and outlining of words facilitates attention to the salient features of symbols, letters, or numbers.

- **Movement:** Words or passages may be more easily read if the text is paired with movement (e.g., scrolling text or words on the electronic screen of a computer, tablet, or video magnifier that are programmed to move dynamically).

- **Latency:** Students are allowed additional time to process visual information.

- **Visual fields:** A raised or slanted surface is used to accommodate for commonly occurring lower visual field dysfunction, and materials are presented off midline, generally in the student's preferred field of view.

- **Visual complexity:** Materials must be presented in a simple array, the sensory environment must be controlled, and the salient features must be isolated in the instructional phase.

- **Light:** Backlighting is critical for inspection of salient features and other details associated with letters, words, or symbols.

- **Distance:** Instruction associated with literacy must be conducted within the range of a student's viewing abilities; complexity in the environment may result in reduced ability to perceive a target or to learn from demonstration.

- **Novelty:** New materials require explanation and instruction in their salient visual features. Students with CVI have little ability to learn incidentally from information in the environment, such as materials on bulletin boards or posters on walls, and, therefore, the visual information they obtain is significantly reduced.

- **Visual motor:** A student with CVI may not be able to direct his or her hand to a precise detail when asked to respond to a specific aspect of a letter, word, or symbol.

The approach for individuals with CVI incorporates factors from across the four traditional reading methods previously described. Phonemic awareness is used to teach letter-sound association. Individuals with CVI should be taught the sounds made by letters of the alphabet, even if they are not able to independently identify each letter by name. It is more important for the individual with CVI to recognize that the letter *b* says "buh" than to be able to name all 26 letters of the alphabet. Learning the sounds of the letters is especially important for helping individuals with CVI recognize the beginning or ending sound of a word.

The sight-word approach provides another critical factor for literacy instruction for students with CVI. Not all students with CVI will access literacy using words, but if the educational team decides to offer word reading, sight words will likely be a better match for the student's needs than learning individual letters. Students with CVI have difficulty with complexity and the crowding effect that occurs when visual elements are very close together. Words contain letters that might be viewed as a complex array of letters; phrases and paragraphs incorporate even more visual information presented in a dense or crowded manner. Sight words are more visually accessible when they are presented as a single-shaped form. They are essentially memorized as whole shapes with salient visual features, as detailed in the next section, and thus do not require the visual inspection of individual letters contained within the word itself. Students with CVI can read these individual units more quickly than would be possible by phonetically sounding out each word letter by letter. The use of sight words may also promote greater fluency in reading and therefore greater comprehension of what was read (Therrien, 2004).

The language experience and context support methods are also incorporated into literacy for students with CVI. It is useful to begin by selecting words that represent something that is highly motivating to the student. The student's own experiences and preferences will dictate which words are selected and then used to create short, personal stories. Students with CVI experience significant deficits in incidental visual learning, therefore, their interests may be more limited than those of their peers. Parents or teachers are likely to know which words have the greatest impact for a student, and it is important to select words that come from students' own interests, not from the interests of their age mates.

Children who are taught to read braille often use curricula that are designed to incorporate specific skills that are different from the skills taught to children who are sighted. According to the catalog of the American Printing House for the Blind (APH, 2017), the *Building on Patterns* series "addresses vocabulary, fluency, comprehension, phonemic awareness (ability to hear and interpret sounds in speech), and phonics (the association of written symbols with the sounds they represent)" (p. 103). These skills are generally considered important for all children who are learning to read. *Building on Patterns* also addresses specific skill areas needed by children who are blind, such as language development, sound discrimination, tactile discrimination, and concept development: "Braille contractions are introduced from the beginning along with sound and letter associations" (p. 106).

Just as children learning to read braille need to learn both the foundational skills and concepts of reading paired with the mechanics of braille reading, so too, instruction for children with CVI needs to address the mechanics of learning to read paired with the CVI-specific skill areas needed to increase language and concept development. Also, similar to the way the *Building on Patterns* program introduces braille contractions at the same time letters are being learned, the CVI approach to reading introduces words even before all the letters of the alphabet are memorized. Learning words, learning concepts, and learning language occur simultaneously.

Suggested Procedures for Learning Words

The following procedures can be implemented to assist in learning sight words. Although some of the elements of these procedures can be found in other methods intended for children with visual impairments (for example, Wormsley, 2016), this approach is rooted in the visual and behavioral characteristics that are the core of CVI. Sidebar 2.2 provides an overview of methods of teaching words, phrases, and paragraphs and the use of supports for literacy with individuals who have CVI.

1. Select two words that are visually discrepant, for example, a short word and a long word.

2. The initial two words must be of high interest to the student with CVI; for example, if the child likes sports, the words *baseball* and *run* can be chosen.

3. The words are written in black on a white or neutral (not colored) background, in a font that uses traditional versions of letters.

4. Outline the shapes of the sight words (using a bright color, preferably the student's preferred color if one exists), adhering tightly to the contours of the words.

SIDEBAR 2.2

Overview of Methods for Teaching Words, Phrases, and Paragraphs and Use of Supports for Literacy with Individuals Who Have CVI

Words

- The student matches a sight word to the correct word shape from a choice of several word shapes.

- The student matches a word shape to the correct word from a choice of several words.

- The student discriminates, recognizes, and identifies individual words.

Phrases

- Introduce a color-outlined sight word in a short phrase; the adult reads the phrase.

- Introduce a color-outlined sight-word shape in a short phrase; the student places the word into the empty shape within the phrase.

- The student reads the word in the phrase without color highlighting.

- Introduce a color-outlined sight-word shape in a short phrase; the student selects the correct word from a bank of two to six sight words.

- The color-outlined word is in the text of the short phrase; the student reads the color-outlined sight word.

- The student writes stories with or without adult assistance using the words that have been learned.

Paragraphs

- Increase numbers of lines of words systematically.

- Insert word shapes of words being learned into the paragraph—one per line of print.
  - The student selects the appropriate word for the word shapes from a list of familiar sight words.
  - Color word shapes are faded as new words are learned.

Supports

- Add increasing numbers of words with extra space between words.

- Use a line marker or occluder as necessary.

- Use a backlit device to help lessen visual fatigue and increase ability of the student to see the salient features.

5. Say the words one at a time. Next, spell each word and emphasize the sound of the beginning and ending letters. Say each word again.

6. Show the word shape and printed word separately.

7. Describe the visual salient features of the brightly colored word shape.

8. Use a cutout of the printed word and demonstrate how the printed word fits into the colored word shape like a puzzle piece.

Two visually discrepant sight words, baseball *and* run, *are tightly outlined in a bright, contrasting color.*

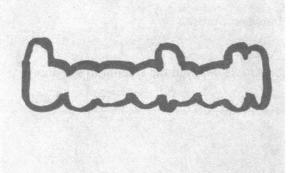

The cutout word is fitted into the colored word shape.

One of the words, baseball, *is shown separately from its colored shape.*

The second word, run, *is shown separately from its colored shape and then fitted into the shape.*

9. Repeat steps 6–8 with the second printed word and word shape.

10. Offer two word shapes and place the matching printed word in the appropriate shape; offer two printed words and place one in the corresponding word shape.

11. Offer two printed words and a sentence with one of the colored word shapes replacing the corresponding word. One of the two words fits into the word shape and completes the sentence. An adult or peer reads the sentence except for the word that is missing. The student with CVI is asked to select a word for the colored word shape. The sentence is then reread to determine if the word selected is appropriate for the context of the sentence. If it is incorrect, the salient features of the two printed words are reinforced, and a new sentence is presented.

12. Once a set of words is learned, apply these words to a new and increasingly longer passage. Colored word shapes replace several words in the passage, and the student with CVI selects the appropriate words to complete each sentence from a selection of words, using context to help make the choice.

13. Continue to add new words based on high-interest topics. As words are memorized, remove the color highlighting. Color shape outlining and descriptions of salient visual features are added to new words until the word is learned and can be used in context.

14. Once words and reading are integrated into memory, color highlighting can be eliminated from new word learning.

This process combines phonics, sight words, language experience, and context. It also addresses the use of CVI-specific supports such as the use of color, selection of known rather than novel content, decreased amounts of visual complexity of array, and the use of salient visual features. These supports are intentionally used as a method to provide access to the visual features of the literacy materials and to support the development of thinking skills used to analyze symbols, such as words. It is hoped that eventually the student with CVI will develop a metacognitive approach to interpreting new symbols or words. In other words, the student needs to learn to reflect on the shape of the symbol or word, identify the salient or key features, and then consider the possible answers.

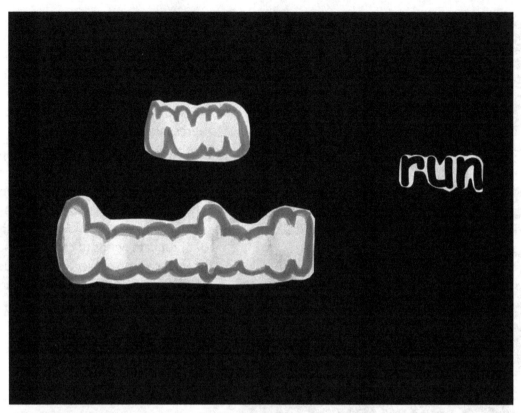

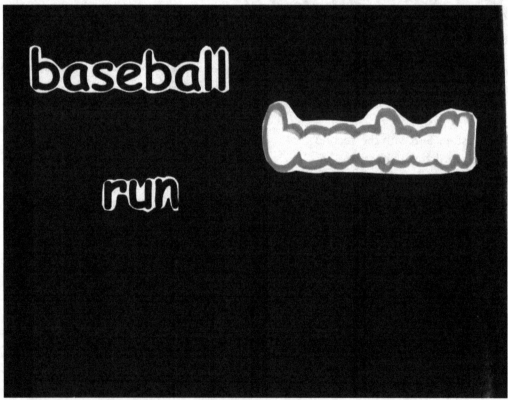

The correct one of two word shapes is matched with a printed word (top). The correct one of the two printed words is matched with a word shape (bottom).

54

The player hit the ball over the fence and had

a home

A word shape replaces one of the words in a sentence, and the student with CVI picks one of the two words that match the shape.

In the next section, a sample lesson provides an example of the adaptations and methods used to support reading for individuals with CVI. The example features a girl who is able to respond verbally, but the same methods can be adjusted for those who have expressive communication challenges.

Jamallah's Lesson

Jamallah is a 6-year-old girl with CVI who is in an elementary classroom with special education support. She has been working with the same teacher of students with visual impairments, Ms. Grimaldi, since infancy. Jamallah's CVI Range scores have moved from Phase I to Phase III. She is currently able to match sets of objects. Jamallah can also discriminate, recognize, and occasionally identify the salient features of animal figures, familiar images, and indoor environments. Jamallah can point to the unique internal features of some images, such as Elmo's big eyes and the triangle-shaped nose on

a rabbit. Ms. Grimaldi worked with Jamallah's preschool and elementary classroom teachers to introduce and reinforce phonemic awareness and phonics. Jamallah is now able to point to some letters of the alphabet when named and can match the sounds associated with a letter with the letter name. Her educational team has decided it is time for her to begin formal reading instruction.

Jamallah's favorite story is *Goldilocks and the Three Bears*. Jamallah's mother reports that this book has been read to Jamallah since she was a toddler. Jamallah can point to images of Goldilocks in the book, and although she confuses the mother, father, and baby bear, Jamallah can touch images of bears in the book as well. Key words from *Goldilocks and the Three Bears* were selected to begin teaching word reading. Ms. Grimaldi selected two visually discrepant words: *Goldilocks* and *bear*. She prepared the words by tightly outlining the printed words with fluorescent yellow, Jamallah's preferred color. Ms. Grimaldi photographed the

run   baseball

score

It was a beautiful day for a [colored word shape]

game. The whole family went to the park

to watch. The batter came to home plate

hoping he could hit the ball and [colored word shape]

a home [colored word shape]

Colored word shapes replace the printed words in a longer passage, and the student chooses the printed words that match the appropriate shapes.

outlined words using a tablet so that Jamallah could inspect the words on a backlit system. She described the words to Jamallah in the following way: "There are two words on the screen outlined in yellow. We will look at them one at a time. The first word is *bear*. It is a short word spelled b-e-a-r. The word *bear* begins with the letter *b*. The letter *b* says 'buh.' The letter *b* is a tall letter that has a circle at the right of the straight line. The word *bear* ends with the letter *r*. The letter *r* sounds like 'err.' The letter *r* is a short letter that has a straight line with a little curved line at the top of the straight line. Let's look at the shape of the word by following the yellow word shape as I spell the word: b-e-a-r."

Next, Ms. Grimaldi described the second word. "The second word is *Goldilocks*. It is a long word spelled G-o-l-d-i-l-o-c-k-s. The word *Goldilocks* be-

gins with the letter *G*. *G* says 'guh.' *G* is a curved letter that has a short, straight line at the bottom of the opening of the curve. The word *Goldilocks* ends with the letter *s*. The letter *s* sounds like 'sss.' *S* is a letter with two curves, one at the top and one at the bottom of the letter. The open part of the curve on top is at the right; the open part of the curve at the bottom is on the left. Let's look at the shape of the word by following the yellow word shape as I spell the word: *G-o-l-d-i-l-o-c-k-s.*"

Ms. Grimaldi presents both words and word shapes to reinforce the outline of the sight words. She presents the printed words without the outlining and the colored word outlines without the print words. They are displayed on cardstock paper so that Jamallah can handle them easily.

New words are added to the sight words the student has learned.

"Now let's look at the shape of the words. I will show you a colored word shape and two words. One of the words is *Goldilocks*, the other word is *bear*. Find the word that fits into the word shape I have given you. It will be like finding a puzzle piece that fits exactly into the correct place in the puzzle."

Once the correct match is found, Ms. Grimaldi reinforces the action by repeating the salient features of the word shape and respelling the printed word that fits into the word shape. Next, two colored word shapes and one printed word are offered.

"I have given you two word shapes and one word. Find the colored word shape that goes with the word I gave you. Remember that the word will match the correct word shape just like a puzzle piece fits into the correct opening in the puzzle."

Once the correct match is found, Ms. Grimaldi reinforces the action by repeating the salient features of the word shape and respelling the correct printed word that aligns with the colored word shape presented. Next, she presents a word shape without a printed word and then the printed word without the word shape.

"Jamallah, I am going to show you a word shape. The word shape will be the colored outline of either the word *Goldilocks* or the word *bear*. When I show you the word shape, look carefully at the colored outline and think about the tall parts, the curved parts, and the beginning and

end of the word. Then I will show you the printed word. Look carefully at the printed word and think about the tall parts, the curved parts, and the beginning and end of the word. Then, tell me the word."

Ms. Grimaldi and Jamallah's classroom teacher adapted a short written passage from *Goldilocks and the Three Bears*. Ms. Grimaldi reads the sentence, leaving out one of the targeted words, and Jamallah selects the correct printed word from a selection of two to be placed into the colored word shape to complete the sentence. The passages and selections of words become more complex as Jamallah learns more sight words associated with her favorite story. She also draws simple pictures of experiences that remind her of the characters in the story.

Once Jamallah demonstrates consistent competence with new words taught with colored shape highlighting, the words are used in new applications. Eventually, Jamallah writes her own passages using a combination of the words she knows, plus words provided by Ms. Grimaldi and her classroom teacher. She calls her first story "Jamallah's Just-Right Wheelchair."

Conclusion

It is important to offer opportunities for literacy that may include reading words to individuals with CVI. As previously stated, a learning media assessment may not be the best way to guide decisions about the selection of the most appropriate media for all individuals with CVI in all phases. Some individuals with CVI are exposed to braille instruction, especially if they score in Phase I or early Phase II. However, it is unlikely that braille will be an appropriate choice for those who score above 5 on the CVI Range, because they have sufficient vision to use visual symbols. Individuals who use vision for much of their learning may be less efficient with braille due to the consistent use of vision and the ability to discriminate details. As with all literacy-related decisions, however, the final determination depends on the input of the entire educational team and the wishes of the family.

REFERENCES

American Printing House for the Blind. (2010). *Building on patterns.* Louisville, KY: Author.

American Printing House for the Blind. (2017). *APH instructional products catalog 2017–2018.* Louisville, KY: Author.

Beukelman, D. R., & Mirenda, P. (1998). *Augmentative and alternative communication: Management of severe communication disorders in children and adults* (2nd ed.). Baltimore, MD: Paul H. Brookes.

Cushman, C. (2016). Functional literacy. In S. Z. Sacks & M. C. Zatta (Eds.), *Keys to educational success: Teaching students with visual impairments and multiple disabilities* (pp. 260–293). New York, NY: AFB Press.

Gillingham, A., & Stillman, B. W. (1997). *The Gillingham manual: Remedial training for children with specific disability in reading, spelling, and penmanship* (8th ed.). Cambridge, MA: Educators Publishing Service.

Griggs, I. (2000). Four main methods learning to read. Teaching Treasures Publications. Retrieved from https://www.teachingtreasures .com.au/homeschool/reading-methods/reading -methods.htm

Kamei-Hannan, C., & Ricci, L. A. (2015). *Reading connections: Strategies for teaching students with visual impairments.* New York, NY: AFB Press.

Koenig, A. J., & Holbrook, M. C. (1995). *Learning media assessment of students with visual impairments: A resource guide for teachers* (2nd ed.). Austin: Texas School for the Blind and Visually Impaired.

Lehman, S. S. (2013). A primer on cortical visual impairment. *Review of Ophthalmology.* Retrieved from https://www.reviewofophthal mology.com/article/a-primer-on-cortical-visual -impairment-42791

Milner, A. D., & Goodale, M. A. (2006). *The visual brain in action* (2nd ed.). Oxford, UK: Oxford University Press.

Milner, A. D., & Goodale, M. A. (2008). Two visual systems re-viewed. *Neuropsychologia, 46*(3), 774–785.

Steelman, J. D., Pierce, P. L., & Koppenhaver, D. A. (1994). The role of computers in promoting literacy in children with severe speech and physical impairments (SSPI). In K. G. Butler (Ed.), *Severe communication disorders: Intervention strategies* (pp. 200–212). Gaithersburg, MD: Aspen.

Stock, P. (2012, June). Reflections about the meaning of literacy [weblog post]. *Literacy in Learning Exchange.*

Swenson, A. M. (2016). *Beginning with braille: Firsthand experiences with a balanced approach to literacy* (2nd ed.). New York, NY: AFB Press.

Therrien, W. J. (2004). Fluency and comprehension gains as a result of repeated reading: A meta-analysis. *Remedial and Special Education, 25(*4), 252–261.

UNESCO Education Sector. (2004). *The plurality of literacy and its implications for policies and programmes.* UNESCO Education Sector Position Paper. Paris, France: United Nations Educational, Scientific and Cultural Organization. Retrieved from http://unesdoc.unesco .org/images/0013/001362/136246e.pdf

Wormsley, D. P. (2016). *I-M-ABLE: Individualized meaning-centered approach to braille literacy education.* New York, NY: AFB Press.

3

Children with CVI and Complex Communication Needs

Sarah Blackstone and Christine Roman-Lantzy

Coauthors' Note

We met at the Pennsylvania Speech and Hearing Association Conference in 2011. Christine was presenting on cortical visual impairment. Sarah was doing a workshop on patient-provider communication. At a break, a colleague of Sarah's said, "Hey, you've got to hear Christine Roman, she's really good."

Fast forward to 2018. We have become best friends, often engaging in lengthy, even raucous conversations that cover a broad range of topics. We share a passion for the rights of children and their families and, most specifically, for the rights of children with cortical visual impairment (CVI) and complex communication needs (CCN) who require augmentative and alternative communication (AAC). We know that these conditions often overlap because of the diagnoses underlying them. We also understand that these children are at high risk across many developmental domains and that it is difficult for them to access their right to an "appropriate" education or the human and civil rights that can enable them to communicate, learn, and actively participate in their families, schools, and communities.

We are also all about knocking down professional silos. When our professions divide up children into body parts or body functions to assess and treat them, we lose opportunities for interprofessional collaboration, and children too often lose the opportunity to see better and understand what they see, to develop robust language and literacy skills, and to learn about their world and how to "be" in it. Without broad-based appropriate interventions, these children will not and cannot communicate effectively with anyone, anywhere, at any time, or be able to develop their interests or realize their dreams.

The framework and many of the insights presented in this chapter were developed based on the authors' work at the Bridge School, a school for children with severe speech and physical impairments in Hillsborough, California, and the Centro de Apoyo Tecnológico para la Comunicación y el Aprendizaje (CATIC), a center in Mexico City for children who use AAC. The teachers, speech-language pathologists, occupational therapists, assistive technologists, instructional assistants, aides, and family members at these facilities have truly created lighthouses for learning. All their students have complex communication needs, and between 50 and 70 percent also have CVI. Most have mobility limitations and other challenges. Sarah has worked with both programs for decades. Christine began to work with each in 2012 and has since visited CATIC in Mexico City and made several trips to the Bridge School. Christine has taught staff in both places to administer the CVI Range and to adapt materials and modify their classrooms to support children with CVI. Most important, perhaps, we both have been privileged to listen to and learn from the staff and family members at these facilities.

We have observed substantial progress in these children. Their functional vision has improved (as measured by the CVI Range and validated through observations in natural settings) and they can now use a broader variety of AAC tools, techniques, and technologies. Some are becoming literate; all are completing school assignments; and all are more able to express their unique personalities, preferences, and interests.

This chapter introduces a framework aimed at helping to transcend the persistent professional silos that act as barriers to effective intervention for children who have both cortical visual impairment (CVI) and complex communication needs (CCN). The first half of the chapter explains the complex needs of children with CVI and CCN and describes a variety of augmentative and alternative communication (AAC) approaches that are available to support their communication over time. The second half of the chapter introduces the Vision Language Learning Communication Framework, which aims to provide a systematic and integrated approach to organizing interprofessional interventions with children who have a diagnosis of CVI and CCN. This chapter is not designed for use with all children who have visual impairment, but specifically those who demonstrate the unique visual and behavioral characteristics associated with CVI as described in sidebar 3.1.

We also seek to raise some critical questions, such as, do children with CVI and CCN lose out on opportunities for early learning? Do they experience unique barriers to their development of language and literacy skills? Is their access to appropriate educational materials limited? Are their social skills compromised because of their vision as well as their communication challenges? Are professionals who specialize in AAC prepared to work with children who have CVI, and are vision specialists prepared to work with children who have CCN? Do parents and teachers understand the unique needs of these children at their various ages and stages?

We encourage our colleagues to act and to do so collaboratively. There is a critical, unmet need to describe and document longitudinally not only the prevalence of CVI and CCN in children, but also (and importantly) the medical, clinical, and educational factors that can have an impact on their outcomes. To date, we know of no published demographic or intervention studies that systematically investigate the efficacy of interventions with these children, even though it is clear that without access to early identification, assessment and treatment programs, appropriate environmental accommodations and adaptive tools and assistive technologies, they will not thrive, reach their

---

SIDEBAR 3.1

Visual and Behavioral Characteristics Associated with CVI

1. **Attraction to color**. Strong color preference, especially for red or yellow.
2. **Need for movement to elicit or sustain visual attention**. Either the viewer or the object viewed needs to be moving to maximize the viewer's ability to "see" the object.
3. **Visual latency**. Delayed responses in looking at objects.
4. **Atypical visual field function**. The presence of unusual field locations. Loss of visual fields, especially in lower quadrants.
5. **Attraction to light**. Light-gazing and non-purposeful gaze.
6. **Difficulty with visual complexity**. For example, inability to see a familiar object against a patterned background.
7. **Difficulty with distance viewing**. For example, inability to see a familiar object beyond a certain distance.
8. **Absent or atypical visual reflexes**. Impaired blink reflex in response to an approaching object.
9. **Difficulty with visual novelty**. Preference for viewing, discriminating, and recognizing familiar objects.
10. **Absence of visually guided reach**. Can't look at and touch an object at the same time. These two actions are performed sequentially.

Courtesy of the Bridge School

Using adaptations for CVI at the Bridge School in Hillsborough, California.

potential, or contribute to society to their full ability.

It is also important to acknowledge that the approach used in this chapter, and in fact this entire text, intentionally differentiates CVI from ocular causes of visual impairment. Although there are other textbooks or articles that address the needs of children with visual impairments and complex

needs (for example, Allman & Lewis, 2014; Holbrook, McCarthy, & Kamei-Hannan, 2017; Sacks & Zatta, 2016), none of these works are specifically dedicated to an approach that begins with the CVI Range as a measure of functional vision. No other program uses the CVI characteristics as the framework for adaptations or specialized methods of instruction. The authors' fundamental belief is that the guiding principles of assessment and intervention with CVI are different from those used for individuals with ocular visual impairment, and therefore the approach used in this chapter is not considered appropriate for individuals whose visual impairment is primarily from ocular disorders.

AAC: A Quick Overview

While many readers may be familiar with CVI and the CVI Range, fewer may know about children with CCN or AAC intervention approaches. AAC refers to an area of practice that addresses the language and communication needs of children and adults who are unable to use their natural speech to communicate effectively across their social circles, such as with family, friends, acquaintances, paid workers, and unfamiliar communication partners (Beukelman & Mirenda, 2013; Blackstone & Berg, 2012). AAC approaches vary widely and depend on a child's physical and cognitive abilities, age, understanding of language, literacy skills, and need to access meaningful vocabulary so he or she can communicate effectively.

The development of literacy skills is especially critical for children with CCN, because when individuals are unable to speak, they are likely to remain forever dependent on others to communicate their thoughts and ideas. Traditional AAC interventions teach very young, preliterate children with CCN to use manual signs, graphic symbol sets, or photographs to represent language concepts prior to teaching them literacy skills. However, graphic symbols and photographs are often visually complex, and what is an obvious representation of a "cup" or "someone sitting" to a child with normal visual acuity may need to be taught to a child with CVI. Although traditional solutions such as minimizing clutter or using yellow or black backgrounds may help some children, graphic symbols or photographs are often not a best or a long-term solution for children with CVI and CCN. The time spent learning hundreds of graphic symbols or photographs might be better spent on teaching these children to recognize 26 letters of the alphabet so they can focus on developing basic literacy skills. Only then will they be able to "say" anything, anywhere, anytime, to anyone, about anything, and do so independently. (Information about the accommodations these children need to develop their literacy skills are described in Chapter 2.) Of course, AAC interventions need to take into account other key variables, such as children's preferences and interests, their purposes for communicating, the needs, skills, and abilities of their communication partners (both peers and adults), contextual variables, and the availability of appropriate AAC tools and assistive technologies.

Courtesy of the Bridge School

Using CVI adaptations for early literacy.

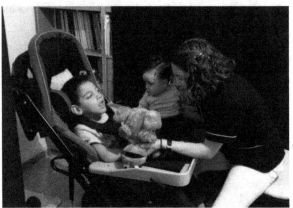

Courtesy of CATIC

A boy with CVI using body-based communication (smiling and looking) during an interaction with a baby and a toy.

Individuals who use AAC, like everyone else, rely on multiple modalities throughout the day to meet their communication needs. These include (Beukelman & Mirenda, 2013):

- *Unaided, body-based approaches* (no-tech), such as body language, gestures, facial expressions, and manual signs
- *Aided, nonelectronic approaches* (low-tech), such as a paper and pencil; an eye transfer or eye gaze communication board; and other communication books, cards, and boards
- *Aided approaches using electronic devices and technologies* (high-tech),

Courtesy of CATIC

Children with CVI communicating using an aided, non-electronic board.

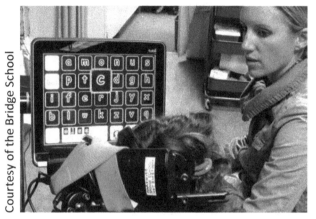

Courtesy of the Bridge School

A girl with CVI communicating using an aided electronic device.

such as a speech-generating device or a phone, tablet, or computer with communication apps or software

In addition, children with physical disabilities may require additional devices, known as access or assistive technologies, to use communication boards or devices—for example, switches that activate a scanning program or eye-tracking technology, infrared technology, a modified mouse device, an adapted keyboard, or a head stick to select items from a display. Without these assistive technologies, children who are not able to use their hands, for example, might be unable to use the communication technologies they need to communicate effectively.

Over the past 40 years, AAC techniques, strategies, and technologies have enabled millions of children and adults to communicate more effectively and independently. In addition, because of the proliferation and sophistication of mainstream technologies today, people with CCN now have access to lower-cost, portable, and more powerful communication options.

Historical Perspective

It is important to acknowledge the long history associated with children who are blind or visually impaired, as well as the relatively short history of efforts to place a special focus on children with severe speech and language impairments. The Institut National des Jeunes Aveugles in Paris, founded in 1785, was one of the first special schools for children who were blind. In the United States, schools for children who are blind or visually impaired have provided specialized instruction since 1829. Over the years, specific disease outbreaks have served to energize medical communities and resulted in significant policy shifts for children with visual impairments.

For example, from 1943 to 1951, an estimated 7,000 infants in the United States became blind from retinopathy of prematurity (ROP), a disease in which the retinal blood vessels of premature infants can grow atypically (Phelps, 1981). The international medical community responded in a dramatic manner, and, as a result, the incidence and severity of ROP has significantly decreased around the world (Bullard, Donahue, Feman, Sinatra, & Walsh, 1999). Together, pediatric ophthalmologists, retinal specialists, and prematurity experts developed a consensus statement known as *An International Classification of Retinopathy of Prematurity* (Committee for the Classification of Retinopathy of Prematurity, 1984), which led to seminal research and effective treatment (Kamholz, Cole, Gray, & Zupancic, 2009).

During the 1962–65 rubella epidemics in the United States, 20,000 children were born with disabilities (Plotkin, 2001). Of these, 12,000 were deaf; 3,580 were blind; and 1,800 had severe cognitive disabilities. Again, the medical community responded quickly. Currently, 131 countries are using the measles-rubella vaccine as part of the World Health Organization's international immunization program. A 74 percent reduction in measles deaths was reported globally between 1980 and 2008 (Wolfson, Grais, Luquero, Birmingham, & Strebel, 2009). The World Health Organization's most recent strategic plan for measles and rubella aims to eradicate the disease and its sequelae in all countries by 2020 (World Health Organization, 2012).

No disease outbreak has ever drawn attention to the medical needs or educational outcomes of children with CCN. In fact, prior to 1975, few children with CCN went to school, and many adults with CCN (including those who were cognitively intact) resided in institutions without a way to communicate. Access to education and clinical services for children with CCN occurred only after 1975, when the U.S. Congress enacted the Education for All Handicapped Children Act (EHA).

The goal of the EHA was to ensure that all children with disabilities (including those with severe and multiple challenges) gained access to "free appropriate public education." Under the EHA, public schools were granted federal funding so they could provide equal access to education for children with physical and mental disabilities. In 1990, amendments to the law were passed, changing the name to the Individuals with Disabilities Education Act (IDEA). In 1997 and again in 2004, additional amendments clarified and extended coverage, with final regulations published in August 2006 (Part B, for school-aged children) and in September 2011 (Part C, for babies and toddlers).

The US Department of Education, Office of Special Education Programs, publishes information about the numbers of students served under IDEA, by primary diagnosis. The most recently reported data from 2015–16 (National Center for Education Statistics, 2018) shows that, of the 6.7 million children served (13 percent of the total public-school enrollment), 54 percent had a primary diagnosis of "specific learning disability" or "speech or language impairment," as shown in Figure 3.1. The category "other health impairment" (14 percent) included children with chronic or acute health problems, such as diabetes, asthma, sickle cell anemia, epilepsy, and lead poisoning. Children with visual impairment, deafblindness, and traumatic brain injury are not included in Figure 3.1 because "each account for less than 0.5 percent of students served."

This data provides no information about children with CVI or CCN. Their numbers are likely buried within multiple categories, such as visual impairment, multiple disabilities, developmental delay, orthopedic impairment, speech or language impairment, intellectual disability, traumatic brain injury, and autism.

Prevalence of CVI and CCN Today

Children with CVI

CVI is the most prevalent cause of visual impairment in first-world nations today; however, it is a condition that is underreported, underdiagnosed, and undertreated (Gardo, 2005; Good, Jan, Burden, Skoczenski, & Candy, 2001; Good et al., 1994; Hoyt, 2003; Jan, Good, & Hoyt, 2006; Khetpal & Donahue, 2007). As summarized by Carden and Good (2012), the Oxford Register of Early Childhood Impairments reported that, as early as 1988, the overall incidence of bilateral visual impairment was at 0.14 percent of the population, with 29.5 percent of cases due to CVI and 14.1 percent due to nystagmus, the second major cause of impairment in the study population. In a study of five Nordic countries, Rosenberg et al. (1996) noted that brain damage accounted for a growing number of cases of visual impairment in childhood. Rogers (1996) also found that CVI was the most common cause of visual impairment in children in the United Kingdom (49 percent of their study population). In northern California, CVI was cited as the leading cause of visual impairment in children under the age of 5 years (Murphy & Good, 1997).

Many children with CVI have multiple disabilities and require support from multiple service providers over their lifetimes. Although studies have shown that CVI can be identified in infancy

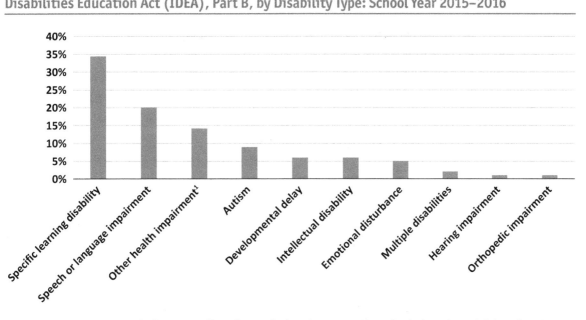

FIGURE 3.1 Percentage Distribution of Students Ages 3–21 Served under the Individuals with Disabilities Education Act (IDEA), Part B, by Disability Type: School Year 2015–2016

SOURCE: U.S. Department of Education, Office of Special Education Programs, Individuals with Disabilities Education Act (IDEA) database, retrieved July 10, 2017, from https://www2.ed.gov/programs/osepidea/618-data/state-level-data-files/index.html#bcc. See *Digest of Education Statistics 2017*, table 204.30.

[1]Other health impairments include having limited strength, vitality, or alertness due to chronic or acute health problems such as a heart condition, tuberculosis, rheumatic fever, nephritis, asthma, sickle cell anemia, hemophilia, epilepsy, lead poisoning, leukemia, or diabetes.

NOTE: Deafblindness, traumatic brain injury, and visual impairment are not shown because they each account for less than 0.5 percent of students served under IDEA. Due to categories not shown, detail does not sum to 100 percent. Although rounded numbers are displayed, the figures are based on unrounded estimates.

Source: Adapted from National Center for Education Statistics. (2018, April). Children and youth with disabilities. In *The Condition of Education*. Retrieved from https://nces.ed.gov/programs/coe/indicator_cgg.asp

(Roman-Lantzy & Lantzy, 2010), there is still no established protocol for screening infants at risk for CVI, and there are no consistent medical criteria utilized to diagnose and track CVI (Jan et al., 2013).

Children with CCN

Multiple demographic studies have found that approximately 3 to 5 percent of children enrolled in special education in the United States have CCN and can benefit from AAC interventions (Beukelman & Mirenda, 2013). Similar data are reported in other Western nations. However, the prevalence of adults with CCN is difficult to determine.

Adults who rely on AAC may have developmental, acquired, or degenerative conditions. They span all age groups and are served in multiple community, educational, and health care settings.

As noted earlier, there was an almost complete lack of services for children and adults with CCN until 1975. However, 40 years later, the field of AAC is now well established and the number of children and adults who benefit has expanded exponentially. AAC is now a recognized area of clinical practice with a robust research base and an industry that supports professionals and consumers. The following list illustrates the broad group of individuals who are invested in using, understanding, developing, and researching the impact of AAC on the lives of people with CCN:

- Children and adults with severe speech and language challenges (chronic, acute, or temporary), their family members and caregivers.

- Professionals from multiple disciplines, including speech-language pathology, education, occupational and physical therapy, assistive technology, vision specialists, and others who provide clinical services in schools, hospitals, clinics, rehabilitation centers, and the like.

- An industry comprised of developers and manufacturers that design, build, and sell speech-generating devices, communication apps and software, switches, and books and other educational materials.

- Public and private insurers that cover some of the costs associated with clinical services and AAC technologies.

- University programs and professors who teach AAC course content to students from multiple disciplines.

- Researchers who conduct AAC-related studies with funding from multiple sources, including universities, health care facilities, governments, and organizations.

- Academic journals that publish research and other media sources that produce information about AAC for multiple stakeholder groups.

- Consumer and professional organizations that represent people who use AAC and their families, as well as the professionals who support them. Examples include the American Speech-Language-Hearing Association, United States Society for Augmentative and Alternative Communication, International Society for Augmentative and Alternative Communication, Assistive Technology Industry Association, American Occupational Therapy Association, Autism Society of America, National Joint Committee for the Communication Needs of Persons with Severe Disabilities, and many others.

Children with CVI and CCN

Because of advances in neonatal and pediatric intensive care practices, younger and more fragile children survive today than previously, and they are at greater risk for neurodevelopmental impairments and multiple disabilities, including CVI and CCN. Similarly, advances in trauma medicine and medical technologies have reduced mortality rates in older children and adults who have experienced trauma or other neurological conditions, leaving many with significant and complex sequelae. Etiologies associated with CVI and CCN in children are often the same, as shown in Table 3.1.

Early Intervention and Interprofessional Collaboration

Assessment and intervention protocols for children with CVI and CCN need to focus on developing functional vision as well as speech, language, and communication skills. This requires close collaboration among vision specialists, speech-language pathologists, teachers, and family members. These children require access to early identification, assessment, and treatment programs; appropriate environmental accommodations; and adaptive tools and assistive technologies, or they will not thrive, reach their potential, or contribute to society to their full ability. They will be unable to access their education or actively participate in their families and communities as children, youths, and ultimately as adults.

Speech-language pathologists who work with children who have vision problems have often

TABLE 3.1

Diagnostic Categories Associated with CVI and CCN in Children

Diagnostic Category	Etiology/Cause	Risk Factor for:	
Congenital and Perinatal Conditions		*CVI*	*CCN*
Asphyxia	Oxygen deprivation to brain resulting in excess carbon dioxide	X	X
Perinatal hypoxic-ischemic encephalopathy, hypoxic-ischemic encephalopathy (HIE)	Lack of sufficient oxygen in body cells or blood (hypoxia); not enough blood being supplied to the brain (ischemia); diffuse, permanent brain damage due to profound asphyxia (HIE)	X	X
Intraventricular hemorrhage (IVH)	Bleeding that occurs in the germinal matrix or ventricles and surrounding tissues of the brain	X	X
Periventricular leukomalacia (PVL)	Injury or death of white matter in the brain (generally associated with prematurity)	X	X
Cerebral vascular accident, cerebral artery infarction	Neonatal stroke that occurs when blood capillaries in the brain rupture or when blood flow is blocked	X	X
Infections that affect the central nervous system	TORCH infections (toxoplasmosis, other [syphilis, varicella-zoster, parvovirus B19], rubella, cytomegalovirus, and herpes), meningitis, group B strep, etc., that can pass from mother to fetus in utero or occur after birth	X	X
Structural abnormalities	Alteration in normal progression of brain development (e.g., Dandy-Walker syndrome, primary microcephaly, hydrocephalus, lissencephaly, etc.); often secondary to chromosomal disorders	X	X
Metabolic conditions	Severe hypoglycemia, kernicterus, hyperbilirubinemia, mitochondrial disorders	X	X
Cerebral palsy	A catchall diagnostic term for motor impairments acquired during the perinatal period or early childhood	X	X
Autism spectrum disorder	Cause undetermined; may include multiple factors		X
Chromosomal anomalies	Chromosomal translocations or deletions and certain syndromes	X	X
Acquired Conditions			
Acquired hypoxia	Near-drowning, near-SIDS, etc.	X	X
Open-head injuries related to blow to head or gunshot wound	Brain damage located in areas affected by penetrating trauma	X	X
Closed-head injury related to vehicle accidents, shaken baby syndrome	Contusions, hemorrhaging in multiple locations of the brain, concussion	X	X
Childhood infection	Meningitis, encephalitis, etc.	X	X
Tumor	Growth that can affect brain function; surgical treatment of tumor can also result in CVI/CCN	X	X
Cerebral vascular accident (CVA)	Stroke that occurs during childhood	X	X

introduced tactile symbols or relied solely on auditory scanning strategies. (*Auditory scanning* refers to the announcing of vocabulary items, one at a time, by a communication partner or a speech-generating device, allowing the individual without speech to select a word or message when he or she hears it using a switch or a body-based signal such as a smile or vocalization.) With these approaches, they are treating children with CVI and CCN in ways similar to children with ocular impairments, even in instances in which ophthalmologists had indicated that an ocular disorder, if present, could not explain a child's lack of functional vision. While capitalizing on existing strengths, AAC professionals too often have failed to capitalize on the fact that these children can develop functional vision over time.

It is essential that vision and communication therapies be integrated and that visual specialists, speech-language pathologists, and other professionals work collaboratively with family members to increase each child's ability to use his or her functional vision so he or she can access language, learn, communicate, and participate. Very simply, to do a good job treating children with CVI and CCN, educational teams need to understand the children's current functional vision (as measured by the CVI Range assessment) and know how to support their use of vision to access language and literacy over time. The goal is to improve functional vision through meaningful activities and participation. In short, it is critical that team members work together to identify these children in a timely manner so they can address the multiplicity of issues they face.

Children with CVI

Early identification of children with CVI is critical, because vision is not a static capacity (Christou & Bulthoff, 2000). It develops over time in response to the environment and as a result of the maturation of the visual system. The human brain has parallel visual pathways with more than 30 specialized areas of the cortex involved in relaying and interpreting visual information. Aspects of visual processing occur in approximately 70 percent of the

sensory processing areas in the cerebral cortex (Eagleman, 2015). We now know that undamaged parts of the brain can reroute visual information from damaged areas as a direct result of new experiences and learning. This means that children with CVI who have access to appropriate vision and educational services can be expected to gain visual skills as more intact areas of their brains gain function (Hoyt, 2002; Hyvärinen, 2006). Because vision affects a young child's ability to move, develop concepts, establish joint attention, learn language, engage with objects and activities, and communicate effectively with others, it is essential to focus on improving a child's functional vision from an early age as part of an integrated intervention program.

Children with CCN

The development of speech, language, and communication skills also begins at birth. By the age of 2 years, typically developing children know the meaning of hundreds of words and are using multi-word utterances. Children at risk of acquiring speech or who have significant language delays require early intervention services. There is now substantial evidence that using AAC approaches can support a child's development of speech (Millar, Light, & Schlosser, 2006; Romski & Sevcik, 2005). Also, a comprehensive review of the outcomes of early intervention programs for children with CCN over the past 35 years demonstrates that young children benefit from using AAC approaches in multiple ways (Romski, Sevcik, Barton-Hulsey, & Whitmore, 2015).

Children with CVI and CCN

AAC professionals have long recognized that many children with CCN have problems with their vision. Higginbotham and Welch (2006) and Kovach and Kenyon (2003) have reported that as many as 48 to 75 percent of children and adults with development delays and cerebral palsy and 75 to 90 percent of children with severe and profound cognitive disabilities demonstrate significant visual problems, including reduced visual acuity, visual field cuts or losses, reduced contrast sensitivity, oculomotor problems, and difficulties with visual processing. However, we know of few case examples and no systematic studies today of interventions with children who have CCN and any form of vision loss, including CVI, to inform our clinical or educational practices with these children.

This current lack of information is a cause for concern. For example, we know that vision is a key component of *joint attention*—sharing of attention to an object or event with a partner (Carpenter & Liebal, 2011; Tomasello, 1995)—and that young children with CVI may fail to see a partner's pointing cues or any supplemental cues, such as where a communication partner is looking. We also know that early communication and joint attention underlie the development of language, and that joint attention is strongly associated with later vocabulary growth in children with and without disabilities (Fallon, Light, & Paige, 2001; Watt, Wetherby, & Shumway, 2006; Yoder & McDuffie, 2006). However, it is not yet routine practice to support the development of joint attention in infants and toddlers at risk for CVI or CCN.

In addition, we know that the quantity and quality of language provided to very young children affects their development across several domains (Cartmill et al., 2013; Hart & Risley, 1995). Children with CVI benefit from "mediators" to help them attach meaning to what they see (see Chapter 1). Children with CCN benefit from the use of modeling, also known as aided language input or augmented input (Bruno & Trembath, 2006; Dada & Alant, 2009; Harris & Reichle, 2004; Romski & Sevcik, 1996). Young children with CVI and CCN need skilled communication partners to provide appropriate language input. Children can benefit if parents, teachers, and therapists learn more about how and when to speak, taking into account a child's visual as well as language abilities.

Intervention Challenges

AAC professionals struggle to find ways for children with limited vision to gain maximum benefit from AAC tools and technologies (Wilkinson & Hennig, 2007) because most AAC strategies, tools, and technologies rely heavily on a child's ability to attend, understand, process semantic information, and select targets on visual displays (Light & Drager, 2007; Wilkinson & Jagaroo, 2004). As a result, many children with CVI and CCN are almost exclusively offered a limited number of tactile symbols or auditory scanning approaches. Auditory scanning systems are notoriously slow; however, they can provide access to a lot of vocabulary using "branching techniques," an important factor in the maturation of these children's communication capacities. Branching is a way to access vocabulary more efficiently by organizing it into categories, such as places, people, things, activities, phrases, and so on. For example, if a child selects "places," the system or communication partner might provide specific places the child might want to talk about, such as school, home, or playground. This organizational strategy enables children with limited functional vision to access large vocabularies and formulate sentences.

Traditionally, AAC displays are organized by associating background colors with types of words, concepts, or parts of speech to make it easier for users to locate symbols. For example, symbols, line drawings, or words related to *people* might be grouped using yellow backgrounds, while *action words* (verbs) might have green backgrounds, *places* might have purple backgrounds, and so on. Also, line drawings or symbols are typically placed on grids, often on 8½ × 11-inch paper or screens located on tablets, computers, or phones. Efforts to increase the number of symbols on displays so a user can access more vocabulary can result in crowding. Clinicians often use symbols or pictures on displays taken from commercially available symbols sets or graphic scenes, which are unfamiliar to most children, and must be taught.

These practices persist despite research that strongly contradicts their use, at least for some groups. There is a need for researchers to demonstrate whether (and which) background colors, if any, facilitate the ability of children with CVI and CCN to locate target symbols on a display. There is also a need to learn more about how to organize vocabulary for children with CVI. For now, clinicians

Courtesy of CATIC

The black background in this display is better for the child with CVI, rather than a vibrant color, as often used with children who have CCN.

who work with children with CVI and CCN should proceed with caution after careful assessment of each child. Recent research with other groups has determined that traditional ways of organizing displays, selecting symbols, and using background colors are often not optimal or effective:

- Traditional AAC displays (symbols in grids) place significant visual and cognitive demands on young, typically developing children with normal vision (Light & Drager, 2007; Wilkinson, Light, & Drager, 2012).

- Young children without disabilities have difficulty identifying, learning, and using even a small number of pictographic symbols arranged on a grid display (Drager et al., 2004; Drager, Light, Speltz, Fallon, & Jeffries, 2003).

- Children with and without disabilities find it easier to learn and use personalized photographs of familiar people, events, and locations (visual scenes) than to learn and use pictographic symbols in grids, especially before the age of 4 to 5 years (Light et al., 2004).

- How graphic symbols are arranged on traditional grid displays affects how fast and how accurately children with and without intellectual disabilities are able to locate a target symbol (Wilkinson & Light, 2014).

- Finally, while characteristics such as internal color, semantic class membership, and shared features (such as emotion type) can facilitate search for a symbol among an array of symbols, the widely used clinical practice of using background color as a cue either has no effect on performance, or in some cases, actually interferes with search (Thistle & Wilkinson, 2012; Wilkinson, Carlin, & Thistle, 2008; Wilkinson & Snell, 2011).

Recently, Wilkinson and her colleagues also demonstrated that even small changes to the physical features on an AAC display can make a significant difference in the speed and accuracy with which individuals, with and without intellectual disabilities, can select a target symbol from among an array of symbols on an AAC display (Wilkinson, Carlin, & Jagaroo, 2006; Wilkinson & Coombs, 2010; Wilkinson et al., 2015; Wilkinson & McIlvane, 2013; Wilkinson, O'Neill, & McIlvane, 2014). Also, individuals with Down syndrome and fragile X syndrome have difficulty inhibiting attention to the nontarget symbols on the display, which likely would affect their ability to use an AAC display (Brady, 2008; Lanfranchi, Jerman, Dal Pont, Alberti, & Vianello, 2010; Lanfranchi, Jerman, & Vianello, 2009; Munir, Cornish, & Wilding, 2000).

Because new eye-tracking technologies are beginning to enable researchers to study visual behaviors in children as young as 6 months (Kooiker, Pel, van der Steen-Kant, & van der Steen, 2016), they may soon be able to (1) characterize the visual capacities of very young children and populations with a range of disabilities and, consequently, help identify evidence-based early intervention; (2) compare risk groups, such as children with ocular impairments, CVI, Down syndrome, autism, or fragile X; (3) follow visual development over time; and (4) construct individual visual profiles for children, track their progress, and report their outcomes. In other words, we may be on the cusp of asking and answering some very important questions about children with CVI and CCN.

Some clinical practices, however, continue to negatively impact intervention programs for children who have CVI and CCN. One example is the notion that the approaches used with children with ocular visual impairments work with children with CVI. Another is that the vision of children with CVI is variable, that it changes from day to day or even hour to hour. It is far more likely that aspects of the child's environment change throughout the day, *not* the child's neurological status or vision. Another misconstrued "factoid" is that children with CVI require a simple, black, plain background to see objects, photographs, or other materials. While definitely helpful for children in Phase I CVI, the same children in Phases II and III are able to use their vision in more complex environments and should be given the chance to do so. Finally, decisions about where and how to present objects, materials, and activities should not be based on a belief that midline presentations are preferable. Some children with CVI and CCN are far more apt to see and attach meaning to objects, images, and people using their peripheral (dorsal stream) vision. Also, children with CVI may have lower visual field cuts or losses and be unaware of objects at midline. Decisions about where and how to provide visual input to children with CVI and CCN should be made only after careful assessment.

Presenting materials to a student away from midline in his preferred visual field.

Courtesy of CATIC

Vision, Language, Learning, Communication: An Integrated Framework

The Vision Language Learning Communication (VLLC) Framework provides a systematic and integrated approach to organizing interprofessional interventions with children who have a diagnosis of CVI and CCN. It also strives to make it easier for family members to understand the barriers and opportunities their children face each day. The VLLC Framework is not prescriptive, but rather offers a road map to support the teams who support these children. The VLLC Framework grew out of the authors' collaborations with staff at the Bridge School and CATIC and has been presented at both national and international conferences to clinicians, educators, and family members over the past few years. The VLLC Framework envisions a journey whose destination for each child is clear: functional vision; access to lifelong learning; an ability to use complex language to communicate; meaningful participation at home, in school, and in the community; and self-determination.

Each child's journey varies, but along the way there will be "rest areas" and "points of interest." Rest areas signal teams to stop, reassess progress, and rethink objectives and strategies. Points of interest represent the potential for breakthroughs—access to new knowledge, new technologies, or unique approaches.

The VLLC Framework is anchored by the phases of the CVI Range. The following are the principles underlying the framework:

1. Vision, language, learning, and communication goals should be integrated and addressed holistically and collaboratively by teams that include speech-language pathologists, vision specialists, teachers, occupational therapists, physical therapists, physicians, family members, and others as needed.

2. Improvement in functional vision and other developmental domains should be expected.

3. The quality and quantity of nonverbal and linguistic input to children with CVI helps them process visual information, as well as understand and interpret what they see and experience. (See also Chapter 1 for a discussion of the mediator's role with children who have CVI.)

4. An integrated approach to intervention can have a positive impact on academic success, social and emotional development, self-determination, and the ability to actively participate in family, school, and community.

5. Access to sufficiently large vocabularies is essential to a child's long-term linguistic, cognitive, educational, social, emotional, and communicative development.

6. Children with CVI and CCN need access to assistive technologies and a variety of AAC tools and strategies across their life span.

Components of the VLLC Framework

Figure 3.2 provides an overview of the components of the VLLC Framework. The journey begins with

identification of children at risk for CVI and CCN. *Assessment* confirms the presence of CVI and the need for AAC approaches. Assessments require the participation of multiple team members, are dynamic, and are conducted periodically (at least yearly). They enable teams to track progress, identify next steps, and measure outcomes.

Intervention is a complex, longitudinal process that involves a series of short-term steps. Teams juggle a multiplicity of variables. A first step is to establish integrated goals based on the needs and characteristics of a child. Then, teams prioritize objectives and determine intervention strategies by addressing contextual accommodations (modifying materials and engineering the environment), coaching communication partners, and providing access to a range of AAC strategies and assistive technologies.

It is important to remember that all children with CVI and CCN display unique developmental patterns. For example, one child may have very limited functional vision (Phase I), but relatively intact cognitive, language, or motor skills. Another child may function at Phase III on the CVI Range, but demonstrate delayed cognitive and language abilities. In other words, their development is likely to be asynchronous. What these children are capable of achieving is not known and is difficult to

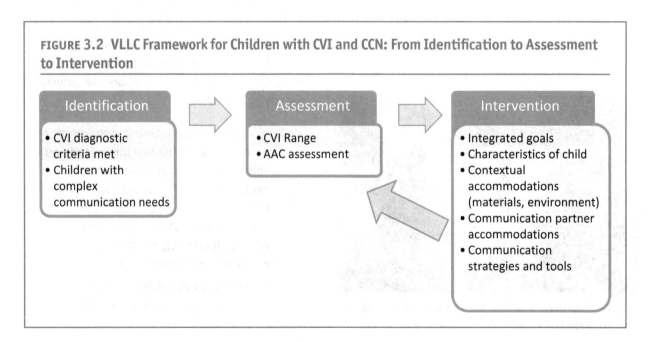

FIGURE 3.2 VLLC Framework for Children with CVI and CCN: From Identification to Assessment to Intervention

determine. Therefore, it is essential that we never underestimate their potential.

The VLLC Framework is illustrated with the story of Danny, a young boy with CVI and CCN who, when initially assessed at age 3, scored a 2 on the CVI Range (Phase I CVI) and was unable to communicate. Four years later, he scored a 7 on the CVI Range (Phase III CVI) and used a variety of AAC methods to communicate.

Identification

Identification of a child with CVI and CCN may require multidisciplinary referrals and assessments. When problems with vision are suspected, a referral is made to an ophthalmologist. If (1) an eye exam does not explain the child's limited use of vision, (2) the child has a medical history that includes one of the etiologies associated with CVI (see Table 3.1), and (3) the child demonstrates the unique visual and behavioral characteristics associated with CVI, a referral is made for a CVI assessment (see Roman-Lantzy, 2018). When delays in speech and language development are noted, a referral is made to a speech-language pathologist to assess the child's speech and language development. It is also necessary to rule out hearing difficulties, so the child may also need to see an audiologist. Children found to be at risk for the development of functional speech are subsequently referred for an AAC assessment. If motor delays are also present, occupational and physical therapy assessments are conducted. Children at risk for CVI and CCN may require multiple assessments by teams of professionals who have the expertise to support their development over time.

At age 3, Danny's parents brought him to an AAC clinic because he was unable to speak. His diagnoses included periventricular leukomalacia, severe dysarthria, and quadriplegia. His hearing was within normal limits. The speech-language pathologist noted that Danny did not look at faces or appear to see objects, and his visual behaviors were consistent with CVI. Upon request, Danny's mother provided the team with an ophthalmologist's report, which

indicated Danny had a normal eye exam. However, results of a visually evoked response test showed abnormalities in conduction. Danny was immediately referred for a CVI assessment. The AAC team decided to wait to develop language and communication goals until after they knew more about Danny's visual processing abilities.

Assessment

Assessment of CVI

The CVI Range (Roman-Lantzy, 2018) identifies children according to their scores (0–10) as being in Phases I, II, or III. It is the anchor for the VLLC Framework.

AAC Assessment

AAC assessments gather information about a child's communication needs and language skills and abilities across partners and environments (Beukelman & Mirenda, 2013). Family members are key participants in the assessment process because they are their child's primary communication partners. Speech-language pathologists evaluate a child's speech production abilities, receptive and expressive language skills, literacy skills, and nonverbal communication behaviors. They also consider a child's vocabulary needs across settings and how best to represent language using a combination of manual signs, photographs, graphic symbols, or spoken messages (auditory scanning). AAC assessments may also include consideration of how to arrange photographs or symbols on aided AAC systems. Occupational and physical therapists determine how to support a child so he or she can move, access materials, and use AAC tools and assistive technologies during everyday activities. They also assess a child's use of hands, head, eyes, and other body parts and ability to sit, stand, reach, walk, and so forth.

Throughout the assessment process, team members observe how a child participates in activities, what the child is interested in, and how the child engages and interacts with familiar and unfamiliar communication partners across multiple contexts. Depending on the child's needs, other professionals (such as behavioral psychologists; educators; pediatricians; mobility, seating, or assistive technology specialists; and social workers) may also participate.

Danny's initial AAC assessment revealed that he had no speech and was unable to sit independently or use his hands. He rarely vocalized and did not have a yes or no response. Although he smiled in response to some sounds and enjoyed music, his mother was uncertain whether he understood any words. (At age 3, typically developing children have receptive vocabularies that approach 1,000 words, so Danny's understanding of language appeared to be significantly delayed.) She reported that he recognized her voice and enjoyed interacting with family members and playing with his sister. Professionals on the team noted that Danny seemed alert and was easy to engage. At the time of the initial assessment, Danny had no way to reliably express language. He was unable to use his natural speech, manual signs, graphic symbols, photographs, drawings, or text.

During the initial CVI Range assessment, Danny's family reported that he frequently gazed at a red lampshade after it was turned on, but it took him up to 15 seconds to look at it. He didn't seem to recognize objects except for a favorite green squeaky frog toy, a gift he had received as an infant. The assessment also revealed that Danny's visual attention was very brief and that objects had to be held very close to his face, presented to his left side, and paired with movement before he became aware of them. Danny did not look directly into the faces of even the most familiar adults and did not appear to recognize his own mirror image. His mother reported that when they were in a store, a restaurant, or visiting friends, he seemed to "shut down," keeping his eyes closed and appearing to sleep though these multisensory experiences, with only occasional

peeks at ceiling lights, fans, or windows. Danny scored a 2 on the CVI Range. His visual behaviors were consistent with a child in Phase I.

The team of family members, teachers, a teacher of students with visual impairments, a speech-language pathologist, and an occupational therapist decided that a major priority for Danny was to focus on increasing his use of vision and to support his development of concepts, building vocabulary and encouraging him to become a more active participant in learning activities. Reassessments would be an inherent component of the intervention process as Danny's skills developed.

Children with very limited access to language, like Danny, are considered "emerging communicators," and AAC goals typically focus on providing access to symbolic communication (Dowden, 1999; Dowden & Cook, 2002).

Intervention

The VLLC Framework provides a way to organize and individualize intervention programs using the phases of CVI. As noted in Figure 3.2, the components of intervention are:

- *Integrated goals:* focusing on vision, language, and communication, as well as other areas that affect learning and participation (such as positioning, mobility, and movement)
- *Characteristics of child*: recognizing areas of strength as well as challenges, based on assessment results
- *Contextual accommodations:* making adaptations to materials and the environment
- *Communication partner accommodations:* teaching or coaching interactants to support the use of functional vision, build concepts, encourage language growth, and promote effective communication

- *Communication strategies and tools:* providing access to no-tech, low-tech, and high-tech strategies and technologies to support learning, language, and communication and to increase participation across daily activities and natural routines

Interventions in Phase I

Children with CVI and CCN in Phase I are limited in what they can experience, learn, and communicate about. Some, like Danny, are not able to move independently or explore their environment so incidental learning opportunities are rare. To optimize learning at home and in the classroom, the following are guidelines for interventions with children in Phase I:

- Provide short practice sessions to encourage the use of vision every day, across multiple but controlled environments, both at home and in school.
- Minimize extraneous sensory input to increase the likelihood of the child using his or her vision.
- Encourage the use of speech or vocalizations and body-based signals, if possible.
- Introduce auditory scanning approaches.
- Explore the use of a backlit, dynamic display, such as a tablet with apps, to support the use of vision, highlighting color, and movement.
- Introduce a simple digitized speech-output device to enable the child to express messages.

Table 3.2 summarizes the characteristics of children who are in Phase I and the goals for working with them and provides specific suggestions for interventions. Integrated goals for this phase are to provide multiple learning opportunities each day in order to build stable visual responses and at the same time expand concepts and vocabulary.

Because children in Phase I are unable to use their vision functionally, they do not establish joint attention, regard faces, or respond to photographs or pictures and symbols. Therefore, familiar communication partners must learn to restrict sensory input and use language mindfully to describe familiar objects, actions, and routines. They also need to support children to express language and communicate with familiar partners. Significant accommodations to materials, environments, and activities are required for these children to use vision and to facilitate their learning, understanding, use of language, and communication development. AAC approaches focus on partner-assisted auditory scanning and use of light boxes, supplemental light, movement, and backlit screens to highlight objects to support conceptual development and language, switch-activated messages, and body-based modes. Tablets with apps that highlight colors and movement can also support vision.

Danny's team worked on increasing his visual attention and building his language understanding. Objects selected for viewing were of a single, preferred color: red. Communication partners—Danny's aide, mother, teacher, speech-language pathologist, and occupational therapist—wore dark, plain clothing. They scheduled short sessions every day in a darkened room to present him with familiar objects, paired with movement. They used shiny objects and a flashlight or a light box to draw his attention. They sometimes waited quietly for up to 15 seconds for him to look to allow for visual latency. Although they generally presented objects to Danny's left, his preferred visual field, they also stimulated his attention in other visual fields. Light, movement, and color gradually drew his attention to familiar objects.

AAC interventions initially focused on language input. Although a simple listener-assisted auditory scanning technique was considered, the team initially decided to focus on increasing

TABLE 3.2

Phase I VLLC Framework Summary and Suggestions

Integrated Goals

- Build stable visual responses.
- Provide multiple learning opportunities throughout the day.
- Attach meaning to familiar, preferred objects in the environment using vision.
- Develop understanding of concepts and words that represent a broad range of objects, actions, events, and activities experienced throughout the day.
- Enable the child to produce language and communicate with familiar partners.

Characteristics of Child

Area	Characteristics
Language and communication	<ul><li>No facial attention</li><li>No joint attention</li><li>May give confusing cues</li><li>Attends to auditory sounds, spoken language</li><li>*Child who talks:* may label object and say, "I see it," "I want that"<ul><li>Spoken language may be concrete, dependent on others, focused on here and now</li><li>May be echolalic</li></ul></li><li>*Child with CCN:* may vocalize, smile, move body</li><li>Not able to use two-dimensional materials</li></ul>
Vision	<ul><li>Child may turn in direction of target using dorsal stream (peripheral) vision</li><li>No eye-to-object or eye-to-person contact</li><li>Intermittent and brief visual responses</li></ul>
Physical	<ul><li>Child may need physical supports to maintain a stable position</li></ul>

Suggestions for Intervention

Type of Intervention	Suggestions
Contextual Accommodations	
Environment	<ul><li>All sensory input (auditory, tactile, visual, language, olfactory) needs to be controlled</li><li>Use of a light box or light source can support vision</li><li>A darkened room can minimize distractions</li><li>Familiar contexts are essential</li></ul>
Materials	Use three-dimensional objects:<ul><li>Present one at a time</li><li>Use the preferred color (or red)</li><li>Pair with light</li><li>Use movement or shiny objects</li><li>Have a plain background</li><li>Use familiar/preferred objects</li><li>Tablet device with apps (using color and movement, and without auditory output) can be helpful</li></ul>

TABLE 3.2 *(continued)*

Communication Partner Accommodations	
Communication partner accommodations	■ Wear black or dark clothing, no patterns ■ Limit the number of interactive partners ■ Time and control language input (see sample script in Figure 3.3) ■ Speak slowly and calmly ■ Wait: respect latency ■ Present objects in the child's preferred or usable visual fields ■ Pair objects with light or movement ■ Provide lots of opportunities to practice
Communication Strategies and Tools	

No-tech (body based)	■ Encourage:
	  □ Reliable yes/no responses
	  □ Speech (approximations)
	  □ Gestures/signs
	■ Use partner-assisted auditory scanning (with branching if child is able) to provide access to large vocabulary
	  □ Typically useful with familiar partners only

Low-tech (nonelectronic)	■ Highlight objects with light, movement ■ If using auditory scanning, partners can use card with list of targeted vocabulary (organized by category, if relevant) to encourage consistency across partners
High-tech (electronic)	■ Use a tablet (without sound/voice) ■ Use switches/devices with simple messages that can be activated by partner and/or child

Danny's receptive language skills, teaching vocabulary for familiar objects, activities, routines, people, and toys. His structured sessions paired visual attention with carefully timed language input. Communication partners found that using few words, a slow rate of speech, and timing their verbal input so it supported Danny's visual experience was very helpful.

The sample script for Phase I described in Figure 3.3 illustrates how such sessions might proceed.

Danny made steady progress. His visual attention to familiar objects became more consistent.

Visual latency decreased, except when he was tired or after a seizure. He no longer stared at overhead lights, although he continued to benefit when objects were backlit using a light box or highlighted with a flashlight. His parents also reported that Danny began to notice objects at greater distances, sometimes up to 10 feet away. After one year, the team reassessed his use of vision. He scored 5 on the CVI Range, placing him in Phase II.

Within that year, Danny learned to understand words for objects, activities, places, people, colors, shapes, and actions, with a focus on familiar

FIGURE 3.3 Sample Script for Phase I

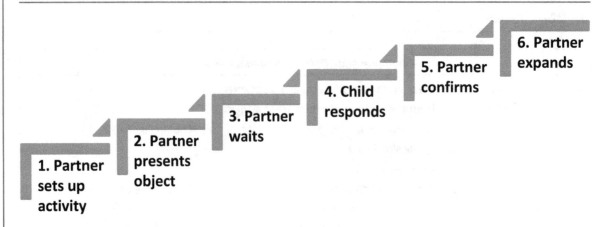

1. **Partner sets up activity.** Partner may say:
   a. "I'm going to ask you to look."
   b. "See if you can find _____."
   c. "See if you know what I have."
   d. "Let's find it again."
   e. "I have something red that you know."
   f. "Here's your _____."

2. **Partner presents a favorite, brightly colored, shiny object.** A backlit device or light box can highlight an object. Movement may also help. If possible, present the object so the child can feel as well as see it. Use favorite, familiar objects, such as a red cup, Elmo, green frog, toy car, Slinky, wind chime, pinwheel, or gold beads.

3. **Partner waits.** Latency can be quite prolonged. The partner is silent and waits for the child to look.

4. **Child responds.** Behaviors that suggest a child has seen the object may include a smile, vocalization, movement of a body part, or turning in the direction of the object. A child who speaks may label the object or comment on seeing it.

5. **Partner confirms.** Partner may say:
   a. "You looked at the _____."
   b. "Yes, you can drink from your red cup."
   c. "You like to play with your frog."
   d. "The ball is bouncing."
   e. "It's the fluffy chicken."

   The partner might activate a switch for the child that says, "My red cup" or other appropriate language. Later on, the child can do this.

6. **Partner expands learning experience.** Partner may:
   a. Help the child touch the object.
   b. Repeat the activity using a different object.
   c. Give the child another opportunity to "find" the object.
   d. Allow the child to "take a rest."

   Expanding the experience can introduce new vocabulary.

routines. Key team members kept updating and sharing the list of words he knew so that all team members could use them consistently. Although Danny's expressive communication repertoire continued to be limited, team members could now interpret a smile to mean yes. A partner-assisted auditory scanning system was introduced, as well as a simple voice-output device. Initially, team members activated a switch (placed near Danny's head) so he would hear words or messages expressed after he saw an object. Recorded messages included: "I see that," "It's my green frog," and "My red cup. Let's have a drink." The team also introduced a tablet with a backlit dynamic display. Although bright colors paired with movement engaged Danny's attention, he did not yet recognize photographs, even of familiar objects.

Interventions in Phase II

Children in Phase II have begun to use their vision functionally. However, they continue to require significant and ongoing accommodations, and team members must constantly reassess ways to support them. Controlling sensory input continues to be a significant factor. The following are guidelines for optimizing learning at home and in the classroom for children in Phase II:

- Provide lots of opportunities to practice using vision functionally, across the day, and in multiple environments.

- Continue to control sensory input to support the child's use of vision.

- Introduce two-dimensional materials and teach the child to attach meaning to photographs of familiar objects and activities.

- Gradually increase the complexity and functionality of dynamic display tools with backlighting, such as a tablet, light box, computer, or communication device.

- Encourage the use of speech or vocalizations and relevant AAC approaches

A child in Phase II CVI using adapted two-dimensional materials.

Courtesy of the Bridge School

to express language and build vocabulary.

- Adapt educational materials and activities to support learning and enhance participation.

Suggestions for intervention during Phase II are summarized in Table 3.3. Integrated goals include increasing the child's use of functional vision across events, activities, and interactions; and developing larger vocabularies that include salient features and reflect comparative thought. Accommodations to materials and the environment, as well as coaching communication partners to support more complex language, continue to be important. Expressive communication now can expand beyond auditory scanning and body-based modes as the child begins to recognize two-dimensional photos and pictures. Teaching literacy skills also becomes a focus for some children during Phase II.

Early in Phase II, Danny's parents noted that although he continued to prefer the colors red and green, he now looked at and recognized other colors and more objects. Also, he had begun to look at and recognize the faces of familiar adults and children and make eye-to-eye contact with his own mirror image. He no longer stared at lights, but did continue to benefit when objects were backlit.

Professionals and family members continued to work together to coordinate efforts to support

TABLE 3.3

Phase II VLLC Framework Summary and Suggestions

Integrated Goals

- Improve the use of vision with intent (i.e., functional vision).
- Increase the child's ability to have an impact on objects, events, activities, and interactions with communication partners.
- Develop concepts by identifying salient features and encouraging comparative thought.
- Provide access to increasingly complex language, both expressive and receptive.
- Support participation in academic/pre-academic activities by modifying materials and the environment.

Characteristics of Child

Area	Characteristics
Language and communication	- May try to reach, swat, touch - May move nearer to object - May use familiar objects functionally throughout the day - *Child who talks:* may label or describe object - *Child with CCN:* may continue to rely on no-tech body-based signals - AAC strategies need to increase access to more diverse, complex vocabulary and literacy - Partners begin to introduce two-dimensional materials - Partners continue to support use of low-tech and high-tech technology across the day
Vision	- Child may orient toward faces but will not have sustained or direct eye-to-eye contact with all partners
Physical	- Child may be positioned, with physical support, to use vision *and* interact with objects - Child may be positioned to hit a switch to make something happen

Suggestions for Intervention

Type of Intervention	Suggestions
Contextual Accommodations	
Environment	- Variability from early to late in Phase II - Child can tolerate low to medium levels of additional sensory input while using vision - May be able to increase complexity and volume of sound (from single voice to several voices in the environment) while maintaining visual attention - Familiar contexts still necessary
Materials	- Child begins to see objects with additional vibrant colors, up to three or four colors on surface of object - Progression seen in two-dimensional images, from photographs of familiar objects to images with two to three elements - Color still important (do not use black and white) - Child begins to generalize from familiar to novel objects based on consistent salient visual features (e.g., cats have whiskers and triangle-shaped ears) - Child is able to deal with increasingly complex materials in natural environments

TABLE 3.3 *(continued)*

Communication Partner Accommodations	

Communication partner accommodations	■ Be mindful of clothing and other backgrounds or arrays
	■ Think about when and how to provide language input
	■ Use wait time to accommodate for latency
	■ Offer objects closer to midline (in preferred or usable field), but not yet at midline
	■ Label objects, actions, and characteristics of object as child uses it (see sample script in Figure 3.4)
	■ When describing salient features of objects, keep in mind the interests and age of the child
	■ When talking or using music, observe whether child can visually attend *while* sound is present
	  □ May vary according to type, volume, and novelty of input, as well as other variables
	  □ If child looks away, the child's sensory threshold may have been exceeded
	■ If child acknowledges partner's face, interpret it as a sign of visual attention and reinforce looking as a communication signal and a shared experience (avoid saying "good looking")

Communication Strategies and Tools	
No-tech (body based)	■ Continue to use strategies that support interactions ■ Skilled partners can provide access to more and more vocabulary, beyond objects and actions, using partner-assisted auditory scanning (branching can expand) ■ Child can make choices using objects and photographs ■ Child may use more recognizable signals and language (gestures, signs, head shakes, etc.)
Low-tech (nonelectronic)	■ Provide objects ■ Provide two-dimensional materials ■ Present communication display or book ■ Use simple visual scanning system ■ Use simple eye-transfer (Etran) system ■ Employ card that partners can use to organize vocabulary for assisted auditory scanning with branching
High-tech (electronic)	■ Use tablet (with sound) and communication apps ■ Use switches that activate toys and provide speech output ■ Use computer with software (photographs and other meaningful graphics) ■ Communication devices: may be accessed directly using fingers, hand, fist, etc., or switches (touch, infrared, etc.) ■ Consider introducing eye-gaze technologies

Danny's use of vision while teaching language and communication skills. Several accommodations helped him use his vision during most daily routines, such as hygiene, play, therapies, and meals. At home, the family placed objects against simple backgrounds—for example, placing his bright red toothbrush on a black washcloth—and used bright colors, such as an orange towel. At mealtimes, Danny drank from his yellow cup and was fed with a bright green spoon. In addition, the team began to introduce two-dimensional materials, helping Danny attach meaning to photographs of familiar objects presented on a backlit screen. He began to understand that his use of vision could affect what happened next.

His receptive vocabulary had grown significantly. Danny was consistently smiling to signal yes, and the team now routinely presented him with auditory choices using a low-tech, listener-assisted auditory scanning system that enabled him to access a larger number of vocabulary items within familiar routines. He also began to use a slight vertical head shake to signal no. The AAC team worked diligently to increase his ability to understand and use two-dimensional materials. He began to recognize photographs of favorite objects when they were presented one at a time on a tablet. However, he could not yet match a two-dimensional photo mounted on a display to a familiar object. During some therapy sessions, he used a switch to make choices provided by a simple auditory scanning speech-generating device.

The quality and quantity of language input from communication partners continued to be an essential component of Danny's program. Figure 3.4 illustrates how communication partners describe salient features of objects, people, and activities in more detail, teaching concepts related to color, shape, texture, and features of

daily routines such as drinking, washing, brushing, and playing. Also, when Danny seemed to look at a partner's face, the partner acknowledged this nonverbally, for example, by smiling. As eye-to-object and eye-to-person behavior (joint attention) became more consistent, partners interpreted Danny's looking as a signal (e.g., "Ah! You want this or that?" or "Okay, I'll keep going?" "Yes, we are having fun"). They did not say "Good looking!" or "Use your eyes," but, rather, reinforced Danny's participation in a shared activity. Also, Danny was learning to sort some objects using language (e.g., "Which one of these is red?" "Can you find another one of these with buggy eyes like Elmo?").

Team members noted that in environments with competing sensory information, Danny had more trouble using his vision. They learned how to help him visually attend when competing sensory stimuli were present and to "back off" when his sensory threshold was exceeded.

Danny was becoming a *context-dependent communicator* (Dowden, 1999; Dowden & Cook, 2002), meaning he had begun to use symbolic communication reliably, even though his access to language continued to be limited and dependent on specific contexts and partners. To be an *independent communicator* (Dowden, 1999; Dowden & Cook, 2002), Danny would need to learn to spell, so that he could "say" anything to anyone.

Interventions in Phase III

In Phase III, children can use their vision functionally to have an impact on objects, activities, and people within familiar routines and across more contexts. However, they continue to require adjustments to their educational program, and team members need to constantly reassess ways to support them by controlling sensory input. Classrooms can pose especially significant challenges. Guidelines for optimizing learning at home and in the classroom in Phase III include:

FIGURE 3.4 Sample Script for Phase II

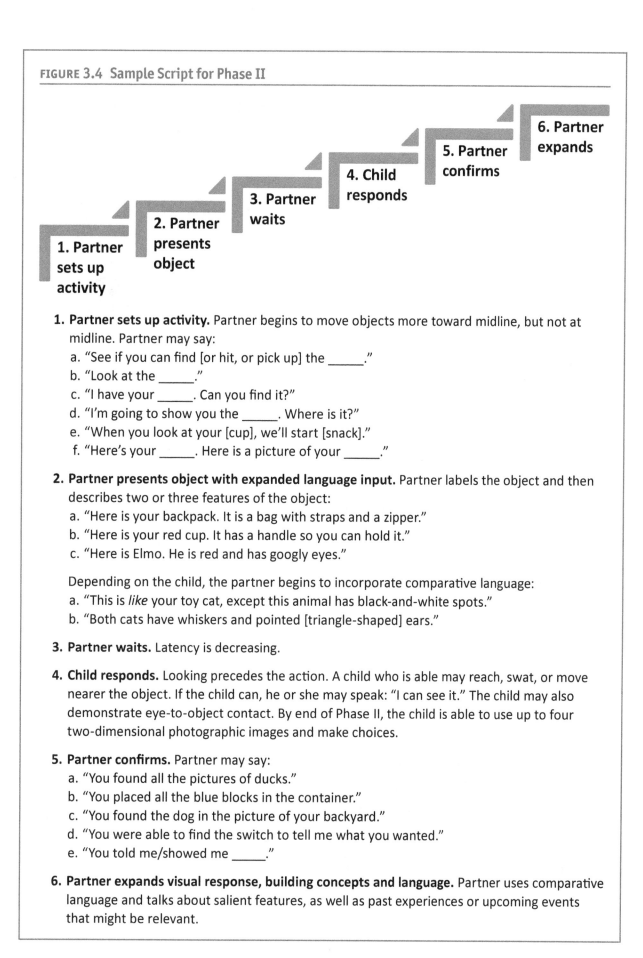

1. **Partner sets up activity.** Partner begins to move objects more toward midline, but not at midline. Partner may say:
   a. "See if you can find [or hit, or pick up] the _____."
   b. "Look at the _____."
   c. "I have your _____. Can you find it?"
   d. "I'm going to show you the _____. Where is it?"
   e. "When you look at your [cup], we'll start [snack]."
   f. "Here's your _____. Here is a picture of your _____."

2. **Partner presents object with expanded language input.** Partner labels the object and then describes two or three features of the object:
   a. "Here is your backpack. It is a bag with straps and a zipper."
   b. "Here is your red cup. It has a handle so you can hold it."
   c. "Here is Elmo. He is red and has googly eyes."

   Depending on the child, the partner begins to incorporate comparative language:
   a. "This is *like* your toy cat, except this animal has black-and-white spots."
   b. "Both cats have whiskers and pointed [triangle-shaped] ears."

3. **Partner waits.** Latency is decreasing.

4. **Child responds.** Looking precedes the action. A child who is able may reach, swat, or move nearer the object. If the child can, he or she may speak: "I can see it." The child may also demonstrate eye-to-object contact. By end of Phase II, the child is able to use up to four two-dimensional photographic images and make choices.

5. **Partner confirms.** Partner may say:
   a. "You found all the pictures of ducks."
   b. "You placed all the blue blocks in the container."
   c. "You found the dog in the picture of your backyard."
   d. "You were able to find the switch to tell me what you wanted."
   e. "You told me/showed me _____."

6. **Partner expands visual response, building concepts and language.** Partner uses comparative language and talks about salient features, as well as past experiences or upcoming events that might be relevant.

- Provide lots of opportunities to use vision across the day and in multiple environments.

- Continue to control sensory input, as needed.

- Support use of two-dimensional materials in providing access to communication and learning materials and, whenever possible, to develop literacy skills.

- Use dynamic displays with backlighting as tools for learning.

- Encourage the use of AAC strategies and technologies while simultaneously building vocabulary and providing opportunities for meaningful interactions with familiar and unfamiliar communication partners.

- Make necessary accommodations to materials and environments.

In Phase III, team members continue to coordinate efforts to integrate functional vision with language, learning, and communication goals. Children in Phase III are also learning how to request the accommodations they need. Integrated goals include increasing these children's use of vision with intent during interactions with objects and people, as well as during activities and events across environments, and developing concepts and using more complex language. Having access to AAC strategies, tools, and technologies continues

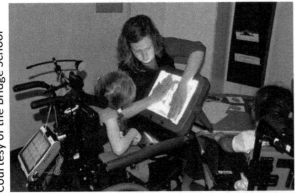

Courtesy of the Bridge School

In Phase III, communication methods a child may use include speech-generating devices.

Courtesy of the Bridge School

Children with CVI and CCN can learn to access large vocabularies as they develop literacy skills.

to be essential to their improved ability to learn, communicate, and participate.

In designing materials for individuals with CVI and CCN, teams continue to provide a range of accommodations to the environment and materials, as shown in Table 3.4. The focus on providing access to two-dimensional materials increases gradually. Team members start with a single, simple image of a familiar object on a neutral background and then add elements and details as appropriate. They may use spacing between elements as well as highlight salient features using color. Most important, team members must remember that they also need to teach the meaning of photographs, letters, and words and gradually increase complexity. Figure 3.5 provides information about how communication partners can use language to support functional vision for children in Phase III.

Approximately 4 years after Danny's initial assessment, family members report that he now appears curious about the elements of new environments. His mother reports that he sometimes seems "nosy," looking around familiar and new places, but still acts shy in the presence of people he does not know. Danny enjoys looking at himself in the mirror and can establish eye contact with most people. He can now visually locate familiar targets at distances up to 20 feet, but not in new or busy environments. He continues to

TABLE 3.4

Phase III VLLC Framework Summary and Suggestions

Integrated Goals

- Refine and integrate use of vision for increasingly complex tasks.
- Use distance vision to support attention to action, location, and persons.
- Increase access to incidental learning.
- Increase access to increasingly robust and large vocabularies.
- Support learning (academic/pre-academic), modifying instruction and materials as needed.
- Increase independence during functional activities across familiar environments.

Characteristics of Child

Area	Characteristics
Language and communication	■ If speaking, child may appear to have rigid concepts; may not be able to describe the salient features of a target (e.g., "a giraffe has a long neck and brown spots") ■ If unable to use natural speech, child should have access to a large vocabulary and be able to use a variety of strategies and tools across activities throughout the day to support continued development of vision and learning and to foster successful communication with peers, family, and teachers (see Communication Strategies and Tools for ideas) ■ Encourage meta-talk about characteristics of objects, function, personal experiences
Vision	■ Looking and describing ■ Use of no-, low-, and high-tech tools and strategies ■ Can learn from and use more abstract visual information, including letters, words, and numbers
Physical	■ Position the child with back to the complexity inherent in the environment to support success with vision, learning, and language input and output ■ Position and support the child to enable easy access to instruction, incidental learning, relationships, and communication tools

Suggestions for Intervention

Type of Intervention	Suggestions
	Contextual Accommodations
Environment	■ Adaptations needed for complexity, novelty, and visual fields ■ Highly complex and novel environments are still difficult ■ Address orientation and mobility (O&M) implications ■ Lower visual fields are often affected ■ Unexpected changes in the environment can result in decreased ability to orient in space, move efficiently through space, and use materials ■ Child is still dependent on familiar schema

(continued on next page)

TABLE 3.4 *(continued)*

	■ Child may appear to have attention difficulties if materials are overly complex or in environments that have random moving targets (e.g., people, video, or computer activities)
	■ Child may avoid near-point, ventral stream, high-acuity, and potentially overly complex tasks and prefer movement (e.g., rocking, moving head, walking, using power mobility device)
	■ Child may function better when moving
Materials	■ Use of slant board may help compensate for lower visual field issues
	■ O&M: use maps to help identify salient features of routes and generalize to larger environments
	■ Two-dimensional materials paired with movement or dynamic displays may continue to assist and support visual attention, with important implications for literacy
Communication Partner Accommodations	
Communication partner accommodations	■ Continue use of comparative language and description to draw attention to the similarities and differences of classes of objects, actions, and environments and to support increase in schema development
	■ Continue to respect latency and integrate the use of wait time
	■ Adjust materials based on assessed CVI Range score and on the child's behavior
	■ Continue to teach and support the child's generalization of vision-language-learning schemes
	■ Support child's "output" efforts by
	☐ encouraging meta-talk (characteristics and function of objects, actions, and environments)
	☐ asking for personal experiences (see sample script in Figure 3.5)
Communication Strategies and Tools	
No-tech (body based)	■ Use same strategies as in Phase II but more consistently
	■ Skilled partners continue to provide access to large vocabulary through partner-assisted auditory scanning to enable the child to create many types of messages
	■ Increase use of recognizable signals and speech approximations across environments and communication partners
Low-tech (nonelectronic)	■ Use same strategies as in Phase II but with more vocabulary
	■ Possible use of coding, such as by color or number
High-tech (electronic)	■ Use tablet and apps with sound and voice
	■ Use computer with software having meaningful graphics
	■ Highlight letters and words to support the development of literacy skills
	■ Communication devices: consider possible use of eye-gaze technology and visual scanning, as well as other speech-generating technologies

FIGURE 3.5 Sample Script for Phase III

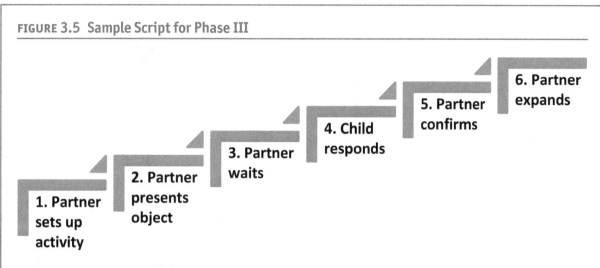

1. **Partner sets up activity.** Partner may say:
   a. "Tell me what you see."
   b. "Show me how these things go together."
   c. "You've seen things like this before."
   d. "Tell me what you notice while we are walking."
   e. "Let me know when you see the _____."
   f. "Find all the pictures that look just like this one."
   g. "Which pictures of faces are girls?"
   h. "Show something you have seen [not seen] before."
   i. "You've seen things like this before because _____."

2. **Partner presents object with expanded language input.** Partner describes object, events, activities, or people using salient features and comparative language.

3. **Partners waits.** May continue to need "wait time" on occasion.

4. **Child responds.** Child uses more complex language, using speech or AAC strategies and tools. Responses may include:
   a. Expressions of personal contributions
   b. Expressions of how objects, images, environments, people are alike and different
   c. Planning an action based on salient features of routes (orientation and mobility)
   d. Connecting novel experiences to past visual information

5 and 6. **Partner confirms and expands visual response, building concepts and language:**
   a. Verbal acknowledgment of the child's competence
   b. Building depth and breadth of existing schema (vision, language, and learning)
   c. Affirmation of ability to solve a problem

Next Steps: Partner continues to use language to support vision and learning; uses descriptive and comparative language and encourages the child to talk about what and how he or she sees, navigates, and learns; and encourages independence and self-directed learning and interactions.

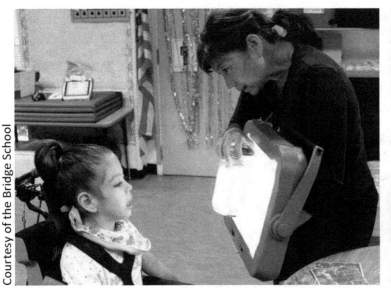
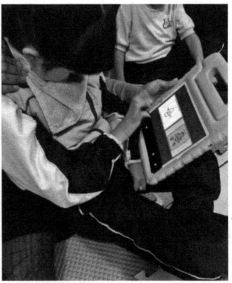

Courtesy of the Bridge School

Courtesy of CATIC

Adaptations for CVI and communication increase access to learning, language, participation, and self-determination.

have difficulty with lower visual field function. Even so, he detects objects or people positioned to his right, left, and even superior visual fields. Danny's teachers note that his vision more consistently supports his learning.

Danny uses AAC materials that include photographs and simple drawings as well as three-dimensional objects. He can now recognize some novel images by identifying their salient features. He is learning to recognize letters (highlighted) and has a sight word vocabulary that currently includes 10 single words if isolated on a plain background. Color highlighting of internal details or defining aspects of letters and words help him attach meaning to two-dimensional materials. According to his teachers and family, Danny occasionally recognizes his own written name when it occurs out of general context.

Conclusion

Children (and adults) with CVI and CCN have medical histories that include brain damage. These children require ongoing medical and educational interventions that begin early and persist over many years. So far, the plight of these children has produced many more words than actions. The

authors' goal is for families and professionals who support children with CVI and CCN to recognize their shared role in ensuring that these children have a chance to develop to their potential.

Operating in professional silos creates unnecessary barriers to successful treatment. Failure to evaluate a child's visual-cognitive processing or to provide a child who is unable to speak access to language restricts critical learning opportunities and negatively affects the child's participation, quality of life, and future opportunities. Children like Danny will continue to require accommodations that support his vision, language, learning, and participation. However, the progression described in Danny's example represents a replicable, feasible trajectory. It also includes a glimpse into how increases in functional vision can support learning, language development, and functional communication. Over time, children with CVI can begin in Phase I and systematically progress to Phases II and III with the support of appropriate interventions paired with meaningful routines. It is critical, therefore, that professionals treat vision, language, and learning as an integrated concept in the identification, assessment, and treatment of these children. This is the responsibility of vision educators, speech-language pathologists, and the entire educational team.

We know significantly more about what to do to help children with both CVI and CNN make steady, significant progress in seeing, learning, and communicating. The challenge going forward is to convert new knowledge into new actions that enable these children to get access to relevant assessments and appropriate interventions.

REFERENCES

Allman, C. B., & Lewis, S. (Eds.). (2014). *ECC essentials: Teaching the expanded core curriculum to students with visual impairments.* New York, NY: AFB Press.

Beukelman, D. R., & Mirenda, P. (2013). *Augmentative and alternative communication: Supporting children and adults with complex communication needs* (4th ed.). Baltimore, MD: Paul H. Brookes.

Blackstone, S. W., & Berg, M. H. (2012). *Social networks: A communication inventory for individuals with complex communication needs and their communication partners* (Rev. ed.). Verona, WI: Attainment Company.

Brady, N. C. (2008). Augmentative and alternative communication for children with Down syndrome or fragile X syndrome. In J. E. Roberts, R. S. Chapman, & S. F. Warren (Eds.), *Speech and language development and intervention in Down syndrome and fragile X syndrome* (pp. 255–274). Baltimore, MD: Paul H. Brookes.

Bruno, J., & Trembath, D. (2006). Use of aided language stimulation to improve syntactic performance during a weeklong intervention program. *Augmentative and Alternative Communication, 22*(4), 300–313.

Bullard, S. R., Donahue, S. P., Feman, S. S., Sinatra, R. B., & Walsh, W. F. (1999). The decreasing incidence and severity of retinopathy of prematurity. *Journal of the American Association for Pediatric Ophthalmology and Strabismus, 3*(1), 46–52.

Carden, S. M., & Good, W. V. (2012). Cortical visual impairment. In K. W. Wright & Y. N. J. Strube (Eds.), *Pediatric ophthalmology and strabismus* (3rd ed., pp. 487–490). New York, NY: Oxford University Press.

Carpenter, M., & Liebal, K. (2011). Joint attention, communication, and knowing together in infancy. In A. Seemann (Ed.), *Joint attention: New developments in psychology, philosophy of mind, and social neuroscience* (pp. 159–181). Cambridge, MA: MIT Press.

Cartmill, E. A., Armstrong, B. F., Gleitman, L. R., Goldin-Meadow, S., Medina, T. N., & Trueswell, J. C. (2013). Quality of early parent input predicts child vocabulary 3 years later. *Proceedings of the National Academy of Sciences of the United States of America, 110*(28), 11278–11283.

Christou, C., & Bulthoff, H. H. (2000). Perception, representation and recognition: A holistic view of recognition. *Spatial Vision, 13*(2–3), 265–275.

Committee for the Classification of Retinopathy of Prematurity. (1984). An international classification of retinopathy of prematurity. *Archives of Ophthalmology, 102*(8), 1130–1134.

Dada, S., & Alant, E. (2009). The effect of aided language stimulation on vocabulary acquisition in children with little or no functional speech. *American Journal of Speech-Language Pathology, 18*(1), 50–64.

Dowden, P. A. (1999). Augmentative and alternative communication for children with motor speech disorders. In A. J. Caruso & E. A. Strand (Eds.), *Clinical management of motor speech disorders in children* (pp. 345–385). New York, NY: Thieme.

Dowden, P. A., & Cook, A. (2002). Choosing effective selection techniques for beginning communicators. In J. Reichle, D. R. Beukelman, & J. C. Light (Eds.), *Exemplary practices for beginning communicators: Implications for AAC* (pp. 395–431). Baltimore, MD: Paul H. Brookes.

Drager, K. D. R., Light, J. C., Carlson, R., D'Silva, K., Larsson, B., Pitkin, L., & Stopper, G. (2004). Learning of dynamic display AAC technologies by typically developing 3-year-olds: Effect of different layouts and menu approaches. *Journal of Speech, Language, and Hearing Research, 47*(5), 1133–1148.

90 Cortical Visual Impairment

Drager, K. D. R., Light, J. C., Speltz, J. C., Fallon, K. A., & Jeffries, L. Z. (2003). The performance of typically developing 2½-year-olds on dynamic display AAC technologies with different system layouts and language organizations. *Journal of Speech, Language, and Hearing Research, 46*(2), 298–312.

Eagleman, D. (2015). *The brain: The story of you.* New York, NY: Pantheon Books.

Education for All Handicapped Children Act, Pub. L. No. 94-142 (1975).

Fallon, K. A., Light, J. C., & Paige, T. K. (2001). Enhancing vocabulary selection for preschoolers who require augmentative and alternative communication (AAC). *American Journal of Speech-Language Pathology, 10*, 81–94.

Gardo, M. (2005, August). Cortical visual impairment. In *Conference report: Education—aiming for excellence* (pp. 98–100). ICEVI European Conference, Chemnitz, Germany. Retrieved from http://www.icevi-europe.org /chemnitz2005/icevi-chemnitz2005.pdf

Good, W. V., Jan, J. E., Burden, S. K., Skoczenski, A., & Candy, R. (2001). Recent advances in cortical visual impairment. *Developmental Medicine & Child Neurology, 43*(1), 56–60.

Good, W. V., Jan, J. E., DeSa, L., Barkovich, A. J., Groenveld, M., & Hoyt, C. S. (1994). Cortical visual impairment in children. *Survey of Ophthalmology, 38*(4), 351–364.

Harris, M. D., & Reichle, J. (2004). The impact of aided language stimulation on symbol comprehension and production in children with moderate cognitive disabilities. *American Journal of Speech-Language Pathology, 13*(2), 155–167.

Hart, B., & Risley T. R. (1995). *Meaningful differences in the everyday experience of young American children.* Baltimore, MD: Paul H. Brookes.

Higginbotham, D. J., & Welch, T. (2006, January). *Visual considerations for individuals with complex communication needs.* Presentation at the annual conference of the Assistive Technology Industry Association, Orlando, FL.

Holbrook, M. C., McCarthy, T., & Kamei-Hannan, C. (Eds.). (2017). *Foundations of education* (3rd ed., Vols. I–II). New York, NY: AFB Press.

Hoyt, C. S. (2002, July). *Visual function in the brain-damaged child.* Presentation at the Doyne Lecture, Oxford, UK.

Hoyt, C. S. (2003). Visual function in the brain-damaged child. *Eye, 17,* 371–386.

Hyvärinen, L. (2006). Cerebral visual impairment (CVI) or brain damage related vision loss. In E. Dennison & A. H. Lueck (Eds.), *Proceedings of the summit on cerebral/cortical visual impairment: Educational, family, and medical perspectives, April 30, 2005* (pp. 35–48). New York, NY: AFB Press.

Individuals with Disabilities Education Act (IDEA), Pub. L. No. 101-467 (1990).

Individuals with Disabilities Education Act Amendments of 1997, Pub. L. No. 105-17 (1997).

Individuals with Disabilities Education Improvement Act (IDEA), 20 U.S.C. § 1400 (2004).

Jan, J. E., Good, W. V., & Hoyt, C. S. (2006). An international classification of neurological visual disorders in children. In E. Dennison & A. H. Lueck (Eds.), *Proceedings of the summit on cerebral/cortical visual impairment: Educational, family, and medical perspectives, April 30, 2005* (pp. 61–64). New York, NY: AFB Press.

Jan, J. E., Heaven, R. K. B., Matsuba, C., Langley, M. B., Roman-Lantzy, C., & Anthony, T. L. (2013). Windows into the visual brain: New discoveries about the visual system, its functions, and implications for practitioners. *Journal of Visual Impairment & Blindness, 107*(4), 251–261.

Kamholz, K. L., Cole, C. H., Gray, J. E., & Zupancic, J. A. (2009). Cost-effectiveness of early treatment for retinopathy of prematurity. *Pediatrics, 123*(1), 262–269.

Khetpal, V., & Donahue, S. P. (2007). Cortical visual impairment: Etiology, associated findings, and prognosis in a tertiary care setting. *Journal of the American Association for Pediatric Ophthalmology and Strabismus, 11*(3), 235–239.

Kooiker, M. J., Pel, J. J., van der Steen-Kant, S. P., & van der Steen, J. (2016). A method to quantify visual information processing in children using eye tracking. *Journal of Visualized Experiments, 113.*

Kovach, T., & Kenyon, P. B. (2003). Visual issues and access to AAC. In J. C. Light, D. R. Beukelman, & J. Reichle (Eds.), *Communicative competence for individuals who use AAC* (pp. 277–319). Baltimore, MD: Paul H. Brookes.

Lanfranchi, S., Jerman, O., Dal Pont, E., Alberti, A., & Vianello, R. (2010). Executive function in adolescents with Down syndrome. *Journal of Intellectual Disability Research, 54*(4), 308–319.

Lanfranchi, S., Jerman, O., & Vianello, R. (2009). Working memory and cognitive skills in individuals with Down syndrome. *Child Neuropsychology, 15*(4), 397–416.

Light, J., & Drager, K. (2007). AAC technologies for young children with complex communication needs: State of the science and future research directions. *Augmentative and Alternative Communication, 23*(3), 204–216.

Light, J., Drager, K., McCarthy, J., Mellott, S., Millar, D., Parrish, C., . . . Welliver, M. (2004). Performance of typically developing four- and five-year-old children with AAC systems using different language organization techniques. *Augmentative and Alternative Communication, 20*(2), 63–88.

Millar, D. C., Light, J. C., & Schlosser, R. W. (2006). The impact of augmentative and alternative communication intervention on the speech production of individuals with developmental disabilities: A research review. *Journal of Speech, Language, and Hearing Research, 49*(2), 248–264.

Munir, F., Cornish, K. M., & Wilding, J. (2000). A neuropsychological profile of attention deficits in young males with fragile X syndrome. *Neuropsychologia, 38*(9), 1261–1270.

Murphy, D., & Good, W. V. (1997). *The epidemiology of blindness in children* [Abstract]. Paper presented at the American Academy of Ophthalmology, San Francisco, CA.

National Center for Education Statistics. (2018, April). Children and youth with disabilities. In *The Condition of Education*. Retrieved from https://nces.ed.gov/programs/coe/indicator _cgg.asp

Phelps, D. L. (1981). Retinopathy of prematurity: An estimate of vision loss in the United States—1979. *Pediatrics, 67*(6), 924–925.

Plotkin, S. A. (2001). Rubella eradication. *Vaccine, 19*(25–26), 3311–3319.

Rogers, M. (1996). Vision impairment in Liverpool: Prevalence and morbidity. *Archives of Disease in Childhood, 74*(4), 299–303.

Roman-Lantzy, C. (2018). *Cortical visual impairment: An approach to assessment and intervention* (2nd ed.). New York, NY: AFB Press.

Roman-Lantzy, C. A., & Lantzy, A. (2010). Outcomes and opportunities: A study of children with cortical visual impairment. *Journal of Visual Impairment & Blindness, 104*(10), 649–653.

Romski, M. A., & Sevcik, R. A. (1996). *Breaking the speech barrier: Language development through augmented means*. Baltimore, MD: Paul H. Brookes.

Romski, M. A., & Sevcik, R. A. (2005). Augmentative communication and early intervention: Myths and realities. *Infants & Young Children, 18*(3), 174–185.

Romski, M. A., Sevcik, R. A., Barton-Hulsey, A., & Whitmore, A. S. (2015). Early intervention and AAC: What a difference 30 years makes. *Augmentative and Alternative Communication, 31*(3), 181–202.

Rosenberg, T., Flage, T., Hansen, E., Riise, R., Rudanko, S. L., Viggosson, G., & Tornqvist, K. (1996). Incidence of registered visual impairment in the Nordic child population. *British Journal of Ophthalmology, 80*(1), 49–53.

Sacks, S. Z., & Zatta, M. C. (Eds.). (2016). *Keys to educational success: Teaching students with visual impairments and multiple disabilities*. New York, NY: AFB Press.

Thistle, J. J., & Wilkinson, K. M. (2012). What are the attention demands of aided AAC? *Perspectives on Augmentative and Alternative Communication, 21*, 17–22.

Tomasello, M. (1995). Joint attention as social cognition. In C. Moore & P. J. Dunham (Eds.), *Joint attention: Its origins and role in development* (pp. 103–130). Hillsdale, NJ: Lawrence Erlbaum Associates.

Watt, N., Wetherby, A., & Shumway, S. (2006). Prelinguistic predictors of language outcome at 3 years of age. *Journal of Speech, Language, and Hearing Research, 49*(6), 1224–1237.

Wilkinson, K. M., Carlin, M., & Jagaroo, V. (2006). Preschoolers' speed of locating a target symbol under different color conditions. *Augmentative and Alternative Communication, 22*(2), 123–133.

Wilkinson, K. M., Carlin, M., & Thistle, J. (2008). The role of color cues in facilitating accurate and rapid location of aided symbols by children with and without Down syndrome. *American Journal of Speech-Language Pathology, 17*(2), 179–193.

Wilkinson, K. M., & Coombs, B. (2010). Preliminary exploration of the effect of background color on the speed and accuracy of search for an aided symbol target by typically developing preschoolers. *Early Childhood Services (San Diego), 4*(3), 171–183.

Wilkinson, K. M., Dennis, N. A., Webb, C. E., Therrien, M., Stradtman, M., Farmer, J., . . . Zeuner, C. (2015). Neural activity associated with visual search for line drawings on AAC displays: An exploration of the use of fMRI. *Augmentative and Alternative Communication, 31*(4), 310–324.

Wilkinson, K. M., & Hennig, S. (2007). The state of research and practice in augmentative and alternative communication for children with developmental/intellectual disabilities. *Mental Retardation and Developmental Disabilities Research Reviews, 13*(1), 58–69.

Wilkinson, K. M., & Jagaroo, V. (2004). Contributions of principles of visual cognitive science to AAC system display design. *Augmentative and Alternative Communication, 20*(3), 123–136.

Wilkinson, K. M., & Light, J. (2014). Preliminary study of gaze toward humans in photographs by individuals with autism, Down syndrome, or other intellectual disabilities: Implications for design of visual scene displays. *Augmentative and Alternative Communication, 30*(2), 130–146.

Wilkinson, K. M., Light, J., & Drager, K. (2012). Considerations for the composition of visual scene displays: Potential contributions of information from visual and cognitive sciences. *Augmentative and Alternative Communication, 28*(3), 137–147.

Wilkinson, K. M., & McIlvane, W. J. (2013). Perceptual factors influence visual search for meaningful symbols in individuals with intellectual disabilities and Down syndrome or autism spectrum disorders. *American Journal on Intellectual and Developmental Disabilities, 118*(5), 353–364.

Wilkinson, K. M., O'Neill, T., & McIlvane, W. J. (2014). Eye-tracking measures reveal how changes in the design of aided AAC displays influence the efficiency of locating symbols by school-age children without disabilities. *Journal of Speech, Language, and Hearing Research, 57*(2), 455–466.

Wilkinson, K. M., & Snell, J. (2011). Facilitating children's ability to distinguish symbols for emotions: The effects of background color cues and spatial arrangement of symbols on accuracy and speed of search. *American Journal of Speech-Language Pathology, 20*(4), 288–301.

Wolfson, L. J., Grais, R. F., Luquero, F. J., Birmingham, M. E., & Strebel, P. M. (2009). Estimates of measles case fatality ratios: A comprehensive review of community-based studies. *International Journal of Epidemiology, 38*(1), 192–205.

World Health Organization. (2012). *Global measles and rubella: Strategic plan 2012–2020*. Geneva, Switzerland: Author. Retrieved from http://apps.who.int/iris/bitstream/10665/44855/1/9789241503396_eng.pdf

Yoder, P. J., & McDuffie, A. S. (2006). Treatment of responding to and initiating joint attention. In T. Charman & W. Stone (Eds.), *Social and communication development in autism spectrum disorders: Early intervention, diagnosis, and intervention* (pp. 117–142). New York, NY: Guilford Press.

The 'What's the Complexity?' Framework

Matthew Tietjen

Author's Note

My motivation to create the 'What's the Complexity?' Framework arose from a conviction that individuals with cortical visual impairment (CVI) deserve a visually accessible school day. I believe that this is their right and that ensuring this right is one of the primary responsibilities of the educational team. I also believe that difficulty with visual complexity is one of the most fundamental visual deficits in individuals with CVI and, therefore, one of the primary barriers to visual access. Many of the other CVI characteristics are intimately related to difficulty with visual complexity, so that any effort to design an accessible school schedule for an individual with CVI should be centered on that characteristic.

If service providers are to succeed in their efforts to offer students with CVI a visually accessible school day, they must understand visual complexity. As a teacher of students with visual impairments, it became clear to me that there were significant gaps in providers' understanding of visual complexity and how it affects the functional vision of their students with CVI. These gaps transcended any one team or school. Despite my detailed functional vision reports and regular consultations, and despite the good intentions and dedication of most educational teams, I often left schools with the sinking feeling that we were coming up short in providing students with the visually accessible school day they deserved.

Too often, teachers were expecting students with CVI to accomplish tasks that were simply outside their visual abilities. Other times, I observed these students struggling to complete tasks that likely would have been achievable in less complex environments. During visits when I was able to observe several consecutive activities, I noticed that many teams were not giving adequate attention to the distribution of visual complexity throughout the student's schedule. Often, the student might have three or more consecutive highly complex activities without opportunities for visual breaks. In these instances of cumulative complexity, many students would appear fatigued by the third or fourth activity and often demonstrated increased visual latency, light gazing, or what was often described as "off-task" behavior.

Even in situations in which I thought an educational team had a sound understanding of visual complexity, I noticed that their application of this knowledge seemed inconsistent. Many of their students had schedules in which just a few activities were well adapted to the student's visual abilities. These activities were the exception, however, dotting their schedules like lone islands of intervention.

As a result of their incomplete understanding of visual complexity, many teams misinterpreted their students' behavior. We know that students with CVI may be overwhelmed and experience stress when in a complex environment, which "may lead to withdrawal, an angry outburst, or anxiety" (Pawletko, Chokron, & Dutton, 2015, p. 146). Children with CVI may be "labeled as 'noncompliant,' 'oppositional,' or 'irritable' when they avoid or refuse to do a task, when in fact they have become visually fatigued . . . and need better scheduling of activities" (Pawletko et al., 2015, p. 148). After too many visits in which I heard team members characterize a student's behavior as "inappropriate," "off-task," or "just behavioral," I knew I needed to help them see how a student's "inappropriate" behavior could actually be an understandable response to an inappropriate activity. I needed to give them a systematic framework for understanding what constitutes visual complexity for their student, how to recognize the presence of complexity in their student's day, and how to address it.

Individuals with CVI deserve a school day that falls within their visual abilities. Using the 'What's the Complexity?' Framework has helped me significantly in this effort and I hope that it will help others as well.

The 'What's the Complexity?' Framework offers a structured, systematic approach to designing a visually accessible school day for individuals with cortical visual impairment (CVI). It asks providers to look closely at each activity in a child's school day and ask, "What is the level of visual complexity?" The framework guides the provider in determining the degree and source of visual complexity in each task and environment and in developing a systematic plan for addressing it and guiding the team.

Meet Ava

Ava is slouching in her seat, her arms dangling by her sides. "Let's finish up those worksheets, boys and girls," chimes Ms. Anderson, Ava's first-grade teacher. Ava sits up a little straighter and manages to find her pencil after some effort. She wants to comply, but as she searches the scene in front of her for her math worksheet, someone in a pink shirt walks by. Ava watches the pink shirt slide past until it disappears into the swirl of colors just beyond her desk. "Ava, you need to look at the paper," chides a familiar voice. Ava searches for her worksheet, but instead, her eyes fall briefly on a yellow sight word poster in the background, then on something red that might be a hat, and then on some stripes in front of her that could belong to a classmate's shirt. Ava starts to feel that swoopy hot feeling again—the one that usually means her teachers are going to start using their disappointed voice. After an increasingly desperate search, her math worksheet finally emerges into view out of all the surrounding materials. At first, all the numbers seem to blend together, like someone just dropped them randomly onto the page. Ava leans in so close that her nose almost touches the paper and, finally, she finds the first problem. She readies her pencil and begins to read, "3 + . . ."

Grrrwrrrwrrwrr, growls the pencil sharpener. And once again, Ava loses sight of the worksheet. She feels herself start to sweat as she realizes that she must start all over again. Now a group of classmates who are already finished are talking right next to her, and Ava's eyes are drawn to the steady, colorful parade of classmates walking by on their way to turn in their completed worksheets.

"Ava, you need to look," warns a disappointed-sounding adult voice. "Don't you want to earn your smiley face?" Ava does want to earn her smiley face. But part of her just wants to crinkle up her math worksheet and escape from Ms. Anderson's busy, noisy room.

After the math lesson, Ms. Anderson steps into the hallway to talk with Mr. Meadows, Ava's teacher of students with visual impairments, who had come in to observe. Ava has been a first grader for close to a month, and her educational team is growing concerned about her increasingly off-task and "inappropriate" behavior during math lessons in Ms. Anderson's classroom.

"We know she can do these math worksheets," Ms. Anderson tells Mr. Meadows. After all, Ava has been doing them successfully in her individual workspace in the resource room. Mr. Meadows reminds Ms. Anderson that Ava's resource room workspace is quiet and visually simple, unlike Ms. Anderson's classroom. He suggests that the complexity of Ms. Anderson's classroom environment—specifically the complex visual background, competing noise, and movement of other students—could be impeding Ava's ability to complete the work.

Ms. Anderson responds dismissively. "She does just fine in my classroom during other activities like snack and story time," she says. "We don't think this is a visual problem. If she would just look at her paper, she would be able to see it. Instead, she seems to be looking everywhere but at her paper. We feel this is just a behavioral problem."

Taking Vision for Granted

While it can be very difficult to know how a student is feeling at any given moment, we can certainly empathize and imagine how he or she might feel when expected to do something he or she is incapable of. We can all probably recall a circumstance when we felt that another's expectations of us exceeded our abilities. We may have felt a sense of pressure, anxiety, inadequacy, or even frustration. We have no reason to doubt that students with CVI feel the same way when confronted with inappropriate expectations.

But while all of us encounter situations in which we fail to complete a task as a result of its cognitive or physical demands, those of us without a visual impairment rarely need to worry about failing a task because of its visual demands. Chances are the visual demands of all or most of our daily activities—such as brushing teeth, making breakfast, or driving to work—fall well within our abilities. (If vision is not your primary sensory modality, consider the auditory or tactile demands of your daily activities instead.) This is not because we possess unlimited visual capabilities. Anyone who has ever struggled to find the book character Waldo in a complex scene or find a friend in a crowded stadium understands that our visual systems, just like all of our other faculties, come with certain limitations. Yet we have designed our daily routines, the tasks we do and the environments we do them in, to fall within our visual abilities. As Dutton (2013) writes, "Society chooses to present information in a way that the majority of people can see clearly, by ensuring that it falls within these 'normal limitations'" (p. 10). In other words, our houses, highways, movie theaters, airports, and classrooms—and the tasks we do in them—have been engineered to match the visual abilities of the vast majority of people. This is why most of us can go through our day without consciously thinking about our vision.

But what if we couldn't take our vision for granted? While it is difficult for people without visual impairments to imagine a day in which the majority of visual demands were at the upper end or completely outside of their abilities, it is an important first step in helping individuals with CVI. To help students like Ava experience a school day that falls within their visual abilities, we must understand the nature of their visual limitations, identify the main barriers to visual access in a given activity, and then address those barriers in a systematic way.

If those of us without visual impairments walked into Ms. Anderson's classroom, we would likely know right away what we were looking at. We would immediately organize the countless pieces of visual information into a coherent scene without any conscious thought. Our brains would take the fragmented visual data bombarding our eyes—edges, corners, shadows, and so forth—and turn them into chairs, desks, computers, posters, children, and crayons. Without any effort, we would likely know what each of these things is, and where they all are in relation to one another and in relation to ourselves. Even if the room were busy and loud, we could scan the entire scene, find what we were looking for, and maintain visual attention on it. In other words, when confronted with the visual complexity of most environments, the typically functioning visual brain is able to create meaning. After all, these environments were designed, consciously or subconsciously, to fall within the typically sighted person's visual abilities.

An individual with CVI, however, spends his or her day in a visual world that was designed for someone else. He or she has difficulty converting the raw data from the eyes into a meaningful visual representation of the world that can be interpreted and acted upon. We call this "difficulty with visual complexity" (Roman-Lantzy, 2018), and it can render even the most ordinary environments and tasks inaccessible. Materials may be too complex to interpret or interact with. Environments may present too much visual information, competing sensory input, or background movement and

derail the individual's use of vision. Missed educational opportunities, visual fatigue, frustration, and a general sense of incompetence are just some of the possible consequences (Pawletko et al., 2015).

However, when a student's educational team understands his or her difficulty with visual complexity, their relationship to school activities, and corresponding intervention strategies, they can engineer a school day that falls within the student's visual abilities—giving him or her a daily experience that more closely resembles that of peers. In doing so, they give the student the opportunity for success. That is the primary goal of the 'What's the Complexity?' Framework.

As Mr. Meadows pulls out of the parking lot of Ava's school, he cannot stop thinking about his conversation with Ms. Anderson. Sure, Ava does well in Ms. Anderson's classroom during snack and story time. Those tasks are well within her visual abilities. Interpreting printed math problems, however, is at the upper end of her visual abilities and is more difficult for her to do in a complex environment. It is likely that neither the complexity of the math worksheet nor the classroom environment alone is causing the problem, but rather the combination of the two.

Mr. Meadows is disappointed in Ms. Anderson's assertion that Ava's conduct in math class is "just behavioral." After all, he had spent hours with her and the rest of the educational team prior to the start of the school year teaching them about visual complexity and how CVI affects Ava's ability to use her vision. Ava's most recent CVI Range report places her at a 6–7 on the CVI Range, and Mr. Meadows has explained to Ava's team that this score means she will need a great deal of support to make school activities accessible. He has explained that Ava has difficulty using her vision with crowded materials or environments and that competing movement and sound are big distractors for her. He has also emphasized that Ava's ability to interpret more complex two-dimensional materials, such as printed words and numbers, is emerging but challenging for her. In addition, he has stressed the importance of using materials that are familiar to her.

Mr. Meadows has observed the team applying this knowledge in some areas of Ava's day, such as in their design of the minimally complex individual workspace in Ava's resource room. After observing the math lesson in the general education classroom, however, it was clear to Mr. Meadows that Ava's team was not generalizing their understanding of visual complexity across all school activities. Mr. Meadows knows he needs to demonstrate to Ava's team how her difficulty with visual complexity impacts her access to her entire school day. He must then support the team in applying appropriate interventions systematically throughout her school day. But how will he accomplish this?

Introducing the 'What's the Complexity?' Framework

To guide the educational team toward designing a more visually accessible school day for a student with CVI, a teacher of students with visual impairments or other education provider uses the 'What's the Complexity?' Framework to outline what constitutes visual complexity for the particular student, identify the sources of visual complexity in the student's school day, and work with the team to address them. Depending on the needs of the student and the team, the provider may choose to evaluate a single activity in the student's day, a cluster of activities, or the entire school day.

Within this framework, an *activity* is any event on the student's schedule such as a morning meeting, math or literacy lesson, or lunch. Each activity is made up of two parts: (1) the environment in which it takes place and (2) the task that the student is expected to perform. By determining the level of visual complexity of the environment and the task separately, the provider can better pinpoint the source of complexity in a given activity

and address it in a targeted way. If an activity seems to exceed the visual abilities of a student, the provider can determine whether it is the environment, the task, or both, that needs to be addressed.

Assessing the environment and task separately also allows the provider to identify any mismatch between the complexity of the environment and the complexity of the task. As a general rule, the complexity levels of the environment and the task should complement, or balance, each other. In other words, when one is high, the other should be low. Thus, a *balanced activity* is one in which the complexity level of the task is an appropriate fit for the complexity level of the environment.

When determining whether a task is an appropriate fit for a given environment, the provider is not looking at whether a student *can* do the task in that environment but whether he or she *should* do it. Some people could do their taxes in the middle of chaotic and noisy Grand Central Station if they absolutely had to, but the mismatch between the complexity of the task and that of the environment would likely leave them fatigued, stressed, and irritable. Ava's math lesson, described earlier, illustrates the potential consequences when the environment and the task in an activity are both very complex.

A balanced activity also allows the student to engage in the activity regularly, for an extended period of time, without undue stress. 'What's the Complexity?' allows the provider to identify unbalanced activities throughout the student's schedule and address them accordingly. In addition to ensuring balanced activities, another central goal of 'What's the Complexity?' is to achieve a *balanced schedule,* in which visual complexity is distributed appropriately and intentionally throughout the student's entire day. Often, teams can pinpoint times of the day when their students with CVI seem to become visually fatigued and less available for learning. The aim of a balanced schedule is to help the student maintain a charged "visual battery" throughout the school day. Providers can do this by looking for areas of the student's schedule with too many successive complex activities.

Once they have pinpointed these problem areas of cumulative complexity, they can proactively offer visual breaks between certain activities or rearrange the order of activities to create a more balanced schedule.

The 'What's the Complexity?' Framework consists of three main parts:

1. Individual Complexity Profile
   a. Companion A: Task Bank
   b. Companion B: Balanced Activity Guide
2. Rating Guides
   a. Environment Rating Guide
   b. Task Rating Guide
3. Recording Forms
   a. Single Activity Recording Form or Schedule Recording Form

These elements are described briefly here, but the forms themselves are provided at points later in the chapter where they are discussed in more detail.

The Individual Complexity Profile is the core of the 'What's the Complexity?' Framework and provides the backbone of individualization for the entire process. It is a one-page overview listing which specific types of tasks are complex for a specific student and in what types of environments the student could reasonably be expected to perform those tasks (that is, a balanced activity). The Individual Complexity Profile has two supporting companion documents that can help the provider complete it: the Task Bank and the Balanced Activity Guide.

The Environment Rating Guide and Task Rating Guide are used to determine the complexity levels of the environment and the task in a given activity. While the Environment Rating Guide is mostly objective and is not student centered, the Task Rating Guide is subjective and reflects the visual abilities of each individual student. Finally, the Single Activity Recording Form and the Schedule Recording Form are intended for recording and sharing results with the educational team.

Just as it is important to understand what the 'What's the Complexity?' Framework is, it is equally important to understand what it is not. 'What's the Complexity?' is not a functional vision assessment. In addition to reading the student's eye report, it is vitally important to complete a functional vision assessment using the CVI Range before beginning assessment of activities using the 'What's the Complexity?' Framework. 'What's the Complexity?' is also not an intervention in and of itself. Rather, it is a framework for designing and applying interventions in an intentional, systematic way.

Finally, the intent of 'What's the Complexity?' is not to shelter individuals with CVI from complex environments altogether. Rather, the goal is to help providers understand the interplay between the task and environment in a given activity and achieve a balance that works best for the individual student.

Language and Terms

The components used in the 'What's the Complexity?' Framework to describe the complexity of the environment and specific tasks are based on the CVI characteristic of difficulties with visual complexity and its subcategories, including difficulties with complexity of the object (target), array, and sensory inputs, as well as the closely related characteristics of difficulty with distance viewing, visual-motor demands (absence of visually guided reach), visual latency, and difficulty with visual novelty (Roman-Lantzy, 2018).

Describing the Environment

In the 'What's the Complexity?' Framework, the environment is the setting in which an activity takes place. The Environment Rating Guide in Figure 4.1 is used as a reference to determine the complexity level of a student's environment and shows the levels used to describe the environment.

The framework describes four levels of environmental complexity:

1. A *minimally complex environment* poses little or no visual complexity. An example would be a completely quiet individual workspace with all or most competing visual input blocked out.

FIGURE 4.1 Environment Rating Guide

Environment Rating Guide

Directions: Rate the complexity level for each of the five components that make up the environment. The highest-rated component determines the overall complexity level of the environment.

Complexity Level	Complexity of Array	Complexity of Sensory Input	Visual Movement	Impact of Lighting	Visual Novelty	Description and Examples
Extreme	Extreme amount of competing background information in student's visual field	Intense, constant level of competing sensory input	Intense level of movement in visual field	Lighting in this environment prevents student from attending to task	Setting and or characteristics of setting may be highly unfamiliar	Complexity of array, sensory input, and/or movement is **greater than in a typical, unadapted general education classroom** (e.g., school cafeteria, gymnasium, crowded hallway)
High	High amount of competing background information in student's visual field	High level of steady, competing sensory input	Frequent background movement in visual field	Lighting in this environment is consistently distracting for student	Setting and/or characteristics of setting may be unfamiliar	Complexity of array, sensory input, and/or movement is **similar to or slightly less than that of a typical, unadapted general education classroom**
Moderate	Low to moderate amount of competing background information in student's visual field	Low to moderate amount of competing sensory input at somewhat regular intervals	Occasional background movement in visual field	Lighting in this environment is occasionally distracting for student	Setting and/or characteristics of setting are basically familiar	Complexity of array, sensory input, and/or movement is **far less than in a typical, unadapted general education classroom** (e.g., generally quiet resource room with some competing visual information in student's visual field)
Minimal	No, or very little, competing background information in student's visual field	Quiet; no, or very infrequent, competing sensory input	No background movement in visual field	Lighting in this environment does not seem to be distracting for student	Setting and/or characteristics of setting are very familiar	Complexity of array, sensory and/or movement is **eliminated or nearly eliminated** (e.g., a quiet one-on-one setting with visual complexity reduced using black trifold boards or a plain wall)

2. A *moderately complex environment* is somewhere in between a minimally and highly complex environment. It is not as "busy" as a typical classroom environment but not as simple as a quiet individual workspace.

3. A *highly complex environment* resembles the typical general education setting, in which there is often a significant amount of competing visual input, background noise, and movement.

4. An *extremely complex environment* presents an intense degree of competing visual input, movement, and noise. Typical examples are a cafeteria or gymnasium.

Each environment has five main components that are examined to determine its overall rating:

- *Complexity of array* is concerned with the amount of visual information in the student's visual field. When evaluating the complexity of array in any given environment, it can help to sit in the student's seat and experience for yourself what he or she is seeing. Consider taking a photograph of the room from the student's perspective and counting the pieces of visual information in the picture. This is the amount of visual information the student has to contend with in order to attend to a particular task.

- *Complexity of sensory input* looks at the amount of competing auditory input in the environment. Students with CVI often have difficulty listening and using their vision at the same time (Roman-Lantzy, 2018). Too much auditory input in an environment, such as people talking, papers shuffling, or the noise of a pencil sharpener, may limit the student's ability to engage visually in a task. Sitting in a student's seat and taking a brief video from his or her perspective can offer a sense of the level of auditory input competing with the student's visual attention.

- *Visual movement* refers to the amount of extraneous movement in a student's visual field, such as teachers and classmates walking by or classmates moving around in their seats. Movement is often visually captivating for individuals with CVI (Roman-Lantzy, 2018). Shifting attention away from extraneous movement to attend to a task may be difficult. Also, in the author's experience, excessive amounts of movement in the environment can seem to overwhelm some students with CVI. Again, taking a short video of the environment from the student's vantage point can be helpful. In addition to capturing competing auditory information, videos will reflect any extraneous background movement competing for the student's attention. In the author's experience, showing a student's educational team the level of visual complexity in a given environment is far more powerful than just describing it. Videos can be very helpful to that end.

- *Impact of lighting* refers to the degree of distracting sources of light in the environment. Like movement, primary sources of light can be captivating, and therefore distracting, to many students with CVI (Roman-Lantzy, 2018).

- *Visual novelty* refers to how familiar or unfamiliar an environment is. Students with CVI often demonstrate their best visual abilities in familiar environments and may struggle to use their vision in novel settings, such as a new classroom or school (Roman-Lantzy, 2013).

Describing the Task

In addition to determining the level of visual complexity stemming from the environment in a given activity, it is also critical to examine the level of complexity posed by the task itself. The task consists of the materials the student is expected to interact with during the activity and what he or she is expected to do with them. The Task Rating Guide shown in Figure 4.2 is used as a reference to rate the complexity of a student's tasks; it defines the levels used to describe a given task.

The 'What's the Complexity?' Framework describes four levels of task complexity:

1. A *low-visual-demands task* is one that places few, or no, demands on the student's visual abilities. Such a task can take two different forms. It can be a nonvisual learning task, such as a verbal speech-language lesson, a listening activity in music class, or listening to an audiobook. A low-visual-demands task can also be a leisure activity or visual break. In these cases, the student may be using vision in a task but in a self-directed or preferred activity with no adult-imposed visual demands. In this case, the student is choosing whether to engage visually with materials and has the freedom to disengage at any time. Visual breaks can be as diverse as swinging in a dark sensory space with one's eyes closed, listening to music, or playing a favorite, highly familiar video game. Sidebar 4.1 provides more information about visual breaks and some additional examples.

2. A *comfortable task* is well within the student's visual abilities. While comfortable-level visual tasks still require a student to think about or act upon what is seen, they do not "stretch" the student's visual abilities. We can think of comfortable-level tasks as those the student has mastered. These tasks may have once been difficult for the student but are now relatively easy.

3. A *challenging task* is at the upper end of a student's visual abilities. While he or she can perform challenging-level tasks, they require the student to stretch his or her visual abilities. Challenging tasks necessitate a level of concentration that comfortable-level tasks do not. Visual goals and objectives that appear in the student's Individualized Education Program (IEP), if appropriate, likely represent challenging-level tasks. The student can and should perform challenging-level tasks but with proper consideration of the pacing, placement within the schedule, opportunity for visual breaks, complexity of the environment, and other factors discussed later in the chapter.

4. A *frustrational task* is beyond or outside of a student's current visual abilities. Generally, a student should not be expected to perform frustrational visual tasks in any environment. In some cases, the educational team may decide to modify a frustrational task or add extra supports in order to bring the task down to a student's challenging or comfortable level. Even with extra supports in place, providers should engage in consistent monitoring to determine if the task is meaningful for the student. If it is not, the team should discuss whether the task should be taught differently or discontinued altogether.

The 'What's the Complexity?' Framework considers seven different components to evaluate the effect each has on the complexity of a task:

- *Complexity of target* centers on the student's ability to look at a visual target and identify or recognize the target. This component is closely related to the subcategory of visual complexity referred to as "difficulty with complexity of object" on the CVI Range Assessment (Roman-Lantzy,

FIGURE 4.2 Task Rating Guide

Task Rating Guide

Directions: Rate the complexity level for each of the seven components that make up a task. The highest-rated component determines the overall complexity level of the task.

Visual Complexity	Complexity of Target	Complexity of Array	Complexity of Sensory Inputs	Distance of Materials	Visual-Motor Demands	Visual Latency	Visual Novelty
Frustrational	Targets are **outside student's ability** to look at and interpret	Array of materials is **outside student's ability** to look at, interpret, and interact with	Sensory demands of materials are **outside student's ability** to look at, interpret, and maintain visual attention	Distance of materials is **outside student's ability** to look at, interpret, and maintain visual attention	Visual-motor demands are **outside student's ability**	Pacing of task is **outside student's ability** to engage visually	Novelty of materials is **outside student's ability** to look at and interpret
Challenging	Targets are **at the upper end of student's ability** to look at and interpret	Array of materials is **at the upper end of student's ability** to look at, interpret, and interact with	Sensory demands of materials are **at the upper end of student's ability** to look at, interpret, and maintain visual attention	Distance of materials is **at the upper end of student's ability** to look at, interpret, and maintain visual attention	Visual-motor demands are **at the upper end of student's ability**	Pacing of task is **at the upper end of student's ability** to engage visually	Novelty of materials is **at the upper end of student's ability** to look at and interpret
Comfortable	Targets are **well within student's ability** to look at and interpret	Array of materials is **well within student's ability** to look at, interpret, and interact with	Sensory demands of materials are **well within student's ability** to look at, interpret, and maintain visual attention	Distance of materials is **well within student's ability** to look at, interpret, and maintain visual attention	Visual-motor demands are **well within student's ability**	Pacing of task is **well within student's ability** to engage visually	Novelty of materials is **well within student's ability** to look at and interpret
Low Visual Demands	**Low visual demands**	**Low visual demands**	**Low visual demands**	**Low visual demands**	**Low visual demands**	**Low visual demands**	**Low visual demands**

Visual Breaks

A visual break is:

- The absence of direct visual demands

- A preferred student activity

- An activity that helps the student "recharge"

- An activity in which any visual aspects are student-directed

- Individualized to each student

A visual break can be:

- Swinging in a sensory space with the lights out

- Taking a rest in a break area with the lights out

- Listening to music with the lights out

- Coloring

- Playing with favorite blocks

- Playing with toy trucks

- Playing a game on a tablet device

- Exploring sensory bins

- Bouncing on an exercise ball

- Going for a walk

When to schedule a visual break:

- Proactively throughout the day; don't wait for the student's "visual battery" to drain

- In areas of the student's schedule with high cumulative complexity

- At regular intervals during any activity in which the environment is highly complex or greater, or the task is at the challenging level or greater

- When a student shows increased visual latency or fatigue

- When a student asks for a break

Important points:

- A visual break is not something a student earns through good behavior or compliance; it is a right

- Students can be taught to recognize when they need a visual break and how to request one

- Students can exercise self-determination by choosing the activities they do during their visual break

    - A student can make this choice using words, signals, signs, pointing to pictures, eye gaze, or other forms of communication

2018). While this component refers to the student's ability to look at and interpret objects, it also applies to his or her ability to do so with images, letters, words, shapes, and other kinds of visual targets. Some students with CVI may be able to recognize three-dimensional objects of solid colors, while others may also be able to identify words and photographs.

- *Complexity of array* refers to the amount of simultaneous visual information presented by the task itself. When rating this component, the provider should consider how much visual information the student can interpret or interact with at once. How many pieces of visual information, such as objects or images, are on the student's desk during a particular task? How much visual information is on a particular worksheet or communication display? Too much simultaneous visual information may make the task challenging or even frustrational for the student. Providers should think about what constitutes a complex array for each student.

- *Complexity of sensory inputs* is evaluated by considering competing sensory demands from the materials themselves, not from the environment. (Sensory complexity of the environment is factored in separately using the Environment Rating Guide.) For example, some students with CVI may be unable to look at a toy while it is producing music (Roman-Lantzy, 2018). Other students may be able to read a passage of text during silent reading but may need to look away from the print in order to listen when the teacher reads the same passage out loud. Although this component primarily considers the effects of competing

auditory input, competition from the tactile and olfactory senses may be considered as well, if they seem to have an impact on the student's use of vision.

- *Distance of the materials* is concerned with how far away the visual target is. This component is intimately tied to the characteristic of difficulty with complexity of array (Roman-Lantzy, 2018). The further away an object is, the more complex the visual array surrounding that object (see Chapter 1). The student has to sort through more visual information in his or her visual field in order to see objects at greater distances. Two-dimensional materials, such as images and text, may be inaccessible to a student beyond his or her preferred viewing distance (the distance that student chooses when holding the materials or when leaning into them).

  Furthermore, the distance at which a student may notice a familiar landmark or a moving person is likely different than the distance at which the same student can maintain meaningful visual attention on a presentation or display. These distinctions are important when rating the distance demands of a given task. For example, spotting the water fountain from 15 feet away on a familiar route may be a comfortable-level task for a student, while sustaining meaningful attention on a math presentation from half that distance may be a frustrational-level task for the same student.

- *Visual-motor demands* refers to a student's ability to use vision to guide fine or gross motor tasks such as reaching, stepping, zipping, buttoning, or using a spoon or fork. Students with CVI often have difficulty pairing vision with motor tasks (Lueck & Dutton, 2015; Roman-Lantzy, 2018). When visual-motor demands are too complex for a student, he or she may look away while attempting to perform the task tactilely.

- *Visual latency* describes a delay in noticing or processing visual information. There may be activities in which the pacing of the task makes it a challenging- or frustrational-level task for a student. Understanding how much time a student needs to process visual information is critical in determining whether the pacing of a task falls within or outside of the student's visual abilities.

- *Visual novelty,* like the distance component, is closely related to difficulty with visual complexity. A student who has difficulty recognizing objects or images by their salient features may recognize familiar versions of an object but have difficulty with novel exemplars. For example, a student who recognizes his or her own dog because it is yellow, large, and has short hair may see a small, white, fluffy dog and not realize it is also a dog even though they both have snouts, paws, and a tail.

  Some students with CVI may have difficulty looking at or identifying a novel object, while others may do fine with novel objects but struggle with novel two-dimensional images and text (Roman-Lantzy, 2013). Similarly, a student who has difficulty interpreting crowded or "busy" visual displays (complexity of array) may do better with such a display if it is one that he or she has had a lot of experience with versus one that is completely novel.

Table 4.1 gives examples of tasks that were comfortable, challenging, and frustrational for specific students in Phases I, II, and III.

Using the 'What's the Complexity?' Framework

Using the 'What's the Complexity?' Framework is a simple process that involves three stages: preparation, observation, and sharing. This brief overview of the process is followed by a step-by-step guide to each stage:

1. **Preparation:** Begin completing the Individual Complexity Profile to outline what types of visual tasks are complex for an individual and what combination of environment and task constitutes a balanced activity for him or her. Information for the Individual Complexity Profile may come from eye reports, current CVI Range assessment results, and interviews with parents and school staff, as well as the two companion documents (Task Bank and the Balanced Activity Guide). Once the Individual Complexity Profile is started, consider it a working draft that can be consulted and updated throughout the observation and sharing stages.

2. **Observation:** Observe the student in an activity, sequence of activities, or entire school day. Use the Environment and Task Rating Guides (consulting the Individual Complexity Profile as needed) to determine the complexity level of each environment and task observed. Summarize the results using the recording form (Single Activity or Schedule). Finally, for any activity in which the complexity level is troublesome, use the recording form to communicate recommendations for addressing that activity.

3. **Sharing:** Meet with the educational team to share your results and review your recommendations.

Preparation
During the preparation stage, the provider gathers information about the individual's visual abilities

TABLE 4.1

Sample Tasks at Different Levels of Complexity for Individual Students

Student	Comfortable Level	Challenging Level	Frustrational Level
Daphne, early Phase I	For some students in Phase I, any intentional use of vision may be at the upper end of their visual abilities For some students in Phase I, especially early Phase I, there may not be any comfortable visual tasks	Looking at a red Mylar pom-pom	Looking at a red, non-shiny stuffed bear
Cameron, late Phase I	Visually locating his shiny red water bottle on a black placemat with no other objects in his visual field	Visually locating his shiny red water bottle on a black placemat when his plate is also on the placemat	Visually locating his shiny red water bottle on a black placemat when his plate, spoon, and bag of chips are also on the placemat
Aisha, mid-Phase II	Looking at and recognizing a familiar multicolored stuffed bear	Recognizing a photograph of the familiar multicolored stuffed bear	Reading the word *bear*
Dylan, mid-Phase II	Indicating a lunch choice by gazing at a preferred item from an array of two objects	Indicating a lunch choice by gazing at a preferred item from an array of four color photographs	Indicating a lunch choice by gazing at a preferred item from an array of six color photographs
Bella, late Phase II	Reaching for finger foods at lunchtime	Using fork to spear food during quiet snack time	Using vision to guide buttoning of clothing
Natalie, late Phase II	Reading familiar sight words outlined in her preferred color, one at a time	Reading connected text with each word outlined in her preferred color and separated by three spaces	Reading unmodified connected text
Ben, early Phase III	Recognizing photographs of personal items	Recognizing novel photographs of common items like a chair, cup, car, brush, etc.	Recognizing black-and-white line drawings or abstract picture symbols
Danielle, early Phase III	Reading connected text with two lines visible at once	Reading connected text with an entire paragraph visible at once	Reading connected text with an entire page visible at once
Alex, mid-Phase III	Recognizing novel photographs of common objects like a chair, cup, car, brush, etc.	Identifying black-and-white line drawings and picture symbols	Recognizing peers by their faces

FIGURE 4.3 Individual Complexity Profile

Individual Complexity Profile

Student's name: _____   School year: _____

Directions: In the Sample Tasks column, write examples of tasks that currently represent each level of visual complexity for this student. Use the Appropriate Environment box to check off which level or levels of environmental complexity would be a good fit for the tasks in that row (i.e., to make it a balanced activity).

Complexity of Task	Sample Tasks for This Student	Appropriate Environment
Frustrational		Frustrational-level tasks should not be attempted in any environment. Tasks may be modified or supports added to bring tasks to student's challenging or comfortable level.
Challenging		☐ Extreme ☐ High ☐ Moderate ☐ Minimal
Comfortable		☐ Extreme ☐ High ☐ Moderate ☐ Minimal
Low Visual Demands	The following constitute preferred visual/sensory breaks for the student:	

and begins completing the Individual Complexity Profile.

Individual Complexity Profile

The Individual Complexity Profile grounds the entire 'What's the Complexity?' process within each student's unique visual abilities. It is an overview of what types of tasks constitute complexity for a particular student and the level of environmental complexity in which he or she can reasonably be expected to do those tasks (see Figure 4.3). It is a working document that the provider begins before any other

part of the 'What's the Complexity?' Framework and continues to add to, adjust, and consult throughout the entire 'What's the Complexity?' process.

GENERATING SAMPLE TASKS. The first step in completing the Individual Complexity Profile is to list examples of tasks that are at the student's comfortable, challenging, and frustrational levels. This information comes from prior knowledge of the student's visual abilities (from the CVI Range, past observations, and interviews with family members and school staff) as well as from current observations that take place during the 'What's the Complexity?' process.

In addition to those sources, the Task Bank (see Figure 4.4) is used to generate examples of tasks for inclusion in the student's Individual Complexity Profile. The Task Bank is a list of general visual tasks related to the components of complexity of the target, complexity of array, complexity of sensory input, distance of materials, and visual-motor demands. The list of tasks is first reviewed to indicate whether each one is currently comfortable, challenging, or frustrational for a particular student. Then the most relevant tasks are transferred to the appropriate boxes on the student' Individual Complexity Profile.

The final box on the Individual Complexity Profile is titled Low Visual Demands. In this section, preferred activities that constitute visual breaks for the student are listed (as described previously in Sidebar 4.1).

DETERMINING WHAT CONSTITUTES A BALANCED ACTIVITY. After recording a list of sample tasks for each complexity level, the Appropriate Environment column is used to indicate the environment level or levels that are an appropriate match for each task level. In other words, this column indicates which combinations of task and environment constitute a balanced activity for the student. This decision is based on current knowledge of the student from prior and current observations, CVI Range results, and interviews with school staff. It also may be helpful to consult the companion document, the Balanced Activity Guide (see Figure 4.5), which suggests appropriate combinations of environment and task complexity levels based on the student's CVI Range phase.

When deciding what combinations of environment and task levels constitute a balanced activity for a student, it is important to remember that the goal is not to create activities that a student might be able to push through only by expending maximum effort. Rather, the goal is to identify the combinations of environment and task complexity that will result in sustainable activities the student can perform regularly without unnecessary stress and fatigue.

Once the most appropriate environments for each task level are determined, they are checked off on the student's Individual Complexity Profile. The completed profile is a one-page overview of what constitutes comfortable, challenging, and frustrational tasks for the student and in what environments he or she should generally perform these tasks. Since frustrational tasks are outside of a student's visual ability and should not be attempted, any activity in which the task is frustrational is considered unbalanced, regardless of the complexity level of the environment.

Providers can update this document throughout the rest of the 'What's the Complexity?' process, adding examples of specific activities from the student's school day when applicable.

DETERMINING VISUAL LEARNING MEDIA. In the author's experience, even after completing a learning media assessment (Koenig & Holbrook, 1995), educational teams often struggle to determine the most appropriate types of visual learning media for students with CVI. The Individual Complexity Profile can be useful in guiding this process. For guidance in selecting specific types of visual learning media for a student with CVI, the provider can look through the student's completed Individual Complexity Profile for tasks that are examples of visual learning media (such as single-color objects, color photographs, black-and-white symbols, or printed words) to find those that are at the student's comfortable and challenging levels. These represent the student's most appropriate visual learning media.

ASSESSING ABILITY TO INTERPRET TWO-DIMENSIONAL IMAGES. Several statements in the Task Bank (see Figure 4.4) deal with the student's ability to interpret two-dimensional images, from color photographs to more abstract black-and-white illustrations or symbols. Many educational materials rely on images, and images can be a powerful communication medium for many people. Therefore, it is important to know a student's abilities in this area and to be able to provide the educational team with guidance regarding

FIGURE 4.4 Task Bank: Individual Complexity Profile—Companion A

Task Bank

Student's name: _____   Date: _____

Directions: Use check marks to indicate whether each task listed below is comfortable (C), challenging (CH), or frustrational (F) for the student given his or her visual abilities. Information from this worksheet may be used to generate sample tasks for the student's Individual Complexity Profile.

Target

☐ C	☐ CH	☐ F	Look at single-color light-up objects
☐ C	☐ CH	☐ F	Look at highly familiar single-color objects
☐ C	☐ CH	☐ F	Look at generally familiar single-color objects
☐ C	☐ CH	☐ F	Look at single-color novel objects
☐ C	☐ CH	☐ F	Look at highly familiar multicolored/patterned objects
☐ C	☐ CH	☐ F	Look at generally familiar multicolored/patterned objects
☐ C	☐ CH	☐ F	Look at novel multicolored/patterned objects
☐ C	☐ CH	☐ F	Interpret highly familiar single-color objects
☐ C	☐ CH	☐ F	Interpret generally familiar single-color objects
☐ C	☐ CH	☐ F	Interpret novel single-color objects
☐ C	☐ CH	☐ F	Interpret highly familiar multicolored/patterned objects
☐ C	☐ CH	☐ F	Interpret generally familiar multicolored/patterned objects
☐ C	☐ CH	☐ F	Interpret novel multicolored/patterned objects
☐ C	☐ CH	☐ F	Look at two-dimensional images and displays on backlit surface
☐ C	☐ CH	☐ F	Look at two-dimensional images or displays
☐ C	☐ CH	☐ F	Interpret color photographs of highly familiar objects
☐ C	☐ CH	☐ F	Interpret color photographs of general exemplars of familiar objects
☐ C	☐ CH	☐ F	Interpret color photographs of novel or unusual exemplars of familiar objects
☐ C	☐ CH	☐ F	Interpret realistic cartoon illustrations of highly familiar objects
☐ C	☐ CH	☐ F	Interpret realistic cartoon illustrations of generally familiar objects
☐ C	☐ CH	☐ F	Interpret realistic cartoon illustrations of animals
☐ C	☐ CH	☐ F	Interpret abstract cartoon illustrations of highly familiar objects
☐ C	☐ CH	☐ F	Interpret abstract cartoon illustrations of generally familiar objects
☐ C	☐ CH	☐ F	Interpret familiar, practiced, colored symbols or icons

(continued on next page)

FIGURE 4.4 *(continued)*

□ C	□ CH	□ F	Interpret novel colored symbols or icons
□ C	□ CH	□ F	Interpret realistic black-and-white illustrations
□ C	□ CH	□ F	Interpret abstract black-and-white illustrations (e.g., line drawings, symbols)
□ C	□ CH	□ F	Identify basic shapes by sight
□ C	□ CH	□ F	Identify/recognize letters
□ C	□ CH	□ F	Identify/recognize numbers
□ C	□ CH	□ F	Identify/recognize words
□ C	□ CH	□ F	Recognize highly familiar faces
□ C	□ CH	□ F	Recognize generally familiar faces
□ C	□ CH	□ F	Interpret facial expressions
□ C	□ CH	□ F	Recognize photographs of highly familiar faces
□ C	□ CH	□ F	Recognize photographs of generally familiar faces
□ C	□ CH	□ F	Interpret photographs depicting facial expressions
□ C	□ CH	□ F	Interpret abstract symbols or icons depicting facial expressions

Array

□ C	□ CH	□ F	Look at single light-up target in darkened room
□ C	□ CH	□ F	Look at 1 object against plain background
□ C	□ CH	□ F	Look at an array of 2–3 objects
□ C	□ CH	□ F	Look at an array of 1 image against plain background
□ C	□ CH	□ F	Look at an array of 2 images
□ C	□ CH	□ F	Look at illustrations in most age-appropriate picture books
□ C	□ CH	□ F	Look at the display in "busy" tablet apps
□ C	□ CH	□ F	Interpret/interact with an array of 1 object
□ C	□ CH	□ F	Interpret/interact with an array of 2 objects
□ C	□ CH	□ F	Interpret/interact with an array of 3 objects
□ C	□ CH	□ F	Interpret/interact with an array of 4 objects
□ C	□ CH	□ F	Interpret/interact with an array of 5–6 objects
□ C	□ CH	□ F	Interpret/interact with an array of 7–10 objects
□ C	□ CH	□ F	Interpret/interact with an array of more than 10 objects

FIGURE 4.4 *(continued)*

☐ C	☐ CH	☐ F	Interpret/interact with an array of 1 image
☐ C	☐ CH	☐ F	Interpret/interact with an array of 2 images
☐ C	☐ CH	☐ F	Interpret/interact with an array of 3 images
☐ C	☐ CH	☐ F	Interpret/interact with an array of 4 images
☐ C	☐ CH	☐ F	Interpret/interact with an array of 5–6 images
☐ C	☐ CH	☐ F	Interpret/interact with an array of 7–10 images
☐ C	☐ CH	☐ F	Interpret/interact with an array of more than 10 images
☐ C	☐ CH	☐ F	Interpret visual array in most children's books
☐ C	☐ CH	☐ F	Interpret visual array in "busy" tablet apps
☐ C	☐ CH	☐ F	Interpret photographs or illustrations of visual scenes
☐ C	☐ CH	☐ F	Read one word at a time
☐ C	☐ CH	☐ F	Read an isolated line of text with single spacing between words
☐ C	☐ CH	☐ F	Read an isolated line of text with double spacing between words
☐ C	☐ CH	☐ F	Read an isolated line of text with triple spacing between words
☐ C	☐ CH	☐ F	Read two lines of text with double spacing between lines
☐ C	☐ CH	☐ F	Read two lines of text with triple spacing between lines
☐ C	☐ CH	☐ F	Read more than two lines of text with double spacing between lines
☐ C	☐ CH	☐ F	Read more than two lines of text with triple spacing between lines
☐ C	☐ CH	☐ F	Complete a worksheet with one printed question or math problem visible at once
☐ C	☐ CH	☐ F	Complete a worksheet with two or three printed questions or math problems visible at once
☐ C	☐ CH	☐ F	Complete a worksheet with four or five printed questions or math problems visible at once
☐ C	☐ CH	☐ F	Complete a grade-level worksheet of typical complexity
☐ C	☐ CH	☐ F	Complete a grade-level worksheet that is "busier" than average
☐ C	☐ CH	☐ F	Interpret/interact with grade-level maps, charts, and tables of typical complexity
☐ C	☐ CH	☐ F	Interpret/interact with grade-level maps, charts, and tables that are "busier" than average
☐ C	☐ CH	☐ F	Count 1 item at a time
☐ C	☐ CH	☐ F	Count a linear array of 2–3 items with extra spacing between items

(continued on next page)

FIGURE 4.4 *(continued)*

☐ C	☐ CH	☐ F	Count a linear array of 4–6 items with extra spacing between items
☐ C	☐ CH	☐ F	Count a linear array of 7–10 items with extra spacing between items
☐ C	☐ CH	☐ F	Count a linear array without extra spacing between items
☐ C	☐ CH	☐ F	Count a random array of 2–3 items
☐ C	☐ CH	☐ F	Count a random array of 4–6 items
☐ C	☐ CH	☐ F	Count a random array of 7–10 items
☐ C	☐ CH	☐ F	Count a random array of more than 10 items

Sensory Input

☐ C	☐ CH	☐ F	Look at an object or display that is not producing sound
☐ C	☐ CH	☐ F	Look at an object or display that is producing sound
☐ C	☐ CH	☐ F	Maintain visual attention on an object or display that is producing sound
☐ C	☐ CH	☐ F	Visually attend to face when person is speaking
☐ C	☐ CH	☐ F	Maintain visual attention on an object or display when the visual information, auditory information, or both, is especially complex

Distance of Materials

☐ C	☐ CH	☐ F	Look at an object within 12 inches
☐ C	☐ CH	☐ F	Look at an object within 18 inches
☐ C	☐ CH	☐ F	Look at an object within 24 inches
☐ C	☐ CH	☐ F	Look at an object within 2–3 feet
☐ C	☐ CH	☐ F	Look at an object beyond 3 feet
☐ C	☐ CH	☐ F	Maintain visual attention on materials or presentation within 12 inches
☐ C	☐ CH	☐ F	Maintain visual attention on materials or presentation within 18 inches
☐ C	☐ CH	☐ F	Maintain visual attention on materials or presentation within 24 inches
☐ C	☐ CH	☐ F	Maintain visual attention on materials or presentation within 2–3 feet
☐ C	☐ CH	☐ F	Maintain visual attention on materials or presentation within 4–6 feet
☐ C	☐ CH	☐ F	Maintain visual attention on materials or presentation within 7–10 feet
☐ C	☐ CH	☐ F	Maintain visual attention on materials or presentation within 10–20 feet
☐ C	☐ CH	☐ F	Maintain visual attention on materials or presentation beyond 20 feet
☐ C	☐ CH	☐ F	Locate a target or landmark from 2–3 feet in familiar location or routine

FIGURE 4.4 *(continued)*

☐ C	☐ CH	☐ F	Locate a target or landmark from 4–6 feet in familiar location or routine
☐ C	☐ CH	☐ F	Locate a target or landmark from 7–10 feet in familiar location or routine
☐ C	☐ CH	☐ F	Locate a target or landmark from 10–20 feet in familiar location or routine
☐ C	☐ CH	☐ F	Locate a target or landmark from beyond 20 feet in familiar location or routine
☐ C	☐ CH	☐ F	Locate a target or landmark from 2–3 feet in novel location or routine
☐ C	☐ CH	☐ F	Locate a target or landmark from 4–6 feet in novel location or routine
☐ C	☐ CH	☐ F	Locate a target or landmark from 7–10 feet in novel location or routine
☐ C	☐ CH	☐ F	Locate a target or landmark from 10–20 feet in novel location or routine
☐ C	☐ CH	☐ F	Locate a target or landmark from beyond 20 feet in novel location or routine

Visual-Motor Demands

☐ C	☐ CH	☐ F	Use vision to guide reach for single item within a simple array
☐ C	☐ CH	☐ F	Use vision to guide activation of adaptive switch
☐ C	☐ CH	☐ F	Use vision to guide reach for an item within a complex array
☐ C	☐ CH	☐ F	Use vision to guide lower extremities over surface terrain such as curbs, steps, surface boundaries, door thresholds, etc.
☐ C	☐ CH	☐ F	Complete "put-in" tasks such as placing chips or money in a slot
☐ C	☐ CH	☐ F	Use vision to guide hanging up items such as coats, backpacks, etc.
☐ C	☐ CH	☐ F	Use vision to guide touch on an AAC display (tablet based or physical materials)
☐ C	☐ CH	☐ F	Use vision to guide spoon during a meal
☐ C	☐ CH	☐ F	Use vision to guide fork during a meal
☐ C	☐ CH	☐ F	Use vision to guide knife to cut food
☐ C	☐ CH	☐ F	Use vision to guide zipping and unzipping clothing
☐ C	☐ CH	☐ F	Use vision to guide buttoning and unbuttoning clothing
☐ C	☐ CH	☐ F	Use vision to guide scissors in a cutting activity
☐ C	☐ CH	☐ F	Use vision to guide placement of puzzle pieces
☐ C	☐ CH	☐ F	Use vision to guide coloring onto a piece of paper
☐ C	☐ CH	☐ F	Use vision to trace lines or letters
☐ C	☐ CH	☐ F	Use vision to write letters or numbers

Balanced Activity Guide (by Phase)

These tables show the combination of task complexity and environmental complexity that is generally balanced or unbalanced for most students in a given phase, based on the author's experience. These combinations are intended only as suggestions and can be used as a guide when completing the Appropriate Environment column on the student's Individual Complexity Profile.

Phase I

		Environment			
		Minimal	*Moderate*	*High*	*Extreme*
Task	Frustrational	unbalanced	unbalanced	unbalanced	unbalanced
	Challenging	balanced	unbalanced	unbalanced	unbalanced
	Comfortable[a]	balanced	unbalanced[b]	unbalanced	unbalanced
	Low Visual Demands	balanced	balanced	balanced	balanced

Phase II

		Environment			
		Minimal	*Moderate*	*High*	*Extreme*
Task	Frustrational	unbalanced	unbalanced	unbalanced	unbalanced
	Challenging	balanced	unbalanced[b]	unbalanced	unbalanced
	Comfortable	balanced	balanced	balanced	balanced[c]
	Low Visual Demands	balanced	balanced	balanced	balanced

Phase III

		Environment			
		Minimal	*Moderate*	*High*	*Extreme*
Task	Frustrational	unbalanced	unbalanced	unbalanced	unbalanced
	Challenging	balanced	balanced	unbalanced[b]	unbalanced
	Comfortable	balanced	balanced	balanced	balanced
	Low Visual Demands	balanced	balanced	balanced	balanced

[a]Many students in Phase I may not yet have a list of comfortable visual tasks. For these students, any visual demands may be considered challenging or frustrational level.

[b]Unbalanced for most children in this phase. May be balanced for some children in this phase, particularly those late in this phase.

[c]Balanced for most children in this phase. May be unbalanced for some children in this phase, particularly those early in this phase.

whether images are appropriate for a student's instructional materials and, if so, what types of images.

The CVI 2D Image Assessment, included in Appendix 4A at the end of this chapter, is a systematic method for assessing a student's ability to interpret two-dimensional images. This information becomes part of the student's Individual Complexity Profile and guides the team in the adaptation of instructional materials, leading to more informed decisions about the types of learning materials to provide. Teams can also look at the 2D Image Assessment results for guidance in planning direct instruction in the interpretation of two-dimensional images.

Observation

After gathering and reviewing information about a student's visual abilities and beginning the Individual Complexity Profile, the provider needs to decide whether to observe the student in a single activity, a series of activities, or an entire school day. During the observation stage, the Environment and Task Rating Guides are used to rate the complexity level of both the environment and the task in each activity, and the results are recorded on either the Single Activity Recording Form or the Schedule Recording Form (shown later in this section).

Rating the Complexity of the Environment

During observation, the Environment Rating Guide (see Figure 4.1) is used as a reference to determine whether the environment in which an activity takes place is minimally, moderately, highly, or extremely complex, based on the five components of complexity of array, complexity of sensory input, visual movement, impact of lighting, and visual novelty. The rater looks for the statement in the Environment Rating Guide that best represents each component's contribution to the environment.

While observing a student performing an activity, the observer should be positioned close to the student's vantage point, so that the observer's view of the room is as close to that of the student as possible. Any complexity in the environment

that is occurring outside of the student's perceptual awareness during that activity (such as a complex array or movement behind the student) is not taken into consideration when evaluating that activity. Therefore, it is possible for the complexity level of an environment to vary from activity to activity, depending on the level of noise and movement in the classroom, as well as where the student is seated at that time. The general education setting, for example, is usually highly complex in terms of the array, visual movement, and sensory input. However, the classroom could become moderately complex if the student with CVI is facing a visually simple area of the room and the class is engaged in independent silent reading. In this case, the complexity of those components would likely be less than their typically high levels.

It is unlikely that all five components of the environment will contribute the same level of complexity in a given activity. Instead, the five statements on the Environment Rating Guide most likely would be scattered across different levels of complexity. The component or components with the highest rating determines the overall level of complexity for the environment. To understand why this makes sense, consider an individual workspace in which all background complexity, movement, and light have been eliminated but which is very noisy due to its close proximity to a cafeteria. In this case, assuming the work area is also highly familiar to the student, complexity of array, visual movement, impact of lighting, and visual novelty would all be rated as minimally complex, but the complexity of sensory input component would be rated as highly complex. The environment of the individual workstation, although minimally complex, would actually be considered highly complex because of the competing noise from the cafeteria.

The first three components used in the Environment Rating Guide—complexity of array, complexity of sensory input, and visual movement—are rated without taking a student's specific abilities into account. For example, a school cafeteria that is rated as highly complex due to the degree of visual clutter (complexity of array), noise (complexity of sensory input), and extraneous visual movement, would be considered a highly complex environment regardless of whether the student being observed in that environment is in Phase I, II, or III. However, the types of visual tasks expected of each student in this environment will depend on his or her CVI Range phase and individual visual ability. The 'What's the Complexity?' Framework accounts for this individualization using the Task Rating Guide and Individual Complexity Profile, as described later in this chapter.

INDIVIDUALS WITH DUAL SENSORY IMPAIRMENTS. Despite the mostly objective approach of the Environment Rating Guide, exceptions may need to be made in case of students with hearing loss. For example, the provider may not need to consider the impact of competing auditory input for a student with profound bilateral hearing loss. Any sounds in the room may fall outside the student's perceptual experience of that environment. In that case, it is permissible to ignore or cross out the sensory component on the Environment Rating Guide and use the other four components to determine the rating. The individual workspace next to the noisy cafeteria just described, while highly complex for most students, may be a minimally complex environment for someone with a profound hearing loss. The decision to discount or adjust the sensory component will depend on the student's degree of hearing loss and should be made in consultation with his or her audiologist or teacher of students with hearing impairments.

Rating the Complexity of the Task
The level of complexity posed by the student's task is rated separately from the environment in which an activity takes place. When observing an activity, the Task Rating Guide (see Figure 4.2) is used as a reference to determine whether the task a student is expected to perform presents a comfortable, challenging, or frustrational level of visual complexity for the student or whether it is presenting low visual demands, based on each of the seven components. Knowledge of a student's visual abilities from prior observations, parent and teacher interviews, CVI Range results, and the Individual Complexity Profile will be helpful when using the

Task Rating Guide. As when rating the environment, the component or components with the highest rating determines the overall complexity level of the task.

Consider an example in which an instructor presents the letters in a student's name, one at a time, and asks him or her to name the letters. Assume that the instructor presents them well within the student's distance abilities and uses the same five letters in each session, making them highly familiar to the student. Furthermore, the instructor allows plenty of quiet wait time for the student to process each letter before answering. However, the instructor reports that the student seems very uninterested in the activity and seems to answer randomly. The teacher of students with visual impairments conducts a CVI Range assessment and determines that the student is just beginning to identify some colored photographs of highly familiar objects, but that more abstract two-dimensional materials such as letters and numbers are currently outside the student's visual abilities. In this case, the task is at the student's frustrational level of visual complexity. This task lies outside of the student's current visual abilities because of the complexity of target component. Even though all the other components in this task are within the student's comfortable level, the student is currently unable to interpret the visual targets that the instructor is presenting, making the entire task frustrational to the student's visual abilities.

When rating the environment and task, there may be times when the provider feels indecisive about what level to rate a particular component. In the author's opinion, when trying to decide between two different ratings, it is generally best to select the higher of the two. The rationale is that it is better to have extra interventions than too few.

Recording the Results
Once the complexity levels of the environment and the task have been determined for a particular activity, record the results and recommendations. If focusing on a single activity in the student's schedule,

the Single Activity Recording Form (see Figure 4.6) is used to record and report the results to the team. If more than one activity or even the student's entire school day is being observed, the Schedule Recording Form (see Figure 4.7) is used instead. The results include a report of the complexity of the environment and task in each activity, and whether these complexity levels are appropriate or need to be balanced for the student. Also included are checkboxes for recommendations to address the activity, as explained next.

Addressing the Activity

In addition to summarizing the ratings for each activity, the recording form is also used to communicate recommendations for addressing an activity or activities. These recommendations can be recorded any time throughout the observation stage and are intended to be reviewed later during the team meeting (sharing stage). In some cases, the recommendations may be accepted as written during the team meeting, and, in other cases, may serve as merely a starting point for further brainstorming and collaborative team discussion. The Comments section of the recording form can be used to list recommendations for addressing an activity.

In the 'What's the Complexity?' Framework, an activity should be addressed if it meets any of the following criteria:

1. The environment is extremely complex.
2. The task is at the student's frustrational level.
3. The activity is unbalanced.
4. The student's schedule is unbalanced; that is, complexity is distributed ineffectively throughout his or her schedule.
5. The task is challenging or the environment is highly complex (duration, visual breaks, and whether the complexity in the task is necessary or unavoidable should be considered).
6. The activity lacks visual opportunity.

Table 4.2 provides suggested courses of action for addressing each one of these six conditions.

These suggestions correspond to the six categories of recommendations in the Single Activity and Schedule Recording Forms and are intended as a guide in determining the appropriate direction for recommendations.

Once it is decided to address an activity, the next step is knowing what tools or supports to use. Although the specific interventions for any individual student with CVI will be as unique and varied as the student and the activity, most of them will make use of one or more of these six general tools to various degrees:

- Color
- Light
- Movement
- Blank space or masking
- Silence
- Tangibles

While these elements of intervention for students with CVI are not tools in a physical sense, they are tools in the sense that they allow the provider to accomplish a task: designing accessible activities for a student with CVI.

These six tools are utilized in countless ways to help sighted individuals better handle visual complexity, such as color coding of sections in textbook pages or websites, lighted and moving billboard signs, blank spaces between words or sections of text, and the silence of a library. However, they are generally more important for individuals with CVI. Table 4.3 provides some examples of how these six tools or supports can be used to reduce the complexity level of the task for individuals with CVI.

COLOR. In general, individuals with CVI have intact color perception (Groenveld, Jan, & Leader, 1990). Their ability to see color is a relative strength compared to their ability to sort through complex visual arrays or identify an object or image based on its salient features. As a result, color becomes an important visual anchor or support for many individuals with CVI (Roman-Lantzy, 2018).

Although some individuals with CVI show a strong preference for a particular color (sometimes

FIGURE 4.6 Single Activity Recording Form

Single Activity Recording Form

Student's name: _____   Date: _____

Directions: For the activity being evaluated, transfer the results of the Environment and Task Rating Guides by the circling the complexity level of each component and filling in the overall complexity level of the environment and the task. Then check off the categories of recommendations for addressing the task and specify in the comments section.

Activity: _____

Environment				
Complexity of Array	Complexity of Sensory Input	Visual Movement	Impact of Lighting	Visual Novelty
extreme	extreme	extreme	extreme	extreme
high	high	high	high	high
moderate	moderate	moderate	moderate	moderate
minimal	minimal	minimal	minimal	minimal

Complexity level of **Environment**: _____

Task						
Complexity of Target	Complexity of Array	Complexity of Sensory Inputs	Distance of Materials	Visual-Motor Demands	Visual Latency	Visual Novelty
frustrational	frustrational	frustrational	frustrational	frustrational	frustrational	frustrational
challenging	challenging	challenging	challenging	challenging	challenging	challenging
comfortable	comfortable	comfortable	comfortable	comfortable	comfortable	comfortable
low demand	low demand	low demand	low demand	low demand	low demand	low demand

Complexity level of **Task**: _____

Recommendations
(Check all that apply)

☐ Balance activity
☐ Address environment
☐ Address task
☐ Duration/breaks
☐ Balance schedule
☐ Create visual opportunity

Comments:

FIGURE 4.7 Schedule Recording Form

Schedule Recording Form

Student's name: _____   Date: _____

Activity (list in chronological order)	Complexity (check one for each)		Recommendations (check all that apply)	Comments (elaborate on recommendations or explain why none are needed)
	Environment	Task		
	☐ Extreme ☐ High ☐ Moderate ☐ Minimal	☐ Frustrational ☐ Challenging ☐ Comfortable ☐ Low visual demands	☐ Balance activity ☐ Address environment ☐ Address task ☐ Duration/breaks ☐ Balance schedule ☐ Visual opportunity	
	☐ Extreme ☐ High ☐ Moderate ☐ Minimal	☐ Frustrational ☐ Challenging ☐ Comfortable ☐ Low visual demands	☐ Balance activity ☐ Address environment ☐ Address task ☐ Duration/breaks ☐ Balance schedule ☐ Visual opportunity	
	☐ Extreme ☐ High ☐ Moderate ☐ Minimal	☐ Frustrational ☐ Challenging ☐ Comfortable ☐ Low visual demands	☐ Balance activity ☐ Address environment ☐ Address task ☐ Duration/breaks ☐ Balance schedule ☐ Visual opportunity	
	☐ Extreme ☐ High ☐ Moderate ☐ Minimal	☐ Frustrational ☐ Challenging ☐ Comfortable ☐ Low visual demands	☐ Balance activity ☐ Address environment ☐ Address task ☐ Duration/breaks ☐ Balance schedule ☐ Visual opportunity	

TABLE 4.2

Addressing an Activity

Reason for Addressing the Activity	Suggested Recommendations
Unbalanced activity	**Balance the activity**: Determine whether the environment or the task needs to be addressed. ■ Address the environment: Reduce the complexity level of the environment through modifications. ■ Address the task: Modify the task to reduce the complexity level. ■ Duration/visual breaks: Consider shortening the task and/or building in proactive visual breaks.
Extremely complex environment	**Address the environment:** ■ Consider reducing or "softening" the complexity level of the environment through modifications. ■ Consider moving the activity to an alternate environment. ■ Have the student try the activity at a time when the environment is not as complex. **Duration/visual breaks:** ■ Consider shortening the activity. ■ Consider proactively building in visual breaks before, during, or after activity.
Frustrational-level task	**Address the task:** ■ Modify: Modify the task to reduce it to the challenging or comfortable level. ■ Add support: Add support to reduce the task to the challenging or comfortable level. ■ Discontinue: Consider whether the task is appropriate for the student with any level of support at this time.
Challenging task or highly complex environment	**Duration/visual breaks:** ■ Consider whether length of task is appropriate and whether built-in visual breaks are necessary. (Offering frequent visual breaks throughout any challenging-level task or within a highly complex environment is helpful for many students with CVI.) *Note*: Determine whether the complexity in a highly complex environment or a challenging-level task is purposeful, necessary, or unavoidable. If not, consider reducing or "softening" complexity as much as possible.
Unbalanced schedule	**Balance the schedule:** ■ Consider offering planned, prolonged visual breaks proactively throughout the schedule. For most students, such breaks should be offered when there are consecutive activities with a highly complex environment or challenging-level activities. ■ Also, consider the distribution of complex activities throughout the student's day and determine if it is appropriate for that student or if the order of activities needs to be rearranged.
Lack of visual opportunity	**Create visual opportunity**: There may be activities in which the student is not expected to use vision at all. For some activities this might be completely appropriate. For others, creating an opportunity for the student to visually engage in the activity may enhance his or her access to and participation in the activity.

TABLE 4.3

Sample Interventions for Reducing Complexity of the Task

Student	Activity	Starting Complexity Level	Modifications	Tools Used to Reduce Complexity	Ending Complexity Level
Lucas, Phase I	Asking Lucas to look at a brown stuffed teddy bear	Frustrational (due to complexity of target)	Replace brown teddy bear with a red teddy bear (Lucas's "power color"). Turn lights off and shine a bright flashlight on the teddy bear while moving it slightly. Allow plenty of quiet wait time for Lucas to look.	Color Light Movement Silence	Challenging
Hannah, early Phase II	Locating and reaching for her flower-patterned cup at her place setting during lunch from an array that includes her lunch box, spoon, plate, bowl, yogurt container, and packet of veggie sticks	Frustrational (due to complexity of array)	Replace the patterned cup with a solid yellow cup (Hannah's "power color") with a strip of yellow Mylar wrapped around the middle. Reduce the array of items at her place setting to include just her cup and plate and one piece of food at a time.	Color Movement Blank space	Challenging
Tucker, mid-Phase II	Making a choice from an array of two black-and-white picture symbols	Frustrational (due to complexity of target)	Replace black-and-white picture symbols with realistic colored photographs of the objects or activities Tucker is choosing from.	Color	Challenging
Nalia, late Phase II	Selecting a printed sight word from an array of 10	Frustrational (due to complexity of target and array)	Tightly outline each sight word in red (Nalia's "power color") to support her awareness of the overall shape and salient features of the word. Ask her to select the word from an array of 4 instead of 10.	Color Blank space	Challenging
Terrance, early Phase III	Reading connected text in a grade-level book	Frustrational (due to complexity of array)	Reduce number of words by masking so that only one line at a time is visible. Triple space between words. Highlight every other word in yellow.	Color Blank space Masking	Challenging
Juanita, mid-Phase III	Using a graphing calculator with a black-and-white display to plot equations in algebra class	Frustrational (due to complexity of array)	Use a version of the graphing calculator with a full-color display, with the axis one color and each equation plotted in a different color so Juanita can tell them apart.	Color	Challenging
Evan, mid-Phase III	Calculating the volume of a prism in geometry	Frustrational (due to complexity of target)	Provide a three-dimensional model of the prism and highlight the length, width, and height of the two-dimensional version each in a different color.	Color Tangibles	Challenging

referred to as their "power color"), the importance of color as a support for individuals with CVI goes much further. At its core, the color preference characteristic is about color being more important to the functional vision of an individual with CVI than it is to his or her typically sighted peers (Roman-Lantzy, 2013, 2018). In the author's experience, an individual's need for color as a visual support is directly related to his or her difficulty with complexity of array and difficulty with complexity of the target. The more difficulty an individual has interpreting a complex visual display or recognizing objects or two-dimensional materials, the more important color will be as a visual support.

For some individuals with CVI, particularly those who are functioning at an early stage on the CVI Range, this need for color may take the form of a preference for a particular color. Others, particularly those in Phase III, for whom a specific color preference has long faded, may still rely on color as a support for interpreting complex environments and two-dimensional materials (Roman-Lantzy, 2013; see also Chapters 1 and 2). For example, a fifth grader in Phase III who struggles to interpret a black-and-white map of the world (due to difficulty with complexity of array) may be able to understand the map when each continent is filled in using a different solid color. Similarly, a first grader in Phase III who struggles to complete a worksheet containing black-and-white images (due to difficulty with complexity of target) may be able to complete the task when colored images are used instead. This same individual may also read more fluently when color is used to reduce the complexity of reading passages—for example, by placing a colored dot at the beginning of each sentence or highlighting every other word in a sentence to help the individual keep his or her place in the text.

LIGHT AND MOVEMENT. Although nonpurposeful sources of visual movement and light can be sources of distraction for individuals with CVI, movement and light can also be important supports when used intentionally. Adding movement or light to a visual target can help an individual locate and attend to it (Roman-Lantzy, 2013, 2018). For most people, the ability to alert to light or movement is a relative strength, compared to the ability to sort through complex visual arrays. Because of their difficulty with visual complexity, light and movement are even more important to the functional vision of individuals with CVI than for their typically sighted peers.

For example, for an individual in early Phase II CVI, finding the spoon on his or her lunch tray may be a frustrational task. Shining a bright flashlight on the spoon, however, and wiggling the light back and forth may help the spoon stand out from the rest of the array, turning a frustrational task into a challenging one.

BLANK SPACE OR MASKING. In addition to color, light, and movement, the use of blank space can be another important tool in supporting individuals with CVI. For those who experience difficulty with complexity of array, one main obstacle to accessing visual information is that there is usually just too much of it. Minimizing extraneous visual information in an environment or in instructional materials may constitute an important step in making an activity accessible for an individual with CVI.

Black trifold boards or fabric can be used to mask extraneous visual information in an environment, including unintended movement in the individual's visual field. This can also be accomplished by seating the individual so that he or she is facing an area of the room that has a minimally complex level of movement and visual array.

In addition to reducing the complexity of the environment, masking and blank space can also be utilized to reduce the complexity of the materials in an activity. Examples include using a piece of black paper to mask extraneous information in a picture book; increasing space between words in text or between problems on a worksheet; or using a tablet to zoom in on a visual scene in a picture book and taking a photograph of only the most important element of the page.

SILENCE. It can be difficult for individuals with CVI to process visual information when there is competing auditory input (Lueck & Dutton, 2015; Roman-Lantzy, 2018). Some individuals with CVI, particularly those who are functioning in the early stages on the CVI Range, may benefit from quiet environments when attempting to engage their vision in any task. Individuals in Phase II or Phase III may need a quieter environment only for challenging visual tasks.

Competing auditory inputs in an activity can be reduced in a variety of ways, including placing a sound-reducing partition near the individual's workspace, scheduling the activity during a time when the environment is quieter, moving the activity to a quieter location, and providing the individual with sound-canceling headphones during a more complex visual task. Providers can also strategically incorporate periods of silence into their instruction to give an individual time to locate or process the instructional materials. For example, when explaining a photograph to an individual, the provider can pause after the description of each feature to give the individual some silent time to process the features visually.

An individual in Phase III may do fine with the sound level of the general education classroom most of the time but may choose to complete more challenging visual tasks, especially exams, in a quieter environment.

TANGIBLES. A tangible is something an individual can perceive by touching it—often a three-dimensional object. In the author's experience, using tangibles can reduce the complexity of a task for individuals with CVI, making the activity more accessible. For example, an individual who has difficulty counting 10 squares on a worksheet because of the complexity of the array may have more success counting 10 cube-shaped blocks. Unlike the two-dimensional squares, the individual can manipulate the blocks, increase the space between them, touch each one as he or she counts, or place each block in a container as he or she counts it. Each of these strategies can help the individual manage the complex array posed by 10 items.

In addition, tangibles can be used to address the complexity of individual objects or images. For example, suppose a teacher is reading a book to the class about different kinds of fruit, and each page of the book features a color photograph of a piece of fruit, such as a banana, an apple, or a grape. Interpreting color photographs is a challenging-level task for a student with CVI in the class. However, the teacher can turn this into a comfortable-level task for the student by incorporating real pieces of fruit into the activity and inviting the student to touch each piece of fruit and explore its salient features before viewing its two-dimensional counterpart.

When pairing tangibles with their two-dimensional representations, it is often best to engage the tactile and visual modalities sequentially, rather than simultaneously, as many individuals with CVI have difficulty using their vision at the same time as their other senses (Roman-Lantzy, 2018).

Sharing

Once the observation stage is complete, a meeting should be scheduled with as many key members of the student's educational team as possible. The purpose of the meeting is to review the results of the observation stage, including proposed recommendations for addressing any particular activities in the student's schedule.

It is important that parents and other family members involved in the student's life have the opportunity to attend and participate fully in the process. Meetings should be scheduled to accommodate their availability.

It may be helpful to begin the meeting with a brief explanation of the 'What's the Complexity?' Framework, if it has not yet been introduced to the team. The Environment and Task Rating Guides may be useful visual aids when explaining complexity of the task and environment. Then the student's Individual Complexity Profile can be shared as an overview of what types of tasks are comfortable, challenging, and frustrational for the student and which levels of environmental complexity are generally an appropriate match for those tasks.

Next, the results of the observations for each activity can be presented, using the completed

Single Activity or Schedule Recording Forms. In many cases, it may be helpful to begin by mentioning some things that the team is doing especially well and celebrating any parts of the day during which visual demands were especially well managed, before turning to any activities that need to be addressed and specific recommendations for doing so. Often, in the most effective meetings, the initial recommendations are really a starting point for collaborative discussion and brainstorming, drawing on the team's collective expertise and knowledge of the student.

Case Study: Ava

Mr. Meadows decides to use the 'What's the Complexity?' Framework to give himself and Ava's educational team a more systematic approach for addressing visual complexity throughout Ava's school day. He contacts Ms. Anderson to share his plans and arranges to observe Ava for the first half of her school day. He plans to return the following week to observe the afternoon portion of her day.

Preparation

Mr. Meadows feels that he knows Ava and her visual abilities quite well. The information about her functional vision that he has gained from previous observations, his CVI Range assessment, and his direct work with Ava will be useful in creating Ava's Individual Complexity Profile.

Mr. Meadows decides to begin filling out this form before his visit to the school. He uses the companion Task Bank (see Figure 4.4) to guide his listing of sample tasks. He reads through each statement in the Task Bank and indicates whether it represents a comfortable, challenging, or frustrational visual task for Ava. Then he looks back at the statements he marked "comfortable" and transfers those that he feels are most relevant into the Comfortable box on her Individual Complexity Profile (see Figure 4.8). He repeats this step to fill in the Challenging and Frustrational boxes.

Next, Mr. Meadows turns to the Appropriate Environment column on the Individual Complexity Profile, where he must indicate which level or levels of environmental complexity will balance each task level for Ava. Since Ava's CVI Range score of 6–7 places her in late Phase II, Mr. Meadows consults the Phase II table on the Balanced Activity Guide (see Figure 4.5) for help. The table indicates that most students in Phase II can be expected to do comfortable-level tasks in a minimally complex, moderately complex, or highly complex environment. The word "balanced" is footnoted in the extreme environment column to indicate that only some students in Phase II, particularly those late in the phase, may be expected to perform comfortable-level visual tasks in an extremely complex environment. Mr. Meadows has observed Ava doing comfortable-level tasks, such as reaching for finger foods, with relative ease in extremely complex environments such as the cafeteria. Therefore, he believes that Ava's team can expect her to perform comfortable-level visual tasks in any of the four types of environments, so he checks all four complexity levels in the Appropriate Environment column for the Comfortable row.

Mr. Meadows repeats this procedure to determine what environment levels will be a good fit for challenging-level tasks for Ava. Consulting the Phase II table on the Balanced Activity Guide, he sees that most individuals in Phase II can be expected to perform challenging tasks in a minimally complex environment and that some children, particularly those in late Phase II, may also perform these tasks in a moderately complex environment. Mr. Meadows knows that Ava does well with challenging tasks in her individual work station, which is typically minimally complex. He has also observed her performing challenging tasks in moderately complex environments, such as the occupational therapy room. Mr. Meadows feels that Ava's team can reasonably expect her to perform challenging-level tasks in both minimally and moderately complex environments. He checks "minimal" and "moderate" in the Appropriate Environment column of Ava's Individual Complexity Profile.

FIGURE 4.8 Ava's Completed Individual Complexity Profile

Individual Complexity Profile

Student's name: _Ava_   School year: _2018–19_

Directions: In the Sample Tasks column, write examples of tasks that currently represent each level of visual complexity for this student. Use the Appropriate Environment box to check off which level or levels of environmental complexity would be a good fit for the tasks in that row (i.e., to make it a balanced activity).

Complexity of Task	Sample Tasks for This Student	Appropriate Environment
Frustrational	*Interpreting color photographs of unusual exemplars of familiar objects, photographs of animals, abstract cartoon illustrations, picture symbols, and black-and-white line drawings; recognizing generally familiar faces; interpreting facial expressions; interpreting array of more than 10 images; interpreting visual array in most children's books or tablet apps; viewing photographs of visual scenes; reading a line of text with single or double spacing between words; completing a worksheet with 4–5 printed math problems visible at once; completing a grade-level worksheet; interpreting grade-level maps, charts, and tables; counting a linear array without extra spacing between items; counting a random array of more than 3 items; visually attending to a face when a person is speaking; maintaining visual attention on presentations beyond 3 feet; locating a landmark from beyond 10 feet in a familiar location or beyond 4 feet in a novel location*	Frustrational-level tasks should not be attempted in any environment. Tasks may be modified or supports added to bring tasks to student's challenging or comfortable level.
Challenging	*Interpreting color photographs of general exemplars of familiar objects, realistic cartoon illustrations of highly familiar objects, and cartoon illustrations of generally familiar objects; identifying basic shapes by sight; recognizing numbers, words, and highly familiar faces; recognizing photographs of highly familiar faces; interpreting photographs depicting facial expressions; interpreting arrays of more than 10 objects or 7–10 images; reading isolated sight words; reading isolated line of text with triple spacing between words; worksheet with 2–3 math problems; counting a random array of 4–6 items; maintaining visual attention on materials or presentation within 24 inches; locating target or landmark from 7–10 feet in a familiar environment or 2–3 feet in a novel environment; using vision to guide hanging up personal items, zipping clothing, and writing; using vision to guide lower extremities over curbs and other surface changes; using vision to guide fork or knife; buttoning clothing*	☐ Extreme ☐ High ☑ Moderate ☑ Minimal
Comfortable	*Interpreting familiar and generally familiar objects; interpreting color photographs of highly familiar objects; recognizing letters; interpreting/interacting with an array of up to 10 objects; interpreting/interacting with an array of up to 5–6 images; reading mastered, isolated sight words; counting a linear array of up to 10 objects with extra space between them; maintaining visual attention on materials within 18 inches; maintaining visual attention on two-dimensional materials within preferred viewing distance; locating landmarks or targets in familiar environments up to a distance of 6 feet; using vision to guide reaching for a single item; using vision to guide spoon during a meal*	☑ Extreme ☑ High ☑ Moderate ☑ Minimal
Low Visual Demands	The following constitute preferred visual/sensory breaks for the student: *Listening to music, swinging in the occupational therapy room, going for a walk*	

Observation: Ava's Morning

Activity 1: Math in the General Education Classroom

RATING THE ENVIRONMENT. The first activity of Ava's day is math in Ms. Anderson's classroom. As the math session begins, Mr. Meadows positions himself next to Ava and kneels down so that he is seeing the classroom from her vantage point. He notes the complex array in the background, with multiple posters and wall materials, desks, and classmates, as well as the steady presence of extraneous visual movement in the background as classmates walk back and forth to Ms. Anderson's desk to ask questions. Just as they did during the last observation by Mr. Meadows, Ava's eyes dart back and forth between these classmates, the materials on the wall, and her math worksheet. Mr. Meadows also takes note of the constant noise in the room—classmates talking to the teacher, chairs sliding back and forth, the door opening and closing, the pencil sharpener grinding—and thinks about how difficult it is for Ava to maintain visual attention in the presence of competing noise.

Taking out a copy of the Environment Rating Guide, Mr. Meadows rates the complexity of array, complexity of sensory input, and visual movement components of Ms. Anderson's classroom as highly complex. (The statements that Mr. Meadows selects for each component of the environment are shown as circled in Figure 4.9 as a visual representation of his thought process; it is unnecessary to circle the statements in practice.) Because Ava is not distracted by the overhead lights and the classroom is highly familiar to her, Mr. Meadows rates the impact of lighting and visual novelty components as minimally complex. Since the highest-rated component determines the overall complexity of the environment, Mr. Meadows rates Ms. Anderson's classroom as highly complex for this activity, and he records this rating on Ava's Schedule Recording Form (see Figure 4.10).

RATING THE TASK. Next, Mr. Meadows turns his attention to the task Ava is expected to do in this environment: completing a math worksheet packet that contains one addition problem per page. Con-

sulting the Task Rating Guide (see Figure 4.11), he looks at the complexity of target column, which deals with a student's ability to interpret the materials. Mr. Meadows has already indicated in Ava's Individual Complexity Profile that reading printed numbers is a challenging task for her, so he selects "challenging" on the target column of the Task Rating Guide. (Again, Figure 4.11 provides a visual representation of the thought process of Mr. Meadows, but it is unnecessary to circle the statements in practice.) He then considers the array column of the Task Rating Guide. Although this specific task is not yet included in Ava's Individual Complexity Profile, Mr. Meadows feels that isolated addition problems, which contain an array of 4–6 numbers and symbols, are possible for Ava to complete but are at the upper end of her visual abilities. He chooses "challenging" for the array component on the Task Rating Guide. He then pencils in "single math problems" in the challenging box on Ava's Individual Complexity Profile so he will remember to add it to the final version later. Mr. Meadows also circles "challenging" for the visual-motor component, since using her vision in writing tasks is currently at the upper end of Ava's visual abilities.

Using the Task Rating Guide, Mr. Meadows determines that the other components of distance, latency, and novelty are all at Ava's comfortable level for this task and that the materials present no competing auditory sensory information. But because the target and array components of this task are at the challenging level, this is a challenging-level task for Ava.

If Mr. Meadows were observing only the math lesson, he would record his results on the Single Activity Recording Form, as in the example shown in Figure 4.12. However, since Mr. Meadows is observing Ava's entire morning today, he begins recording his results on Ava's Schedule Recording Form (see Figure 4.10).

ADDRESSING THE ACTIVITY. After recording the ratings for the task and environment for math class on Ava's Schedule Recording Form (see Figure 4.10), Mr. Meadows fills in the recommendation section. To guide his decisions in making

FIGURE 4.9 Rating the Environment in Ava's Classroom

Environment Rating Guide

Directions: Rate the complexity level for each of the five components that make up the environment. The highest-rated component determines the overall complexity level of the environment.

Complexity Level	Complexity of Array	Complexity of Sensory Input	Visual Movement	Impact of Lighting	Visual Novelty	Description and Examples
Extreme	Extreme amount of competing background information in student's visual field	Intense, constant level of competing sensory input	Intense level of movement in visual field	Lighting in this environment prevents student from attending to task	Setting and or characteristics of setting may be highly unfamiliar	Complexity of array, sensory input, and/or movement is **greater than in a typical, unadapted general education classroom** (e.g., school cafeteria, gymnasium, crowded hallway)
High	High amount of competing background information in student's visual field	High level of steady, competing sensory input	Frequent background movement in visual field	Lighting in this environment is consistently distracting for student	Setting and/or characteristics of setting may be unfamiliar	Complexity of array, sensory input, and/or movement is **similar to or slightly less than that of a typical, unadapted general education classroom**
Moderate	Low to moderate amount of competing background information in student's visual field	Low to moderate amount of competing sensory input at somewhat regular intervals	Occasional background movement in visual field	Lighting in this environment is occasionally distracting for student	Setting and/or characteristics of setting are basically familiar	Complexity of array, sensory input, and/or movement is **far less than in a typical, unadapted general education classroom** (e.g., generally quiet resource room with some competing visual information in student's visual field)
Minimal	No, or very little, competing background information in student's visual field	Quiet; no, or very infrequent, competing sensory input	No background movement in visual field	Lighting in this environment does not seem to be distracting for student	Setting and/or characteristics of setting are very familiar	Complexity of array, sensory and/or movement is **eliminated or nearly eliminated** (e.g., a quiet one-on-one setting with visual complexity reduced using black trifold boards or a plain wall)

FIGURE 4.10 Ava's Schedule Recording Form

Schedule Recording Form

Student's name: _Ava_   Date: _September 22_

Activity (list in chronological order)	Complexity (check one for each)		Recommendations (check all that apply)	Comments (elaborate on recommendations or explain why none are needed)
	Environment	**Task**		
Math in Ms. Anderson's classroom	☐ Extreme ☑ High ☐ Moderate ☐ Minimal	☐ Frustrational ☑ Challenging ☐ Comfortable ☐ Low visual demands	☑ Balance activity ☑ Address environment ☑ Address task ☑ Duration/breaks ☐ Balance schedule ☐ Visual opportunity	The environment is highly complex due to array, movement and sensory input (noise). The task is challenging due to the challenging level for Ava). In order for Ava to stay in Ms. Anderson's classroom during math, we need to "overmodify" the task using manipulatives, and allow Ava to answer verbally instead of using printed math problems or writing answers. These adaptations would bring the task to Ava's comfortable level and balance this activity. We can also take steps to "soften" the complexity of the environment by changing Ava's seat so that she is facing the area of the room to the left of the cubbies, where there is less movement and clutter in her visual field. Placing a black trifold board on the table next to the wall will further reduce complexity of the background array. *Offer brief visual breaks every 5–10 minutes throughout activity.*
Buttoning clothing in the occupational therapy room	☐ Extreme ☐ High ☐ Moderate ☑ Minimal	☑ Frustrational ☐ Challenging ☐ Comfortable ☐ Low visual demands	☑ Balance activity ☐ Address environment ☑ Address task ☑ Duration/breaks ☐ Balance schedule ☐ Visual opportunity	While buttoning tasks are generally at Ava's challenging level, the complex pattern on the fabric used in this activity makes it a frustrational-level task for her. She was unable to button the fabric independently and seemed to have difficulty looking at the fabric. By using plain black fabric with single-color buttons and lining the button holes with a strip of yellow fabric, we can bring this task back to Ava's challenging level. *Offer brief visual breaks every 5–10 minutes throughout activity.*

FIGURE 4.10 *(continued)*

Activity (list in chronological order)	Complexity (check one for each)		Recommendations (check all that apply)	Comments (elaborate on recommendations or explain why none are needed)
	Environment	**Task**		
Weather in Ava's workstation	☐ Extreme ☐ High ☐ Moderate ☑ Minimal	☑ Frustrational ☐ Challenging ☐ Comfortable ☐ Low visual demands	☑ Balance activity ☐ Address environment ☑ Address task ☑ Duration/breaks ☑ Balance schedule ☐ Visual opportunity	*Black-and-white line drawings are at the frustrational level for Ava. Although she can see them, she cannot interpret them. When the black-and-white line drawings were colored in, Ava was able to complete the activity successfully. Use full-color materials with Ava going forward. Two-dimensional images still represent a challenging task for Ava, even when in color, so offer brief visual breaks every 5–10 minutes during such tasks.* *At this point in her schedule, Ava has had three consecutive activities in which the environment was highly complex and/or the task was challenging or greater. Schedule a 10-minute visual break between this activity and her next activity.*
Independent reading in Ms. Anderson's classroom	☐ Extreme ☐ High ☑ Moderate ☐ Minimal	☐ Frustrational ☑ Challenging ☐ Comfortable ☐ Low visual demands	☐ Balance activity ☐ Address environment ☐ Address task ☑ Duration/breaks ☐ Balance schedule ☐ Visual opportunity	*Ms. Anderson's room is relatively quiet during silent reading. Ava's new seating position reduces the movement and array in her visual field. The environment during this activity is moderately complex. Ava can perform challenging-level tasks in a moderately complex environment (see her Individual Complexity Profile), so the activity is balanced. Because reading is a challenging-level task for Ava, offer frequent visual breaks every 5–10 minutes.*
Lunch in cafeteria	☑ Extreme ☐ High ☐ Moderate ☐ Minimal	☐ Frustrational ☑ Challenging ☐ Comfortable ☐ Low visual demands	☑ Balance activity ☐ Address environment ☑ Address task ☑ Duration/breaks ☑ Balance schedule ☐ Visual opportunity	*The environment is extremely complex and the task (using a fork) is challenging. The activity is unbalanced for Ava. Ava can do comfortable-level tasks in an extremely complex environment. Eating with a spoon and picking up finger foods are both comfortable-level visual tasks for Ava and we should limit lunch, for now, to these tasks. Consider carving out a quiet snack time each day in her minimally complex workspace where she can work on the challenging-level task of using a fork.*

(continued on next page)

129

FIGURE 4.10 *(continued)*

Activity (list in chronological order)	Complexity (check one for each)		Recommendations (check all that apply)	Comments (elaborate on recommendations or explain why none are needed)
	Environment	Task		
				We can also take steps to "soften" the environment by moving Ava's class table so that the long end is facing the wall and Ava is seated at the head of the table. This change will reduce the amount of movement and array in her visual field. Even with movement and array reduced, the environment is still extremely complex due to the auditory component. Due to the complexity of the cafeteria and the fact that Ava has an individual math lesson coming up soon, Ava may benefit from leaving lunch 5–10 minutes early for a visual break.
Recess	☑ Extreme ☐ High ☐ Moderate ☐ Minimal	☐ Frustrational ☐ Challenging ☐ Comfortable ☑ Low visual demands	☐ Balance activity ☐ Address environment ☐ Address task ☑ Duration/breaks ☐ Balance schedule ☐ Visual opportunity	*The environment is extremely complex due to array, movement, and sensory input (noise). Ava swung on swings with friends for most of recess, a low visual demands activity. Recess today was a balanced activity. Because the environment was extreme, however, consider offering Ava an extended visual break before her math lesson.*
Math lesson in Ava's work station	☐ Extreme ☐ High ☐ Moderate ☑ Minimal	☐ Frustrational ☑ Challenging ☐ Comfortable ☐ Low visual demands	☐ Balance activity ☐ Address environment ☐ Address task ☑ Duration/breaks ☐ Balance schedule ☐ Visual opportunity	*Ava works with her special education teacher on math skills in her individual workspace. They are using a math worksheet, so the task is challenging for Ava, but the activity is balanced because the environment is minimally complex. As with any challenging-level task, be aware of potential fatigue and the duration of the task, and offer brief visual breaks every 5–10 minutes. As noted above, Ava may benefit from a lengthy visual break at the beginning of this session since she is going from an extremely complex environment to a challenging-level math lesson.*

FIGURE 4.10 *(continued)*

Activity (list in chronological order)	Complexity (check one for each)			Recommendations (check all that apply)	Comments (elaborate on recommendations or explain why none are needed)
	Environment	**Task**			
Physical education—volleyball	☑ Extreme ☐ High ☐ Moderate ☐ Minimal	☑ Frustrational ☐ Challenging ☐ Comfortable ☐ Low visual demands		☑ Balance activity ☑ Address environment ☑ Address task ☑ Duration/breaks ☑ Balance schedule ☐ Visual opportunity	*The environment is extremely complex due to sensory input (noise), array, and movement in Ava's visual field. The task, playing in a volleyball game, is frustrational due to the amount of movement, visual array, and complex visual-motor skills involved. Furthermore, the distance and speed (pacing) at which Ava must maintain visual attention in the game is at her frustrational level. During the game, Ava didn't seem to be able to locate the ball and said several times that she was nervous that the ball would hit her.* *While locating and hitting a volleyball within the fast-paced context of a game is frustrational to Ava's visual ability, practicing her serve one-on-one with a peer in close proximity would be at her comfortable level. When serving, she is already holding the ball and would not have to use her vision to locate and hit the ball in midair. Also, because only half the class is playing the game at any time and the other half is practicing isolated skills in pairs, we can give Ava the opportunity to spend extra time partnering with a peer to practice her serve. Have Ava's partner stand with his or her back to a blank wall about 4 feet from Ava, so that Ava is facing a part of the gym where there is little movement and a simple background array. Positioning Ava and her classmate this way would soften the environment somewhat, although noise will still be a factor, and Ava should have the opportunity for a visual break between PE and her next activity.*

(continued on next page)

FIGURE 4.10 *(continued)*

Activity (list in chronological order)	Complexity (check one for each)		Recommendations (check all that apply)	Comments (elaborate on recommendations or explain why none are needed)
	Environment	*Task*		
Story time in Ms. Anderson's classroom	☐ Extreme ☐ High ☑ Moderate ☐ Minimal	☑ Frustrational ☐ Challenging ☐ Comfortable ☐ Low visual demands	☑ Balance activity ☐ Address environment ☑ Address task ☐ Duration/breaks ☐ Balance schedule ☐ Visual opportunity	Ms. Anderson's room is moderately complex during story time. The lights are out, minimizing complexity of background array, and the class is relatively quiet. There is a moderate degree of sound and movement (classmates fidgeting in place) but not as much as during times of group work. The task itself, however, is frustrational due to the distance component. Ava is in the front row, and the book is about 3 feet from her. While Ava can see some items from 3 feet away, she has difficulty maintaining visual attention on any materials beyond 18 inches. During this activity, Ava demonstrated very little attention to the book and mostly looked around the room as the teacher was showing the class each page. The pictures in this book are realistic color images, which are within Ava's challenging level. Ava's paraeducator can use Ava's tablet to snap a picture of each page of the book prior to story time. While the pages are not too busy, it is still a good idea to zoom in on the most important aspects of each illustration, eliminating any extraneous information. During story time, Ava brings along her tablet to follow along, holding the story at her preferred distance. The task will still be at Ava's challenging level due to the requirement of interpreting color images, but it is okay to expect Ava to do challenging-level tasks in a moderately complex environment (see her Individual Complexity Profile).

FIGURE 4.11 Ava's Task Rating Guide

Task Rating Guide

Directions: Rate the complexity level for each of the seven components that make up a task. The highest-rated component determines the overall complexity level of the task.

Visual Complexity	Complexity of Target	Complexity of Array	Complexity of Sensory Inputs	Distance of Materials	Visual-Motor Demands	Visual Latency	Visual Novelty
Frustrational	Targets are **outside student's ability** to look at and interpret	Array of materials is **outside student's ability** to look at, interpret, and interact with	Sensory demands of materials are **outside student's ability** to look at, interpret, and maintain visual attention	Distance of materials is **outside student's ability** to look at, interpret, and maintain visual attention	Visual-motor demands are **outside student's ability**	Pacing of task is **outside student's ability** to engage visually	Novelty of materials is **outside student's ability** to look at and interpret
Challenging	Targets are **at the upper end of student's ability** to look at and interpret	Array of materials is **at the upper end of student's ability** to look at, interpret, and interact with	Sensory demands of materials are **at the upper end of student's ability** to look at, interpret, and maintain visual attention	Distance of materials is **at the upper end of student's ability** to look at, interpret, and maintain visual attention	Visual-motor demands are **at the upper end of student's ability**	Pacing of task is **at the upper end of student's ability** to engage visually	Novelty of materials is **at the upper end of student's ability** to look at and interpret
Comfortable	Targets are **well within student's ability** to look at and interpret	Array of materials is **well within student's ability** to look at, interpret, and interact with	Sensory demands of materials are **well within student's ability** to look at, interpret, and maintain visual attention	Distance of materials is **well within student's ability** to look at, interpret, and maintain visual attention	Visual-motor demands are **well within student's ability**	Pacing of task is **well within student's ability** to engage visually	Novelty of materials is **well within student's ability** to look at and interpret
Low Visual Demands	**Low visual demands**	**Low visual demands**	**Low visual demands**	**Low visual demands**	**Low visual demands**	**Low visual demands**	**Low visual demands**

133

FIGURE 4.12 Ava's Single Activity Recording Form

Single Activity Recording Form

Student's name: _Ava_   Date: _September 22_

Directions: For the activity being evaluated, transfer the results of the Environment and Task Rating Guides by the circling the complexity level of each component and filling in the overall complexity level of the environment and the task. Then check off the categories of recommendations for addressing the task and specify in the comments section.

Activity: _Math in Ms. Anderson's classroom: Students are working on a math worksheet at their desks. Students are talking with each other and walking back and forth past Ava's desk to ask the teacher questions._

Environment

Complexity of Array	Complexity of Sensory Input	Visual Movement	Impact of Lighting	Visual Novelty
extreme	extreme	extreme	extreme	extreme
(high)	(high)	(high)	high	high
moderate	moderate	moderate	moderate	moderate
minimal	minimal	minimal	(minimal)	(minimal)

Task

Complexity of Target	Complexity of Array	Complexity of Sensory Inputs	Distance of Materials	Visual-Motor Demands	Visual Latency	Visual Novelty
frustrational	frustrational	frustrational	frustrational	frustrational	frustrational	frustrational
(challenging)	(challenging)	challenging	challenging	(challenging)	challenging	challenging
comfortable	comfortable	comfortable	(comfortable)	comfortable	(comfortable)	(comfortable)
low demand	low demand	(low demand)	low demand	low demand	low demand	low demand

Complexity level of Environment: _High_   Complexity level of Task: _Challenging_

Recommendations: (Check all that apply)

- ☑ Balance activity
- ☑ Address environment
- ☑ Address task
- ☑ Duration/breaks
- ☐ Balance schedule
- ☐ Create visual opportunity

Comments: _The environment is highly complex due to array, movement, and sensory input (noise). The task is challenging due to the target component (printed numbers are at the challenging level for Ava). In order for Ava to stay in Ms. Anderson's classroom during math, we need to "overmodify" the task use manipulatives, and allow Ava to answer verbally instead of using printed math problems or writing answers._

These adaptations would bring the task to Ava's comfortable level and balance this activity.

We can also take steps to "soften" the complexity of the environment by changing Ava's seat so that she is facing the area of the room to the left of the cubbies, where there is less movement and clutter in her visual field. Placing a black trifold board on the table next to the wall will further reduce complexity of the background array.

Offer brief visual breaks every 5–10 minutes throughout activity.

recommendations, Mr. Meadows consults the suggestions in the Addressing an Activity table (see Table 4.2) and Ava's Individual Complexity Profile (see Figure 4.8) and determines that this math activity meets two of the criteria for interventions.

First, the activity is unbalanced. As he indicated in Ava's Individual Complexity Profile, Ava should be expected to complete challenging-level tasks only in environments that are minimally or moderately complex. In this case, however, her team is expecting her to perform a challenging-level task in a highly complex environment. Mr. Meadows checks "balance activity" in the Recommendations section of the Schedule Recording Form. To balance the activity, the team must lower either the complexity of the environment, the task, or both. Mr. Meadows shares Ava's team's belief that she should be included in the general education setting as much as possible. However, he understands that Ava is not truly included in the classroom unless she has the opportunity to be successful there. Mr. Meadows wonders if Ava could complete the same math content in the general education setting in a medium that is visually comfortable for her. He consults the tasks in the Comfortable box on Ava's Individual Complexity Profile and remembers that using three-dimensional objects is a comfortable-level task for Ava. Mr. Meadows reasons that, if Ava's team modifies her math work in the general education setting, allowing her to receive the problems verbally and solve them using physical manipulatives, she may be able to do the work and remain included. Using manipulatives instead of printed worksheets, and giving her the option to answer the problems verbally instead of writing them down, would make the math session in Ms. Anderson's room a balanced activity for her, as she would be doing a comfortable-level task in a highly complex environment. She could continue to build her skill at solving printed math problems in her minimally complex individual work setting while using a more visually comfortable learning medium to participate in the general education math curriculum. Mr. Meadows records this recommendation in the Comments section of the Schedule Recording Form.

In addition to being an unbalanced activity, the math session in Ms. Anderson's room meets a second criterion for requiring interventions: the environment is highly complex. While it is appropriate for Ava to work in a highly complex environment, especially when the task is at her comfortable level, the impact of any complexity should still be minimized whenever possible. One way to do this is to offer short visual breaks periodically throughout the activity, consider shortening the duration of the activity, or both. Mr. Meadows checks "duration/breaks" on the Recommendations section of the Schedule Recording Form.

Another way to address the highly complex environment is to consider "softening" the environment, or looking at its individual components (array, movement, sensory input, etc.) and determining whether the complexity of any of these can be reduced. Mr. Meadows looks around the classroom and realizes that it may be possible to move Ava's seat so that she is still next to her classmates but is no longer facing a high-traffic area. This change would reduce the complexity level of the movement component. From Ava's new seat, the visual background would also be less complex with fewer wall materials. Also, placing a 4-foot by 4-foot black trifold board on a table next to the wall would further reduce the amount of background visual information in Ava's field of vision. The environment overall would still be highly complex due to the noise in the room (sensory input), but the total impact of the environment would be "softened" somewhat.

Mr. Meadows records these recommendations on the Schedule Recording Form and plans to propose them to the team during the team meeting (sharing stage). He then moves on with Ava to her next activity.

Activity 2: Buttoning Clothing in the Occupational Therapy Room

Ava and Mr. Meadows enter the occupational therapy room and greet Ms. Lopez, Ava's occupational therapist. As Ava engages in some warm-up activities at her desk, Ms. Lopez informs Mr. Meadows that Ava has been struggling with her buttoning task and usually looks away while attempting to button the practice fabric.

RATING THE ENVIRONMENT. Mr. Meadows gets next to Ava at eye level and takes in the occupational therapy room from her vantage point. While other areas of the room have a moderate amount of clutter, Ava's occupational therapist has placed a large, black trifold board immediately across from Ava, which blocks out nearly all background visual information. Ava is also the only student in the room, so it is very quiet. Using the Environmental Rating Guide, Mr. Meadows rates the occupational therapy room from Ava's vantage point as minimally complex and records the results on her Schedule Recording Form.

RATING THE TASK. Ms. Lopez places the practice shirt on the desk in front of Ava. Mr. Meadows immediately notices the pattern on the fabric—a highly cluttered, multicolored flower pattern with three white buttons. Ms. Lopez asks Ava to get started. Ava looks away from the shirt and feels for a button with her left hand. After some trial and error, she finds the first button, but struggles to find the correct opening for the button with her right hand. Ms. Lopez encourages Ava to "use her eyes," which Ava attempts, glancing briefly toward the fabric but then looking away again.

Mr. Meadows believes that using vision to guide a buttoning task is a challenging-level task for Ava, but that the complex pattern on the practice shirt is preventing her from being successful. Using the Task Rating Guide, Mr. Meadows rates the visual-motor component as challenging and the array component as frustrational. On Ava's Schedule Recording Form, he records the overall task as frustrational and recommends addressing the task in order to balance the activity. In the Comments section, he suggests using a practice shirt made of plain black fabric with three single-color buttons. He recommends lining the buttonholes with a strip of yellow fabric, which is a visually alerting color for Ava.

In this case, the task was the primary source of complexity. By following Mr. Meadows's recommendations, Ava's team will reduce the complexity

of the task, resulting in a balanced activity in which Ava can be successful.

Activity 3: Weather in Individual Workspace
Next, Mr. Meadows accompanies Ava to her individual workspace in the special education resource room. Her resource teacher, Mr. Yang, explains that part of Ava's morning routine is to report the day's weather by circling the correct picture from a field of three. Mr. Meadows notices that the three pictures are black-and-white line drawings representing different weather conditions: a sun with two small clouds in the background, a cloud with raindrops coming out of it, and a cluster of clouds.

It is a sunny day. Mr. Yang and Ava open the classroom door and take a few steps outside to check on the weather. Returning to Ava's desk, Mr. Yang asks Ava to look at the worksheet and circle the picture that depicts the weather outside. Ava hesitates for several seconds and then circles the picture of the cloud with raindrops coming out of it. Mr. Yang quietly mentions to Mr. Meadows that Ava is consistently inaccurate with this activity.

Mr. Meadows explains that black-and-white line drawings are at Ava's frustrational level and that colored pictures are much easier for her to interpret. He requests a box of crayons, and on a second copy of the worksheet he colors the clouds gray, the rain blue, and the sun yellow. Then he asks Ava to circle the picture that matches the weather outside. After searching the array for a few seconds, she correctly circles the picture of the sun.

Mr. Meadows rates the environment as minimally complex and the task as frustrational, due to the complexity of the target component (the use of black-and-white drawings). In the Recommendations section, he indicates that Ava's team needs to balance the activity by addressing the task. He recommends using colored images instead of black-and-white ones. Implementing Mr. Meadows's recommendations will bring the task from a frustrational to a challenging level for Ava, which is well suited for the minimally complex environment of the workspace. Because most of the tasks

Ava does in the individual workspace are at her challenging level, Mr. Meadows recommends giving her opportunities for visual breaks every 5 to 10 minutes throughout each activity.

Balancing the Schedule

Mr. Meadows looks at the first three activities in Ava's schedule and notices that each of them has either an environment that is highly complex or a task that is at the challenging level or greater. He realizes that this would be a good time to consider the effects of cumulative complexity in Ava's schedule and build in a prolonged visual break. He checks "balance schedule" in the Recommendations section of the Schedule Recording Form and elaborates in the Comments section.

Activity 4: Independent Reading in General Education Classroom

After a 10-minute visual break listening to music in Mr. Yang's room with the lights out, Ava returns to Ms. Anderson's room for independent reading, the final activity before lunch. This time, Ms. Anderson's room is quieter. Now in her designated independent reading area, Ava sits in a beanbag chair facing a sparsely decorated wall. This seating arrangement results in a moderately complex background array and eliminates any sources of environmental movement in her visual field. Using the Environment Rating Guide, Mr. Meadows determines that Ms. Anderson's room is a moderately complex environment during this activity.

Mr. Meadows then considers the task. Ava is reading a familiar book in which the words have been triple spaced. This task is at her challenging level of visual complexity. Mr. Meadows consults Ava's Individual Complexity Profile, on which he had indicated that Ava's team can expect her to perform challenging-level tasks in a moderately complex environment. The activity is balanced. In the Comments section of the Schedule Recording Form, Mr. Meadows explains why Ms. Anderson's classroom is less complex during this activity and adds that the team should not expect Ava to do the same task under more typical classroom conditions.

Activity 5: Lunch in the School Cafeteria

As Mr. Meadows and Ava enter the lunchroom with Ava's paraprofessional, Ms. Williams, Mr. Meadows is struck by the wall of noise they encounter. Ms. Williams helps Ava find her seat, and Mr. Meadows crouches down beside her in order to take in the room from her vantage point. There is a large window to the right of the table, about 5 feet from Ava's seat, and sunlight is pouring in. The background in Ava's visual field is basically a view of the entire cafeteria. There is constant movement, as other students walk by, wiggle in their seats, and gesture energetically to their friends. Wondering how many thousands of pieces of visual information are in Ava's visual field at that moment, Mr. Meadows snaps a picture of the room from her vantage point to show her team.

Ms. Williams cuts up Ava's sandwich and hands her a fork, explaining to Mr. Meadows that the occupational therapist wants her to practice using her fork during lunchtime. As Ava holds the fork, her gaze seems to move from the vast sea of moving bodies in front of her to the window on her left, as she stabs her fork randomly on her tray. Ms. Williams comments, "I usually have to help her with her fork in here. I think there is just too much going on for her to concentrate." She adds that Ava is often so tired and stressed by the end of lunch that she starts to become less compliant.

Although Mr. Meadows knows instinctively that the cafeteria is an extremely complex environment, he consults the Environment Rating Guide to document it for Ava's team. He rates array, movement, and sensory input as extremely complex and light as highly complex. Mr. Meadows also consults Ava's Individual Complexity Profile to confirm that using vision to guide her fork is currently a challenging-level task.

On Ava's Schedule Recording Form, Mr. Meadows checks "extremely complex" for environment and "challenging" for task. Lunch is an unbalanced activity for Ava. Mr. Meadows recommends balancing the activity by addressing the task: allowing Ava to eat finger foods at lunch or use a spoon, two tasks at her comfortable level, and practice using the fork in a less-complex setting. Recognizing the importance of practicing skills within repetitive, meaningful contexts, he suggests that the team give Ava the opportunity to have a short snack each day in her quiet individual workstation. She can then practice using her fork during that time, saving her finger foods for the cafeteria.

While Mr. Meadows believes Ava can do comfortable-level tasks in an extremely complex environment, he knows that one purpose of the 'What's the Complexity?' Framework is to reduce any unnecessary or avoidable complexity in a student's day. He scans the room, wondering if there are any seating locations that would allow Ava to stay in the cafeteria with her friends while also softening the complexity of the environment. The cafeteria will always be loud, regardless of Ava's location in it, so the extreme level of sensory input is unavoidable. However, Mr. Meadows is confident he can reduce the complexity of array and movement for Ava. He spots a row of tables positioned perpendicular to the plain cafeteria wall. If Ava's class were to move to that table, and Ava sat at the head of the table, there would be a drastic reduction in the amount of movement and visual information in her visual field. She would also have her back to the windows, reducing the complexity of the light component. Mr. Meadows writes these recommendations in the Comments section of Ava's Schedule Recording Form. In addition, he checks "duration/breaks" and advises Ava's team to consider allowing Ava to leave lunch 5 to 10 minutes early to take a visual break in a quiet setting.

Observation: Ava's Afternoon
The following week, Mr. Meadows returns to Ava's school to observe and evaluate her afternoon activities in order to get a complete picture of her day. He continues to record his ratings and recommendations on Ava's Schedule Recording Form (see Figure 4.10 for details).

Sharing
Meeting with Ava's Team
When Mr. Meadows is finished with his observations, he prepares a 'What's the Complexity?' re-

port for Ava's educational team, which includes her Individual Complexity Profile, Environment and Task Rating Guides for the team's reference, and Ava's completed Schedule Recording Form encompassing her full school day. He adds a summary at the end into which he has inserted some pictures of various environments from Ava's vantage point.

The following week, he meets with Ava's team at the end of the school day, reviews Ava's 'What's the Complexity?' report, and leads a team brainstorming session on ways to implement his recommendations. Now that Ava's team members have a deeper understanding of visual complexity and its impact on Ava's day, they seem better able to generate their own ideas for interventions. At the end of the meeting, Mr. Meadows thanks everyone for their time, tells them he will generate a list of next steps and email it to them, and schedules a date to visit the school again to support the team in implementing the next steps.

Mr. Meadows hopes that using the 'What's the Complexity?' Framework with Ava's team has given them a greater sense of confidence in designing a more visually appropriate school day for her. He hopes that he has helped the team transform a schedule that required Ava to drift between islands of intervention into one that will place her on solid ground all day. As he drives away from Ava's school that afternoon, he imagines her arriving at school and encountering a visual world that was designed for her, one in which she can be successful and demonstrate her true abilities.

Additional Considerations
Expecting Progress
The brain's cerebral cortex is not static or hardwired as was once believed. Instead, it responds to experience by forming new connections and developing new capacities (Catteneo & Merabet, 2015). The brain's ability to change and adapt based on experience is called *neuroplasticity.* A growing body of research, as well as advances in brain im-

aging technology, is leading to a deeper understanding of neuroplasticity and its implications for educating individuals with CVI. Studies on adults and older children have also demonstrated that neuroplasticity is not confined to early childhood, as once thought, but is instead a capability we carry with us throughout our lives (Catteneo & Merabet, 2015).

As a result of our deeper appreciation of neuroplasticity, many providers are looking at individuals' abilities from a growth mindset (Dweck, 2016) rather than a fixed mindset. Visual abilities are no exception. Research and experience tell us that improvement in visual functioning is likely in individuals with CVI (Roman-Lantzy, 2018).

Like the visual abilities of individuals with CVI, the Individual Complexity Profile is a dynamic entity. A student's Individual Complexity Profile should be updated to capture changes in his or her visual abilities as they occur. A task that is challenging for a student today may be comfortable for him or her six months from now.

Providers sometimes question the need to modify the environment for individuals with CVI. "The real world is complex," the reasoning goes. "Don't our students have to get used to using their vision in the real world?" This is an understandable but misguided question, rooted in the view of functional vision as a fixed entity. However, when providers recognize vision as a dynamic ability, with the potential to improve like other skill areas, the logic in supporting visual development becomes obvious. When first teaching children to swim, for example, they cannot be expected to jump into the deep end without support, even though that is hopefully what they will eventually be able to do. Instead, the swimming instructor matches instruction and supports to the child's current swimming ability and raises the expectations as the child's ability grows. The supports initially given to the child provide him or her with access, or an entry point, to the water—a prerequisite for both present success and future development as a swimmer.

It is important to apply the same mindset when providing visual supports for a student with CVI.

While it is not possible to predict what a student's visual abilities will be in the future, the provider can use the CVI Range to determine a student's present visual abilities. The 'What's the Complexity?' Framework can then be used to ensure that the environments and tasks in the student's day are matched to those abilities. This approach provides the student with an entry point to the visual world, giving him or her access now so that he or she can experience success in the present and develop skills for the future.

Working toward Frustrational-Level Tasks

Just because a particular task is currently outside of a student's visual ability does not mean that it always will be. Frustrational tasks may one day become challenging or even comfortable tasks as a student's visual abilities develop. The provider can facilitate this process by taking what is currently a frustrational-level task and adding enough supports and modifications to bring it to the student's challenging or comfortable level. The provider can then gradually remove these supports and modifications over time as the student's ability progresses, ensuring that the activity never rises above the student's challenging level. Before deciding to initiate this process, however, here are some guiding questions that may be helpful:

- Is the task meaningful to the student? Would introducing it have a clear purpose and the potential for long-term benefits? If not, the task is likely not appropriate.

- Has the student already mastered any tasks (that is, at the comfortable level) that are related to the frustrational task? If so, could the frustrational materials be paired with those at the student's comfortable level?

- Are there options for supports and modifications so that the student can participate in the task at his or her comfortable or challenging level?

Consider, for example, the support offered to Daniel while working toward a frustrational-level task.

Daniel is a student with CVI who uses a daily schedule with an object representing each activity. He has used this schedule for a year, and recognizing objects is now at his comfortable level. While Daniel is able to look at two-dimensional images, interpreting them is currently a frustrational-level task. However, the team hopes to help him transition to two-dimensional learning media.

Daniel's teacher takes color photographs of each object on Daniel's schedule. Each time she reviews the schedule with Daniel, she pairs the familiar object with its photograph and draws Daniel's attention to the salient features of both. For four months, Daniel looks at the photographs, a comfortable-level task, but is not required to identify them.

Finally, Daniel's teacher removes one of the objects from the schedule altogether and uses the photograph in its place. Within a matter of days, Daniel grows accustomed to the change and demonstrates anticipation of the upcoming activity after seeing just the photograph. His teacher then replaces a second object with its photograph, then a third, and so on as Daniel demonstrates readiness, until his schedule is entirely made up of photographs. Eight months after Daniel's team first introduced pictures, he now uses a daily picture schedule and even sets it up independently each morning.

Daniel's team helped him learn to recognize photographs, once a frustrational-level task. They did so by providing a level of support that allowed him to practice this skill at a level that was within his visual abilities. Furthermore, they embedded the task into a meaningful routine that Daniel would repeat several times daily. They put no pressure on Daniel to identify the photographs until they felt he was ready. Furthermore, they always ensured that his environment was an appropriate match for the task. Although the details of whether and how to work toward frustrational tasks will vary with each individual and circumstance, the spirit with which Daniel's team approached the endeavor is broadly applicable.

Not Every Activity Will Be Balanced

Although achieving balanced activities is one of the central goals of the 'What's the Complexity?' Framework, there may be certain situations in which it is not necessary to balance an activity. For example, Nasir, a first grader with CVI, has begun identifying photographs of familiar objects. Using a tablet with a communication app, he is becoming proficient at making highly motivating recreation and leisure and mealtime choices by selecting photographs from an array of four. While Nasir is making excellent progress with this task, it is at the upper end of his visual abilities and is, therefore, a challenging-level task.

Nasir is beginning to take the tablet with him to all his activities, and he uses it to make choices in minimally, moderately, and highly complex environments. His speech-language pathologist expresses concern that when he is using the tablet to make choices in a highly complex environment, it is an unbalanced activity. "Should we simplify his tablet display to make the task less complex?" she wonders. Her question, and this particular situation, illustrate the importance of considering the duration and motivation level of the task. In this case, the task is very short. It takes Nasir less than a minute to make his choice on the tablet, after which he is rewarded with the chosen, highly motivating activity that lasts several minutes. Were Nasir practicing his communication app for an extended period of time in a speech-language lesson, the nature of the task would be more worklike and the duration longer. In that case it would be important to ensure an appropriately matched environment. As it is, however, using his tablet to make a quick choice in a highly complex environment constitutes only a momentary imbalance, making further modification unnecessary.

Adjusting Expectations during Stressful Situations

Nasir's story illustrates another important consideration. Most people can think of particular situations or events that were stressful or anxiety producing, perhaps a public speaking engagement, a job interview, or a lost smartphone. For Nasir, it is transitions. Ever since entering preschool, Nasir has had difficulty making the transition from one activity to another, especially when it involved leaving his resource room to go to another area of the building. During these times, he shows visible signs of stress and can engage in behavior that is harmful to himself or others.

In his kindergarten year, his educational team introduced a schedule system of tangible objects, with one object representing each activity in his schedule. At the end of each activity, staff members support Nasir as he places the object for that activity in the "all done" box and picks up the object representing the next activity. The object schedule has since become a staple of Nasir's daily routine. Although transitions are still stressful for him, holding onto a concrete object as he travels from one activity to the next seems to give him a level of anticipation and comfort that was previously absent.

Given his recent growth in interpreting photographs and using them to make choices, Nasir's team also decides to try replacing his schedule transition objects with photographs. At first they pair the photographs with the original objects, presenting them sequentially to Nasir. Once he seems comfortable with the change, they begin removing the objects one by one and using only the photographs. This change does not go well. During transitions, Nasir pushes the photographs away and does not look at them. He seems to become more anxious around transitions. The photographs don't seem to be providing the same sense of comfort that the objects had.

When we remember that interpreting photographs is a challenging task for Nasir, his aversion to photographs during transitions begins to make sense. Challenging tasks that are possible under normal circumstances may be too difficult under stress. Consider, for example, the task of learning and speaking a second language. Even those who have become fluent in a second language would likely be most comfortable using their native language when in an unusually stressful situation. If photographs can be thought of as type of second language for Nasir, then it is no wonder he prefers his native language of objects when experiencing stress. Sometimes, even when an activity appears balanced, it is important to consider whether the emotions evoked by the situation necessitate comfortable- rather than challenging-level tasks.

"Cloudy" Days

Most people have days in which they feel well-rested, healthy, and up to performing the tasks of the day. And most people have days when they do not. Maybe they are feeling ill or they didn't get enough sleep the night before. Whatever the reason, there are days when many of the tasks we are normally capable of may seem overwhelming. Individuals with CVI are no different.

One parent who favored weather analogies used the term "cloudy days" to describe days when her son, Brian, was ill or was tired from being awake most of the night before. Brian's CVI Range assessment, his present levels of performance documented in his IEP, and his Individual Complexity Profile all gave a clear picture of his visual and cognitive abilities. However, on "cloudy days," Brian's teachers adjusted their expectations accordingly, just as they would have done for themselves. Depending on how Brian was feeling, they might shorten the length of his challenging tasks or even forgo them altogether. Sometimes Brian's teachers would offer more frequent and longer breaks and skip an activity like art or physical education that took place in an extremely complex environment. Anyone using the 'What's the Complexity?' Framework should feel the same latitude in adjusting expectations based on the immediate needs of their students.

Conclusion

The 'What's the Complexity?' Framework offers a systematic way to intentionally design a student's entire school day to fall within his or her visual abilities. It ensures that tasks and environments are individualized and balanced to the abilities of each student. Educational teams can use the Individual Complexity Profile as a guide for evaluating existing activities, designing new ones, and selecting the most appropriate visual learning media for each student.

Individuals with CVI confront visual complexity and the related CVI characteristics during every part of their day. When left unaddressed, this complexity stands between the individual and an accessible, appropriate education. To avoid such an outcome, CVI interventions must be applied rigorously and consistently across an individual's entire school day. Visual complexity must be evaluated and addressed at every turn. A team that decides to make this effort is taking the first step in an ongoing collaborative process that sends the individual with CVI a clear message: "You are valued; you are welcome here; and this school is yours, too."

REFERENCES

Catteneo, Z., & Merabet, L. B. (2015). Brain plasticity and development. In A. H. Lueck & G. N. Dutton (Eds.), *Vision and the brain: Understanding cerebral visual impairment in children* (pp. 105–123). New York, NY: AFB Press.

Dutton, G. N. (2013, January). *Types of impaired vision in children related to damage to the brain, and approaches towards their management.* Paper presented at the Proceedings of South Pacific Educators in Vision Impairment. Retrieved from http://media.wix.com/ugd/f88b42_432b79fb375a4d37b9ed1b5714e2a6b8.pdf

Dweck, C. S. (2016). *Mindset: The new psychology of success.* New York, NY: Ballantine Books.

Farah, M. J. (2000). *The cognitive neuroscience of vision.* Malden, MA: Blackwell Publishers.

Groenveld, M., Jan, J. E., & Leader, P. (1990). Observations on the habilitation of children with cortical visual impairment. *Journal of Visual Impairment & Blindness, 84*(1), 11–15.

Humphreys, G., & Riddoch, J. (2014). *A case study in visual agnosia revisited: To see but not to see* (2nd ed.). New York, NY: Psychology Press.

Koenig, A. J., & Holbrook, M. C. (1995). *Learning media assessment of students with visual impairments: A resource guide for teachers* (2nd ed.). Austin: Texas School for the Blind and Visually Impaired.

Lueck, A. H., & Dutton, G. N. (2015). Assessment of children with CVI: Introduction and overview. In A. H. Lueck & G. N. Dutton (Eds.), *Vision and the brain: Understanding cerebral visual impairment in children* (pp. 207–260). New York, NY: AFB Press.

Pawletko, T., Chokron, S., & Dutton, G. N. (2015). Considerations in the behavioral diagnosis of CVI: Issues, cautions, and potential outcomes. In A. H. Lueck & G. N. Dutton (Eds.), *Vision and the brain: Understanding cerebral visual impairment in children* (pp. 145–173). New York, NY: AFB Press.

Roman-Lantzy, C. (2013, June). *CVI Phase III.* Presentation at the Connections Beyond Sight and Sound summer institute, College Park, MD.

Roman-Lantzy, C. (2018). *Cortical visual impairment: An approach to assessment and intervention* (2nd ed.). New York, NY: AFB Press.

Zuidhoek, S., Hyvärinen, L., Jacob, N., & Henriksen, A. (2015). Assessment of functional vision: Assessment of visual processing in children with CVI. In A. H. Lueck & G. N. Dutton (Eds.), *Vision and the brain: Understanding cerebral visual impairment in children* (pp. 343–390). New York, NY: AFB Press.

APPENDIX 4A

CVI 2D Image Assessment

Ava knows what scissors are. She uses them nearly every day in school. She can even find a pair on the cluttered table in the art room. For Ava, recognizing or identifying common objects is a comfortable-level visual task. Ms. Anderson is confused, then, when Ava fails to circle a black-and-white illustration of a pair of scissors from an array of three images on a recent assessment.

During Mr. Meadows's next visit, Ms. Anderson shows him the assessment and points out the illustration of the scissors, which is oriented so that the blade is open and facing up and the round handles are spread out and facing down. "I know they are big enough for Ava to see," says Ms. Anderson. She turns to Ava, pointing at the scissors and says, "Ava, can you see this picture?" Ava replies that she can. "So why," asks Ms. Anderson, "did she circle the image of the pencil instead?"

Mr. Meadows knows that black-and-white illustrations tend to be more difficult than color images for many individuals with CVI, and he suspects this may be true for Ava. He decides to ask her a different question. "Ava, what do you see?" he asks, pointing to the illustration of the scissors. Ava studies the image and, after a few minutes, responds, "I think it's a bicycle." Mr. Meadows gazes at the image and thinks for a moment.

"Ava, can you point to one of its wheels?" he asks. Ava reaches out and touches her index finger to one of the handles on the scissors. "Wheel," she says. Ms. Anderson and Mr. Meadows look at each other and nod.

Of course, Ava had been able to see the illustration. But what no one had realized until this moment, is that she had been seeing a bicycle instead of a pair of scissors. On his tablet, Mr. Meadows pulls up a color photograph of a real pair of scissors that look like the kind Ava uses in art class (see Figure 4A.1). He positions the image with the handles down, so that the orientation matches that of the black-and-white version. "What do you see here?" he asks Ava. "Scissors!" she exclaims after a brief pause.

Individuals with CVI may have difficulty identifying or recognizing what they are looking at, even if they can see it clearly, including objects, images, shapes, letters, numbers, and other symbols (Roman-Lantzy, 2013). While there is no one-size-fits-all hierarchy to describe the order in which individuals with CVI begin to recognize different kinds of materials, there do seem to be some general patterns. In the author's experience, for example, individuals with CVI usually have more difficulty identifying images than objects. This finding is supported in the literature on brain-based visual impairments (Farah, 2000).

Individuals with CVI often have difficulty recognizing objects based on their salient defining features (Roman-Lantzy, 2018). Instead, they may rely on more basic visual cues, such as the object's actual color, size, texture, and reflectance (Farah, 2000). When one photographs an object, some of these cues are lost immediately, such as the object's actual size. The progression from color photographs to colored illustrations to black-and-white illustrations involves the increasing removal of these important visual cues. For many individuals with CVI, the further removed an image is from the way its subject actually looks in the physical

FIGURE 4A.1 Two Images of Scissors

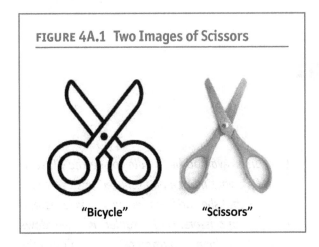

"Bicycle"   "Scissors"

FIGURE 4A.2 Difficulty in Recognizing Images

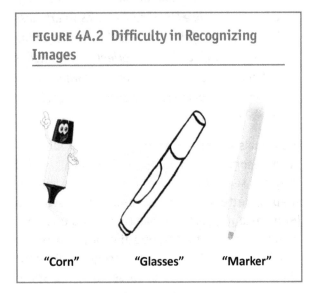

"Corn"   "Glasses"   "Marker"

world, the more difficult it will be to recognize. In general, objects are easiest to identify, then photographs, and then black-and-white illustrations (Farah, 2000).

Figure 4A.2 illustrates this general order of difficulty. A third-grade student in mid-Phase II was shown the three images of a marker and asked, "What do you see?" She identified the black-and-white illustration as "glasses," the abstract color illustration as "corn," and correctly identified the color photograph, which most closely resembles the kind of marker she uses in class. For this student, objects are at her comfortable level of visual complexity, color photographs at the challenging level, and abstract color or black-and-white illustrations at her frustrational level.

Because the functional vision of individuals with CVI is dynamic, some students may progress along this continuum of objects, photographs, and more abstract illustrations, given appropriate instruction and support, and learn to recognize types of materials that were previously frustrational for them. However, to ensure that instruction and support is appropriate and that the student's ability to interpret two-dimensional images is accurately reflected in his or her Individual Complexity Profile, more targeted assessment may be needed. It is important to determine whether the student can currently interpret images and, if so, what types. Many educational materials, such as worksheets, picture books, and textbooks, use images that are more abstract than photographs. Therefore, to ensure that instructional materials are appropriate for each student, the provider needs to assess the student's ability to identify or recognize both realistic and abstract images, in color and in black and white (Zuidhoek, Hyvärinen, Jacob, & Henriksen, 2015).

The provider can use the 2D Image Assessment presented here to accomplish this task for some students with CVI. This assessment helps to determine whether a student is able to recognize images and, if so, which types are at his or her comfortable, challenging, and frustrational levels. This information can be entered into the student's Individual Complexity Profile and can be used to drive instruction and ensure that he or she is given two-dimensional materials that are within his or her current visual abilities. This assessment is based on the five categories of images that, in the author's experience, best represent those found in most instructional materials: color photographs, realistic color illustrations, abstract color illustrations, realistic black-and-white illustrations, and abstract black-and-white illustrations.

Using the 2D Image Assessment

When and Where to Start?
The right time to start assessing and teaching interpretation of two-dimensional images will vary with each individual. However, in the author's

experience, many individuals in early to mid-Phase II may be ready to begin the transition from objects to photographs. At this point, identifying or recognizing familiar objects may be a comfortable-level task for the individual. The provider can then use the 2D Image Assessment to determine whether the individual's ability to recognize photographs is emerging.

Of the two assessment categories included in this appendix, common objects and animals, common objects is often the best place to start. In the author's experience, and according to the literature on brain-based visual impairments (Humphreys & Riddoch, 2014), animals tend to be more difficult to recognize than other things. Allowing an individual to experience success with the common objects category before attempting the animals category may be the best approach.

For individuals who have already demonstrated some ability in recognizing two-dimensional images, it may be best to begin the assessment with the most abstract images in a category and work backward toward color photographs, so that the easier images do not give the individual clues about the identity of the more abstract images.

If a provider is attempting this assessment with an individual who has never been asked to interpret two-dimensional materials, or with one whose ability to interpret images is just emerging, it may be best to begin the assessment with color photographs. Many individuals may be able to interpret photographs of highly familiar personal objects (such as their own toothbrush with a cartoon character's face) before those of more generally familiar objects (a general picture of a toothbrush), like those included in the everyday things category of the 2D Image Assessment. If the provider suspects this to be the case, it may make sense to begin with photographs of highly familiar personal items, rather than the images suggested in the 2D Image Assessment.

Procedure

The provider begins the 2D Image Assessment by showing the student a series of images and asking, "What do you see?" The size and presentation of each image may vary depending on the student's visual abilities, but, in the author's experience, presenting each image full screen on a backlit tablet is an effective approach. (For full-size digital versions of each image in the 2D Image Assessment, please see http://learn.aph.org/CVI-advanced -principles.) The provider should not give students any feedback on the accuracy of their answers, although it is acceptable to thank them for each response or praise them for effort. Repeated administrations of this assessment will be less useful if the student has memorized the answers to images he or she previously answered incorrectly.

The student's answers are recorded on the Response Record forms, which feature small versions of the images for the provider's reference (not for showing to students). There are separate forms for the common objects and animals categories, and separate pages for each type of image (see Figures 4A.3 and 4A.4). A check mark is placed next to each image the student recognized or identified correctly, and the student's approximation is recorded next to each image that is identified incorrectly. At the bottom of each page is a row to record the percentage of correct answers for the type of image on that page, as well as the level of complexity that type of image poses for the student. There are multiple columns for recording answers on different dates to track a student's progress over time.

There may be cases in which an image in the 2D Image Assessment is not appropriate for a particular individual. For example, while the images in the common objects category may be familiar to many individuals, there may be some items that are not part of a particular individual's experience. In these instances, the provider may choose to omit the item and calculate the individual's percentage score using the adjusted number of items.

For individuals who cannot verbalize what they are seeing, it may not be possible to assess identification. In many cases, however, it may still be possible to assess *recognition* of images. One approach is to embed new images within the context of a familiar routine and assess whether the

Response Record: Common Objects

Student's name: _____   Response method (check one): ☐ Identification ☐ Recognition

Indicate correct answers with a check mark. If incorrect, write student's approximation.

		Color Photographs			
Image	*Date:*	*Date:*	*Date:*	*Date:*	*Date:*
Percentage correct					
Complexity level					

Rating Key: 100% = Comfortable   60–99% = Challenging   0–59% = Frustrational

Response Record: Common Objects

Student's name: _____ Response method (check one): ☐ Identification ☐ Recognition

Indicate correct answers with a check mark. If incorrect, write student's approximation.

Realistic Color Illustrations					
Image	*Date:*	*Date:*	*Date:*	*Date:*	*Date:*
Percentage correct					
Complexity level					

Rating Key: 100% = Comfortable   60–99% = Challenging   0–59% = Frustrational

Response Record: Common Objects

Student's name: _____   Response method (check one): ☐ Identification ☐ Recognition

Indicate correct answers with a check mark. If incorrect, write student's approximation.

Image	Date:	Date:	Date:	Date:	Date:
Abstract Color Illustrations					
(shoe)					
(airplane)					
(lamp)					
(scissors)					
(cup of coffee)					
(bed)					
(couch)					
(backpack)					
(car)					
(toothbrush)					
Percentage correct					
Complexity level					

Rating Key: 100% = Comfortable   60–99% = Challenging   0–59% = Frustrational

Response Record: Common Objects

Student's name: _____   Response method (check one): ☐ Identification   ☐ Recognition

Indicate correct answers with a check mark. If incorrect, write student's approximation.

Realistic Black-and-White Illustrations					
Image	*Date:*	*Date:*	*Date:*	*Date:*	*Date:*
Percentage correct					
Complexity level					

Rating Key: 100% = Comfortable   60–99% = Challenging   0–59% = Frustrational

Response Record: Common Objects

Student's name: _____   Response method (check one): ☐ Identification ☐ Recognition

Indicate correct answers with a check mark. If incorrect, write student's approximation.

Abstract Black-and-White Illustrations					
Image	*Date:*	*Date:*	*Date:*	*Date:*	*Date:*
Percentage correct					
Complexity level					

Rating Key: 100% = Comfortable   60–99% = Challenging   0–59% = Frustrational

Response Record: Animals

Student's name: _____   Response method (check one): ☐ Identification ☐ Recognition

Indicate correct answers with a check mark. If incorrect, write student's approximation.

Color Photographs					
Image	*Date:*	*Date:*	*Date:*	*Date:*	*Date:*
Percentage correct					
Complexity level					

Rating Key: 100% = Comfortable   60–99% = Challenging   0–59% = Frustrational

Response Record: Animals

Student's name: _____ Response method (check one): ☐ Identification ☐ Recognition

Indicate correct answers with a check mark. If incorrect, write student's approximation.

Realistic Color Illustrations					
Image	*Date:*	*Date:*	*Date:*	*Date:*	*Date:*
(dog)					
(cow)					
(cat)					
(fish)					
(bird)					
(elephant)					
(rabbit)					
(horse)					
(spider)					
(snake)					
Percentage correct					
Complexity level					

Rating Key: 100% = Comfortable   60–99% = Challenging   0–59% = Frustrational

Response Record: Animals

Student's name: _____   Response method (check one): ☐ Identification ☐ Recognition

Indicate correct answers with a check mark. If incorrect, write student's approximation.

Abstract Color Illustrations					
Image	*Date:*	*Date:*	*Date:*	*Date:*	*Date:*
(dog)					
(cow)					
(cat)					
(fish)					
(owl)					
(elephant)					
(rabbit)					
(horse)					
(spider)					
(snake)					
Percentage correct					
Complexity level					

Rating Key: 100% = Comfortable   60–99% = Challenging   0–59% = Frustrational

Response Record: Animals

Student's name: _____ Response method (check one): ☐ Identification ☐ Recognition

Indicate correct answers with a check mark. If incorrect, write student's approximation.

Realistic Black-and-White Illustrations					
Image	*Date:*	*Date:*	*Date:*	*Date:*	*Date:*
Percentage correct					
Complexity level					

Rating Key: 100% = Comfortable   60–99% = Challenging   0–59% = Frustrational

Response Record: Animals

Student's name: _____   Response method (check one): ☐ Identification ☐ Recognition

Indicate correct answers with a check mark. If incorrect, write student's approximation.

Abstract Black-and-White Illustrations					
Image	*Date:*	*Date:*	*Date:*	*Date:*	*Date:*
Percentage correct					
Complexity level					

Rating Key: 100% = Comfortable   60–99% = Challenging   0–59% = Frustrational

images seem to hold meaning for the individual within that routine. For example, a child who travels to her cubby to get her lunchbox after the teacher shows her the spoon that represents "lunch" is giving a pretty clear indication that she visually recognizes the spoon and understands what it signifies. To assess whether the child can recognize a photograph of that same spoon, the provider can substitute the photograph for the object and hand it to the student when it is time for lunch, with no additional verbal cues. If the child then travels to her cubby to retrieve her lunchbox, she is indicating that she recognizes the photograph of the spoon. Embedding images into the context of natural daily routines can also be an effective way to teach image recognition, especially when the images are paired with a medium that is already at the individual's comfortable level, such as objects.

Some individuals who cannot verbalize a response may still be able to demonstrate recognition of images in a more formal but still modified assessment situation. For example, a student may be able to select an image from a field of two choices through touch, eye gaze, or other means to demonstrate recognition of a named image. Others may be able to indicate yes or no reliably using vocalizations, body movements, or assistive technology. The provider can assess these students by showing them a series of pictures and asking them, "Is this a _____?" The provider can fill in the blank with both correct and incorrect answers and note their yes or no responses. The response record and category summary sheets include a place to check either "identification" or "recognition" to indicate the method used. When interpreting the results, it is important to remember that identifying an image is generally more difficult than recognizing a named image (Roman-Lantzy, 2013).

As already noted, the Response Record forms capture how a student performs across a series of assessment dates. It can be useful to track any changes in the student's ability to identify images over time, especially if he or she is receiving instruction in this skill. The three Category Summary

Sheets (Figures 4A.5, 4A.6, and 4A.7) offer a one-page overview of how a student performed with all images on one particular date. They provide an at-a-glance perspective of which types of images and which items were more difficult for the student. Both types of forms can be useful in different ways, and it is up to the provider to decide which one to use or whether to use both. Note that the third Category Summary Sheet, Highly Familiar Personal Items (Figure 4A.7) is used when a student who is at the beginning of image identification is being shown photographs of his or her own personal items. The Items column on this form is blank so that the form can be customized to reflect this unique set of images.

Interpretation

The Response Record forms and the Category Summary Sheets each have rows for recording the percentage of correct answers as well as the complexity level for each type of image. A score of 100 percent for a particular type of image indicates a comfortable level of visual complexity. A score of 60–99 percent corresponds to a challenging level of visual complexity. The rationale is that any incorrect answer in a category indicates that interpreting images from that category is more difficult for the individual with CVI than it is for typically sighted peers. Finally, a score of 0–59 percent indicates a frustrational level of visual complexity.

In addition to the percentage of correct answers for each image type, students' incorrect identifications, or approximations, are just as useful, offering clues as to how and why they incorrectly identified particular images.

In general, the types of images that are currently at the student's comfortable or challenging levels are the most appropriate to include in instructional materials. For example, a student should not receive a worksheet that requires the ability to interpret black-and-white line drawings if black-and-white line drawings are currently at his or her frustrational level. However, it is important to keep in mind that the 2D Image Assessment

Category Summary Sheet: Common Objects

Student's name: _____   Date: _____

Response method (check one): ☐ Identification ☐ Recognition

Indicate correct answers with a check mark. If incorrect, write student's approximation.

Item	Color Photographs	Realistic Color Illustrations	Abstract Color Illustrations	Realistic Black-and-White Illustrations	Abstract Black-and-White Illustrations	Average
Shoe						
Plane						
Lamp						
Scissors						
Cup						
Bed						
Couch						
Backpack						
Car						
Toothbrush						
Percentage correct						
Complexity level						

Rating Key: 100% = Comfortable   60–99% = Challenging   0–59% = Frustrational

FIGURE 4A.6 Category Summary Sheet for Animals

Category Summary Sheet: Animals

Student's name: _____   Date: _____

Response method (check one): ☐ Identification ☐ Recognition

Indicate correct answers with a check mark. If incorrect, write student's approximation.

Item	Color Photographs	Realistic Color Illustrations	Abstract Color Illustrations	Realistic Black-and-White Illustrations	Abstract Black-and-White Illustrations	Average
Dog						
Cow						
Cat						
Fish						
Bird						
Elephant						
Rabbit						
Horse						
Spider						
Snake						
Percentage correct						
Complexity level						

Rating Key: 100% = Comfortable   60–99% = Challenging   0–59% = Frustrational

Category Summary Sheet: Highly Familiar Personal Items

Student's name: _____   Date: _____

Response method (check one): ☐ Identification ☐ Recognition

Indicate correct answers with a check mark. If incorrect, write student's approximation.

Item	Color Photographs	Realistic Color Illustrations	Abstract Color Illustrations	Realistic Black-and-White Illustrations	Abstract Black-and-White Illustrations	Average
Percentage correct						
Complexity level						

Rating Key: 100% = Comfortable   60–99% = Challenging   0–59% = Frustrational

evaluates a student's ability to identify a set of novel images the student has had no previous exposure to. Poor performance on a particular type of image does not necessarily mean that a student would be unable to learn a specific, limited set of that type of image within a meaningful, functional, and routine context, such as a communication system. While the 2D Image Assessment can provide valuable information for choosing the most appropriate type of images for a student with CVI, it is only one component of the individualized, collaborative process of determining what will work best for each student in each situation.

Direct Instruction and Progress

Although individuals with typical functional vision learn to interpret two-dimensional materials incidentally, those with CVI may need direct instruction and guidance to develop this skill. They may benefit from support in identifying the salient visual features of an object or image and then generalizing those salient features across different variations of that item, as discussed in Chapter 1 (see also Roman-Lantzy, 2018).

Although the 2D Image Assessment does not give guidance on strategies for teaching image recognition, it can help determine where to begin. Since each student will have his or her own combination of visual abilities and learning needs, the 2D Image Assessment does not prescribe a one-size-fits-all set of rules to apply the data to direct instruction. In general, however, any image type at the student's comfortable level (receiving 100 percent correct responses) probably does not need to be taught. Instead, the provider can use the student's comfortable-level learning medium

to support instruction in the types of images that are challenging or frustrational for him or her. If, for instance, identifying familiar objects is at a student's comfortable level and her ability to interpret color photographs is at her challenging level, the provider can pair photographs with the real objects they depict during instructional activities. If the student is learning to recognize a photograph of her spoon, for example, the provider can review the salient features of the spoon with her (long, skinny handle; curved scoop) and ask her to touch the handle. The provider can then highlight the handle of the spoon on the photograph and ask the student to touch it. Similarly, for a student who comfortably identifies color photographs, the provider can use photographs to support instruction in the types of images that are more challenging.

In addition to indicating what types of images are more difficult for a student, the data recorded in the final column of the Category Summary Sheet indicates whether any particular items were also more challenging. For example, if a student correctly identified a couch in only one out of five image types in the Common Objects category, the provider would reflect this by recording 20 percent in the Average column. The provider may decide to use this information when determining which items may need more attention in direct instruction activities.

Just as in all areas of the 'What's the Complexity?' Framework, the decision of whether and when to work toward a frustrational-level task requires thoughtful consideration based on the unique needs and abilities of each individual. Any work toward a frustrational-level task needs to be done with appropriate supports in place.

5

CVI and the Development of Social Skills

Christine Roman-Lantzy

Author's Note

Several years ago, I was at a conference listening to a presentation about cortical visual impairment (CVI). A parent of a child with CVI was sitting next to me. When the presenter mentioned ways that CVI affects learning, the parent whispered that it also affects her child's social skills. I turned the conference outline paper over to the blank side and began to jot down all the ways I imagined CVI could interfere with social development. The list was lengthy. Later, I thought about whether these challenges were different for individuals with CVI than for those with ocular issues. For a moment, I was appalled at my previous lack of insight regarding this question.

Thus, I began to formalize my thoughts around the social skill challenges associated with CVI. I realized that the underlying obstacle may be that the public, and even family or peers, do not readily perceive the individual with CVI to be visually impaired. No visual or behavioral features can be read on the faces of those with CVI to indicate their condition. As a result, there may be expectations of social behaviors that are not appropriate and, unfortunately, may suggest disinterest, social avoidance, or, in the extreme, autism.

This chapter presents the ways in which cortical visual impairment (CVI) affects the development of social skills. The presence of the CVI characteristics affects social development and opportunities for socialization in a variety of ways. Delayed development of social skills also affects educational and community inclusion and the ability of the individual to participate in gratifying relationships with peers. Teachers of students with visual impairments and others who work with students with CVI are obligated not only to provide appropriate educational opportunities but also to facilitate the development of meaningful social relationships. It is not uncommon for students with CVI to bond with their adult instructors, one-on-one assistants, or family members, but these are arguably obligatory relationships and do not fulfill the basic need for friendships formed from mutual experiences. The individual with CVI requires intentionally designed opportunities intended to bridge the barriers to social inclusion that are heightened by the effects of CVI.

Social Learning

The role of social interaction in human development has long been studied. Vygotsky was a social psychologist whose main work was in developmental psychology. Vygotsky (1978) described a theory of the development of cognitive function in children as emerging from activities that occur in social environments. He posited that social interaction is the foundation of conscious thought and cognition.

A social learning theory proposed by Bandura (1977) describes how people learn primarily from socialization, specifically through observation, imitation, and modeling. Social learning theory has been useful in explaining how people can learn new things and develop new behaviors incidentally by watching and imitating the actions of others. This theory was used as an alternate approach to Skinner's (1985) behavioral theory, in which learned behaviors were believed to be the result of direct forms of reinforcement for desirable or undesirable behaviors.

According to Bandura's social learning theory, there are four elements that contribute to learning in a social context. The first, *attention*, is defined by Bandura as arousal that is triggered by novelty. Some new event, person, activity, or object signals the individual to regard the target, and attention is created. The second element is *retention*, which refers to remembering and coding the information or action. The third element is *reproduction*, by which the individual is able to recall the visual imagery held in memory. Finally, in the fourth element, *motivation and reinforcement*, rewards and incentives drive the individual to do well and succeed.

Bandura's theory is dependent on the use of vision as a means of initiating and maintaining so-

cial skill learning and competence. Starting from Bandura's first element, attention, and all through his model, vision is used to mediate social learning. Mehrabian (1972/2007) described how much critical social learning occurs through visual information and estimated that only 7 percent of emotional meaning is conveyed in the words we speak, while 55 percent is through facial expression and body language, and 38 percent is through tone of voice.

Consequently, the presence of either CVI or ocular visual impairment significantly impacts access to social experiences. However, individuals with CVI are not readily perceived to be visually impaired; the appearance of their eyes is generally typical, and at times they can look directly into faces. The visual and behavioral cues associated with ocular visual impairment or blindness are not the same in those associated with CVI. Thus, others may assume that the individual with CVI is accessing social information from their environment that in fact they are missing.

Although children with ocular forms of visual impairment may also have difficulty accessing information derived from incidental or direct experiences, children with CVI face a set of unique challenges. Because of their abilities to perceive and interpret some types of information but not others, their needs can often be misunderstood, especially when the environment is novel or complex. With many forms of ocular visual impairment, individuals can more readily interpret targets when the object is brought closer or made larger or when contrast is enhanced. These adaptations are not commonly useful for individuals with CVI. The CVI characteristics are the key to understanding the visual challenges and abilities, not the constructs associated with ocular visual impairment.

The following example illustrates the potential influences of CVI on visual attention used to drive social learning.

Savannah was diagnosed with CVI when she was 18 months of age. She is now 11 and attends a fifth-grade class in her local public school.

Savannah also participates in Girl Scouts and swimming lessons with children who are from either her school or the community.

In the fall, her Girl Scout troop attended an autumn festival at a local farm. Savannah was accompanied by her adult teaching assistant and her mother. The 12 girls in the scout troop gathered in a rustic barn that was converted into a gathering center. During the girls' orientation to the afternoon's activities, a lamb unexpectedly wandered across the far end of the room. Suddenly, 11 girls' heads turned to watch the lamb. Savannah did not change her posture or acknowledge the presence of the animal.

The Girl Scouts all participated in a horse-drawn hayride through the farm fields and an adjoining wooded area. Savannah sat between her mother and the teaching assistant on the hay wagon. The ride consisted of a two-mile loop around the grounds. Some of the girls waved at several young men who were harvesting pumpkins in the field. Savannah did not wave or even turn in the direction of the men. As the hay ride neared its end, the horses suddenly reared up. Some of the girls yelled and others laughed as they saw a snake slither under the horse's feet and into the surrounding field.

Later, while the girls were having apple cider in the gathering center, they chatted about the boys they had seen in the field. One girl mentioned that one of the boys was a person who attends her school. She said she was going to talk to him about his experiences working in the pumpkin patch. Another girl brought up the snake. The girls talked about their feelings regarding snakes and about seeing the horses rear up. Savannah sat with the girls drinking her cider, but until this discussion, was unaware of the boys in the field or the incident with the snake. Later, Savannah asked her mother why some of the girls were shrieking on the hayride. She won-

dered if it was because of the bumpiness of the hay wagon ride.

Savannah's story illustrates how CVI can affect experiences that are initiated through visual attention. It also shows how CVI alters the quantity and quality of social learning experiences. The girls who did not have CVI shared a set of mutual experiences that were initiated through novel visual inputs. Their attention was triggered by incidents or targets that were unexpected. Following Bandura's model, if the initial element of attention is impaired or absent, the additional elements of retention, reproduction, and reinforcement are also likely to be compromised.

An interesting pattern of behavior has been reported to the author by parents who participated in a telephone support group sponsored by the New York Lighthouse for the Blind. Parents of children who were in Phase III CVI commonly described how their children's memories of novel events seemed vague compared to those of their other children who did not have CVI. Is it possible that the novel setting was so visually confusing to the children with CVI that no individual element emerged as novel or interesting? Is it possible that if the children failed to attend to novel targets, their ability to form a visual representation of the new event would be fragmented or absent? If so, it is easier to understand how a child with CVI is then unable to reproduce the experience by talking, drawing, writing, or thinking about it. And, finally, in this situation, Bandura's fourth element of motivation or reinforcement to revisit this novel environment or experience would be vague or even absent.

It is critical for educators and therapists to be aware of the impact of CVI on social learning in the child's school and community settings. The presence of the CVI characteristics affects the child's access to appropriate social interactions with adults and especially with peers. Again, even though children with ocular visual impairment experience similar challenges to social development, these challenges are arguably greater for children with CVI because providers may not be aware of the characteristic behaviors of CVI and may misinterpret a child's social behaviors as a separate issue, not related to visual impairment. And, simply put, children with CVI do not have the appearance of children with ocular visual impairment. They do not "look visually impaired."

Social skill competence and the CVI characteristics intersect in specific and important ways. The following is an overview of some of the CVI characteristics and related factors and the specific risks they pose to social development.

- Difficulty discriminating the features of human faces, primarily as a result of the CVI characteristic of difficulties with visual complexity

- Difficulty learning from imitation, primarily as a result of the CVI characteristics of difficulty with distance viewing, difficulty with visual novelty, and visual latency

- Difficulty interacting with new materials, primarily as a result of the CVI characteristic of difficulty with visual novelty

- Difficulty developing play skills, primarily as a result of the CVI characteristics of difficulty with distance viewing (which interferes with learning from imitation), difficulty with visual novelty, and difficulties with complexity of materials, array, or the sensory environment

- Difficulty with activities that occur at a distance, primarily as a result of the CVI characteristics of difficulty with distance viewing and difficulties with complexity of array

An additional factor related to CVI that affects social development is the role of adults who misread the behavioral cues of a child with CVI and who may unwittingly hinder rather than facilitate social opportunities. The remainder of this chapter describes these factors affecting social development, which are associated with the specific profile of a child with CVI.

Human Faces

Mothers of newborns may tell you that their baby loves to stare at faces. This isn't simply hopeful thinking. According to Farzin, Hou, and Norcia (2012), there may be a physiological reason for an infant's interest in faces. These authors describe the dominant role of faces in the life of an infant and the early emergence of attention to faces. It is accepted that face processing begins at birth (Pascalis et al., 2011), with visual concentration primarily on the outer features of the face, such as the hairline. Progress in refined discrimination of both outer and inner features of faces (the eyes, nose, and mouth) is present by age 5 (Jeffery & Rhodes, 2011) and continues to be refined into adolescence. But the ability to discriminate faces is not merely a function of biology alone. Tanaka and Farah (1993) describe how experience also has an impact on facial recognition as early as 3 months of age. For example, infants' preferences for male or female faces is shaped by the gender of their primary caregivers (Pascalis et al., 2011). Facial discrimination is a complex combination of biology, age, experience, and the use of additional cues, including the features of faces, unique configurations of faces, and holistic cues such as environmental context.

The ability to use recognition of faces for social development is a neurological mechanism that individuals use in society every day. Jeffery and Rhodes (2011) write that faces "convey a wealth of information that we use to guide our social interactions." But what happens when an individual is born without the ability to visually discriminate faces? What happens if the child's visual impairment is not identified in a timely manner? What incorrect assumptions may be made about the child who does not make eye contact with adults or children? What opportunities for social development will be lost without the child's ability to read the facial expressions of others? These are important questions that must be addressed by parents and professionals who have knowledge about the impact of CVI on social development.

TABLE 5.1

Progression of the Development of Facial Recognition

This excerpt from the CVI Range Rating II Scoring Guide shows how the ability to accurately discriminate a face develops as an individual's CVI Range scores on the CVI characteristic of complexity begin to improve.

CVI Characteristic	Rating II Score				
	0	*.25*	*.5*	*.75*	*1*
Complexity of faces	No visual attention on faces	Brief attention or localization in the direction of a familiar face May be reported as "looking through" rather than looking at a person's face	Brief fixations on the faces of familiar people (especially parents) Brief eye-to-contact with own mirror image	Eye-to-eye contact with most people May be less attentive to the faces of new or unfamiliar people Typical responses to mirror image	Visual attention (with eye-to-eye contact) on the human face is present in all social interactions Interpretation of faces occurs even if the target person is in a novel setting

Source: Adapted from Roman-Lantzy, C. (2018). Appendix 5C: CVI Range rating II scoring guide. In *Cortical visual impairment: An approach to assessment and intervention* (2nd ed., p. 168). New York, NY: AFB Press.

The human face is a highly visually complex target for an individual with CVI. The ability to accurately discriminate a face tends to follow a particular sequence that is associated with CVI Range scores and phases. Table 5.1 shows this progression as described in the Rating II Scoring Guide of the CVI Range (Roman-Lantzy, 2018). This progression is based on a general rule of how individuals with CVI develop this ability, but it may vary in some individuals.

In early Phase I, there is little or no attention toward faces. Parents report that their child primarily discriminates their presence by recognizing their voice. At this level, the child may fail to acknowledge the company of even the most familiar adults until they speak. By mid- to late-Phase I, parents or highly familiar individuals report that they notice brief attention toward their faces. This is the time in which parents often report that it seems as though their child is "looking through," rather than directly at, their faces. This behavior may be associated with the strong reliance on dorsal stream visual function, in which direct eye-to-target fixa-

tions are not present. Therefore, the child with CVI may visually locate the form of the head, but not individual internal details of the face.

In Phase I and early Phase II CVI, individuals with CVI may gaze at or in the direction of a mirror. This behavior may be more closely associated with the CVI characteristics of need for light or attention to movement. A mirror has highly reflective properties that may be the motivating factor associated with attention to a mirror in the early phases. In mid- to late-Phase II, individuals with CVI generally have some ventral stream or detail vision. They are able to look directly at a target with eye-to-object contact. In Phase II, individuals with CVI often begin demonstrating eye-to-eye contact with familiar people, usually family members. They also start to notice their own mirror reflection, and by the end of Phase II will generally gaze at their mirror image. By the end of Phase II and into Phase III, individuals with CVI are establishing eye contact with most people. However, eye contact is not synonymous with the ability to visually discriminate faces, as illustrated in the following scenario.

James is a student with CVI who has a CVI Range score of 7–7.5. He is in an integrated first-grade class; half the class consists of children with special needs. James is able to establish eye-to-eye contact with most peers and adults. For this reason, many of the adults who work in James's class do not question whether he recognizes their faces. They do not realize that, despite the fact that he does not wear eyeglasses and has a normal eye exam, he is recognizing people based on their voices, the color of their hair, or some other non-facial feature.

During a class activity James was given a set of cards with female and male images. The cards were faces of adults and children of various ethnicities and ages. James was asked to sort them into two piles, one of girls and one of boys. James was skilled at sorting activities so he happily accepted the task. When James reported that he had completed the activity, his teacher glanced through the two piles. To her surprise, James had sorted the images of faces into groups of images of people with long hair and images of people with short hair. James's teacher was confused by his responses. James was always able to identify the members of his class and was even able to identify them in the photos used every day during morning circle time.

The teacher decided to further investigate James's ability to discriminate faces. She adapted a set of the familiar student pictures by cutting away all the elements of clothing and hair in the images. The teacher asked James to identify the people in the pictures. James guessed incorrectly and finally said he had never seen any of the individuals in the pictures, with one exception. James correctly identified a member of his class who wears bright blue eyeglasses.

Facial attention is not the same thing as facial discrimination. Just as many individuals with CVI are able to visually attend to a complex image, visual attention, or looking, must not be considered

synonymous with the visual-cognitive task of discriminating and understanding what is being seen. Difficulties with discriminating faces can interfere with social interaction and learning in many ways. First, without the individual hearing a voice, it is likely that the presence of even a familiar person may go unnoticed. For example, a parent may quietly enter a room, sit near the child with CVI, but not be recognized. Parents have reported that their children frequently mistake a nonfamily member for their mother or father.

Peer relationships are also affected by the inability to discriminate faces. Children with CVI may look directly at a peer but be unaware of the person's identity. Many unspoken cues are communicated through facial expressions, which may initiate peer-to-peer interaction. For example, a child may make eye contact with another child and then smile as an indicator of a desire to approach. Conversely, a frown or look of disapproval may result in the peer understanding that the frowning person is not inviting interaction. Facial expressions also convey more subtle messages. At times a smile may communicate nervousness or fear. People may shift their gaze upwards or "roll their eyes" in response to an absurdity. These facial signals are part of the incidental social "script" acquired by most children. Children with CVI must be taught directly about these subtle indicators in order to successfully participate in peer activities. Misreading facial cues can make a significant difference in establishing and maintaining peer interactions and, at its worst, can contribute to social isolation from peers.

Difficulty with facial discrimination associated with the CVI characteristic of difficulties with visual complexity should be distinguished from two other facial recognition disorders, prosopagnosia and autism spectrum disorders. According the National Institute of Neurological Disorders and Stroke (2018), "Prosopagnosia is a neurological disorder characterized by the inability to recognize faces" and "can result from stroke, traumatic brain injury, or certain neurodegenerative diseases." *Prosopagnosia* is commonly known as "face blindness." Congenital prosopagnosia is considered to be a lifelong condition that does not resolve (Wilson, Brock, & Palermo, 2010). There may be a genetic link due to the fact that prosopagnosia appears to present across generations in certain families (Farah, 2004). Congenital prosopagnosia usually exists in individuals who do not have other disorders or disabilities (Wilson et al., 2010). Individuals with CVI do not always meet the criteria associated with prosopagnosia. The relationship between prosopagnosia and facial discrimination difficulties associated with CVI is unclear. However, it is important to consider the likelihood that these may not be identical conditions given the incidence of improved facial recognition abilities in individuals who have CVI, especially those who are in Phase III CVI. Those with CVI generally improved their ability to discriminate faces in conjunction with increases in CVI Range scores (Roman-Lantzy & Lantzy, 2002–2017). Also, a diagnosis of CVI is not associated with hereditary causes, except in the cases of certain rare genetic causes of CVI.

Individuals with an autism spectrum disorder constitute the second group of people who frequently demonstrate atypical eye-to-eye contact or facial regard. According to the American Psychiatric Association's (2013) *Diagnostic and Statistical Manual of Mental Disorders,* autism spectrum disorder is defined as "persistent deficits in social communication and social interaction across multiple contexts," including "deficits in social-emotional reciprocity, . . . deficits in nonverbal communicative behaviors used for social interaction, [and] deficits in developing, maintaining, and understanding relationships." According to Golarai, Grill-Spector, and Reiss (2006), individuals with autism have impaired abilities in gaze processing, memory for facial identity, and recognition of facial expressions associated with emotion. However, these difficulties are not correlated with distinct areas of brain damage found in prosopagnosia or CVI. The difficulties associated with facial attention in individuals with an autism spectrum disorder are more likely related to an overarching lack of social cognizance and social reciprocity. In other words, some people on the autism spectrum can visually perceive the human face but are unable to engage

in the social interactions associated with direct eye contact or facial attention.

Research is needed to help identify the important differences among CVI and other disorders in which certain behaviors are shared, but it is important to be clear that shared behaviors are not equivalent to shared diagnoses. Table 5.2 provides examples of traits associated with both CVI and autism spectrum disorders and explanations of the ways in which the shared behaviors differ.

It is important to consider the differences between CVI and autism spectrum disorder when interacting with individuals who have CVI. The use of the CVI Range places difficulties with facial discrimination in the greater context of the characteristics associated with CVI, and it should be approached as a condition that is expected to improve through the application of a systematic approach such as the ones associated with the CVI Range protocol.

Imitations

Imitation and Social Learning

Imitation is the ability to voluntarily repeat the behaviors of others. According to Jones (2009a, 2009b), a child's ability to imitate the actions of others is a critical tool for social learning and for acquiring new information. Imitation is also a form of social learning that leads to the "development of traditions, and ultimately our culture. Imitation allows for the transfer of information (behaviors, customs, etc.) between individuals and down generations without the need for genetic inheritance" (Hopper, 2010, p. 295).

The ability to imitate simple actions emerges very early in life. Imitation in newborns has been studied extensively, and there is evidence that imitation of simple actions, such as tongue protrusion, may emerge in infancy (Anisfeld, 1996, 2005; Jones, 2009a, 2009b). By 8 months of age, babies are capable of imitating simple actions and facial expressions during face-to-face interactions. Around 18 months of age, children imitate actions that they have observed others performing previously, such as rocking a baby doll to sleep

---

TABLE 5.2

Similarities and Differences between Autism Spectrum Disorders and CVI

Feature	Autism Spectrum Disorder	CVI
Etiology	Unknown; likely a combination of genetic and environmental factors	Damage to the posterior visual system in the brain
Eye exam/appearance of the eyes	Generally normal	Generally normal
Response to color	Used to order or align objects	Used to establish attention to objects or environmental elements
Response to sensory complexity	Competing sensory inputs may result in sensory overload or distress	Competing sensory inputs result in decreased ability to use functional vision
Response to facial complexity	Decreased attention to faces as a result of difficulties with social cognizance	Decreased attention to faces as a result of the inability to discriminate facial details
Response to novelty	Markedly restricted repertoire of activities and interests	Unable to visually discriminate or interpret new materials or environments

---

after observing an adult with an infant (Parks, 2004). By 3 years of age, children can demonstrate multistep scenarios observed in day-to-day life (Hart & Risley, 1999). Beyond childhood and into adult life, imitation continues to feed and enrich learning. Adolescents observe and then replicate methods of behavior associated with acceptable behavior to fit into a social group. Adults may use YouTube as a method to learn a new skill or technique.

Gathering knowledge from imitation depends on the use of vision as the primary input mechanism. Many social skills are learned without direct instruction; rather, they are simply observed and integrated into a social context. But what happens if vision is impaired (Sacks & Wolffe, 2006)? How can an individual with CVI become socially competent without the information gathered through everyday visual experiences? How does the absence of this critical information affect inclusion with peers? How do the characteristics associated with CVI affect the individual differently

than those who have ocular forms of visual impairment or blindness? The following example illustrates these issues.

David is a 5-year-old boy who attends a kindergarten class. David was diagnosed with a genetic disorder and has developmental challenges. He was diagnosed with cerebral palsy when he was 18 months old and CVI when he was 2. David also has expressive communication difficulties and is learning to use a communication device. Developmental specialists believe David has normal or near-normal intelligence. Though David is learning the content of the kindergarten curriculum, he has not developed friendships.

Part of the kindergarten curriculum includes learning how to take turns while in a group setting. The teacher instructed the class about appropriate options when a student wants to answer a question, ask a question, or share information. The children quickly respond to the concept of

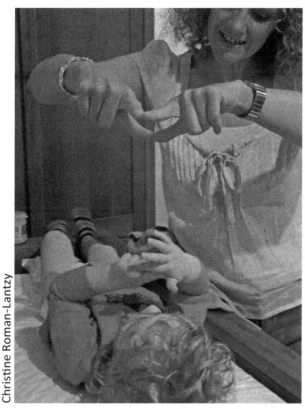

Christine Roman-Lantzy

Now that he is in Phase III, this child with CVI is demonstrating beginning imitation skills by imitating his mother's gestures in simple finger play and song.

raising a hand to indicate a desire to participate. David, too, learns this skill after the teacher physically positions David's arm in a raised pose.

Later in the day, in a larger classroom of 30 students, a number of children, including David, raise their hands when asked to answer questions from a science lesson. However, David does not lower his arm after the teacher calls on a classmate to respond. The other kindergarten children stare at David, who seems unaware that the other kindergarteners were lowering their arms. The classroom teacher is further confused when she remembers how David was able to raise and lower his arm when he was in a small-group setting in a quiet and visually simple room.

This example illustrates the association between access to visual cues used for imitation and social competence. David's peers were likely con-

fused about their classmate who was unable to conform with the behavior implicitly understood by the others. Without the ability to see the everyday behaviors learned through vision, children with CVI can become estranged from members of their social groups. The example also shows how different levels of visual and sensory complexity have different results.

The Mirror Neuron System

The *mirror neuron system* is the name given to the brain mechanism that is responsible for the brain's perception of a shared experience, such as imitation. It is important to consider its potential role in the development of social competence. The first scientific paper on mirror neurons was published by Rizzolatti and his colleagues in 1992 (Di Pellegrino, Fadiga, Fogassi, Gallese, & Rizzolatti, 1992, cited in Rizzolatti & Fabbri-Destro, 2010). They found that there is a part of the brain that is activated equally when either watching an action or performing the same action. These researchers studied the premotor cortex of macaque monkeys and found that a mirror neuron fired, for example, when a monkey grasped for a peanut and also when the monkey saw the experimenter grasp for a peanut.

This concept is important in understanding the development of learning from imitation, but it also has implications for emotions such as empathy (Winerman, 2005). If an individual sees another person fall from a step, for example, mirror neurons recreate the experience at the brain level, resulting in responses that may "mirror" the feelings of the person who fell as if the observer had experienced the fall. The work on mirror neurons is now being duplicated by many other researchers (Iacoboni, 2009; Keysers & Gazzola, 2010; Wicker et al., 2003) and has expanded to include the role of mirror neurons in touch (Keysers & Gazzola, 2006), language development (Hickok, 2010), and the emotional differences associated with autism (Winerman, 2005).

The mirror neuron system is activated when humans imitate behaviors and actions of others. Mirror neurons allow a person to observe and reproduce the actions and emotions of others without physically engaging in the actual activity. The principle of mirror neurons is that as you observe an action or emotion, you are activating the same neurons in your brain as if you were doing the action (Iacoboni & Dapretto, 2006). According to this theory, an individual who is watching an athlete swing a baseball bat activates mirror neurons that are identical to those of the athlete who is performing the physical act. People who attend a movie and cry at a scene in which a character is sad are activating mirror neurons that essentially put them in the shoes of the movie character. Essentially, mirror neurons are a form of subconscious imitation.

Individuals with CVI have diminished ability to access the visual information that activates mirror neurons and fuels understanding of actions or feelings learned and reinforced through imitation. It is critical to consider the potential impact of the healthy development of emotional and social com-

petence. Without this proficiency, the child with CVI, as well as children with ocular forms of visual impairment, may be alienated from the benefits of peers and community. The presence of the CVI characteristics interferes with an individual's ability to learn reliably through imitation. The characteristics of visual latency, difficulties with visual complexity, difficulty with distance viewing, and difficulty with visual novelty all create barriers to accessing social information that can be learned through imitation. Table 5.3 provides examples of the potential obstacles to social opportunities or imitation.

Play

Play has been described as the work of children. It teaches social skills that include turn-taking, sharing, and cooperating with others. Children's lives are enriched by creative play, and it assists in

TABLE 5.3

Effects of CVI Characteristics on Social Learning and Imitation

Characteristic	Challenge	Example
Visual latency	The individual does not notice the action in a timely way.	Children are playing charades, but the child with CVI does not perceive the physical gestures of the leader in time to recognize the meaning, imitate, or follow the action.
Complexity of array	The individual is unable to distinguish the elements of the action or activity due to the visual "clutter" of people, materials, and equipment in the background.	A teacher demonstrates sign language to the class, but the child with CVI is unable to participate because the teacher is wearing a multi-colored shirt and the child cannot discriminate the teacher's hand positions from the background pattern of the clothing.
Difficulty with distance viewing	The individual is unable to perceive activities that occur at distances at which their peers are able to view similar activities.	A group of children use colored chalk to draw on a sidewalk 15 feet from the position of the child with CVI. The child with CVI does not see the activity and does not approach the group.
Visual novelty	The individual with CVI does not alert to or investigate new objects, materials, environments, or people.	Children who are on a school excursion to a museum all gather to look at the massive reproduction of a dinosaur. The child with CVI prefers to stay by the adults rather than inspect the dinosaur model.

their emotional and intellectual growth (Fantuzzo, McWayne, Perry, & Childs, 2004). Play is considered an activity that is freely chosen and motivating to the child. It is directed by the child, not the adult. Sociologist Mildred Parten's (1932) seminal work on the development of play describes specific stages that are associated with age:

- Unoccupied play, primarily seen in infants

- Solitary play, around 2 to 3 years of age

- Onlooker play, 2½ to 3½ years of age

- Parallel play, 2 to 3½ years of age and older

- Associative play, 3 to 4 years of age and older

- Cooperative play, 4 to 6 years of age and older

Elements of facial attention, imitation, and incidental learning are crucial in the development of play, and children with CVI face considerable challenges in this realm, as in the following scenario.

Hayley is a 6-year-old who has CVI. She attends a private school that emphasizes learning through play and cooperation. Hayley's parents selected this setting for their daughter because it follows a curriculum that fosters order and peer learning in the classroom. Hayley seems to be able to attend to her learning materials in this setting but is struggling with the elements of instruction that are incorporated in cooperative play. She generally waits for the teacher or teaching assistant to direct her to the shelf containing a choice of several bins, which contain blocks, pegs, paper, crayons, puzzles, and animal figures.

Today, Hayley was led to an area where three other 6-year-olds were sitting at a table with puzzles. The children decided to work together on a puzzle that had 15 interlocking pieces. One child directed the activity by informing the other children about their respective roles in the process of completing the puzzle. He asked Hayley to lo-

Many children with CVI commonly engage in solitary play or parallel play beyond the time frame of their non-CVI peers.

Anna Ault

cate all the pieces that had a straight edge. Hayley agreed, but within minutes, began to stack puzzle pieces into a tower, which she knocked over and then restacked. Hayley did not engage with the other children's conversation and after a few minutes, the other children gathered her puzzle pieces and completed the puzzle without her participation.

In this example, Hayley is clearly in a different stage of play than her classmates. Hayley is playing near other children but has little contact with them and is unaware of a common goal. Hayley's play is likely either parallel play or associative play. She is not able to join her peers in cooperative play, in which there is teamwork toward a mutual goal. Because of her CVI, Hayley is less capable of learning about the key elements that lead to age-appropriate play. Without appropriate intervention, Hayley is likely to continue playing on her own or relying on the partnership of adults rather than peers. It is important for teachers and other educational providers to provide supports that illuminate the information that is fragmented or absent in children who have CVI.

Distance Viewing

Individuals with the CVI characteristic of difficulty with distance viewing are unable to visually locate or discriminate targets that exist at distances at which their peers are able to view similar targets. In general, individuals with CVI view targets from a close range, at times within inches of the target. This may occur for several reasons, including the complexity of the array and other effects of the environment, as well as the effects of novelty and movement. For example, when an individual with CVI has difficulty with complexity of the viewing array, the further away the object, the greater the number of elements in view. Near viewing may be an effective way to block out the complexity that exists beyond the target.

Even individuals with CVI who have normal or near normal eye exams experience difficulty with distance viewing. Their ability to view a target at a distance is not necessarily a reflection of their ocular refractive abilities. Although it is critical for individuals with CVI to have a thorough eye exam and to be provided with corrective lenses when a refractive error is identified, individuals with CVI generally demonstrate an inability to locate targets at typical distances even with appropriate corrective lenses.

The principles associated with functional acuity for individuals with ocular conditions do not hold true for individuals with CVI. Traditional, ocular-based functional vision assessment includes an assessment of distance vision in which the evaluator determines the smallest size object the individual is able to detect at the greatest distance. This test helps guide educators and parents about the relatively stable range in which an individual with ocular visual impairment can locate a target. The use of this measurement for an individual with CVI is not meaningful. The degree of complexity of viewing array, competing sensory information, novelty, and movement may all affect the ability to detect a target at a prescribed distance.

For example, a student with CVI may demonstrate the ability to visually locate a yellow spoon offered to him from 10 feet away. The next day, when confronted with an identical request to locate the spoon, the student stares off into space, appearing to be unaware of the familiar object. The size of the object and the presentation distance are the same as the previous day, but the response is not. The environmental and sensory factors surrounding the presentation of the object are the likely reasons for the different responses. And, in fact, on day 1:

- The teacher wore a black sweater and pants.
- The teacher stood in front of a plain beige wall.
- All adults and children were in stationary positions.
- The classroom was quiet.

On day 2:

- The teacher wore a brightly colored floral dress.
- The teacher stood in front of the classroom windows.
- An adult entered the room with another classmate who moved freely through the classroom.
- One child in the classroom was crying, and music was playing on a radio.

Thus, it is critical to consider the impact of the environment when assessing the distance-viewing abilities of an individual with CVI. Even when the size of the object and the viewing distance remain consistent, the response of the individual with CVI may vary. These seemingly different abilities illustrate the effect of the CVI characteristics. Therefore, the construct of size plus distance used with students who have ocular visual impairment is not a reliable method to measure the functional distance abilities of individuals with CVI.

The presence of difficulty with distance viewing has an impact on the acquisition of social skills. The activities that occur beyond arm's reach can spark curiosity and result in "approach behaviors" in children with typical vision, but often do not do so in children with CVI. For example, a child may see an activity, person, or object at a distance and then be motivated to move toward it, while a child with CVI may be engaged in solitary play, unaware of the group games occurring across the play yard. Without an awareness of the activities occurring at a distance, the child with CVI is denied the opportunity to join in the play.

Approach behaviors help children follow a source of interest or curiosity and therefore can support new learning that children with CVI miss out on. The effects of difficulty with distance viewing may result in children with CVI missing new opportunities to socialize with peers and can contribute to a tendency to stay within the familiar

Louisa Tratt

Difficulties with distance viewing can result in a child with CVI missing events that would add to their experience of the world.

forms of play. The risk of remaining in solitary or redundant play is a barrier to learning important social skills that include turn-taking, rule following, and negotiating group norms.

Additional factors that affect the quality and quantity of experiences gathered through distance viewing include:

- *Targets or activities that change rapidly as a result of movement or environmental complexity.* For example, a ball thrown from a distance may not be perceived in time for the child with CVI to adjust his or her position. The action occurring in a movie may be overly fast, complex, or novel. A moving swing on the playground may become a potential hazard for the child who has difficulty with distance or visual latency, or who has visual field difficulties.

- *Targets that cannot be approached for safety reasons.* Some objects or activities are not safe for close inspection. For example, a child with CVI may not be able to directly inspect a lion at a zoo or learn how railway cars are connected. These activities must be viewed from a safe distance, and thus may be part of a shared experience for children without CVI, but inaccessible to children who have CVI.

The Role of Adults

Vygotsky (1978) believed that learning occurs in what he called the *zone of proximal development.* The zone of proximal development is the distance between a student's ability to perform a task under adult guidance or with peer collaboration and the student's ability to solve the problem independently. He also emphasized the importance of learning that begins in a social setting and that competence in a skill occurs within a group before the skill can be demonstrated independently. Peers or adults who have more advance knowledge provide supports or scaffolds (Wood, Bruner, & Ross,

1976) that help a student work through the zone of proximal development. The more skilled person provides the scaffolds but fades them away as the student becomes more skilled. In other words, those who provide the scaffolds must also be focused on the goal of enabling the student to ultimately perform the task on his or her own. Much as the construction of a building requires outside supports, or scaffolds, the building is not truly finished until the scaffolds are removed.

Thus, it is imperative that adults who work with or care for children with CVI not only fill in the gaps associated with learning and social competence, but also be aware of the potential pitfalls in their own behavior that may interfere with a child's ability to move from dependence to independence. They may need to examine the extent to which they provide scaffolding or support and ask themselves:

- Do I manage all aspects of the social interactions?

- Do I design play activities that guarantee the child's success?

- Do I insert myself into peer interactions as a kind of pseudo-peer?

If an adult or older peer engages in these behaviors, the child with CVI is unlikely to move through the zone of proximal dependence to independence. Parents, therapists, educators, support staff, and teaching assistants can support children with CVI by intentionally providing scaffolds that help a child develop age-appropriate skills for learning and social interaction. Table 5.4 presents guidelines that may support the goals necessary for increased social competence, as well as examples of what those guidelines look like in practice.

Failure can also be an important element of social learning. Children who are given the opportunity to both succeed and fail may learn to become more resilient. In *The Gift of Failure*, Lahey (2015) explains that it is crucial for children to experience disappointment and frustration so they can learn

to develop into resilient and independent adults. Adults who support children with CVI may be caught in the pitfall of manipulating the outcome of an activity to make the interaction positive for the child with CVI. There may be an intrinsic need for some adults, and even some peers, to treat children with CVI as though they need to be protected from naturally occurring obstacles, as if they are somehow emotionally incapable of experiencing the positive and negative aspects of social encounters. This attitude can have a lifelong impact. Mulder, Bollen, de Jong, and Lazonder (2016) state that there is

> an insidious attitude—that society doesn't expect people with disabilities to perform up to standard, and when people with disabilities do, they are somehow courageous. This attitude has the effect of patronizing people with disabilities, usually relegating them to low-skill jobs, setting different job standards (sometimes lower standards which tend to alienate co-workers, sometimes higher standards to prove they cannot handle a job), or expecting a worker with a disability to appreciate the opportunity to work instead of demanding equal pay, equal benefits, equal opportunity and equal access to workplace amenities. (p. 518)

This was Tara's experience with her classmates:

Tara is a third-grade student who has CVI. She has friendly relationships with a group of six other girls in her class. They usually eat lunch together and gather as a group on the playground. One day, three of the girls, including Tara, left class to use the restroom. The teacher had clear rules that the students were only permitted to use the restroom closest to their classroom, not restrooms that were in other hallways of the school building. Even though the three girls knew the rules, they ventured to a restroom that was off limits. The classroom teacher discovered the

TABLE 5.4

Guidelines for Supporting Increased Social Competence for Children with CVI

Guidelines	Examples
1. Learn to become "quietly available." Remain near the child without hovering or being intrusive.	The adult remains watchful but not within arm's length during independent work time.
2. Facilitate, mediate, and frame an experience. Provide information that may include concepts, salient features, and previous experiences. Vision is the anticipatory sense; it helps children perceive information and begin to predict what might happen. Children with CVI may demonstrate reluctance to participate until an adult previews the activity or environment that is about to be encountered.	The adult lets the child with CVI know about an upcoming school assembly by describing the guest performers, showing isolated images of their costumes on a tablet, and comparing the similarities and differences of this new experience to a previous musical assembly. The adult also walks through the assembly room with the child prior to the event, showing the child the salient elements of seats, visual displays, and other novel information that will be included in the assembly.
3. Provide verbal descriptions of remote information.	The adult describes the activities occurring on the playground each day so the child with CVI can be aware of the events occurring and make choices about play, rather than always engaging in the same routines during recess. The adult shares images or brief videos of the activities on a tablet to help support the child's understanding of the activities and provides the names of the children who are in each play area.
4. Do not play *for* the child with CVI, but describe the experience, the children present, and the activity.	During a game of catch, rather than catching the ball on behalf of the child, the adult allows the child with CVI to attempt to catch the ball, even if the child's skills or motor abilities are not conducive to doing so successfully.
5. Give the child time to work it out.	The adult provides verbal descriptions of the rules of a game to a group of children that includes a child with CVI. At first, the child with CVI follows the rules incorrectly, and the other children, rather than the adult, tell the child with CVI that he is not following the rules. The adult does not interfere, but rather watches to see if the child with CVI adjusts his actions in accordance to his classmates' instructions. Even if it takes several attempts, the adult waits to see if the children can work it out amongst themselves.
6. Help the child with CVI understand consequences.	The child with CVI learns that when playing a game with other children or adults, sometimes she may win and sometimes someone else may win. The adult does not manipulate the outcome of the game in favor of the child with CVI.
7. Stand back; provide enough physical space so that the child with CVI has more natural opportunities to initiate interactions with peers.	The adult provides verbal input regarding the options for activities at a classmate's birthday party. If the child with CVI does not initiate interactions with peers, the adult tells the child with CVI about the children present, naming and describing the location of the children in a given space. The child with CVI moves toward the children and, using their names, asks if they want to play, but the adult remains with the other adults watching from across the room.

three friends returning from the direction opposite from the girl's restroom in the third-grade hallway. As the girls entered the classroom, they all admitted that they had violated the rules. Two of the girls were told they would not be permitted to attend recess that day. Tara was not punished.

Later in the day, Tara was at the lunch table with her usual group. She thought it was odd that none of the girls included her in the conversations about breaking the rules. The following day, she heard the girls discussing their telephone conversations about getting in trouble. No one had called Tara the previous night.

By not punishing Tara even though the other girls were punished, the teacher may be conveying a message that Tara is not the same as the other girls. The implication inherent in the teacher's actions is that Tara is not capable of accepting the same consequences as her peers. In turn, the other classmates may begin to perceive Tara as needing special rules, that she is somehow an outsider. Such a seeming act of kindness by the teacher may in fact result in social isolation for the student with CVI.

Ego strength is the ability to cope with reality and stress while maintaining emotional stability (Colman, 2008). The opportunity for children with CVI to experience the natural consequences of social experiences can contribute to their dignity and help support the development of ego strength, thus preparing the child to enter the broader social communities of work and meaningful lifelong relationships. Adults who support children with CVI need to prepare them to

- participate in peer interactions,
- solve difficulties inherent in social conflict,
- recover from disappointment,
- learn to ask questions and advocate for their own needs, and

- develop a sense of self-confidence and independence.

When this type of support isn't offered, the self-image of the child with CVI can suffer, as in the following example.

Jake is a 4-year-old boy whose CVI was diagnosed in infancy. He attends a preschool class in his community. Jake enjoys the three-day-a-week sessions and especially looks forward to spending time with Ms. Bauer, the classroom assistant. Ms. Bauer helps Jake in ways that she does not assist the other children. During tabletop activities, Ms. Bauer sits next to Jake. When the class is outdoors or during active play, Ms. Bauer is Jake's partner. At lunchtime, Ms. Bauer brings Jake's lunch tray to the table and places a straw in Jake's juice bottle. The other children in the class sometimes ask Ms. Bauer for assistance but are often told that "they are big boys and girls and should try to do it themselves." The classmates notice that Jake is not held to the same standard and sometimes ask, "Why can't Jake do it himself?" No explanation is given. At the end of each preschool session, Ms. Bauer walks with Jake hand in hand down the hallway to meet his mother. Jake's mother always asks about her son's day and his peer interactions. Ms. Bauer generally reports that Jake has had a good day and that, "He doesn't even know there is anything different about him."

The well-intentioned behavior of Jake's assistant places Jake at risk for impaired self-image and exclusion from peer activities.

Adults can also facilitate social inclusion by helping children with CVI understand their visual impairment. If the child can understand his or her visual issues, there is a greater likelihood that the child can explain it to others. The ability to describe one's CVI can lead to greater self-advocacy. One definition of self-advocacy is

learning how to speak up for yourself, making your own decisions about your

Christine Roman-Lantzy

John Cleary

Brenda Biernat

Children with CVI often require adult assistance in pretend and play situations in which other children would learn from their peers.

own life, learning how to get information so that you can understand things that are of interest to you, finding out who will support you in your journey, knowing your rights and responsibilities, problem solving, listening and learning, reaching out to others when you need help and friendship, and learning about self-determination. (Wrightslaw, 2017)

Helping a child with CVI understand his or her visual impairment can

- help the child recognize his or her abilities, as well as challenges, in naturally occurring opportunities;
- increase the child's potential for self-esteem and positive self-image; and
- incorporate realistic self-perception as a healthy goal.

Although no two humans perceive the world in precisely the same way, there are common factors that can be used to explain CVI to the individual.

Depending on the age of the individual, the following statements are examples of ways to describe CVI to the individual:

- Your eyes work normally, but the part of your brain that makes sense of what your eyes see is not the same as in people who do not have CVI.

- When you were a baby, something happened to your brain. The same thing that caused your difficulties with walking and speaking also made your vision different.

- I know it must be frustrating to see how quickly others find the ball in the yard. You are just as smart as those children, but you have CVI, so it takes you a bit longer to see the ball when it is far away.

- You have a vision condition called CVI that affects the way you see things that are far away or in a complicated scene.

- When things are familiar to you, it is easier for you to understand what you are seeing.

- Sometimes it is hard for you to know who is near you until you hear their voice. That's because your CVI makes it very hard for you to see faces the same way other people see faces.

It is important for children with CVI to understand that their visual impairment is a feature of their person but not the essence of their person. Descriptions of a child's CVI should be unemotional explanations meant to provide a fuller understanding of the child's visual functioning. These accounts should help clarify any visual limitations the child may have and not be used to elicit sympathy or sadness. If talking about CVI is a sensitive experience, some parents may wish to have another trusted adult provide the initial explanations. An accurate explanation to the child will, hopefully, become integrated into their overall self-image, not as a negative or positive feature, but as a neutral set of factors that explain certain behaviors, needs, and potential obstacles.

Conclusion

Social learning is critical to the ability of the child with CVI to develop necessary thinking skills and to facilitate greater access to people, environments, and materials. Social learning is a challenge for children with CVI and must be an integral part of their specially designed instruction.

REFERENCES

American Psychiatric Association. (2013). *Diagnostic and statistical manual of mental disorders (DSM-V)* (5th ed.). Washington, DC: Author.

Anisfeld, M. (1996). Only tongue protrusion modeling is matched by neonates. *Developmental Review, 16*(2), 149–161.

Anisfeld, M. (2005). No compelling evidence to dispute Piaget's timetable of the development of representational imitation in infancy. In S. Hurley & N. Chater (Eds.), *Perspectives on imitation: From neuroscience to social science: Vol. 2. Imitation, human development, and culture* (pp. 107–131). Cambridge, MA: MIT Press.

Bandura, A. (1977). *Social learning theory.* Englewood Cliffs, NJ: Prentice Hall.

Colman, A. M. (2008). *A dictionary of psychology* (3rd ed.). New York, NY: Oxford University Press.

Di Pellegrino, G., Fadiga, L., Fogassi, L., Gallese, V., & Rizzolatti, G. (1992). Understanding motor events: A neurophysiological study. *Experimental Brain Research, 91*(1), 176–180.

Fantuzzo, J., McWayne, C. M., Perry, M. A., & Childs, S. (2004). Multiple dimensions of family involvement and their relations to behavioral and learning competencies for urban, low-income children. *School Psychology Review, 33*(4), 467–480.

Farah, M. J. (2004). *Visual agnosia* (2nd ed.). Cambridge, MA: MIT Press.

Farzin, F., Hou, C., & Norcia, A. M. (2012). Piecing it together: Infants' neural responses to face and object structure. *Journal of Vision, 12*(13), 6.

Golarai, G., Grill-Spector, K., & Reiss, A. L. (2006). Autism and the development of face processing. *Clinical Neuroscience Research, 6*(3), 145–160.

Hart, B., & Risley, T. R. (1999). *The social world of children learning to talk.* Baltimore, MD: Paul H. Brookes.

Hickok, G. (2010). The role of mirror neurons in speech and language processing. *Brain and Language, 112*(1), 1–2.

Hopper, L. M. (2010). Deferred imitation in children and apes. *Psychologist, 23*(4), 294–297.

Iacoboni, M. (2009). Imitation, empathy, and mirror neurons. *Annual Review of Psychology, 60,* 653–670.

Iacoboni, M., & Dapretto, M. (2006). The mirror neuron system and the consequences of its dysfunction. *Nature Reviews Neuroscience, 7*(12), 942–951.

Jeffery, L., & Rhodes, G. (2011). Insights into the development of face recognition mechanisms revealed by face aftereffects. *British Journal of Psychology, 102*(4), 799–815.

Jones, S. S. (2009a). The development of imitation in infancy. *Philosophical Transactions of the Royal Society B: Biological Sciences, 364*(1528), 2325–2335.

Jones, S. S. (2009b). Imitation and empathy in infancy. *Cognition, Brain, & Behavior, 13*(4), 391–413.

Keysers, C., & Gazzola, V. (2006). Towards a unifying neural theory of social cognition. *Progress in Brain Research, 156,* 379–401.

Keysers, C., & Gazzola, V. (2010). Social neuroscience: Mirror neurons recorded in humans. *Current Biology, 20*(8), R353–R354.

Lahey, J. (2015). *The gift of failure: How the best parents learn to let go so their children can succeed.* New York, NY: HarperCollins.

Mehrabian, A. (2007). *Nonverbal communication.* New Brunswick, NJ: Aldine Transaction. (Original work published 1972)

Mulder, Y. G., Bollen, L., de Jong, T., & Lazonder, A. W. (2016). Scaffolding learning by modelling: The effects of partially worked-out models. *Journal of Research in Science Teaching, 53*(3), 502–523.

National Institute of Neurological Disorders and Stroke. (2018). Prosopagnosia information page. Bethesda, MD: National Institutes of Health. Retrieved from https://www.ninds.nih.gov/Disorders/All-Disorders/Prosopagnosia-Information-Page

Parks, S. (2004). *Inside HELP: Administration and reference manual for using the Hawaii Early Learning Profile as a birth to three, curriculum-based assessment.* Menlo Park, CA: VORT Corporation.

Parten, M. B. (1932). Social participation among pre-school children. *Journal of Abnormal and Social Psychology, 27*(3), 243–269.

Pascalis, O., de Viviés, X. M., Anzures, G., Quinn, P. C., Slater, A. M., Tanaka, J. W., & Lee, K. (2011). Development of face processing. *WIREs Cognitive Science, 2*(6), 666–675.

Rizzolatti, G., & Fabbri-Destro, M. (2010). Mirror neurons: From discovery to autism. *Experimental Brain Research, 200*(3–4), 223–237.

Roman-Lantzy, C. (2018). *Cortical visual impairment: An approach to assessment and intervention* (2nd ed.). New York, NY: AFB Press.

Roman-Lantzy, C. A., & Lantzy, A. (2002–2017). Pediatric VIEW data bank (unpublished data). Pittsburgh, PA: Western Pennsylvania Hospital.

Sacks, S. Z., & Wolffe, K. E. (Eds.). (2006). *Teaching social skills to students with visual impairments: From theory to practice.* New York, NY: AFB Press.

Skinner, B. F. (1985). Cognitive science and behaviourism. *British Journal of Psychology, 76*(3), 291–301.

Tanaka, J. W., & Farah, M. J. (1993). Parts and wholes in face recognition. *The Quarterly Journal of Experimental Psychology, 46A*(2), 225–245.

Vygotsky, L. S. (1978). *Mind in society: The development of higher psychological processes* (M. Cole, V. John-Steiner, S. Scribner, & E. Souberman, Eds.). Cambridge, MA: Harvard University Press.

Wicker, B., Keysers, C., Plailly, J., Royet, J. P., Gallese, V., & Rizzolatti, G. (2003). Both of us disgusted in *my* insula: The common neural basis of seeing and feeling disgust. *Neuron, 40*(3)*,* 655–664.

Wilson, C. E., Brock, J., & Palermo, R. (2010). Attention to social stimuli and facial identity recognition skills in autism spectrum disorder. *Journal of Intellectual Disability Research, 54*(12), 1104–1115.

Winerman, L. (2005). The mind's mirror. *Monitor on Psychology, 36*(9), 100–148.

Wood, D., Bruner, J. S., & Ross, G. (1976). The role of tutoring in problem solving. *The Journal of Child Psychology and Psychiatry, 17*(2), 89–100.

Wrightslaw. (2017). Self-advocacy. Retrieved from http://www.wrightslaw.com/info/self.advocacy .htm

6

CVI and Orientation and Mobility

Alisha Waugh and Christine Roman-Lantzy

Coauthor's Note: Alisha Waugh

My interest in cortical visual impairment came about through personal experience. My background in serving adults and children with various types of impairments began when I was a physical therapist in the 1990s. After my second child was born 4 months early at 24 weeks' gestation, weighing 1 pound, 10 ounces, the world of visual impairment personally touched my reality.

Within the first year of life, Griffen was diagnosed with cortical visual impairment (CVI). That was the catalyst to the beginning of my quest, and now lifelong passion, to expand my understanding of CVI. Based on my professional experience with infants and personal experience of having another child, I knew my son should have been making eye contact, smiling and cooing to my facial expressions, reaching out for rattles, and lifting his head to look at the world around him. But this was not happening despite my best efforts of doing what I knew to do as a pediatric physical therapist. When Griffen was 9 months old, an ophthalmologist diagnosed him with CVI. He told me that his vision would never be normal, but that there might be "some" improvement as he grew older.

As Griffen grew older and should have been navigating our home with confidence and independence, I noticed that he could not leave a room in our house without following closely behind someone. If he was left alone in a room, he stayed there until someone came back in to get him. It was then that I realized his great need for orientation and mobility (O&M), despite his improved ability to use his vision over the previous few years. With a specific approach based on his unresolved CVI characteristics, we addressed his O&M within our home so that he learned to navigate it without needing someone to follow. After realizing the importance of O&M to all areas of life, I pursued O&M training, became a certified O&M specialist, and have also obtained the Perkins-Roman CVI Range Endorsement (Perkins School for the Blind, n.d.) to help other families and service providers learn how to foster their child's visual functioning and increase their visual access within their everyday lives.

Coauthor's Note: Christine Roman-Lantzy

When I became an O&M professional I imagined that the techniques would be consistent for both individuals with ocular forms of visual impairment and those with CVI. I quickly learned that my initial instincts were incorrect. I noticed that my O&M students with CVI were orienting to features of the environment that had vibrant color. I noticed that my O&M students with CVI were able to navigate a route when there was little pedestrian traffic but clung to doorways when the sidewalks were busy. I noticed that these students could locate a moving car but did not identify the presence of a parked car. The visual and behavioral characteristics associated with CVI have a strong impact on students' ability to travel and require practitioners to adjust instruction accordingly. The data collected at the Pediatric VIEW Program (Roman-Lantzy & Lantzy, 2002–2017) shows that only about one-third of individuals with CVI have ever received services from an O&M specialist. This confused me. I hope that the information in this chapter will illuminate both the need for individuals with CVI to be considered for O&M services and will guide readers about the key differences in O&M for those with CVI.

Orientation and mobility (O&M) instruction is necessary for the development of foundational skills for individuals with cortical visual impairment (CVI) to become more fully aware and participatory in their environments and communities. O&M is age-appropriate, ongoing instruction used to teach individuals with visual impairments to move safely and efficiently, and as independently as possible, in home, school, work, and community settings (Pogrund et al., 2012). Orientation is the ability to establish and maintain an awareness of one's position in space. Mobility is the act of moving through space in a safe and efficient manner.

O&M is a key related service for individuals with visual impairments, including CVI, under the Individuals with Disabilities Education Improvement Act (IDEA, 2004) "to ensure that all children with disabilities have available to them a free appropriate public education . . . and related services designed to meet their unique needs and prepare them for further education, employment, and independent living" (34 C.F.R. § 300.1[a]).

Yet, data collected at the Pediatric VIEW Program showed that only 24 percent of 431 individuals identified with CVI have received O&M services (Roman-Lantzy & Lantzy, 2002–2017). Possible reasons may be a lack of awareness about O&M services and incorrect interpretations of who is eligible for them. Some professionals may assume that individuals who are not ambulatory do not require O&M instruction. Some may be uninformed about how an individual with multiple disabilities can receive any benefits from O&M instruction. A provider may believe that an individual with cognitive delays would not benefit from such instruction, or that if an individual can travel from one location to another without unintentional contact, no O&M instruction is needed. And in less-populated geographic areas, a lack of qualified personnel may prevent an individual from receiving O&M instruction.

This chapter begins with a rationale for providing O&M instruction to individuals with CVI and considerations for assessment. Next, integration of CVI phases and characteristics into various areas of instruction is discussed, first in orientation and then in mobility. Guidelines are then offered for targets and strategies to be used in both orientation and mobility instruction based on each CVI characteristic and phase, followed by special considerations for individuals with CVI who are ambulatory and nonambulatory and for those with additional disabilities. The chapter concludes with brief case examples highlighting how consideration of the CVI characteristics can inform O&M instruction.

Rationale for Providing O&M Instruction to Students with CVI

O&M is essential for individuals with CVI to be able to function with the greatest level of independence and attain the skills required for self-determination, given the expectation that individuals with CVI can make significant progress in the use of their functional vision (Roman-Lantzy, 2018). The guidelines for O&M for individuals with CVI presented in this chapter are based on the premise that each time an individual uses vision to attend to a visually accessible target in the environment, the connections among the brain cells responsible for visually processing that target are potentially strengthened to support greater use of vision in the future. O&M instruction for individuals with CVI needs to be systematic and intentional, and materials, targets, and landmarks need to be selected based on an individual's CVI phase. O&M specialists need to take into account the specific behavioral characteristics of an individual with CVI in order to implement an effective O&M program that allows the individual, at minimum, to become oriented to his or her environment.

Compared to the visual system, other sensory systems have more intermittent input, and sensory input seems diminished or reduced without visual access to the environment. Without visual access, individuals receive inconsistent, discrete, and generally unverified fragments of information (Strickling, n.d.). However, this fragmented view of their everyday world can be replaced with a more coherent representation as their visual access is increased. This can be done by making activities and environments throughout the day compatible with

learning through adaptations and controlling for CVI characteristics. And, greater visual access on a consistent basis leads to improvement in the overall visual functioning of individuals with CVI.

O&M instruction also aims to decrease the frequency and intensity of anxiety-provoking situations by providing individuals with a greater understanding of their environments and a framework for analyzing them. Providing orientation to environments adapted to meet an individual's visual functioning at its current level reduces anxiety and enables anticipation of upcoming events. This allows individuals some level of control over their daily life, which is likely to decrease their anxiety about the unknown.

If an individual is pushed everywhere in a wheelchair and does not have any personal control to independently navigate through the environment, then appropriate instruction needs to be implemented with materials that orient the individual to his or her regular environments and provide some level of visual accessibility. This orientation will provide a sense of familiarity and purpose, as well as some visual input to access within each routine space. In turn, this may dampen anxiety and foster greater participation as the individual is more oriented and has a basic understanding of and visual accessibility to activities and routines carried out in each particular area.

For example, a young preschooler who is moved from sitting at circle time to the restroom, but who has not been adequately oriented to the various areas and activities within the room, will not be able to spontaneously access the visual information to infer her location. She may have access using auditory clues if her auditory processing and hearing are intact. She may have positional detection if her vestibular system adequately registers postural changes. Tactile and cutaneous input from the skin may provide some sensation. But all this input takes place without confirmation by the visual system about the source of the stimuli. This can be extremely disconcerting, as, for example, sound without visual verification is only noise coming from nowhere. Only after much tactile, motor, and auditory interaction does sound acquire meaning and only then can sound provide information about the location, cause, or source of an object or event (Strickling, n.d.).

O&M instruction should aim to enable individuals' visual access within their environments and routines. This will help them be better able to interpret the sensory array of information that they must assimilate. Individuals are then able to develop broader concepts and spatial understanding of the world around them. The orientation aspect of O&M should be addressed within individuals' regular environments, whether or not they can move from one place to another, so that they may interpret the sensory information that is accessible to them in order to participate more fully in routines. Mobility can include skills that are components of locomotion. This may simply mean moving a body part while staying in one place, such as turning the head to orient to a person, target, or activity or reaching to grasp something in the immediate environment.

The intention of the framework and the guidelines presented in this chapter is initially to allow individuals in Phase I CVI to have opportunities to use their vision to access the objects, spaces, and activities that make up their day-to-day routines. As the individuals' visual behaviors develop and they begin to function in Phase II, the intent is to provide visual access to use their vision to guide how they act upon their world. Ultimately, by Phase III, the end goal is to teach a system to analyze novel situations and environments in order to critically solve problems, determine alternate solutions when issues arise, and achieve the greatest level of independence possible.

O&M Assessment

As noted, O&M is a related service under IDEA, and individuals with visual impairment and blindness, including those who have CVI, qualify for a comprehensive O&M evaluation. Just as individuals with CVI require a specialized method for assessment of functional vision, so too, O&M assessment for them must be rooted in the principles of CVI rather than of ocular forms of visual impairment. For individuals with CVI, this means using the CVI Range as a protocol to determine the extent of the effect of the visual and behavioral characteristics associated with CVI and then to apply those findings to O&M programming.

O&M must be a key consideration for any individual who is blind or visually impaired, including those scoring in any phase of CVI on the CVI Range. If the results of a CVI Range assessment don't already exist in the individual's recent evaluation records, the CVI Range should be administered as part of the O&M assessment. The CVI Range should be administered in both familiar as well as more novel settings. Once a CVI Range score has been obtained, the CVI Orientation and Mobility Progress Chart should also be used to assist in program planning and tracking progress of the individual (Roman-Lantzy, 2010, 2018).

It is important to assess an individual in less familiar environments with less familiar visual targets and in unpredictable locations. In environments the individual already knows, familiarity and memorization can compensate for and mask the interference of difficulty with visual novelty, difficulties with visual complexity, and visual latency, as he or she may appear to see most everything in the environment. For example, an individual who has developed the cognitive understanding that soap is typically found at a sink to wash his hands may indeed appear to locate it easily because he knows where to look. But if the soap is in an unpredictable location in the room, would he find it?

Once an environment becomes familiar, an individual may have memorized the locations of objects in the room and is using that knowledge instead of visually processing elements in the environment. If a certain visual target is very familiar and assigned significance by an individual, he or she may find it visually, regardless of its size, even in complex situations. To the untrained observer, this appears to be "finding a needle in a haystack." It can be difficult for the untrained observer to understand that the individual in this situation has a visual impairment, as this observer might have had difficulty finding that target him- or herself. But the untrained observer with typical sight is visually processing and sorting through all the elements in the scene to determine the ones he or she wishes to focus attention on, whereas the individual with CVI is visually processing the one element he or she knows without visually processing and sorting through the rest.

The CVI characteristics in Phase III can be hidden when assessing them in familiar settings (see Chapter 1). In an unfamiliar environment, the individual's visual processing can be more precisely assessed by asking the individual with CVI to report the features and items seen so the evaluator can determine the specific environmental features that have been attended to and interpreted. This is necessary because the presence of eye-to-object visual fixation is not a guarantee that visual processing and understanding have occurred. Questioning should be conducted without offering cues to avoid the possibility that the individual will simply look for a target that is similar to the one requested. Unlike a verbal prompt that includes the name of the target object, prompts such as "Tell me what you see" or "Can you find all the toys that have been placed in the hallway?" require the individual to notice something novel or unprompted. If an individual is looking directly at an item, but does not visually interpret what is seen or cannot adequately disembed it from the background elements to be able to sort and classify it, then it cannot be intentionally perceived on a conscious level. Put simply, looking at an object is not the same as understanding what is seen.

Assessment in unfamiliar environments also provides valuable information in determining an individual's level of difficulty with the characteristics of visual complexity, visual novelty, visual latency, and visually guided reach. It is also essential for determining an individual's current capacity for independent living and the need for lessons in the community to prepare the individual for future independence. Encountering novel environments is a necessary aspect of life, and the individual needs to be taught a framework for analyzing novel situations to achieve independence.

Integrating CVI Phases and Characteristics in Teaching Orientation

The information derived from the CVI Range, including determination of an individual's CVI Range score, will provide the O&M specialist with a starting point for selecting appropriate environments, materials, and instructional techniques, as well as measuring an individual's present levels of performance and long-term progress with intervention. Having access to visual aspects of the environment elicits an individual's desire to move toward visual targets in that environment. If an individual has never been intentionally provided an environment conducive and adapted to his or her specific CVI characteristics, he or she has not had adequate visual access that would provoke an interest to move. If O&M instruction appropriately considers the individual's CVI Range score in regard to the environment and instructional methods, it is more likely the individual will achieve mobility with that intentional setup in place. Ultimately, the instructional environment can integrate greater levels of visual and sensory complexity, as neural pathways are created over time to support greater visual behaviors. Modifying the instructional environment appropriately for individuals in each phase of CVI is discussed in detail later in this chapter.

Teaching the orientation skills of concept development and cognitive mapping, including map representation and interpretation, is discussed in the following sections, with considerations for each CVI phase. Guidelines for teaching each of these skills in each phase of CVI are summarized in Table 6.1. Basic mobility techniques are discussed in the subsequent section.

Teaching Concept Development

One description of O&M notes that "Learning about the world and how to navigate through it is a developmental process, in which each new experience builds on previously acquired knowledge. Each new piece strengthens an overall understanding and broader sense of increasingly larger environments" (Family Connect, n.d., para. 5).

TABLE 6.1

Guidelines for Orientation Instruction for Each Phase of CVI

Area of Instruction	Guidelines		
	Phase I	*Phase II*	*Phase III*
Concept development	Provide description for any items that the student visually regards by describing two or three defining features about those items. Teach geometric shapes with manipulatives adapted to appeal to student's CVI characteristics. Teach color names using the labels for items visually regarded by the student as a bridge to the corresponding color label. Teach positional/spatial concepts using the student's body as a point of reference.	Teach that number labels indicate a specific quantity using manipulatives and materials compatible with the student's visual access, at least for small numbers. Focus on recognition of objects based on giving the student a label of an object or category rather than just having student match identical objects. Teach environmental concepts for components of spaces, such as *floor, ceiling, wall,* and *door,* and signify transitions between spaces by adapting a permanent feature at each transition.	Focus on identification of objects and categories in familiar environments. Focus on recognition of objects in novel environments based on giving the student a label of an object or category. Focus on regularities of the environmental layout of common public establishments. Teach temporal sequence of activities in routines and temporal sequence and temporal relationship of landmarks within routes.
Use of maps	Use three-dimensional objects, compatible with the student's visual access, to represent significant near-space landmarks in common routines for the student. Limit object cues to two for each near space.	Use photos of maps for familiar intermediate spaces on a tablet, laptop, or other backlit medium. Limit map icons to three for each intermediate space. Use enlarged photos of the mapped landmarks and present them in the order in which they will be encountered along common routes before the student travels a route.	Limit map icons to five for each large space. Introduce new landmarks in the mapped space by replacing icons one at a time on the map once the student demonstrates a solid conceptualization of current map icons' representation of actual landmarks in space. Provide instruction and activities using backlit photos for temporal relationships from various reference points to ensure that the student's cognitive map is solid (e.g., "Which is closer to the front door, the stairs or the water fountain?").
Cognitive mapping	Use an *egocentric* frame of reference to teach landmarks or features in highly routine routes or activities. (An egocentric frame of reference relates the location of a landmark to the student's position.)	Use explicit teaching of environmental features and landmarks and their function in familiar spaces to help the student develop a more solid cognitive map.	Use an *allocentric* frame of reference to teach landmarks or features in familiar spaces. (An allocentric frame of reference relates the location of a landmark to the position of another landmark.)

Teaching concept development to a student with CVI needs to be systematic and intentional in order for him or her to develop stable visual schemes and be able to generalize those schemes. Visual schemes for O&M can be defined as sets of static information that can be accessed and sorted by a visual feature (such as shape, color, or texture) to allow for classification of an object, person, or place. This process can help a student develop, store, and retrieve stored information about a place or event.

The need for concept development that is generated through O&M instruction cannot be overestimated. For a student with CVI, concepts are not spontaneously generalized from environment to environment, object to object, or activity to activity, even into Phase III. In students with CVI, the lack of diverse visual experiences may result in visual schemes that can be rigid and inflexible. O&M instruction needs to facilitate appropriate generalization of concepts to allow more flexible thinking so that salient features are used as guidelines to aid in recognizing and identifying unfamiliar items, but not as hard and fast rules that do not allow any variation.

Variations within a particular concept need to be explained and demonstrated to the student once he or she understands the primary salient features that generally characterize an object. This may prevent undergeneralization. For example, a student may be unable to identify a green apple cut into wedges as an "apple" because the student has a rigid scheme that an apple can only be a red, round, whole item with a stem that is smaller at its bottom and wider at its top. A student may be able to travel to a particular center or location within his or her preschool classroom, but be unable to manipulate the materials at that center in more than one way because he or she has minimal conceptual knowledge of different ways to interact with the specific materials or toys. The incidental learning support to acquire this knowledge by observing peers has not been accessible to this student. Similarly, a student may be able to identify a chair in a familiar environment, like the home or the classroom, but fail to generalize that concept to identify chairs in a novel environment, such as a library, due to differences in furniture style or fabric from chairs the student already knows. By implementing explicit teaching during concept development activities, generalization of concepts can be taught to allow for more spontaneous identification of environmental features, items, schemes, and places.

Salient features also need to be expanded on to avoid overgeneralization of a concept. An example of overgeneralizing a concept would be a student who has been taught the salient description of a "window" as an "opening in a wall that is filled with clear glass to see through," and repeatedly labels a mirror in the bathroom as a window. Another example is when a student classifies any large, four-legged animal as a "cow" based on its size and four legs, without regarding the distinctive salient features that uniquely distinguish it from other four-legged animals. Similarly, a student mistaking every tall, brunette woman with eyeglasses as her math teacher is overgeneralizing personal attributes that are shared by multiple people.

Explicitly addressing concept development in specific, intentional ways allows for greater carryover of skills across both familiar and unfamiliar environments. Simply assessing a student's ability to move from point A to point B without unwanted contact with obstacles in his or her environment and to negotiate changes of elevation is not enough to adequately determine the student's need for O&M services. Parents and other service providers need to be interviewed as part of a routine assessment. In doing this, the O&M specialist can recognize the concepts that have already been explicitly taught to avoid mistaking a student's gravitation toward certain activities or items within the environments as his or her intentional preference for that activity or item among the variety of choices. It may just be that the particular activity or item the student gravitates toward is one of the few in the environment that make visual sense as a result of explicit teaching and previous experience. All other visual features may go unnoticed due to difficulty visually processing them to the extent that is needed to interact with them. Especially with

Alisha Waugh

Without color, a viewer must carefully analyze the multiple internal salient features to categorize the farm animals whose front halves protrude out of each white cup. Without paying visual attention to the ear shape, snout or nose, and stature that distinguishes each animal, it would be easy to overgeneralize that they are the same since they all have two front legs with hooves.

students in Phase III, the O&M specialist must be able to recognize and make fine distinctions regarding their visual processing abilities. Despite scoring in Phase III, which indicates the student is able to use vision to gather some environmental information, the student may not be able to determine that he or she is missing key visual information in order to request clarification of concepts, events, and elements within the environment. Clarification and elaboration are necessary for developing comprehensive concepts in light of incomplete visual information. The area of concept development must be sufficiently addressed to allow students with CVI to use visual information with purpose and accuracy. The following sections provide specific information about teaching concept development to individuals in different phases of CVI.

Phase I

Rudimentary concept development begins with eliciting the student's visual regard for routine, three-dimensional, concrete items found within familiar environments and activities. When visual regard of an item is elicited, a caregiver or provider can help the student form meaning for commonly

used objects. By describing the object's salient features in a consistent way, visual regularities can begin to emerge and be given meaning with an assigned language label that the student can adopt. Once the student has come to recognize several objects, he or she can start to cognitively connect two or more objects by extracting their common characteristics to form a scheme that may continue to broaden as the student's repertoire of regarded visual imagery expands.

Instruction in concept development begins in Phase I. Basic orientation concepts of body awareness, positional and spatial perception, and recognition of geometric shapes and colors form a basis of understanding salient features and developing comparative thought.

SHAPES. Teaching shapes using simple manipulatives modified to appeal to a student's specific CVI characteristics profile is fundamental for his or her understanding of salient features of objects. For example, traditional shape sorter blocks can be adapted by adding Mylar of the student's preferred color. Blocks can be presented one at a time within the student's preferred fields and viewing distance

Alisha Waugh

A traditional shape sorter toy is adapted to encourage visual attention to a square shape for a student in Phase I CVI.

in a dim room with a flashlight shining on it to elicit visual attention. The name of the particular shape should be stated before and after presenting it, not during the presentation. The shape's corresponding opening on the shape sorter can be highlighted to encourage visual attention to the overall outline of the shape. These adaptations appeal to the CVI characteristics of color preference, difficulties with visual complexity, attraction to light and movement, difficulty with distance viewing, and so on. Once a student has been explicitly introduced to a particular shape, that shape label can be used in descriptions of salient features for routine items that he or she regularly encounters to reinforce its meaning.

COLORS. It may be helpful for students to learn color names using their preferred items they look at, appealing to the CVI characteristic of difficulty with visual novelty (for example, "Elmo is the color red"; "Your sippy cup is the color yellow"; or "Your ball is the color green"). By relating something abstract, like color, to something concrete that the student has already come to understand, he or she can begin to make the cognitive connection for the meaning of color.

POSITIONAL CONCEPTS. Teaching positional concepts with an *egocentric* frame of reference (using the student's own body as the positional reference point in relation to another object) is important to assist in developing spatial relationship concepts that will be used in descriptions of salient features. When a provider moves a student or the student moves him- or herself through space, positional words, like "up," "in," and "out," should be used consistently at every opportunity so that concepts communicating one's location ultimately form a meaningful representation in the student's mind. An accessible visual target positioned in common areas that the student visits for specific purposes may also provide cues to recognize his or her location in space. For example, a light-up canopy hanging down from the ceiling provides the cue that the student is lying on the bed.

Caregivers and providers need to describe salient features of naturally occurring, frequently encountered items in the student's routine environments. All caregivers and providers should use the same salient feature language to describe those objects when the student encounters them. Selecting two or three defining salient features for each item allows consistency among providers to describe the item in the same way without confusing the student with CVI.

Phase II
NUMBER CONCEPTS. Concept development activities for students in Phase II CVI continue to be a significant component of the O&M program. The concept of number quantities is important for comprehending details of salient features and taking directions for routes. At minimum, quantities up to 4 should be taught, as salient feature descriptions often include the specific number of certain features (such as four legs or two circles), and most directions entail multiple turns. Teaching that a number label represents a specific amount of some entity is important in Phase II.

Using manipulatives that appeal to the student's unresolved CVI characteristics to represent various quantities can be a starting point. A light box can be adapted by covering its surface with an

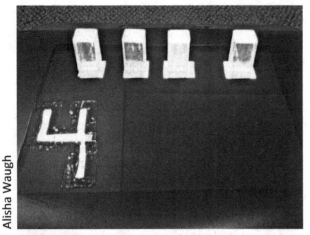

Alisha Waugh

To teach the quantity of 4 and the salient shape of the number to a student in Phase II, a light box has been adapted to shine light through four colored, translucent manipulatives and a template for the symbol 4 outlined in Mylar.

opaque template of cut-out holes that correspond to the specific number the student is working on. When a translucent manipulative is placed in each hole, the light shines only through the manipulatives, rather than the entire light box surface, guiding the student's visual attention to a specific target. A template for the number symbol that allows light to shine through its shape can be created and outlined in a highly saturated color.

This adaptation may prove helpful when teaching specific methods for developing a sense of quantities and *numerosity,* the ability to discriminate arrays of objects based on the number of items presented. Lessons to teach one-to-one correspondence or *subitization,* the ability to perceive small quantities at a glance, may elicit more directed and longer visual attention if presented with these adapted materials and assistive technology appealing to the student's specific CVI characteristics. This activity should be pursued whether or not a student is verbal, as infants who are preverbal can represent quantities up to 3 (Feigenson & Carey, 2005).

VISUAL OBJECT RECOGNITION. Once a student has a foundation of basic orientation concepts (including body awareness, color, geometric shapes, and positional awareness), has developed a beginning

sense of number concepts, and has learned the salient features for some common items, the O&M specialist can begin asking him or her to recognize objects that match a given salient feature description within familiar environments. Sequential teaching progresses from simply discriminating "same" from "not same," which consists of finding something that matches the visual characteristics of something else, and moves to recognizing an object. Once a student has been given a label for an object and taught its salient features, he or she can pull up a visual scheme within his or her repertoire of concepts to match it to one of the visual targets. For example, the O&M specialist can give a student the description that "a shelf is a rectangle-shaped object, flat on top, and is used to hold smaller items," and then ask the student to "find all the shelves" in his or her familiar home environment.

ENVIRONMENTAL CONCEPTS. Environmental concepts need to be introduced to address the student's understanding of components of a space, such as walls, doors, and floors. Environmental access in larger spaces needs to be addressed in Phase II. Independence in moving from one room to another can be challenging as a result of the unresolved CVI characteristic of difficulty with distance viewing, as well as the increased visual complexity that results from looking at greater distances and having to simultaneously process a greater number of elements within the scene (as described in Chapter 1). For example, a student may have difficulty visually perceiving the doorway from greater distances and be unable to move purposefully toward it from a more distant location within the room. When the student gets closer to the doorway, however, he or she may be able to perceive it more fully and move purposefully and efficiently toward it. Increasing the student's access to information in the environment by appealing to the CVI characteristic of color preference, using color highlighting (such as bold-colored duct tape in the student's preferred color to line the edge of a doorframe or outline a piece of furniture) at transition points (such as doorways, partitions, or shelves dividing areas within the classroom)

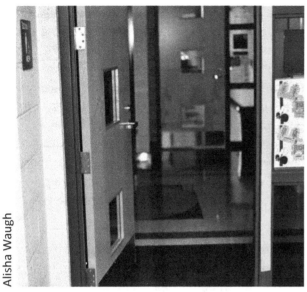

Alisha Waugh

The color highlighting on this doorframe in the student's preferred color of bright green is intended to elicit visual regard from a distance and help the student recognize that this is a transition point to another space.

is important to increase the student's ability to move independently between rooms within a building or between locations within a larger space. Explicitly teaching the student the specific color highlighting at transition points between specific rooms or areas within a room will help the student become better oriented and seek out that additional cue from a distance.

Phase III

IDENTIFYING AND RECOGNIZING OBJECTS IN FAMILIAR AND NOVEL ENVIRONMENTS.

Once students' visual recognition of objects is more reliable, they can progress in Phase III CVI to identifying an object based on analyzing its visual characteristics and pulling up the label on their own. Describing salient features of routine and meaningful items in the environment lays the necessary foundation for students to be able to build concepts that will be used to orient to the space around them in order to travel safely, efficiently, and independently. After students develop an even greater repertoire of object schemes and environmental concepts, the O&M specialist can ask them to *identify* objects and describe their salient features in familiar envi-

ronments. For instance, a student can be asked "What is this?" for any known scheme or concept in a familiar environment.

In novel environments, the O&M specialist can begin asking the student to *recognize* objects that belong to already familiar categories previously taught through explicit concept-development lessons. For example, a student can be asked to locate all the various styles of seating in an unfamiliar library if he or she has already been explicitly instructed in the salient features of a seat, including variations within the category of seat, such as armchairs, benches, and stools.

FAMILIARIZING TO AN UNKNOWN SPACE. In Phase III, a student can be familiarized with an unknown space before traveling through it by using a map (discussed in the next section) and comparative language to describe similarities and differences with already known environments. Such familiarization can prove extremely helpful in decreasing anxiety so that the student is more willing to participate in the novel environment. For example, an unfamiliar playground with new equipment and other children yelling and running around can be quite distressing and unfriendly to an elementary school–aged child, even one in Phase III, who may resort to wandering without purpose on the perimeter of the playground to escape the chaotic, high level of complexity this environment entails.

LAYOUTS OF COMMERCIAL ESTABLISHMENTS. Environmental concept teaching focused on layout regularities within commercial establishments may be helpful for students in Phase III CVI to provide them with some orientation in unfamiliar environments. They can use explicitly taught environmental concepts to generalize features across similar settings. For instance, a wall of windows is typically found in the front of a grocery store, and the checkout counters can generally be found in this front area as well. This general knowledge can serve as a compensatory strategy for students with unresolved difficulty with distance viewing. For example, even if not fully familiarized to the novel shopping environment, a student can find the store exit by locating the sunlight streaming into the space to guide him or her toward the checkout counters.

TEMPORAL CONCEPTS. Temporal concepts, which involve having an awareness of the time and distance it takes to travel from a given reference point, should be addressed in Phase III to assist in cognitive mapping of familiar spaces (discussed in the next section). Asking the student to compare distances between known features within familiar environments from a provided starting point will help the O&M specialist glean awareness of the accuracy of the student's cognitive map of a space. Determining "Which is closer to your classroom door, the stairs or the library?" without traveling the route requires the student to access a cognitive map to analyze the temporal relationships among features in the environment.

Increasing students' mastery in discerning distance and time by addressing their accuracy for sequencing events within routines or sequencing landmarks in order of encounter along routes is a significant component of O&M. This will aid students in confirming their location in space, determining when they have traveled off-route, and managing their time successfully, skills that are necessary to eventually become an independent traveler.

Use of Maps

To support students with CVI in developing a working cognitive map, or mental image of space, O&M specialists can utilize actual three-dimensional object models, photographic representations, or visual maps. These materials need to be adapted to fit students' visual needs based on their CVI Range scores. Having concrete, tangible materials to reference provides students with a bridge from concrete representation of space to higher levels of abstract thinking involved in visualizing environmental features. The environmental features that are represented by physical materials (such as object cues, photographic images, and map icons) can become more solidly represented in the individual's "mind's eye" through familiarization activities, with the O&M specialist describing the salient

details of selected environmental landmarks. Repetitive instruction is also key to addressing the CVI characteristic of difficulty with visual novelty. The following sections provide recommendations to consider when creating maps and models to represent environments for students in the three phases of CVI and photographs for students in Phases II and III. Instruction in models, maps, and photographs will provide a foundation for those with CVI to begin to develop cognitive maps, or mental representations, of their environments.

Phase I

In Phase I, three-dimensional items should be used to represent elements found within common routines in the student's near space in familiar environments. The selected items should be limited to two for each near space in the natural environment. The items used need to be visually discrepant and relevant to the routine and space that they represent. For example, the restroom can be represented by a roll of toilet paper. The art center can be represented by a paintbrush. The locker or cubby can be represented by a metal hook. The selected object cues should be compatible with the student's identified CVI characteristics—for example, in the student's preferred color with no pattern,

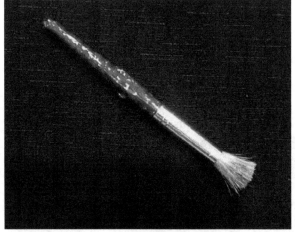

Alisha Waugh

This object cue, used with a preschool student, represents the familiar activity of painting at the art easel center in her classroom. It is compatible with her CVI characteristics of need for light and movement, difficulty with visual novelty and complexity, and color preference of red.

or adapted with reflective tape for a student who is visually attracted to movement and light.

Phase II

Once a student achieves a score of at least 5 on the CVI Range, backlit two-dimensional materials may be introduced if an assessment finds that the student demonstrates the ability to sustain visual attention to assistive technology, such as a tablet or light box. A backlit photo of a map displayed on a tablet or laptop encourages visual attention. The landmarks on the map should be limited to three for a familiar intermediate space, and a different-shaped icon should be used for each landmark represented on the map. Photographs presented with backlighting can also be utilized to represent familiar landmarks found at intermediate distances within familiar spaces. The photographs should be enlarged images of specific landmarks that the student will encounter along a particular route. The images of the landmarks should be reviewed with the student in the order they will be encountered before traveling the familiar route to prime him or her to visually attend to those specific landmarks. Ultimately, it will aid the student in developing a temporal understanding of where he or she is along a route—for example, at the beginning of the route, mid-route, or at the end destination. Having the student match the backlit photograph of each landmark to its corresponding icon on the map can assist the O&M specialist in determining how accurate the student is in understanding the map's representation of actual space.

Phase III

For a student in Phase III, up to five landmarks can be represented on a map for larger environments if an assessment finds that the student can handle the level of visual complexity and simultaneously process that number of elements. Care should be taken to make sure that the student is not identifying landmarks on the map based on memorizing the icons' colors or shapes. Instead, the student should be using the location of an icon in relation to other icons and features on the map as the cue for identifying a landmark. If the student appears to be memorizing icons by their attributes, rather than by their location on the map, the same type of icon can be used for each landmark. Once the map landmarks appear to be well conceptualized in the student's corresponding cognitive map, the landmarks on the physical map can be changed, one at a time, to introduce new landmarks to learn and to incorporate into the student's developing cognitive map of that space.

This photo of a map for a student in Phase II is displayed on a tablet so the backlighting promotes extended visual attention. The icons representing different landmarks of a familiar intermediate space are distinct and are limited to three to avoid increasing visual complexity.

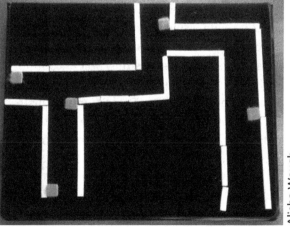

This map of a larger space for a student in Phase III uses identical icons to ensure that the student is accurately conceptualizing each icon's location in relation to other elements in the space, not by its color or shape.

Alisha Waugh

Alisha Waugh

Creative activities can be developed to assess students' temporal understanding of landmarks along a route. For example, backlit photographs of landmarks can be presented all at once on the screen in random order for a student to then sequence in the order in which they will be encountered along a selected route. Games exploring alternate routes to the same destination within familiar environments can also be created using the map and backlit photographs of landmarks. For example, immediately before traveling an alternate route, a student can be shown a few photographs of different landmarks found along the alternate route that lead up to the final known destination. A photograph of a motivating and familiar item (such as putty or a die cast car) that will be found at the end destination to reward the student can be previewed as well. The incentive of winning the prize previewed in the photograph will help the student push through the challenge of using his or her vision to sort through the visual scene to find the landmarks. The student then travels this alternate route, using the map to plan travel directions and photos to correspond with landmarks marked on the map, as he or she looks for these previewed landmarks during actual travel along the route. Once the student reaches the final landmark for this route, he or she can scan for the prize within the immediate environment. Often, reinforcing students with a small reward will motivate them to use top-down visual attention strategies; that is, access their background knowledge and expectations of the visual targets they will encounter to allow them to more quickly perceive the landmarks along a non-rote route. These types of instructional activities can help to improve the student's ability to think flexibly about alternate routes to become a more independent traveler.

Developing Cognitive Representation of Space

A cognitive map is a mental representation of one's environment or geographic space. Having a solid cognitive map is extremely challenging for individuals with CVI. Developing a visual "mental picture" of environments requires an individual to generate a visual image of salient landmarks of a particular environment in his or her mind's eye and to construct spatial relationships among landmarks on demand. This must be supported by solid representations of landmarks from long-term memory.

However, the CVI characteristics can affect the ability to form stable visual representations of the surrounding space. If there is an actual concrete landmark in front of you to hold in your mind, you can refresh that mind's-eye image periodically by viewing the landmark to maintain that mental imagery without having to cognitively pull up a stored visual representation of it. But without an actual tangible landmark to reference, its abstract mental representation must be retrieved from long-term memory. To have a landmark in long-term memory, sufficient visual attention to its features must have been previously achieved to create a solid mental representation of it. If an individual with CVI has not been instructed to visually attend to the salient features of a particular landmark, that landmark might simply be part of visual "white noise" and go unnoticed. But, if an individual has been instructed with intentionality to notice the landmark's salient details and therefore develop a solid mental representation of that landmark, he or she can retrieve it from stored images to assist in informing navigational decisions.

Moreover, individuals with CVI must learn to access their vision to notice details in order to form allocentric, or survey-type, mental representations, as other sensory modes typically do not provide the simultaneously available details to spontaneously create such representations, as vision does. Unlike individuals with ocular visual impairments, in which "the rest of the downstream processing structures within the brain appear to remain largely intact despite the loss of visual sensory input early in development" (Martín et al., 2016, para. 2), individuals with CVI have sustained damage to the visual pathways, the primary visual cortex, or both. This means that visual input taken in by the eyes may not get converted into meaningful representations in the brain to guide behavior.

In regard to ocular visual impairment, studies support the view that the brain can undergo structural and functional changes after vision loss, with an accumulation of evidence suggesting "that individuals with ocular blindness (particularly, when blind from birth or very early in life) demonstrate comparable, and in some cases even superior, behavioral skills in the tactile and auditory domains as compared to their sighted counterparts" (Merabet & Pascual-Leone, 2010, p. 45; see, for example, Amedi, Raz, Pianka, Malach, & Zohary, 2003; Gougoux, Lepore, Lassonde, Voss, Zatorre, & Belin, 2004; Lessard, Paré, Lepore, & Lassonde, 1998; Van Boven, Hamilton, Kauffman, Keenan, & Pascual-Leone, 2000; Wong, Gnanakumaran, & Goldreich, 2011). Neuroimaging studies have shown significant activation in the occipital cortex region in individuals with ocular blindness during the performance of nonvisual tasks (Martín et al., 2016), which allows for additional and alternative means to process sensory information for those individuals. For those with ocular blindness, these changes allow for increased, or at least comparable, tactile and auditory skills to those of sighted individuals and the development of tactile and auditory markers that can take the place of visual landmarks in their cognitive representation of space. In addition, individuals with acquired vision loss have access to visual memories to aid them in developing new mental representations after vision loss.

Thus, individuals with ocular visual impairments have the capacity to develop more robust cognitive representations to guide their understanding of space and travel decisions than those with CVI. Individuals with CVI, who are unable to fully access their functional vision, and whose other systems and abilities (such as motor control, haptic awareness, auditory processing, and integration of sensory input) also may be impaired by neurological injury, have less reliable sensory input from which to develop a cognitive representation of space.

Having a cognitive map of space is essential to becoming an independent traveler. Independent travelers are able to travel a route, making corrections as needed and determining new or alternate routes in order to find their way to a destination,

as opposed to rote route travelers who only follow a specific set of directions to get from one place to another. Without a mental representation of a route and its landmarks, if a rote route traveler makes a wrong turn or if part of the known route is not accessible, he or she is stuck. To become independent travelers, individuals need to have developed sufficient cognitive representations of their environments so that they can have greater flexibility and options in their travel.

Assessment of the development or accuracy of a cognitive map for a familiar space may be determined by asking verbal individuals to respond to questions based on an already known reference point that would require a firm mental representation of space to answer. Nonverbal individuals may need to be given the choice of two options to which they can respond through alternative modes of communication or through their behavior (for example, "Walk to the landmark that is farther away from the door—the sink or the computer"). An individual's lack of response to such an inquiry would lend credence that mental representation of space has not been created and needs to be addressed. A cognitive impairment does not mean that an individual cannot establish routines and cognitive representations of space, but it may take longer and require more repetition, instruction built into natural routines, and teaching in smaller chunks and with specific strategies such as fading prompts and chaining.

Phase I

Forming a cognitive map of even a highly familiar space is generally a rote task for an individual in Phase I. It occurs within a highly practiced and familiar area and is based on an egocentric (self-to-object) perspective rather than an allocentric (object-to-object) one. Ultimately, an allocentric cognitive map is necessary to change route directions and have flexibility in thinking about moving through space.

The following vignette illustrates how a non-verbal student in Phase I CVI can begin to form a cognitive understanding of his familiar environment and demonstrate that understanding.

Quinton is a 7-year-old boy with Phase I CVI who was diagnosed with a rare genetic disorder. He is nonverbal and has frequent seizures that are poorly controlled by medication. He can ambulate short distances with decreased balance and posture, but typically uses a wheelchair or adapted bicycle to achieve mobility for longer distances. He is working with a speech therapist to learn how to use a switch to communicate simple phrases. Quinton is educated in a resource room and has a paraeducator to assist him.

The O&M specialist addresses cognitive mapping through opportunities for Quinton to use his vision within mini-routes by setting up the resource room environment with visually accessible adaptations on features in the room and daily reinforcement of these adapted features by the paraeducator. Quinton's first stop in the classroom each morning is his cubby, which stands out with its back interior wall completely covered in red Mylar, while the other cubbies in the row have just a white background. Next, Quinton is pushed in the wheelchair to his destination on the rug area, where his large, red beanbag chair sits.

To start prompting Quinton for this mini-route, the paraeducator describes the visual features of his cubby: "We will move to your cubby. It is on the wall. It is red, has a shiny hook, and is shaped like a rectangle." Then she pushes Quinton in his wheelchair to the cubby, stating, "When you come in the door, it is on your left side," and taps his left arm to tactilely indicate the direction. Squaring off before pushing Quinton's chair to the bean bag, she states, "Now we will move to your seat on the rug. It is a big, red, round seat on the floor."

After two weeks of consistent, daily practice with the paraeducator through reinforcement within this natural routine, Quinton is ready to make a decision on what feature he sees first in the mini-route. The paraeducator pushes him in the wheelchair and instructs him to activate a switch when he is moved close to the feature that represents the first location he visits each morning when he comes in the door. She first presents the beanbag, then the cubby. When Quinton sees the cubby, he activates the switch. Through his behavior, Quinton demonstrates that he is beginning to notice the adapted visual features within his familiar environment.

Phase II

An environment would likely need to be extremely familiar, such as an individual's home, for that individual to be able to form any semblance of a cognitive map for that space. Even then, the individual might fail to perceive many features within that highly familiar space and require explicit concept development activities. Most likely, only highly salient features with which the individual has had frequent direct contacts and has assigned meaning to—such as a closet that the individual has taken things out of and put things into it many times—would be mentally represented.

The following scenario illustrates the type of concept development required to help a student begin to develop cognitive mapping.

Karlie is a 13-year-old middle school student with Phase II CVI who had a stroke in utero. She ambulates independently and is functionally verbal but requires prompting for problem solving in novel situations. She is educated in a resource room for language arts and math instruction, but participates in the general education curriculum for science, social studies, and elective classes. She is independent in getting around her homeroom classroom but needs a classmate to guide her through the hallways.

Mr. George, the O&M specialist, noticed that Karlie was missing visual features that would indicate she was close to the media center when traveling from her homeroom. When asked what she noticed on the route, she was unable to come up with any features and said she knows she's in the right place when she sees the tables with computers and the bookshelves.

Mr. George implemented explicit concept activities for features along the route to help Karlie develop a meaningful memory and visual regard of salient features that indicate she is nearing the media center. For instance, he encouraged her to stop and drink from the water fountain at the halfway point on the route. He also explained the visual features of the water fountain and showed her simple photographs of other water fountains on a tablet to generalize the concept of a water fountain's characteristics. Karlie was asked to drop off documents at the office, located near the media center, and to have an interaction at the office counter. Mr. George verbally highlighted the features of the office counter and window to point out their unique visual characteristics. A vending machine with snacks was the final landmark encountered before the media center door, and Mr. George incentivized Karlie for noticing the previous landmarks by giving her change to buy a bag of chips. The interaction with the vending machine, along with description of its salient visual aspects, helped to reinforce this environmental feature in Karlie's mental imagery. Mr. George continued to work on Karlie's cognitive mapping by posing questions about what she would encounter along the route, in order, from her homeroom to the media center. Based on these explicit experiences, and as Karlie became more accurate in her answers, Mr. George was able to assess that she was developing a cognitive map of the route.

Phase III

Individuals in Phase III CVI may be able to generate object-to-object cognitive maps of a few highly familiar environments. Without being in the actual environment and visually regarding a feature within a familiar space, however, the individual may still have difficulty pulling up a particular environmental feature within his or her cognitive map. To ensure that individuals have formed a solid representation of a specific space in their mind, they must be able to develop a visual image with-

out prompts for landmarks or environmental features. While developing this skill of forming a solid representation of the space, they may need to be given a category or specific feature in that environment to prime the mental visualization. They may not be able to mentally pull up any salient feature to anchor the cognitive map when it is cognitively represented in a fragmented or fragile way, as shown in the example of Garrett that follows. Individuals need to be assessed in this area of O&M as it is an essential component of independent, flexible travel in large spaces.

Garrett is a 16-year-old boy in Phase III CVI with a diagnosis of periventricular leukomalacia. He participates in the general education curriculum with some small-group and individualized interventions for academic areas. He developed an accurate cognitive representation of salient features within familiar environments that he traveled on a regular basis, like his school and home. But with less-frequented environments, like the mall or his large church, he easily became disoriented. When asked, "Which location is closest to the mall's front parking lot entrance?" he needed a category prompt of restaurant to accurately answer "Panera Bread."

Garrett's O&M specialist developed activities to address the cognitive representation of large spaces and layout generalities to help with less-frequented establishments. They visited multiple community locations and analyzed locations of visual features and types of establishments common for public places. For example, restaurants are often by mall entrances to allow non-shoppers easy access without entering the mall. Restaurants look visually different from stores in that they are darker for ambiance, have a tall counter or hostess stand by the door, and contain tables and chairs. Escalators are found in the middle of an open space at a mall. They look like stairs but are metal with ridges and move to transport people to an upper or lower floor.

The cognitive mapping activities focused on the relationship of certain landmarks to one another (such as the location of Panera Bread in relation to the parking lot entrance). With the concept development activities and cognitive mapping practice, Garrett developed an expectation of what he might visually encounter when he navigates in less-familiar locations and became better able to use his vision.

Integrating CVI Phases and Characteristics in Teaching Mobility

This section provides considerations for teaching basic mobility techniques, such as human guide and trailing, to students in each phase of CVI. Table 6.2 provides a summary of these guidelines.

Teaching Basic Mobility Techniques

Basic mobility techniques can be challenging to master for students with CVI. The tactile, auditory, and visual input created by moving through space without an underlying understanding of the space can result in confusion. While visual input is helpful for orienting in one's environment, it can be disorienting if there are no familiar visual anchors or reliable elements that have been assigned meaning. The visual input can become a bombardment of colors, patterns, and shapes without any attached meaning to support interpreting the vast array of stimuli.

Phase I

HUMAN GUIDE. Human guide technique is a specific method in which another individual guides the student with a visual impairment and takes responsibility for negotiating the environment by establishing a path of travel, avoiding obstacles and surface changes that interfere with travel, and safely guiding the student's navigation (LaGrow, 2010). The student with a visual impairment holds the guide's arm just above the elbow—or in the case of a small child, at the guide's wrist—and walks approximately a half-step behind the guide and off to one side. If the student with a visual impairment uses a wheelchair or mobility device, modifications are made to the traditional human guide technique. (Detailed descriptions of these modifications can be found in Rosen & Crawford, 2010).

Human guide can be adapted for Phase I CVI to lead the student within a few feet of particular environmental features that are encountered during routine travel. The particular environmental features selected should be visually accessible based on the student's color preference, attraction to light or movement, visual field preferences, and level of familiarity. Also, giving the student extended time to visually regard the specific environmental feature while providing its label and a description of a few of its salient features may help the student begin to develop a visual-cognitive connection for that particular item. This use of human guide affords the student an opportunity to visually regard features along routes in a way that may be commensurate with his or her present level of visual functioning.

TRAILING. Trailing is a basic mobility technique for maintaining one's direction and finding objects and destinations along a wall (Jacobson, 2013) by lightly touching the back of the hand against a wall surface as one moves along a straight path. Teaching trailing may initially provide a means for students in Phase I to achieve constant contact and to remain tactilely oriented when moving through the environment. However, students still will not be able to visually regard and touch the environment simultaneously. For a student to achieve some visual regard of any feature in his or her space, the student will need to discontinue trailing and be provided plenty of time to visually regard a feature that appeals to his or her preferred color, is simple and located against a plain background in a quiet environment, is familiar, has movement or light qualities, and is located within near space and within his or her preferred visual field.

Phase II

HUMAN GUIDE. For students in Phase II CVI, human guide technique can be adapted to allow them extended viewing of key environmental features

TABLE 6.2

Guidelines for Mobility Instruction for Each Phase of CVI

Area of Instruction	Guidelines		
	Phase I	Phase II	Phase III
Basic mobility techniques	**Human guide:** Lead the student within a few feet of landmarks in familiar environments that are accessible or have been made accessible to the student's vision. Provide extended time for viewing without simultaneous auditory input. Describe salient features of the landmark before and after providing viewing opportunity.	**Human guide:** Lead the student within 5 feet of landmarks on routine routes that are accessible or have been made accessible to the student's vision. Review two or three salient features of these landmarks. Low ambient noise may be tolerated during viewing.	**Human guide:** Human guide technique may be adapted, as the student is able, to allow the student to closely follow another trained individual without physical contact, in familiar environments (after environmental features and hazards have been previewed and explicitly taught). Point out salient features of landmarks representing familiar concepts that are located at distances 10+ feet away. Point out salient features of novel landmarks that are located at distances of 5–10 feet.
	Trailing: Do not expect the student to trail and visually regard the environment simultaneously. For visual regard of a particular environmental feature, have the student discontinue trailing.	**Trailing:** The student may be expected to simultaneously view and trail highly familiar environmental features. Trailing will need to be discontinued to view novel features along a route. Review enlarged photos taken of novel features at the end of route and before traveling route on subsequent attempts. Attempt in environments with low ambient noise.	**Trailing:** When the student encounters a novel environmental feature along a route, stimulate the student's comparative thinking by inquiring how it is like something already known by the student and how it is different. Attempt in environments with low ambient noise.
Detection of environmental hazards	Use human guide technique to assist the student with detecting obstacles and elevation changes.	Preview and discuss environmental hazards at the beginning of the route and during the route, immediately before the student encounters them. Highlight hazards to make them more visually accessible to the student.	Preview environmental hazards at the beginning of the route. Select naturally occurring landmarks that are visually appealing to the student as cues of an impending hazard. Adapt landmarks, as needed and able, to elicit the student's visual regard to provide cues of an upcoming hazard.
Mobility cane techniques	Address precane skills, such as maintaining grasp on the cane grip and exploring the immediate environment with the cane tip. Adapt the cane as needed to encourage visual regard of its parts (e.g., grip, tip).	Teach cane techniques separately from requiring simultaneous visual regard of environment. Teach techniques in highly familiar, low-complexity environments. Encourage the student's visual regard for environmental features that the cane tip contacts.	Once the student has become more proficient at using cane techniques in familiar, low-complexity environments, have the student attempt cane techniques in less-familiar and more complex settings. Encourage the student to visually regard more distant (10+ feet) environmental features by maintaining a neutral head position as the cane detects immediate environmental features.

along routine routes by stopping within 5 feet of each key feature and reviewing its two or three most salient details. The environmental features selected should be compatible with the student's CVI characteristics.

TRAILING. Teaching trailing will need to take place in an environment with low ambient noise. After multiple familiarizations to a particular route have occurred, a student may be able to visually regard some familiar items as he or she trails their surfaces during travel. When the student encounters a novel feature while trailing, the O&M specialist should point out its salient details, along with comparative language to connect it to an already familiar concept. The student is not likely to touch and view the novel item simultaneously. Therefore, trailing will need to be discontinued to allow for viewing of the novel feature. A photograph can be taken of the novel feature using a tablet or cell phone to review at the end of the lesson and preview before trailing the route on the next occasion. With intentional familiarization to the novel feature over time, the student may be able to visually regard it while trailing on subsequent opportunities.

Phase III

HUMAN GUIDE. In Phase III CVI, human guide technique may be adapted to allow the student to utilize another individual who is properly trained as a close visual guide (walking 3 to 5 feet ahead of the student) without direct physical contact—if deemed appropriate by the O&M specialist—in environments that have been thoroughly previewed through mapping and explicit teaching. It is of utmost importance that the individual serving as a close visual guide is able to provide sufficient, immediate supervision to intervene as necessary for the student's safety, assuming a much closer distance to the student (within arm's reach) for impending obstacles, drop-offs, street crossings, and other environmental hazards. The student's attention should be directed to the guide's clothing—or some other feature that is salient and visually accessible based on the student's CVI characteristics—to differentiate the guide from other individuals. The guide can verbally point out environmental features along the route that represent familiar concepts to the student at greater distances (10 or more feet) and novel features at closer distances (within 5 to 10 feet), using comparative language to link salient details of new items with already familiar ones.

TRAILING. Teaching trailing to students in Phase III should be attempted in an environment with low ambient noise. Once mastered, trailing may be a helpful technique to maintain a straight line of travel for students in novel environments. When encountering a novel feature, the O&M specialist should elicit the student's perception of its salient features. The student's comparative thinking can be evoked by inquiring whether the feature is like anything else the student knows. If the student is unable to identify any salient features, the specialist can point out details for the student's visual regard. When the salient features are described, the student will more likely be able to touch and view the novel feature simultaneously.

Detection of Environmental Hazards

Students with CVI do not take in all of the many visual elements in their environments. They are missing visual details that would alert them to potential changes in terrain, elevation, and street crossings. O&M specialists need to be cautious about assuming that if a student with CVI traveled without difficulty from point A to point B on one occasion, the route can be repeated without difficulty at another point in time. When the environment changes in its level of complexity (for example, has greater pedestrian or vehicular traffic) and novelty (such as a change in a window display by a known drop-off point), a student can become disoriented and miss the hazard that was previously detected. If the student is not feeling well or is more fatigued, visual latency will have greater impact on his or her ability to efficiently process environmental hazards in adequate time to respond.

If a student has physical disabilities that require assistive devices and assistance of another person for mobility, such as being pushed in a wheelchair, the provider should explicitly alert him or her about any hazards, such as obstacles, drop-offs, and ramps, as they are encountered in the environment. This will allow the student to start to develop the concept of environmental hazards that he or she must attend to for safety, should mobility progress to an independent level in the future.

Phase I

A student in Phase I is not likely to be able to detect surface changes, obstacles, and drop-offs, even within familiar spaces. When moving through space, human guide technique or close supervision is necessary to assist or alert the student to upcoming obstacles and drop-offs to ensure safety.

Phase II

With students in Phase II CVI, surface changes, drop-offs, and obstacles that will be encountered in their travel on specific routes need to be discussed and previewed ahead of time to give advanced notice, as well as pointed out immediately before encountering them, since CVI characteristics may interfere with students' immediate visual access to these environmental hazards. Environmental accommodations to enhance students' safety in their travel environments can be made by highlighting locations of environmental hazards with bright colors, markers that have movement

and backlit qualities, and highly familiar visual targets. Decreasing the visual complexity of the immediate space around an obstacle, drop-off, or terrain change by removing extraneous clutter and patterns is also key to increasing visual access to the environmental hazard.

Phase III

Safety in mobility for students in Phase III requires alerting them to changes in terrain and elevation within their environment by using natural landmarks or adaptations appealing to their unresolved CVI characteristics on specific environmental features as a cue to forewarn them of an impending hazard. Previewing these landmarks in the environment with students before they travel the route so they know what to look for ahead of time is an important part of O&M instruction. An example of an adapted feature may be bold-colored duct tape on the beginning and end of a stair handrail for a student whose color preference characteristic is unresolved to visually notify him or her that an elevation change is coming up. Or, a waving flag by a door could be used as a warning that a curb is near for a student with the unresolved CVI characteristic of attraction to movement.

Benefits of Cane Use

Teaching the use of a mobility cane can be a very important component of O&M instruction for

Alisha Waugh

To visually alert a student in Phase III CVI of impending hazards or elevation changes, marking a stair railing with fluorescent orange tape (left) or placing a waving flag near a curb (right), will appeal to the CVI characteristics of color preference and attraction to movement.

students who have CVI. This is an important safety consideration for those who have decreased visual fields, visual latency, and difficulty with complexity, distance viewing, and visual novelty. The cane can detect drop-offs, obstacles, and surface changes to warn the student of environmental safety hazards.

Using a mobility cane can also serve as a proprioceptive anchor and serve as an additional means of getting input from the environment to achieve greater sensory grounding. Proprioception is the sense or perception of the relative positions and movements of parts of the body, independent of vision (Wiener, Welsh, & Blasch, 2010). Proprioception creates an awareness of one's body in relation to the environment and aids in receiving proximal sensory input that feed into body scheme (the internal awareness of the body and the relationship of body parts to one another), movement, and orientation.

Using a cane for identification purposes also can be a safeguard to alert others that the student does not have typical vision. Visual latency may cause a student's visual regard of motorists to be delayed, so that he or she walks out in front of a moving car. Studies have concluded that for pedestrians waiting to cross a street, using a cane increased drivers' yielding to them from 52 percent to 63 percent, and when the pedestrian walked into the street, preparing to cross, using a cane increased motorists' yielding rate from 41 percent to about 90 percent (Bourquin, Wall Emerson, & Sauerburger, 2011).

Through observation, an O&M specialist can assess a student's awareness and ability to avoid obstacles and detect drop-offs and stairs. Although a student may appear proficient in familiar areas with detecting drop-offs, stairs, and obstacles, novel areas may still pose an issue. Observation in a novel location will provide an insight into the student's level of proficiency for unanticipated or unpracticed hazard detection. The specialist can observe the student's foot position on stairs and drop-offs to determine if he or she compensates by increasing proprioceptive cues at the edge of drop-offs. For example, a student with CVI may position a foot so that the toes are off the edge, unsupported by the step, to feel the drop-off, rather than keeping the whole foot securely supported on the step. This may indicate a need for a cane to provide additional information so the student will not be as likely to compensate with unsafe foot placement and strategies like looking down as he or she travels stairs.

The presence of the following CVI characteristics may indicate that instruction in cane techniques is indicated:

- **Visual latency:** Use of the cane should be carefully considered so that obstacles and drop-offs that have not been visually processed within an efficient time frame can be detected by the cane in sufficient time to avoid unintentional contact.

- **Visual field preferences:** If the student has difficulty accessing his or her lower field or either peripheral field, use of the cane should be carefully considered to increase detection of drop-offs and obstacles in the less regarded fields.

- **Difficulties with visual complexity:** Use of the cane should be carefully considered to allow the student a means to detect environmental obstacles and drop-offs in more complex environments, such as areas with many visual elements, patterns, colors, movements, and sounds, while he or she looks ahead and uses vision to locate more distant salient features to guide the line of travel and navigational choices.

- **Difficulty with distance viewing:** Use of the cane should be carefully considered to increase the student's independence and safety for travel in larger spaces, as he or she may not be able to visually access environmental features at further distances to anticipate upcoming obstacles and drop-offs. It may also help the student to maintain a position with the head up in order to use distance viewing within his or her capability.

- **Difficulty with visual novelty:** Use of the cane needs to be carefully considered for less familiar areas so that unexpected and novel features that go unnoticed visually can be detected by the cane.

Phase I

Precane skills, such as maintaining a grasp on the mobility cane grip and exploring the immediate environment with the cane tip, are foundational precursor skills to using the cane during mobility from one location to another. In Phase I, students may not reach out for the cane and grasp it independently. However, early exposure and experience can be provided in helping students visually regard and hold an adapted cane. Canes can be adapted for unresolved CVI characteristics by wrapping the grip with reflective Mylar tape in the student's preferred color and presenting it to him or her in a highly controlled environment.

Phase II

For students in Phase II, using a cane may help them move within their environment with greater visual awareness by eliciting their attention to visually regard features and obstacles detected by the cane tip in near space. Specific cane techniques need to be taught separately from visually locating and regarding landmarks. The O&M specialist should select familiar and less complex environments when teaching cane techniques, because students might experience increased disorientation in novel and complex environments and be unable to achieve the lesson's objectives.

Phase III

Many people, even some O&M specialists, may question whether students in Phase III need to use a mobility cane if they appear sighted. But if a student has unresolved CVI characteristics, such as visual field preferences or difficulty with distance viewing, novelty, or visual latency, he or she may miss important clues to safety hazards, including drop-offs and other obstacles that a cane might have detected.

Using the cane may also help students with CVI maintain a neutral head position if they tend to move their head around to compensate for less-regarded visual fields. Students who have been visually impaired since birth often maintain a forward head posture, possibly as a protective measure in case of collision with obstacles (Rosen, 2010; Tavares et al., 2014) or as a functional consequence of not having visual access to a point on the horizon. By maintaining a posture in which they look ahead, students in Phase III CVI can regard visually accessible features of the environment located at further distances, such as 10 to 15 feet away. Thus, they can more efficiently scan and regard the environment's salient features by maintaining a better-aligned posture with cane in hand to guide their mobility in a more efficient and safe manner. Cane contact allows the student with CVI to have a constant anchor to the external world and enables more efficient use of vision for recognizing landmarks.

A lesson in both proper cane technique and scanning and searching for landmarks may be too complex a task, even for a student in Phase III and even within familiar environments. Cane technique instruction should follow the traditional progression of learning in familiar indoor environments before moving to less-familiar and outdoor spaces. Lessons should start with simple I (straight travel without any direction changes) and L routes (travel with one direction change) before progressing to more complex U (travel with two turns in the same direction) and Z routes (travel with two turns in opposite directions). Once a student has learned to perform cane techniques in a noncomplex environment, he or she may start to tolerate some increased sensory complexity, such as background noise, and increased novelty, such as navigating less familiar community settings while using the cane for mobility.

Guidelines for Targets, Landmarks, and Strategies

In both orientation and mobility lessons, targets, landmarks, and other supports need to be carefully and intentionally selected for students with CVI so that they will be visually accessible. Likewise, instructional strategies need to be selected based on students' specific unresolved behavioral characteristics in addition to their phase of CVI.

A *target,* as used in this chapter, is a particular object, landmark, or feature in the environment, to which students with CVI need to visually attend in order to know where they are. A *landmark* is a term commonly used in O&M to describe "objects, sounds, odors, temperatures, tactile or visual clues that are easily recognized, are constant, and have discrete, permanent locations in the environment that can give a traveler unique, specific information about the individual's location in space" (Wiener et al., 2010, p. 799).

Targets for students with CVI should be selected based on their visual aspects that make them visually accessible to students. This requires considering students' unresolved CVI characteristics when choosing targets intended to elicit their visual attention so they will know where they are in a specific environment and to guide their line of travel and directional changes while navigating a route. An example of a target or landmark might be a fire hydrant at a particular street corner. The O&M specialist may instruct a student to find the fire hydrant at the southeast corner of the intersection of Miller and Wayne Streets. After the student orients to the fire hydrant to confirm where he or she is, the O&M specialist may have the student turn left at the hydrant to make a directional change in the route. A more visually accessible target for another student with CVI and unresolved characteristics of attraction to movement and attraction to light might be a commercial backlit sign in front of the corner business at the intersection.

Table 6.3 presents guidelines for the characteristics of targets, landmarks, and strategies to be used in both orientation and mobility lessons for individuals in each phase of CVI and for each of the CVI behavioral characteristics.

Special Considerations

O&M instruction for individuals with visual impairments should not be contingent on their attainment of independent mobility, a specific age, particular locomotor skills, cognitive abilities, or other disabilities. This is especially important to remember when serving children with CVI, since, unlike ocular visual impairments, CVI results from a brain disorder, disease, or injury that has the potential to affect an individual's motor skills and development as well as his or her vision. If O&M instruction is postponed until an individual achieves independent mobility, significant opportunities will be lost to learn basic orientation and problem-solving skills for those who develop independent mobility later or not at all. The following sections list some special considerations for individuals with CVI depending on whether or not they are ambulatory.

Special Considerations for Individuals with CVI Who Are Ambulatory

Individuals who have CVI and are ambulatory require careful O&M assessment to determine their degree of orientation while traveling along routes. Is an individual aware of and visually processing salient features and landmarks along the way? Is the individual aimless in his or her movement or does he or she move with purpose and efficiency from one destination to another? Individuals with CVI need to know how they get to where they are going by noticing salient visual features that guide their direction and knowledge of their position along a route. Simply traveling from one location to another is not sufficient to become a purposeful, independent traveler, as that approach only addresses the mobility aspect of traveling and neglects to address orientation.

O&M instruction should be tailored to utilize salient features and landmarks in routes that meet the phase-specific guidelines (see Table 6.3) for students' unresolved characteristics in order to allow orientation to occur simultaneously with mobility.

TABLE 6.3

Guidelines for Orientation and Mobility for Each CVI Characteristic

Characteristic	Orientation Guidelines	Mobility Guidelines
Phase I		
Color preference	Use targets of the student's preferred bright color or adapt targets intended for the student's visual regard using this color.	Provide targets of a highly saturated, preferred color for the student to visually regard to encourage upright head position and posture while moving.
Need for movement	Select targets or landmarks that have movement qualities or mark them with material that has movement properties (such as Mylar). It may be necessary to actually move, shake, or tap the target to elicit the student's visual regard.	Movement activity that activates the student's vestibular system, such as jumping or swinging, before traveling a route, may improve the student's visual regard of targets during the route.
Visual latency	Allow extra time, up to 60 seconds, to achieve visual regard of the target after the student encounters it within the distance and in the visual fields where he or she is consistently able to visually regard objects.	Allow the student to familiarize to the visual target by traveling by and encountering it and stopping within a few feet of it for a minute or so multiple times each day over several days. Four or five trips by the target may need to take place during the lesson before the student can be expected to visually regard the target.
Visual field preferences	Position visual targets or selected landmarks in the student's preferred visual fields and within the distance at which he or she is consistently able to visually regard objects.	Ask the student to move toward only those targets located in his or her preferred visual fields. Use of a mobility cane may need to be considered to detect obstacles and drop-offs located in nonpreferred visual fields.
Difficulties with visual complexity	**Targets:** Use solid-colored, three-dimensional items without patterns as targets to attract the student's visual regard. The selected target should be described with two or three salient characteristics incorporating concepts that have been previously introduced or taught (e.g., a specific shape, color, or texture). Two-dimensional targets will not likely be regarded. **Background array:** The background behind the selected visual targets should be plain, without any additional elements.	**Targets:** Ask the student to move toward a specific, simple target (based on orientation target guidelines). If in a wheelchair, the student can indicate the direction in which to be moved (e.g., by head turn, arm movement, activating switch buttons, etc.). **Background array:** Additional background elements besides the simple visual target itself may result in deterioration of the student's posture (e.g., lowered head or poor body control).

(continued on next page)

TABLE 6.3 *(continued)*

Characteristic	Orientation Guidelines	Mobility Guidelines
	Sensory environment: There should be minimal to no background noise and no visual distractions in the student's visual fields. Present verbal description before and after the target is presented; there should be no auditory input when the student is looking. The student should be well supported posturally, with head support for students with decreased head and body control.	**Sensory environment:** Do not ask the student to move when there are other people or noise in the environment. He or she should be well supported if in a mobility device (i.e., wheelchair, gait trainer, adapted bike, walker, etc.).
	Human faces: Do not ask the student to make eye contact or look at faces, as this task is too complex for students in Phase I, given the multiple features and fine details of the human face.	**Human faces:** The student can be asked to turn or move toward the sound of a person or a voice. The student should not be asked to make eye contact or look at others' faces.
Need for light	Select targets or landmarks that reflect light or are backlit for increased visual regard.	Lighting a target in a dimmed environment can help to elicit movement toward it, such as turning toward, reaching, crawling, or walking.
Difficulty with distance viewing	Orient the student to visual targets from a maximum of 2 to 3 feet away.	Have the student move toward large targets (at least 2 feet by 2 feet in size) at a maximum distance of 5 feet away to reduce the complexity of the array and promote greater visual detection of the intended target.
Absent or atypical visual reflexes	The student may not be aware of bright lights and fast-moving threats.	Head protection needs to be considered when the student is moving through areas with potential upper-body obstacles due to inconsistency of visual threat reflexes.
Difficulty with visual novelty	Present and orient the student to the target multiple times before expecting spontaneous visual regard. Help the student develop cognitive understanding of the target by explicitly describing it. Be sure the target incorporates characteristics that the student has visually regarded in the past.	Encourage movement within familiar environments toward familiar targets during familiar routines and transitions. In unfamiliar environments, use human guide technique and describe salient features before and after travel to help the student build familiarity with the environment.
Absence of visually guided reach	First, elicit visual orientation toward a target by reducing environmental and target complexity. However, the student will not be able to orient efficiently to a target while manipulating it, so provide verbal instructions and hand-under-hand guidance to support execution of motoric actions after visual orientation has been achieved.	Reaching toward a target is likely to occur separately from visual regard.

206

TABLE 6.3 *(continued)*

Characteristic	Orientation Guidelines	Mobility Guidelines
Phase II		
Color preference	Targets intended for the student's visual regard may have two to three colors maximum.	Provide highly saturated colored targets in the intermediate distance range (5–10 feet) for the student to move toward.
Need for movement	Targets and landmarks may need to have movement qualities to elicit visual regard beyond near space (greater than 3–5 feet away).	The student may be able to move toward targets that move or have movement qualities that are located outside near space (greater than 5 feet).
Visual latency	Allow extra processing time for visual understanding of the target to occur.	The student may travel by landmarks or targets during routes without visually processing them due to a delay in visual processing after eye-to-target fixation occurs, even in familiar environments. Ask the student to give an indication that he or she has passed the landmark (e.g., by verbalizing, touching the target, or raising a hand when the student gets to it) to confirm the student's understanding and visual processing of the environment.
Visual field preferences	Visual targets or landmarks that are extremely familiar and motivating may be positioned in the student's less-regarded visual fields. Less-familiar targets or landmarks should be very similar in characteristics to motivating and preferred targets and be positioned within the student's preferred fields.	Generally, the student should be asked to move toward visual targets positioned within his or her preferred visual fields to elicit the optimal visual regard for orientation in order to guide mobility. The student may be asked to visually attend to and move toward targets outside of his or her preferred fields if the target has qualities that have movement or reflect light or are strongly preferred and familiar.
Difficulties with visual complexity	**Targets:** The selected target should be three-dimensional and may have up to one pattern with a maximum of two colors, or no pattern with up to three colors. **Background array:** Backgrounds may have an additional one to two elements that are within view, but not directly behind or close to the intended visual target.	**Targets:** The student may be asked to move from one target to a second target appropriate for Phase II (based on orientation target guidelines) within a mini-route (e.g., from one location or landmark within the classroom to another in the same classroom). **Background array:** The student may be able to move toward visual targets despite a complex background array (e.g., multiple colored and patterned background elements) as his or her environment becomes more familiar.

(continued on next page)

TABLE 6.3 *(continued)*

Characteristic	Orientation Guidelines	Mobility Guidelines
	Sensory environment: The student may now tolerate a low level of background noise and movement while orienting to and looking at a target. **Human faces:** Human faces continue to be complex targets, but the student may spontaneously look at faces of highly familiar people once a familiar person's voice is recognized to support this task.	**Sensory environment:** The student may move in environments with low levels of noise and movement of others. **Human faces:** The student may initiate interaction (e.g., smile, brightening, acknowledgment) with a familiar person within familiar environments. The student may have difficulty initiating interaction with a familiar person in a novel or unexpected environment in which it is out of context to encounter that familiar individual.
Need for light	Two-dimensional targets may be used as landmarks if they are backlit to support visual attention.	The student may be able to move toward backlit targets that are located outside near space (greater than 5 feet).
Difficulty with distance viewing	Most targets will need to be within 3 feet to attract the student's visual regard and movement toward them.	Have the student move toward targets that are within 5 to 10 feet away.
Absent or atypical visual reflexes	Visual threat and blink-to-touch reflexes may be inconsistently present. The student will need to be thoroughly oriented to areas of potential upper-body threats and obstacles to increase safety awareness and caution in the environment.	The student needs to be provided preview of areas of the environment where safety is threatened by fast-moving objects (e.g., swings or moving balls) and to visually scan an area thoroughly before traveling through it. Protective techniques should be taught and their use encouraged.
Difficulty with visual novelty	The selected target or landmark should share characteristics with a known preferred item. Comparative language should be used to link characteristics that are like those of the preferred item and distinguish characteristics that are unlike those of the preferred item in order for the student to build a new visual scheme around the less-familiar target.	Encourage the student's spontaneous, purposeful mobility, encouraging orientation to specific familiar targets within familiar environments. Teach use of a mobility cane or adaptive mobility device, if appropriate, within familiar environments, with the intention of ultimately transferring its use to novel environments. Use human guide technique in less well-known environments with comparative language during travel to help the student make associations and visual schemes to support new learning of concepts and novel landmarks and targets.

TABLE 6.3 *(continued)*

Characteristic	Orientation Guidelines	Mobility Guidelines
Absence of visually guided reach	Looking and reaching toward a target may occur simultaneously in controlled environments. The student will require explicit pre-teaching of routine and familiar visual-motor skills to be able to orient to those movements in his or her environment and routines.	Even when look and reach occur simultaneously, the student may not be able to independently perform multistep visual-motor tasks (e.g., opening doors or removing a backpack hanging on a high hook) within a mobility route. The student will likely be unable to efficiently imitate visual-motor tasks and will require explicit pre-teaching of movements that are part of routines and activities.
Phase III		
Color preference	Targets intended for the student's visual regard may have multiple colors and should be highly saturated in color.	Provide targets of or adapted with a highly saturated color in the intermediate distance (10–20 feet) for the student to move toward.
Need for movement	Targets may need to have movement qualities to elicit visual regard beyond intermediate space (greater than 10 feet away).	The student may be able to move toward targets located outside of his or her intermediate space (10–20 feet away) if selected targets move or have inherent movement qualities.
Visual latency	Even if eye-to-object fixation is achieved with a visual target, latency may still be occurring. Have the student indicate (e.g., verbally or using a switch or raising a hand) when he or she notices the target to ensure that the student is oriented to the selected target.	The student may travel by landmarks or targets during routes without visually processing them due to a delay in visual processing after eye-to-target fixation occurs, particularly in novel environments. Ask the student to give an indication that he or she has passed the landmark (e.g., by verbalizing, touching the target, or raising a hand when the student gets to it) to confirm the student's understanding and visual processing of the environment.
Visual field preferences	Visual targets that are extremely familiar and motivating may be positioned in the student's less-regarded fields. With less-familiar targets, select those that are very similar in characteristics to motivating targets. Positioning of these less-familiar targets should be within the student's preferred visual fields.	The student may be asked to visually attend to and move toward targets outside of his or her preferred fields if the selected targets have salient features the student is familiar with.

(continued on next page)

TABLE 6.3 *(continued)*

Characteristic	Orientation Guidelines	Mobility Guidelines
Difficulties with visual complexity	**Targets:** Selected visual targets can now be two-dimensional and may have several colors if they incorporate a familiar concept.	**Targets:** The student may be asked to move between three targets (based on orientation target complexity guidelines) along a longer route (e.g., from one room as a starting point into a hallway, to a landmark to inform a travel decision, such as "right" or "left" along the route, and on to another room as the final destination).
	Background array: Backgrounds to visual targets or landmarks may have additional elements that are within view, but the additional elements may interfere with the student's recognition or identification of the target and subsequent orientation within the space if not in a highly familiar environment.	**Background array:** The student may be able to move toward visual targets despite a complex background array (e.g., multiple colored and patterned background elements), even in a novel environment, as long as selected visual targets incorporate highly familiar concepts.
	Sensory environment: The student may now tolerate a moderate level of background noise and movement while orienting to and looking at a visual target.	**Sensory environment:** The student may move in environments with moderate levels of noise and movement of others.
	Human faces: Human faces continue to be complex targets, but the student may spontaneously look at faces of highly familiar people within the context of expected environments without needing their voice to support recognition. Providing a description of the salient features of a person's physical appearance may facilitate looking toward novel faces.	**Human faces:** The student may initiate interaction with a familiar person within familiar and novel environments. He or she may have difficulty initiating interaction with a novel person in either a familiar or novel environment.
Need for light	Photographs of salient landmarks used to orient the student to a route need to be presented on a backlit medium (such as a tablet). If a landmark needs to be noticed from a distance greater than the one at which the student typically detects visual targets, it is helpful to select a large element in the environment that has backlit qualities.	The student may be able to move toward backlit targets that are located outside of intermediate space (10–20 feet away).
Difficulty with distance viewing	Most targets will need to be within 10 feet to attract the student's visual regard and movement toward them.	Have the student move toward targets that are within 10–20 feet away.

TABLE 6.3 *(continued)*

Characteristic	Orientation Guidelines	Mobility Guidelines
Absent or atypical visual reflexes	Visual threat and blink-to-touch reflexes may be consistently present except when the student is fatigued, ill, in a postictal state (after an epileptic seizure), or the like. The student needs to be thoroughly oriented to areas of potential upper-body threats and obstacles to increase safety awareness and caution in the environment.	The student needs to be provided pre-views of areas of the environment where safety is threatened by fast-moving objects (e.g., swings, moving balls, bicycles) and to visually scan an area thoroughly before traveling through it. Protective techniques should be taught and their use encouraged whenever the student seems fatigued or ill, as visual processing will be more greatly compro-mised during these times.
Difficulty with visual novelty	Novel targets are appropriate to intro-duce in highly familiar environments.	Encourage the student's spontaneous, purposeful mobility within novel envi-ronments by encouraging orientation to specific familiar targets. Use compara-tive language during travel to help the student make associations to already known concepts and broaden his or her visual schemes to support new learning.
Absence of visually guided reach	Looking and reaching toward a target oc-curs more simultaneously. The student will require explicit pre-teaching of novel visual-motor skills to orient to those movements within routines and activities in the environment.	Even when look and reach occur simultaneously, the student may likely be unable to independently perform novel visual-motor tasks (e.g., manipu-lating an unfamiliar door handle) within a mobility route. The student will require demonstration and step-by-step instruc-tions to perform novel visual-motor tasks.

O&M instruction should also focus on addressing orientation within nonacademic routines and activi-ties during the student's school day, such as physical education class and social opportunities at recess and lunch. Incorporating accessible and salient tar-gets within nonacademic activities affords students greater visual access to all parts of their education, one of the intentions behind the expanded core curriculum for students with visual impairments.

Special Considerations for Individuals with CVI Who Are Nonambulatory

Individuals who have CVI often have other neuro-logical disabilities, such as cerebral palsy, seizures, or genetic syndromes. O&M assessment and in-struction for these individuals must consider not only the impact of CVI, but also the impact of any other disabilities, including those that affect an indi-vidual's motor abilities or cognitive development.

When individuals have motor impairments that impact their ability to ambulate or be indepen-dently mobile, O&M instruction will need to ac-commodate this additional disability. Individuals may need to use wheelchairs, adaptive seating sys-tems, walkers, gait trainers, or mobility canes to achieve mobility in the most independent way pos-sible. Specialty controls for power wheelchairs may need to be considered for those who do not have adequate motor control of their upper extremities to use a joystick. Collaboration with an individual's physical and occupational therapists is essential for determining appropriate assistive devices to achieve mobility and ways to incorporate use of these additional assistive devices into the O&M program.

The movement provided by a power wheelchair may actually assist individuals who cannot move independently through the environment to access their vision if the CVI characteristic of attraction to movement is not resolved. If the individual also needs a mobility cane to detect obstacles and drop-offs and to preview the immediate environment, then specific instruction, as well as potential adaptations, will be needed to use the mobility cane in conjunction with the assistive device. Wheelchairs can be adapted with modifications such as curb feelers to provide an alternative way for the individual to detect walls and obstacles. Traditional mobility cane techniques can be adapted to enable the individual's detection and preview of environmental features by learning modified techniques. Human guide technique can be also implemented with those in wheelchairs. (See Rosen & Crawford, 2010; and Crawford, n.d., for information about wheelchair modifications, teaching cane use with assistive devices, and human guide techniques for individuals in wheelchairs.)

It is also important to address orientation along with assisted mobility for individuals who cannot move through space independently. Independent mobility can also be addressed on a smaller scale. For example, working with an individual to initiate turning toward or reaching toward a visual target in the environment can fall under the scope of O&M instruction.

For individuals who are nonambulatory, it is essential to provide opportunities for movement throughout space, following specific orientation and visual accommodations (described in Table 6.3), whether individuals are pushed in a wheelchair, moving themselves in a power chair, riding an adapted tricycle, or using whatever independent locomotor means is available to them, including crawling or scooting.

Special Considerations for Individuals with CVI Who Have Multiple Disabilities

Although it might seem obvious that decreased interaction with others and with the environment among individuals with CVI who also have multiple disabilities can be attributed to comorbid motor impairments or cognitive delays, vision is the sense that directs these other functions and capacities. In typically sighted individuals, vision motivates exploration and reaching very early in development. Fazzi et al. (2011) studied the ability to reach to sound for children diagnosed with visual impairment, including some with CVI. The study looked at reaching to sound to indicate acquisition of object permanence as a measure of cognitive development. A majority of one group, consisting of children with visual impairment and multiple disabilities, performed more poorly than the group of children who were blind without additional disabilities, which points to the difficulty that additional disabilities pose in assessing cognitive functioning (Gori, Cappagli, Tonelli, Baud-Bovy, & Finocchietti, 2016). This finding heightens the urgency of addressing a child's visual accessibility early on, or the child may not have an opportunity to develop reaching and exploration skills that lay the foundation for later acquisition of cognitive concepts.

There is a danger in assuming decreased cognitive potential exists because it is not confirmed by traditional measures. Many cognitive assessment tools use visual information that is not accessible to individuals with CVI. An individual must be able to respond to the visual information used by such tools in order to register a certain level of cognition. If professionals can give individuals with CVI and multiple disabilities opportunities to develop vision through adapted targets, materials, environments, and specific approaches aimed at helping them regard and interpret visual stimuli, they can enable sufficient vision to guide acquisition and further development of other capabilities. If an individual is capable of movement, even if it is qualitatively poor and imprecise, he or she is still physically interacting with the environment, which will help develop some amount of spatial understanding of the immediate space.

As recommended by Good, Jan, Burden, Skoczenski, and Candy (2001), "a simplified visual environment is more beneficial to children with CVI because it forces them to focus attention on a particular visual stimulus" (p. 59). They also recommend reinforcement with verbal stimulation. Setting up the environment with simple visual targets allows the individual first to become aware that there is something to fixate on and, ultimately, to develop the desire to act on it, even if independent interaction with the visual targets is not possible. Verbal mediation, through describing salient visual details, connects the visual image to specific language, which lays the foundation for cognitive concept development to begin as the quantity of visual targets that are regarded increases and patterns emerge. In other words, when the same type of salient visual detail is detected on another target, and the same language is used to describe that detail, the brain can form a cognitive concept around the visually accessible target with a connection to specific language used to describe its visual appearance. Then the brain can interpret similar details in visual targets encountered in the future with connected language that allows the brain to store and later retrieve a visual memory.

For individuals who have complex needs, facilitating the use of vision should be prioritized and addressed to support the development of other capacities, such as language, cognition, and motor skills. The O&M specialist's role is to work on orienting individuals to accessible visual targets in quiet, simplified environments before moving on to attempting orientation in complex environments, with or without adapted targets and conditions. Orientation can begin to be integrated with mobility by encouraging individuals to initiate purposeful mobility by moving through space toward accessible visual targets in smaller, quiet familiar environments.

Examples of CVI Considerations in Orientation Instruction

This section presents examples of how O&M lessons that teach orientation in space would differ with and without consideration of the CVI Range principles. Vignettes are provided for each CVI characteristic and phase to illustrate how the CVI characteristics can be integrated with O&M concepts and techniques as students progress through the phases of CVI. (Please note that the CVI characteristic of atypical visual reflexes is not used in any type of intervention strategy, including O&M instruction. These reflex differences are part of the CVI Range protocol only.) Orientation is the focus here because orientation is a precursor to purpose-driven mobility. Efficient and purposeful mobility happens as a result of sufficient orientation to a space.

As already noted, the selection of materials, landmarks, and instructional approaches needs to be tailored to students' present level of visual functioning so that they can immediately visually access at least portions of the world around them. Understanding and considering students' visual preferences, aversions, and difficulties when selecting visual targets will allow them to use their vision in a more sustained way. This, in turn, will create brain changes to support greater use of vision in the future—an example of Hebb's (1949/2002) axiom, "neurons that fire together wire together" (p. 62). That is, each time a student uses vision to attend to a visually accessible target in the environment, the connection between the sets of brain cells responsible for visually processing that target is strengthened to support greater use of his or her vision in the future.

The following examples provide dual perspectives on the same situation. The first example for each CVI characteristic depicts a scenario in which the student is not given a visually accessible target to orient to, so the student's use of vision to access the environment is not facilitated. The student must use other senses like touch, hearing, and smell, which are much less efficient and confirming than vision, to know where he or she is in space. The second example for each characteristic depicts a situation in which the student's unresolved characteristics and phase of CVI are carefully considered when selecting appropriate visual targets. This systematic approach to landmark or target selection and instruction elicits the student's vision, at its present level, to access at least some parts of the environment so that the student knows where he or she is in space.

Orientation Instruction Related to Color Preference

Phase I

WITHOUT CVI CONSIDERATIONS. The O&M specialist plans to orient Taylor to her preschool classroom. He uses a natural-toned wooden block against a white background to represent an object cue to designate the block center. Taylor is encouraged to touch this object cue with hand-under-hand guidance to make her aware that she is at the block center.

WITH CVI CONSIDERATIONS. The O&M specialist plans to orient Taylor to her preschool classroom. She has appeared to visually regard red items in the past. The O&M specialist uses a large, bright, red block against a black background to represent an object cue to designate the block center. Taylor is encouraged to orient to this object cue so that she knows that she is at the block center. Other adaptations to address Taylor's unresolved CVI characteristics and enhance Taylor's ability to visually attend to the highly saturated colored object cue consist of a clip-on LED gooseneck light shining on the object cue and reduction of the complexity of the surrounding environment.

Phase II

WITHOUT CVI CONSIDERATIONS. Claude meets with his O&M specialist to be oriented to his new elementary school. The O&M specialist uses a black-and-white drawing that represents the hallways and doorways of the school. He describes the hallways and helps Claude follow along on the paper map. He encourages Claude to count the doorways from the corner of the hallway intersection to the doorway of his classroom destination and has Claude use a black marker to trace the route from the school entrance to the classroom.

WITH CVI CONSIDERATIONS. Claude meets with his O&M specialist to be oriented to his new elementary school. The O&M specialist shows Claude photographic images of key features of the school environment presented on a tablet and enlarged to eliminate background details. The selected key features include a bright yellow reception office door, a red flag that is consistently suspended outside the gymnasium, and windows at the corner of the hallway where Claude's classroom is located. The O&M specialist reviews the images with Claude until he is consistently able to identify the main feature in each image and in the physical space. The O&M specialist also marks the selected key features on a map of the school's main hallways and doorways that she created using a tactile map kit. He takes a photograph of the map on the tablet and imports it into an app that allows the user to draw on top of photographs. In addition to reviewing the photographic images of the key features along the route in sequential order, he has Claude use a fluorescent-colored line to trace the route from the school doorway to the classroom destination on the photograph of the tactile map before he travels the route.

Phase III

WITHOUT CVI CONSIDERATIONS. Chandra's O&M specialist introduces her to a new route in the school. He verbally points out the landmarks to ori-

Alisha Waugh

A photograph of a map created with a tactile map kit has been imported into an app on a tablet that allows a student to trace a route with his finger in his preferred color.

Alisha Waugh

These permanent landmarks along a route have been marked with bright green duct tape to draw the visual attention of a student in Phase III CVI so that she knows where she is along the route.

ent to so that Chandra knows when she is at the beginning, middle, and end of the route and has her feel their texture as she passes by.

WITH CVI CONSIDERATIONS. Chandra's O&M specialist introduces her to a new route in the school. He has her orient to permanent landmarks along the route, such as the classroom doorframe at the beginning of the route, a water fountain midway through, and a display case on the wall by the end destination. All the landmarks are outlined with fluorescent green duct tape to help Chandra dis-

embed the salient landmarks from their background and identify where she is along the route at any given time.

Orientation Instruction Related to Attraction to Movement

Phase I

WITHOUT CVI CONSIDERATIONS. Ben has difficulty visually regarding any stationary items, even when presented for prolonged periods in one position. Ben's O&M specialist instructs the paraeducator to always position Ben's cup by his plate at 10 o'clock, saying that he will eventually orient to it tactilely when he wants a drink.

WITH CVI CONSIDERATIONS. Ben has difficulty visually regarding any stationary items, even when presented for prolonged periods in one position. Ben's O&M specialist has the paraeducator shake Ben's cup in his preferred visual field so that he will notice it and indicate when he wants a drink.

Phase II

WITHOUT CVI CONSIDERATIONS. Isabella struggles with visually locating her lunch bag among her classmates' lunch bags sitting on the shelf. The O&M specialist asks the teacher to give the lunch bag directly to Isabella since it is difficult for her to find it.

WITH CVI CONSIDERATIONS. Isabella struggles with visually locating her lunch bag among her classmates' lunch bags sitting on the shelf. The O&M specialist attaches a bundle of reflective Mylar ribbons onto the bag's handle, which creates the effect of movement to draw Isabella's visual attention to the bag that belongs to her.

Phase III

WITHOUT CVI CONSIDERATIONS. Noah has difficulty finding his friends' location at recess when they are far away. The O&M specialist tells Noah to walk up to groups of kids, scanning the groups until he eventually recognizes his friends.

WITH CVI CONSIDERATIONS. Noah has difficulty finding his friends' location at recess when they are far away. The O&M specialist teaches Noah's friends to wave their arms overhead when they are not close by to attract Noah's visual attention. He also teaches Noah to self-advocate for this need by reminding his friends to do so as needed.

Orientation Instruction Related to Visual Latency

Phase I

WITHOUT CVI CONSIDERATIONS. Aiden has a prolonged period of latency when orienting toward familiar items. The O&M specialist instructs the teacher and teacher's assistant to attempt regular presentations of a variety of items in Aiden's preferred visual field to determine which items he will orient toward.

WITH CVI CONSIDERATIONS. Aiden has a prolonged period of latency when orienting toward familiar items. The O&M specialist instructs the teacher and teacher's assistant to present intentionally selected items for extra-long periods each time, with multiple presentation attempts, before deciding that Aiden will not orient toward them.

Phase II

WITHOUT CVI CONSIDERATIONS. Becca demonstrates visual latency when she is tired, more in the second half of the day. The O&M specialist teaches her to listen to environmental sounds (such as telephones ringing in the office, a piano playing in the music room, and echoing voices in the gym) to orient to the classrooms she must find in the afternoon.

WITH CVI CONSIDERATIONS. Becca demonstrates visual latency when she is tired, more in the second half of the day. The O&M specialist teaches her to think about the salient features of the landmarks she uses to know if she has made it to her destination for the afternoon class before she travels the route. This helps her visually process and orient to the environment more efficiently by knowing what to look for before she gets there.

Phase III

WITHOUT CVI CONSIDERATIONS. Lexi still demonstrates visual latency, particularly in novel environments. She was asked by her O&M specialist to orient to the location of the elevator in a novel setting by listening for auditory cues, like the "ding" before the door opens and the sounds of the opening and closing doors.

WITH CVI CONSIDERATIONS. Lexi still demonstrates visual latency, particularly in novel environments. She was pre-taught the visual concept of "elevator" during an O&M lesson by looking at online images of various elevators before being

Alisha Waugh

Looking up online images of environmental concepts, such as an elevator, during a lesson as part of concept-development activities can help students in Phase III have an image ready to hold in their mind's eye as they try to find an actual one in a novel setting.

asked to find one in a new environment. Then Lexi was asked by her O&M specialist to orient to the location of the elevator in a novel setting by thinking about and visualizing the salient features of an elevator like those she had viewed beforehand online, such as the button panel positioned on the wall a few feet above the floor and the thick, wide frame on the exterior wall that surrounds the elevator opening. This metacognitive activity—sustaining an awareness of her own thinking—helps to decrease the latency Lexi experiences in novel situations.

Orientation Instruction Related to Visual Field Preferences

Phase I
WITHOUT CVI CONSIDERATIONS. When Aisha attempts eye-to-object fixation, she regards items only peripherally, in her left visual field. Her O&M

specialist wants her to be able to orient to the teacher during circle time activities. He has Aisha sit in the circle directly across from the teacher so that the teacher is front and center, directly in Aisha's central viewing field.

WITH CVI CONSIDERATIONS. When Aisha attempts eye-to-object fixation, she regards items only peripherally, in her left visual field. Her O&M specialist wants her to be able to orient to the teacher during circle time activities. He has Aisha sit in the circle directly on the teacher's right side so that the teacher is in her preferred left visual field for instruction during circle time.

Phase II
WITHOUT CVI CONSIDERATIONS. Jayden does not consistently visually regard objects in his upper or left visual fields. The boys' and girls' restrooms are located next to one another, but the signs are located high on the wall and left of each doorway. Jayden needs to be able to orient to the boys' restroom sign before walking in to verify that he is entering the correct restroom. His O&M specialist has him attempt to scan for the sign before he walks in.

WITH CVI CONSIDERATIONS. Jayden does not consistently visually regard objects in his upper or left visual fields. The boys' and girls' restrooms are located next to one another, but the signs are located high on the wall and left of each doorway. Jayden needs to be able to orient to the boys' restroom sign before walking in to verify that he is entering the correct restroom. His O&M specialist places a conspicuous sign lower on the doorframe and on the right side of the doorway, located within Jayden's preferred visual fields, so that he can visually access the sign.

Phase III
WITHOUT CVI CONSIDERATIONS. Sophia often misses visual information in her immediate lower field. Her classroom teacher has assigned her the lowest mailbox cubby closest to the floor. Sophia's O&M specialist encourages her to scan down to the floor to find her mailbox cubby.

WITH CVI CONSIDERATIONS. Sophia often misses visual information in her immediate lower field. Her classroom teacher has assigned her the lowest mailbox cubby closest to the floor. Sophia's O&M specialist asks the teacher to assign Sophia the top mailbox cubby, located 3 feet above the floor, for easier visual access.

Orientation Instruction Related to Difficulties with Visual Complexity

Phase I

WITHOUT CVI CONSIDERATIONS. Thomas's O&M specialist wants him to be able to anticipate the routine schedule of the school day. She uses eight multicolored icons on a page of Thomas's augmentative alternative communication device to represent the different subjects and routines for the day. The O&M specialist reviews the schedule during a transition time when students are moving around and making noise in Thomas's immediate area.

WITH CVI CONSIDERATIONS. Thomas's O&M specialist wants him to be able to anticipate the routine schedule of the school day. She uses objects of a single color that are utilized in each specific routine to represent the different subjects and routines for the day. The O&M specialist presents the objects in isolation, one at a time, against a plain background, in a quiet environment, and in sequential order of the day's activities so that Thomas may anticipate the day's events to come.

Phase II

WITHOUT CVI CONSIDERATIONS. Kaylee meets with her O&M specialist during a class change to learn where her locker is in the hallway. Since all the lockers are identical, her O&M specialist teaches her to count the locker doors, starting at her homeroom door. Many students are opening and closing their lockers and talking all around Kaylee, and there are multiple posters hanging on the wall around her locker.

WITH CVI CONSIDERATIONS. Kaylee meets with her O&M specialist to learn where her locker is in the hallway 10 minutes before a class change, while the hallway is fairly quiet. The wall immediately be-side her locker is free from visual clutter. A three-dimensional object—a tassel—hangs from her locker latch to differentiate it from the others. Her O&M specialist adds an accommodation to Kaylee's Individualized Education Program to allow her five minutes before each class change to orient to her locker in a quieter, less-complex environment.

Phase III

WITHOUT CVI CONSIDERATIONS. Ryan needs to be oriented to the different playground activities available at recess. The O&M specialist visits each item in the playground with Ryan during recess, when students are running around and yelling. As Ryan's fellow classmates speak to him in passing, he appears unable to identify them. The O&M specialist encourages Ryan to respond but does not ask the students to identify themselves, as Ryan appears to look at their faces when they pass by.

WITH CVI CONSIDERATIONS. Ryan needs to be oriented to the different playground activities available at recess. The O&M specialist plans her orientation lessons for quiet times without other students outside. She makes a simple map using a tactile map kit and marks the main playground items on it. She also uses photographs of the same playground items enlarged on a tablet to carefully review their salient features with Ryan. They review the map and photos, discussing each item's salient features multiple times during the lesson: once at the beginning before going up to each specific playground item, again as they are at each specific item, and at the end of the lesson after visiting each item.

After Ryan has been thoroughly oriented to the various playground features over two weeks' time, the O&M specialist observes him at recess with his peers present. When she notices that he is not approaching his friends and not readily responding to peers who speak to him, she realizes that Ryan is not recognizing his friends' faces due to the visual complexity of the human face and creates a plan to address this. With the permission of Ryan and his parents, she provides his classmates with a brief lesson about Ryan's CVI diagnosis and resulting difficulty in recognizing faces. She teaches Ryan's

The locker of a student in Phase II CVI has Mylar fringe hanging from the top to differentiate it from the other lockers and help her locate it despite the complexity of the surrounding environment.

classmates to always say their name when approaching him out of context when outside to help him respond to them. She also suggests that Ryan orient to his friends' coats to avoid the visual complexity of faces and to provide an additional clue for recognition. She tells Ryan to speak up for himself when he doesn't know who is talking to him by politely reminding his classmates to tell him their names.

Orientation Instruction Related to Attraction to Light

Phase I

WITHOUT CVI CONSIDERATIONS. Emily is consistently attracted to lights and often gazes for ex-tended periods at light coming through the window. She needs to orient to her assigned seat in music class. Her O&M specialist consults with the music teacher and decides to seat her directly by the window for the best natural lighting.

WITH CVI CONSIDERATIONS. Emily is consistently attracted to lights and often gazes for extended periods at light coming in through the window. She needs to orient to her assigned seat in music class. Her O&M specialist consults with the music teacher on where to position a light-up foam stick, to be turned on before class begins, to help Emily locate her assigned seat. The O&M specialist recommends that Emily should face away from the windows to decrease her light gazing.

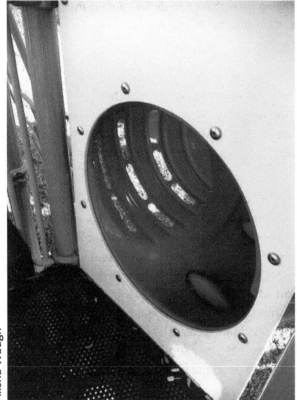

A large, visually complex playground apparatus (top), and photographs enlarged to zoom in on specific parts of the equipment to reduce the complexity when reviewing their salient features (bottom).

Phase II

WITHOUT CVI CONSIDERATIONS. Joey's visual attention is more efficiently focused on backlit or light-emitting targets, resulting in less visual fatigue. When his O&M specialist consults with the physical education teacher, she suggests using a beeper ball during ball games to help Joey orient toward the ball's location.

WITH CVI CONSIDERATIONS. Joey's visual attention is more efficiently focused on backlit or light-emitting targets, resulting in less visual fatigue. When his O&M specialist consults with the physical education teacher, she suggests using LED light-up balls and light-up pylon cones to help Joey orient more efficiently toward the ball and goal boundaries for various games.

Phase III

WITHOUT CVI CONSIDERATIONS. Matthew has difficulty orienting to his locker at the end of the day when he is more visually fatigued. His O&M specialist teaches him to count the locker doors starting from the water fountain to find his own locker later in the school day when visual fatigue has set in and he needs to gather his belongings.

WITH CVI CONSIDERATIONS. Matthew has difficulty orienting to his locker at the end of the day when he is more visually fatigued. His O&M specialist fastens a neon-colored, battery-operated string light to his locker door and teaches him to turn it on daily after lunch to provide a support for him later in the school day when visual fatigue has set in and he needs to gather his belongings.

Orientation Instruction Related to Difficulty with Distance Viewing

Phase I

WITHOUT CVI CONSIDERATIONS. Miguel can demonstrate eye-to-object fixation on preferred items in strictly controlled environments at distances of 12–18 inches. His O&M specialist asks the teacher to use an auditory cue, the "Good Morning" song, in place of an accessible visual cue to indicate that it is circle time.

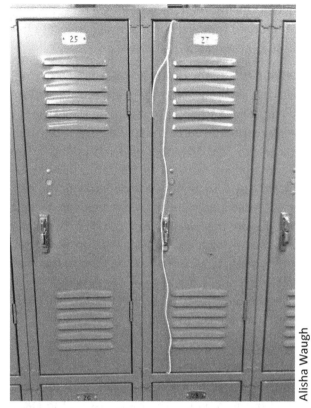

A locker adapted with a neon-colored string light to draw a student's visual attention at times when he experiences visual fatigue.

Alisha Waugh

WITH CVI CONSIDERATIONS. Miguel can demonstrate eye-to-object fixation on preferred items in strictly controlled environments at distances of 12–18 inches. His O&M specialist asks the para-educator to present an object cue for the routine Miguel is about to participate in against a black background within 12 inches of his face in his most regarded visual field.

Phase II

WITHOUT CVI CONSIDERATIONS. Natasha's O&M specialist is orienting her to her new classroom before the upcoming school year begins. He would like her to travel mini-routes independently within her classroom. The O&M specialist sets up the lesson by instructing Natasha to trail an L mini-route. Starting at a home base, the doorway to the hall, she is to travel south along the east wall, then turn right to travel approximately 8 feet west at the south wall until she tactilely locates a bulletin board. Then she is to square off at the bulletin board to travel north in order to locate her desk approximately 10 feet away.

WITH CVI CONSIDERATIONS. Natasha's O&M specialist is orienting her to her new classroom before the upcoming school year begins. He would like her to travel mini-routes independently within her classroom. The O&M specialist sets up the lesson by instructing Natasha to trail an L mini-route. Starting at a home base, the doorway to the hall, she is to visually orient and move south on the east wall toward the filing cabinet with reflective Mylar paper covering the side facing the doorway. From there, she is to square off at the front of the filing cabinet, visually orient to her desk with a Mylar pinwheel attached to the back of the seat, and travel west about 6 feet to reach it.

Phase III

WITHOUT CVI CONSIDERATIONS. Elizabeth needs to be oriented to her class's picnic area during a field trip to a park with other classes. The O&M specialist has the teacher assign a classmate as her human guide to orient Elizabeth and lead her from the grassy area where the activities are occurring to the pavilion area where the food will be available.

WITH CVI CONSIDERATIONS. Elizabeth needs to be oriented to her class's picnic area during a field trip to a park with other classes. The O&M specialist recommends that the teacher bring a bundle of Mylar balloons to place on the table so that Elizabeth can independently orient to the pavilion area where the food will be available from the grassy area where the activities are occurring. With this support in place, Elizabeth will not have to rely on fellow students or staff to guide her between the two locations.

Orientation Instruction Related to Difficulty with Visual Novelty

Phase I

WITHOUT CVI CONSIDERATIONS. Tanner needs to orient to the sink after using the restroom. The O&M specialist instructs the aide to turn on the

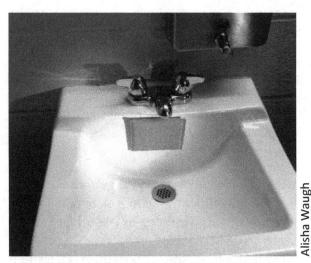

This school sink is adapted with a metallic orange sponge, a familiar, preferred visual target for a student in Phase I CVI, to draw his attention toward the sink.

faucet to help Tanner use the cue of its environmental sound to orient toward it.

WITH CVI CONSIDERATIONS. Tanner needs to orient to the sink after using the restroom. He has briefly and consistently visually oriented recently toward a metallic orange scrub sponge under strictly controlled conditions without competing sounds. The O&M specialist tells the aide to adhere the sponge to the sink bowl to elicit Tanner's visual regard without the water running, as the sound will detract from his ability to look. She recommends that the aide verbalize, "This is a sink," and describe its salient features, for example, "A sink is a big bowl that holds water. There is a metal tube above it called a faucet. Water falls down from the faucet into the bowl called a sink. You can wash your hands or dishes in the sink. A sink also has a small hole at the bottom for the water to empty out of it." The aide is to provide this verbal description before and after giving Tanner the opportunity to look and orient toward the sink and before assisting him in putting his hands into the water.

Phase II

WITHOUT CVI CONSIDERATIONS. Sajda is supposed to place her materials in a bin on the teacher's desk. The O&M specialist teaches Sajda to visually orient to the bin by telling her that it will be located at the near right corner when she is standing in front of the teacher's desk.

WITH CVI CONSIDERATIONS. Sajda is supposed to place her materials in a bin on the teacher's desk. The O&M specialist teaches Sajda to visually orient to the bin by noticing the box on the teacher's desk that is covered with the same colors (green and yellow) and similar pattern (polka dot) as the familiar backpack that she brings to school each day.

Phase III

WITHOUT CVI CONSIDERATIONS. Corey is learning to orient to the computer lab entrance from a hallway with many indistinguishable doors in one area. His O&M specialist plans a lesson to help him to determine whether he has found his correct destination at the end of a route. She tells him to locate the computer lab by counting four doors down on the left after passing the stairwell from the main corridor. This can be an unreliable method to orient to the computer lab entrance, however, in the complex hallway environment when it is filled with many students and noise.

WITH CVI CONSIDERATIONS. Corey is learning to orient to the computer lab entrance from a hallway with many indistinguishable doors in one area. His O&M specialist plans a lesson to help him to determine whether he has found his correct destination

at the end of a route. She instructs him that if he looks into the room and sees tables with multiple computers on them, he will have confirmation that he is in the right place. A computer is a fairly novel concept for Corey, but a flat-screen television is not. From interviewing Corey's mother, the O&M specialist knows that his family has three flat-screen TVs at home that Corey is attracted to. Corey also can easily find TVs in novel situations, such as stores and restaurants. The O&M specialist uses comparative language and the salient features of a computer, a novel concept, to bridge the similarities to a TV, a well-known concept for Corey, for example, stating, "A computer has a rectangle-shaped, dark-colored flat screen just like a television." She also makes sure to point out its differences in order to build a separate concept in Corey's scheme, for example, "A computer is different from a TV because it has a keyboard that is a rectangle shape with square buttons labeled with letters, numbers, and symbols. You can push the buttons to type words so you can look up information from the Internet, write a story, or play a game." The O&M specialist consults with the speech therapist and intervention specialist so that they will also address the concept of computer in their lessons with Corey to build greater familiarity with the concept and its salient features.

Alisha Waugh

A photo of a computer lab (left) and an image on a tablet showing the computer's distinguishing salient feature—its keyboard—enlarged and highlighted in red (right).

Orientation Instruction Related to Absence of Visually Guided Reach

Phase I

WITHOUT CVI CONSIDERATIONS. Cheng Yee's teacher would like him to be able to orient to her gestures during finger-play songs at circle time. His O&M specialist consults on this goal by recommending that the teacher move Cheng Yee's hands using hand-under-hand guidance as she sings the song, with the goal of Cheng Yee eventually being able to visually attend to the movements on his own.

WITH CVI CONSIDERATIONS. Cheng Yee's teacher would like him to be able to orient to her gestures during finger-play songs at circle time. His O&M specialist consults on this goal by educating the teacher that in Phase I CVI, Cheng Yee will have difficulty visually attending to her movements, particularly with the additional sensory input of the sound of her singing and the touch of her hands. He recommends that she sing the song with him daily without gestures to familiarize him with the melody and rhythm. She also recommends reinforcing concepts in the song, such as body parts and positional concepts, by reviewing them separately from circle time on a regular basis, so that the language and associated gestures will eventually acquire some meaning. Once the songs become familiar and the concepts begin to acquire meaning, Cheng Yee should be positioned close enough to the teacher at circle time for opportunities to visually attend briefly to the movements of finger plays.

Phase II

WITHOUT CVI CONSIDERATIONS. Olivia would like to be able to better visually orient to projects she's working on in art class as she uses her hands to manipulate the materials. Her O&M specialist suggests that the art teacher provide Olivia with high-contrast, highly textured materials and an enlarged two-dimensional picture of the finished project to reference as she is working on it.

WITH CVI CONSIDERATIONS. Olivia would like to be able to better visually orient to projects she's working on in art class as she uses her hands to manipulate the materials. Her O&M specialist suggests that the art teacher provide Olivia with familiar three-dimensional materials that have reflective qualities. He also recommends that Olivia's workspace be organized so that it is free from clutter, with a plain background, to help draw Olivia's visual orientation to the materials her hands are manipulating as she uses her vision to guide her hands' movements. He also suggests that a finished three-dimensional model made of familiar, reflective materials be provided for reference as needed, with step-by-step instructions in an accessible format to guide Olivia as the complexity of the task increases and visually guided reach becomes more challenging.

Phase III

WITHOUT CVI CONSIDERATIONS. Tatum has difficulty following along with the physical education teacher's demonstration of novel warm-up stretches at the beginning of gym class. Since Tatum finds it challenging to watch the instructor and perform the novel movement simultaneously, the O&M specialist provides one-on-one auditory mediation during gym class to narrate what is going on as it is happening to help Tatum better keep up in performing the stretches.

WITH CVI CONSIDERATIONS. Tatum has difficulty following along with the physical education teacher's demonstration of novel warm-up stretches at the beginning of gym class. The O&M specialist consults with the physical education teacher ahead of time to find out the specific new stretches that will be added to the planned lessons. He provides previews of the exercises through multiple approaches, including practicing moving through the stretch with auditory instructions and a video preview on a tablet of the teacher performing the stretches. The O&M specialist provides previews of the new stretches several times before gym class that week in a quiet and noncomplex environment. This allows Tatum to become more familiar with the movements motorically so that he can more efficiently visually attend to the teacher's guidance and still participate in the stretches during class.

Conclusion

O&M is an educational related service for individuals with CVI that cannot be disregarded or undervalued. It is essential for individuals with CVI to be able to function with the greatest level of independence and attain skills required for self-determination. However, O&M services cannot be carried out in the usual manner for individuals with CVI. The unique visual and behavioral characteristics that are unresolved in individuals for each phase of CVI must guide the O&M specialist, teacher of students with visual impairments, other professionals, and parents in adapting lessons in O&M, educational curricula, and everyday routines to meet students' present levels of visual functioning and help them to become increasingly independent travelers.

REFERENCES

Amedi, A., Raz, N., Pianka, P., Malach, R., & Zohary, E. (2003). Early "visual" cortex activation correlates with superior verbal memory performance in the blind. *Nature Neuroscience, 6*(7), 758–766.

Bourquin, E., Wall Emerson, R., & Sauerburger, D. (2011). Conditions that influence drivers' yielding behavior for uncontrolled crossings. *Journal of Visual Impairment & Blindness, 105*(11), 760–769.

Crawford, J. S. (n.d.). Orientation and mobility strategies for low vision wheelchair users. Retrieved from http://www.tsbvi.edu/therapy/wc_tip_edit.pdf

FamilyConnect. (n.d.). Orientation and mobility and the expanded core curriculum. Retrieved from http://www.familyconnect.org/info/education/expanded-core-curriculum/orientation-and-mobility/orientation-and-mobility-ecc-6104/1235

Fazzi, E., Signorini, S. G., Bomba, M., Luparia, A., Lanners, J., & Balottin, U. (2011). Reach on sound: A key to object permanence in visually impaired children. *Early Human Development, 87*(4), 289–296.

Feigenson, L., & Carey, S. (2005). On the limits of infants' quantification of small object arrays. *Cognition, 97*(3), 295–313.

Good, W. V., Jan, J. E., Burden, S. K., Skoczenski, A., & Candy, R. (2001). Recent advances in cortical visual impairment. *Developmental Medicine & Child Neurology, 43*(1), 56–60.

Gori, M., Cappagli, G., Tonelli, A., Baud-Bovy, G., & Finocchietti, S. (2016). Devices for visually impaired people: High technological devices with low user acceptance and no adaptability for children. *Neuroscience & Biobehavioral Reviews, 69,* 79–88.

Gougoux, F., Lepore, F., Lassonde, M., Voss, P., Zatorre, R. J., & Belin, P. (2004). Neuropsychology: Pitch discrimination in the early blind. *Nature, 430,* 309.

Hebb, D. O. (2002). *The organization of behavior: A neuropsychological theory.* Mahwah, NJ: Lawrence Erlbaum Associates. (Original work published 1949)

Individuals with Disabilities Education Improvement Act (IDEA), 20 U.S.C. § 1400 (2004).

Jacobson, W. H. (2013). *The art and science of teaching orientation and mobility to persons with visual impairments* (2nd ed.). New York, NY: AFB Press.

LaGrow, S. J. (2010). Improving perception for orientation and mobility. In W. R. Wiener, R. L. Welsh, & B. B. Blasch (Eds.), *Foundations of orientation and mobility: Vol. II. Instructional strategies and practical applications* (3rd ed., pp. 3–26). New York, NY: AFB Press.

Lessard, N., Paré, M., Lepore, F., & Lassonde, M. (1998). Early-blind human subjects localize sound sources better than sighted subjects. *Nature, 395,* 278–280.

Martín, M. B. C., Santos-Lozano, A., Martín-Hernández, J., López-Miguel, A., Maldonado, M., Baladrón, C., Bauer, C., & Merabet, L. B. (2016). Cerebral versus ocular visual impairment: The impact on developmental neuroplasticity. *Frontiers in Psychology, 7.* Retrieved from http://dx.doi.org/10.3389/fpsyg.2016.01958

Merabet, L. B., & Pascual-Leone, A. (2010). Neural reorganization following sensory loss: The opportunity of change. *Nature Reviews Neuroscience, 11*(1), 44–52.

Perkins School for the Blind. (n.d.). About the CVI Range Endorsement. Watertown, MA: Author.

Retrieved from http://www.perkinselearning.org/cvi-endorsement/about

Pogrund, R., Sewell, D., Anderson, H., Calaci, L., Cowart, M. F., Gonzalez, C. M., . . . Roberson-Smith, B. (2012). *TAPS—Teaching age-appropriate purposeful skills: An orientation and mobility curriculum for students with visual impairments* (3rd ed.). Austin: Texas School for the Blind and Visually Impaired.

Roman-Lantzy, C. (2010). Teaching orientation and mobility to students with cortical visual impairment. In W. R. Wiener, R. L. Welsh, & B. B. Blasch (Eds.), *Foundations of orientation and mobility: Vol. II. Instructional strategies and practical applications* (3rd ed., pp. 667–711). New York, NY: AFB Press.

Roman-Lantzy, C. (2018). *Cortical visual impairment: An approach to assessment and intervention* (2nd ed.). New York, NY: AFB Press.

Roman-Lantzy, C. A., & Lantzy, A. (2002–2017). Pediatric VIEW data bank (unpublished data). Pittsburgh, PA: Western Pennsylvania Hospital.

Rosen, S. (2010). Kinesiology and sensorimotor functioning for students with vision loss. In W. R. Wiener, R. L. Welsh, & B. B. Blasch (Eds.), *Foundations of orientation and mobility: Vol. I. History and theory* (3rd ed., pp. 138–172). New York, NY: AFB Press.

Rosen, S., & Crawford, J. S. (2010). Teaching orientation and mobility to learners with visual, physi-cal, and health impairments. In W. R. Wiener, R. L. Welsh, & B. B. Blasch (Eds.), *Foundations of orientation and mobility: Vol. II. Instructional strategies and practical applications* (3rd ed., pp. 564–623). New York, NY: AFB Press.

Strickling, C. (n.d.). Impact of visual impairment on development. Austin: Texas School for the Blind and Visually Impaired. Retrieved from http://www.tsbvi.edu/infants/3293-the-impact-of-visual-impairment-on-development

Tavares, G. M. S., de Espírito Santo, C. C., Santos Calmon, C. M., Nunes, P. M., de Cássia Libardoni, T., Sinhorim, L., . . . Santos, G. M. (2014). Postural characterization in visually impaired young adults: Preliminary study. *Manual Therapy, Posturology & Rehabilitation Journal, 12,* 296–301.

Van Boven, R. W., Hamilton, R. H., Kauffman, T., Keenan, J. P., & Pascual-Leone, A. (2000). Tactile spatial resolution in blind braille readers. *Neurology, 54*(12), 2230–2236.

Wiener, W. R., Welsh, R. L., & Blasch, B. B. (Eds.). (2010). Glossary. In *Foundations of orientation and mobility: Vol. II. Instructional strategies and practical applications* (3rd ed., pp. 789–810). New York, NY: AFB Press.

Wong, M., Gnanakumaran, V., & Goldreich, D. (2011). Tactile spatial acuity enhancement in blindness: Evidence for experience-dependent mechanisms. *Journal of Neuroscience, 31*(19), 7028–7037.

7

CVI and Deafblindness: Considerations for the CVI Range Assessment

Tracy Evans Luiselli and Christine Roman-Lantzy

Coauthor Note: Tracy Evans Luiselli

My career as a deafblind project director and teacher of students with visual impairments has afforded me many opportunities to work with children who have combined vision and hearing loss, or deafblindness. Whether conducting a home visit in a rural town or consulting with an urban school, I often encountered children who were deaf or hard of hearing, had a normal eye exam, and yet didn't respond to typical vision assessment methods. Their families and practitioners were concerned with how best to provide appropriate auditory access, navigate assistive listening devices, and trying to understand why the child wasn't visually regarding people, toys, and instructional materials. While I tried different vision and hearing approaches, many children did not respond to my usual "bag of tricks." They did not follow a penlight, look at my face or that of their parents, visually scan an array of toys, or orient toward a sound-producing toy calibrated to match their degree of hearing loss. Frequently, these children didn't orient toward me or look at my face when I used simple sign language cues. I was stumped but curious. I tried presenting toys with and without sound, and with and without light, and nothing seemed to make a positive difference.

My inspirational moment came at a national conference for state deafblind projects over 10 years ago where I learned about the CVI Range. I listened to stories about children who were similar to those I was challenged by. I returned home from the conference and started to experiment using the CVI Range, collaborating with parents and teachers to engineer home and school environments based on the 10 CVI characteristics. As my knowledge of CVI has evolved, I've come to realize that the more I know, the more I don't know, and the more I want to learn.

Coauthor Note: Christine Roman-Lantzy

Directors from state deafblind projects were the first to extend invitations for me to share my perspectives about CVI. I soon realized that support from this group of highly specialized educators was likely not random, as we had much in common. Those who choose to work in the field of deafblindness embrace the challenges of children with highly complex needs. I learned that the professionals in deafblindness must probe deeply into the needs of the children they serve; there are no easy answers with this population. They taught me that combined hearing and vision loss creates a hybrid of needs that cannot be explained by understanding the fields of visual impairment or hearing impairment alone. I was in awe watching their respectful approach toward communication and instruction. It looked like magic to me! I also learned that many of the neurological conditions associated with CVI are also linked with hearing loss. I felt as if I had met "my people." I have remained closely associated with the professionals in deafblindness long after my initial introduction. I know for certain that the teachers who are trained in deafblindness represent the rarest of educators who find no child too complicated to reach and who have been among the very first to step up to meet the needs of children with CVI.

Cortical visual impairment (CVI) occurs in individuals who have a history of neurological impairment and often results in significant additional disabilities. Combined vision and hearing loss, or deafblindness, is associated with many of the same neurological conditions that cause both ocular and cortical forms of visual impairment. Although diagnosis of potential eye disorders occurs through examinations by an eye care specialist, the diagnosis of CVI in children (infants, school-age children, and youths) with deafblindness may be more elusive. It is important to consider the potential for CVI to occur in individuals with deafblindness even when a co-occurring ocular issue exists. The use of the CVI Range and other CVI-targeted methods may be critical components in understanding the functional vision of these complex individuals. This chapter will provide information about the specialized needs of individuals who have CVI and deafblindness, as well as recommendations for administering the CVI Range assessment to children at risk for these combined conditions.

Deafblind Education in the United States

The term *deafblindness* often conjures up famous images of Helen Keller as she received tactile sign language through the hands of her teacher, Anne Sullivan. However, the belief that all individuals who are deafblind have no vision or hearing at all is misguided. Rather, 90 percent of children identified as deafblind in the United States have some residual vision and hearing and represent a unique and diverse population with a wide range of sensory abilities (Schalock, 2017b).

Combined vision and hearing impairment cannot be viewed as being "additive," in the sense that vision loss plus hearing loss equals deafblindness (Riggio & McLetchie, 2008). Instead, combined vision and hearing impairment presents distinct challenges as the child experiences the world and the myriad visual, auditory, olfactory, and tactile changes that occur throughout the child's day. The impact of vision and hearing loss is unique and should be viewed as a combined sensory disability requiring tailored supports to maximize a child's access to visual, auditory, and tactile information and to facilitate achievement of his or her true learning potential.

The Individuals with Disabilities Education Improvement Act (IDEA, 2004), defines deafblindness as "concomitant hearing and visual impairments, the combination of which causes such severe communication and other developmental and educational needs that they cannot be accommodated in special education programs solely for children with deafness or children with blindness" (34 C.F.R. § 300.8[c][2]). This definition pertains more to educational placement than learning needs and functional abilities, however. More recently, national, state, and local agencies have begun to utilize a more functional categorization of deafblindness such as "combined vision and hearing loss, which may challenge a person's ability to communicate, interact with others, access information, and move about safely" (Miles & Riggio, 1999; New England Consortium for Deafblind Technical Assistance and Training, n.d.b, para. 2).

There are approximately 40,000 people in the United States who are deafblind, of which approximately 10,000 are children who are deafblind, ages birth to 22 (Malloy & Killoran, 2007; Schalock, 2017b). However, there may be underreporting due to inaccurate and inconsistent identification and different referral procedures across educational programs and state agencies (Malloy et al., 2009).

The deafblind population changed considerably following the rubella epidemic in the 1960s, which infected approximately 1 out of every 10 pregnant women (Vernon, Grieve, & Shaver, 1980), and resulted in an estimated 20,000 infants born with multiple disabling conditions and combined sensory loss known as *congenital rubella syndrome* (Congenital Rubella Syndrome, n.d.). With the discovery of the rubella vaccine in the late 1960s, as well as improvements in widespread inoculations and prenatal care, the incidence of children affected by rubella in utero has been virtually eliminated and is now a rare occurrence in the United States (Plotkin, 2006). Conversely, there has been a persistent increase in the number of children with deafblindness and additional disabilities born with more severe medical and neurological conditions and unique syndromes such as CHARGE syndrome (Chen, 1998; Hartshorne, Hefner, & Davenport, 2005; Hatton, Schwietz, Boyer, & Rychwalski, 2007; McInnes & Treffry, 1982; Moss, 2001; Riggio, 1993; Schalock, 2017b). (CHARGE syndrome originally stood for coloboma of the eye, heart defects, atresia of the choanae, retardation of growth and development, and ear abnormalities and deaf-

ness. Although these exact conditions no longer constitute the diagnosis of CHARGE syndrome, the term remains in use.)

Federal funding for deafblind education emerged in the 1960s as a result of strong parental advocacy for specialized educational programs for their children born deafblind. Personnel preparation programs were developed, producing teachers and professionals who formed state and national communities around deafblindness. As the demographics changed over the past half a century, the educational service-delivery system for children born deafblind in the United States also changed. Currently, educational programs are spread out over both public and private programs, rather than substantially separate programs as was the case decades ago. Even as delivery of specialized supports has moved away from regional or separate schools to more inclusive local educational settings, the percentage of children who are deafblind and educated in public and inclusive settings remains low compared to other disability groups (Hatton, 2014; Malloy et al., 2009). The result is an increased need for service providers who are skilled in the area of sensory assessment and intervention and are available across a larger geographical area. There remains a critical shortage of personnel prepared to meet the educational needs of infants, children, and youths who are deafblind (Parker & Ivy, 2014).

Range of Sensory Abilities and Challenges

Through years of investigation in the area of child development and learning, we know children learn about the world using their five senses as they perceive and discriminate changes in their environment. They use the "near" senses of touch and taste, as well as the "distance" senses of vision, hearing, and smell to make meaning of the world. Through use of the distance senses of vision and hearing, children are able to gather a wide breadth of information in a short period of time and across numerous experiences (McInnes & Treffry, 1982; Miles, 2008). So how does learning occur when a child cannot see and hear well? We now know that

Michael Williams

Children who are deafblind are capable of robust learning, including communicating through sign language, such as using a modified sign for CAR that includes larger movements of the arms and hands.

learning for children who are deafblind can still be robust when intervention is matched to meet their sensory and communication needs.

The key ingredients for learning for children who are deafblind include (Ferrell, Bruce, & Luckner, 2014; Nelson & Bruce, 2016):

- Home, school, and work environments that are predictable
- Additional time provided for the child to interpret information and respond accordingly
- Individualized strategies and supports based on assessment findings to maximize sensory abilities (vision, hearing, and touch)
- Repeated exposure to meaningful activities and experiences across environments, people, and materials

Infants, school-age children, and youths who are deafblind represent a diverse group who present with a wide spectrum of sensory abilities and challenges. As depicted in Figure 7.1, there is a continuum of potential configurations of vision and hearing, ranging from mild to severe to total vision and hearing loss, which is the rarest combination. The sensory abilities of individuals who are deafblind fall into general categories or degrees of deafblindness, such as:

- Progressive conditions that are currently mild or less severe with the potential for change
- Moderate or severe loss in one or both sensory modalities
- Severe or profound loss in one or both sensory modalities
- Total lack of perception in both vision and hearing

Only 1 percent of the current population of children identified as deafblind have the latter combination of a profound hearing loss and total blindness (Schalock, 2017b).

Identifying Children Who Have CVI and Deafblindness

Since 1986, the federal Office of Special Education Programs has supported the National Deaf-Blind Child Count for infants, children, and youths (birth to age 21) who are identified as deafblind, with data collected through state deafblind projects (federally funded programs that provide technical assistance and training to teachers and other professionals), and agencies involved with children and youths who are deafblind (National Center on Deaf-Blindness, n.d.). The data collected represents a snapshot of hereditary or chromosomal syndromes and disorders, prenatal and postnatal

Engagement in meaningful experiences within a variety of environments supports vision and learning for children who are deafblind.

231

FIGURE 7.1 Range of Combined Vision and Hearing Loss in Deafblindness

The shaded cells represent areas of combined vision and hearing loss. Cells with no shading indicate that either vision or hearing is within normal rage.

	Degree of Vision Loss and Related Conditions						
Degree of Hearing Loss and Related Conditions		**Mild or No Visual Impairment** (20/40 to 20/70)	**Moderate Visual Impairment or Low Vision** (20/70 to 20/200)	**Severe Visual Impairment or Legal Blindness** (20/200 to 20/400 or visual field < 20°)	**Light Perception Only**	**Total Blindness**	**Diagnosed Progressive Loss**	**Cortical Visual Impairment (CVI)**
Normal −10 to 15 dB								
Slight 16 to 25 dB								
Mild 26 to 40 dB								
Moderate 41 to 55 dB								
Moderately Severe 56 to 70 dB								
Severe 71 to 90 dB								
Profound 91 dB or greater								
Central Auditory Processing Disorder (CAPD)								

Sources: Adapted from American Speech-Language-Hearing Association. (2015). Type, degree, and configuration of hearing loss. Retrieved from https://www.asha.org /uploadedFiles/AIS-Hearing-Loss-Types-Degree-Configuration.pdf; Garber, M., & Huebner, K. M. (2017). Visual impairment: Terminology, demographics, society. In M. C. Holbrook, T. McCarthy, & C. Kamei-Hannan (Eds.), *Foundations of education: Vol. I. History and theory of teaching children and youths with visual impairments* (3rd ed., pp. 50–72). New York, NY: AFB Press; New England Consortium for Deafblind Technical Assistance and Training. (n.d.). Child registration. Retrieved from http://www.nec4db.org/child-registration.html; Schalock, M. D. (2017). *The 2016 national child count of children and youth who are deaf-blind.* Monmouth: Western Oregon University, The Research Institute, National Center on Deaf-Blindness. Retrieved from https://nationaldb.org/reports/national-child-count-2016; World Health Organization. (2012). *Global data on visual impairments 2010.* Geneva, Switzerland: Author. Retrieved from http://www.who.int/blindness/GLOBALDATAFINALforweb.pdf ?ua=1

conditions, vision and hearing characteristics, educational settings, and living arrangements for children and youths identified as deafblind in each state. Data from the National Deaf-Blind Child Count is aggregated, analyzed, and reported by the National Center on Deaf-Blindness. As the longest running and most comprehensive registry of infants, children, and youths who are deafblind, the National Deaf-Blind Child Count is also the only registry of its kind to identify children with CVI and deafblindness. The prevalence of CVI in children also identified as deafblind in the National Child Count has doubled from 15 percent in 2004 to 29 percent in 2015 (Schalock, 2017b). The conditions associated with deafblindness in the National Deaf-Blind Child Count are listed in Table 7.1.

The misperception in our culture and educational system that deafblindness refers to a total lack of both vision and hearing results in under-reporting of children with milder forms of deafblindness, and impacts identification, referral, assessment, and instruction for children who are deafblind. Similarly, children who have CVI and deafblindness are more frequently identified under the larger categories of "multiple disabilities," "global developmental delay," or "visual impairment and additional disabilities" (Müller, 2006). In many states, educational teams focus on one primary disability during the process of disability categorization within the Individualized Education Program (IEP) process. Physical, health, and learning conditions tend to be identified as the primary disability affecting learning, rather than deafblindness, further confounding the process of proper identification and referral of children who are deafblind, including children with CVI who are also deafblind (Hatton, 2014; Müller, 2006; Parker & Ivy, 2014; Wiley, Parnell, & Belhorn, 2016; Wright & Wright, 2007).

The practice of identifying infants, children, and youths who are deafblind or who are deafblind with CVI under the umbrella of multiple disabilities is problematic. First, this practice does not emphasize the child's unique and combined sensory needs and often impedes access to specially trained personnel (such as a teacher of students with vi-

sual impairments, orientation and mobility specialist, teacher of students who are deaf or hard of hearing, consultant with formal training in deafblindness, or intervener) and delivery of appropriate assessment and instruction. Second, using the category of visual impairment and additional disabilities does not identify the critical sensory needs of children who are deaf or hard of hearing, which is necessary for appropriate assessment and intervention strategies for these children. Too often, children identified under the category of multiple disabilities have vision and hearing issues that go undetected, and tend to be described as having a "processing problem" or "global developmental delay," without proper assessment of both vision and hearing systems (Müller, 2006). Promoting accurate identification and referral of children who have CVI and deafblindness or who are at risk for these conditions, as well as facilitating their access to skilled personnel and appropriate services, requires that practitioners consider the following:

- "Red flags" associated with CVI
- Common etiologies and medical conditions related to deafblindness
- Child's specific vision needs pertaining to ocular or cortical visual impairment, along with the degree and type of hearing loss

Although national and state identification efforts are in place, there is not a consistent definition of deafblindness used across and within many educational agencies and state service delivery systems (Parker & Nelson, 2016). For a child who is deafblind, with or without CVI, the impact of approaching deafblindness through the lens of a different primary disability often results in poor service delivery and places the child at distinct educational risk. The likelihood of the child receiving a targeted, appropriate set of supports is often diminished, and successful learning outcomes are unlikely. Consensus across educational and service delivery systems at local, state, and national levels would best support improved identification, referral, and service delivery to children who are deafblind, as well as children with CVI and deafblindness.

TABLE 7.1

Etiologies and Conditions Associated with Deafblindness

Hereditary/Chromosomal Syndromes and Disorders	
101 Aicardi syndrome	130 Marshall syndrome
102 Alport syndrome	131 Maroteaux-Lamy syndrome (MPS VI)
103 Alstrom syndrome	132 Moebius syndrome
104 Apert syndrome (Acrocephalosyndactyly, Type 1)	133 Monosomy 10p
105 Bardet-Biedl syndrome (Laurence Moon-Biedl)	134 Morquio syndrome (MPS IV-B)
	135 NF1 - Neurofibromatosis (von Recklinghausen disease)
106 Batten disease	136 NF2 - Bilateral Acoustic Neurofibromatosis
107 CHARGE Syndrome	137 Norrie disease
108 Chromosome 18, Ring 18	138 Optico-Cochleo-Dentate Degeneration
109 Cockayne syndrome	139 Pfieffer syndrome
110 Cogan Syndrome	140 Prader-Willi
111 Cornelia de Lange	141 Pierre-Robin syndrome
112 Cri du chat syndrome (Chromosome 5p syndrome)	142 Refsum syndrome
113 Crigler-Najjar syndrome	143 Scheie syndrome (MPS I-S)
114 Crouzon syndrome (Craniofacial Dysotosis)	144 Smith-Lemli-Opitz (SLO) syndrome
115 Dandy Walker syndrome	145 Stickler syndrome
116 Down syndrome (Trisomy 21 syndrome)	146 Sturge-Weber syndrome
117 Goldenhar syndrome	147 Treacher Collins syndrome
118 Hand-Schuller-Christian (Histiocytosis X)	148 Trisomy 13 (Trisomy 13-15, Patau syndrome)
119 Hallgren syndrome	149 Trisomy 18 (Edwards syndrome)
120 Herpes-Zoster (or Hunt)	150 Turner syndrome
121 Hunter Syndrome (MPS II)	151 Usher I syndrome
122 Hurler syndrome (MPS I-H)	152 Usher II syndrome
123 Kearns-Sayre syndrome	153 Usher III syndrome
124 Klippel-Feil sequence	154 Vogt-Koyanagi-Harada syndrome
125 Klippel-Trenaunay-Weber syndrome	155 Waardenburg syndrome
126 Kniest Dysplasia	156 Wildervanck syndrome
127 Leber congenital amaurosis	157 Wolf-Hirschhorn syndrome (Trisomy 4p)
128 Leigh Disease	199 Other _____
129 Marfan syndrome	

TABLE 7.1 *(continued)*

Pre-Natal/Congenital Complications		Post-Natal/Non-Congenital Complications	
201	Congenital Rubella	301	Asphyxia
202	Congenital Syphilis	302	Direct Trauma to the eye and/or ear
203	Congenital Toxoplasmosis	303	Encephalitis
204	Cytomegalovirus (CMV)	304	Infections
205	Fetal Alcohol syndrome	305	Meningitis
206	Hydrocephaly	306	Severe Head Injury
207	Maternal Drug Use	307	Stroke
208	Microcephaly	308	Tumors
209	Neonatal Herpes Simplex (HSV)	309	Chemically Induced
299	Other_____	399	Other _____

Codes in the table are used to indicate each condition in the National Child Count Report.

Source: Schalock, M. D. (2017). Child count code sheet. Monmouth: Western Oregon University, The Research Institute, National Center on Deaf-Blindness. Retrieved from https://nationaldb.org/materials/page/1998/11

Associated Medical Conditions

Accurate and early identification and referral of children with CVI and deafblindness facilitates more timely delivery of services and provision of individualized instructional supports. Therefore, service providers should be knowledgeable about medical "red flags" or conditions most commonly associated with CVI and deafblindness. The conditions most commonly associated with CVI and that are also commonly associated with deafblindness are listed in Sidebar 7.1. Administration of the CVI Range assessment should be considered for all children who have any of these risk conditions.

The most prevalent causes or etiologies resulting in children born deafblind and reported on the Annual Deaf-Blind Child Count include undetermined etiology, such as undiagnosed conditions (18.5 percent), complications of prematurity (11 percent), and CHARGE syndrome (10 percent) (Schalock, 2017b). Although premature birth is not a direct cause of CVI or deafblindness, sequelae such as intraventricular hemorrhage and neurodevelopmental impairments often affect visual, au-

ditory, tactile, and vestibular processing and place a child at greater risk for CVI and deafblindness (Wickremasinghe et al., 2013).

Although the cognitive ability in children with CHARGE syndrome ranges from normal cognitive functioning to severe intellectual disability, there is growing evidence of an array of resulting brain anomalies and cranial nerve disorders warranting further investigation of the presence of CVI. These conditions include weak chewing or sucking, facial palsy, sensorineural hearing loss and auditory processing disorders, balance or vestibular problems, swallowing difficulties, and optic nerve damage resulting in visual field deficits (Blake, Hartshorne, Lawand, Dailor, & Thelin, 2008).

In the case of cytomegalovirus (CMV) infection, 3 percent of children identified in the 2016 National Deaf-Blind Child Count were identified as having symptomatic CMV (Schalock, 2017b). Given that CMV is the most common congenital infection in the United States, with neurological, optic nerve, and retinal abnormalities, it appears that children with CMV and deafblindness are underreported (Wiley et al., 2016).

SIDEBAR 7.1

Medical "Red Flags" for CVI and Deafblindness

The following conditions are commonly associated with CVI and deafblindness and should serve to alert practitioners to the possibility that a child has CVI and deafblindness:

- Asphyxia and perinatal hypoxic-ischemic encephalopathy (HIE)

- Intraventricular hemorrhage (IVH)

- Periventricular leukomalacia (PVL)

- Cerebral vascular accident/cerebral artery infarction (stroke)

- Kernicterus

- Infection, such as meningitis or TORCH infections (toxoplasmosis, others [syphilis, listeriosis, varicella, parvovirus B19], rubella, cytomegalovirus, and herpes simplex virus)

- Viral infections, such as HIV in pregnancy and Zika virus

- Structural abnormalities

- Metabolic conditions

- Traumatic/acquired brain injury

Source: Roman-Lantzy, C. (2018). *Cortical visual impairment: An approach to assessment and intervention.* New York, NY: AFB Press.

Children with CVI and deafblindness demonstrate behaviors that sometimes create confusion among diagnosticians, such as turning away from a sound source to direct the ear for better hearing; pushing away materials that feel unfamiliar; repetitive hand movements over surfaces to search for tactile rather than visual information; and "tuning out" or lack of response when the environment is overstimulating or lacks meaningful information. Accurate diagnosis of CVI in infants, children, and youths who are deafblind is critical to prevent misdiagnosis. Children with deafblindness and CVI are at risk of receiving the diagnosis of autism spectrum disorder (ASD) because they share common features related to visual regard, socialization, communication, and repetitive, ritualistic behaviors (Dammeyer, 2014; Dunn, 2008; Gense & Gense, 2005). The potential for misdiagnosis of ASD in persons who are deafblind with CVI may ultimately result in inappropriate assessment and intervention (Belote & Maier, 2014).

Hearing Impairment and CVI

A hearing impairment is often described as a hidden disability. To many, it is not apparent that a child who is deaf or hard of hearing cannot perceive or understand speech and environmental sounds. In contrast, there are more features that can be observed in a child with visual impairment that indicate the presence of the disability, for example, direction of eye gaze, lack of eye gaze, eye deviations, and oculomotor issues. Whereas vision has been described as the key to exploration, mobility, and concept and social development, the ability to detect, discriminate, and understand sound is considered to be the underlying foundation of a child's communication system. Children who are deaf or hard of hearing often have greater difficulty learning vocabulary, grammar, word order, and other aspects of speech. There are strong visual and auditory aspects of speech that support language development for children who are deaf and hard of hearing, such as visual cues that indicate who is speaking, duration of speech sounds, and visual contextual cues that support understanding (Picou, Ricketts, & Hornsby, 2011). A child's perception and identification of an object involves the integration of salient visual features, such as shape, color, and location in the visual field, along with salient auditory features of pitch, loudness, and location of a sound source.

The combined impact of CVI and hearing impairment can present a major barrier to learning and language development if parents and educators are not aware of the child's residual sensory abilities and how to support access to visual and auditory information (Yoshinaga-Itano, Sedey, Coulter, & Mehl, 1998). Although recent studies suggest an increase in the prevalence of vision disorders in children who are deaf, these investigations do not account for CVI or other visual processing issues (Carvill, 2001; Mafong, Pletcher, Hoyt, & Lalwani, 2002).

Hearing loss is categorized according to the affected area of the auditory system into conductive, sensorineural, or mixed type hearing loss; these are explained in Sidebar 7.2. The prevalence of these specific categories of hearing loss in children who are deafblind is currently unknown. However, of the 3,080 children identified on the 2016 Deaf-blind Child Count as having CVI and documented hearing impairment, the prevalence of specific levels or degrees of hearing loss is as follows: mild, 13.6 percent; moderate, 18.6 percent; moderately severe, 13.8 percent; severe, 9.8 percent; profound, 16.8 percent; diagnosed progressive loss, 0.8 percent; further testing needed, 8.5 percent; and functional hearing loss, 18.0 percent (Schalock, 2017b). These numbers suggest that almost half of the population of children who have CVI and deafblindness have residual hearing. Also, there are several progressive conditions, such as Usher Syndrome and mitochondrial disorders, that may result in decreased vision, hearing, or both, over time.

Any hearing impairment in a child with vision loss or CVI, regardless of the degree, is significant and warrants careful assessment of the impact of each sensory loss on learning. Of the total population of children with hearing loss, 30–40 percent have one or more additional disabilities (Burkey, 2015), suggesting that combined hearing loss and CVI is an important topic for those who are responsible for identification and referral of children who are deafblind, deaf or hard of hearing, or visually impaired.

Practitioners should monitor and control the listening environment during the assessment process to ensure auditory access and keep background noise at a minimum (Chen, 2014a; Madell, 2013; Smaldino & Flexer, 2012). In addition, the examiner should be positioned within 2–3 feet of the child, in the child's better visual field, and at his

Vision plays an important role in supporting language development, establishing joint attention, and building anticipation in children who are deaf or hard of hearing.

Catherine Glover

Sheena Smith

SIDEBAR 7.2

Types and Configurations of Hearing Loss

Types of Hearing Loss and Conditions Affecting Hearing

- **Sensorineural hearing loss (SNHL)** is the most common type of hearing loss and involves damage to the inner ear and nerves inside the cochlea or to the nerve pathways from the inner ear to the brain. SNHL cannot be medically or surgically corrected.

- **Conductive hearing loss** involves the outer and middle ear, and may be caused by wax blockage, a punctured eardrum, ear infections, birth defects, or hereditary factors. Almost all conductive hearing loss can be effectively treated with hearing aids.

- **Mixed hearing loss** means that there is a problem in both the outer or middle and inner ear.

- **Auditory neuropathy spectrum disorder (ANSD)** refers to a specific type of hearing loss involving problems in the inner hair cells, connection with the auditory nerve, or the auditory nerve itself. The signal is often intermittent, and the child captures only parts of speech and auditory information.

- **Auditory processing disorder (APD)** is an auditory perception problem in detecting the subtle differences between sounds in words. Typically, a child with this condition is unable to hear well when competing noise is present or is unable to "tune out" extraneous sounds. Children with APD do not have a hearing loss but act as if they do.

Possible Configurations of Hearing Loss

- **Bilateral hearing loss:** loss in both ears

- **Unilateral hearing loss:** loss in one ear

- **Symmetrical hearing loss:** loss that is the same in both ears

- **Asymmetrical hearing loss:** loss that is different in each ear

- **Progressive hearing loss:** hearing will become worse over time

- **Fluctuating hearing loss:** hearing loss changes over time—sometimes better, sometimes worse—and is not stable

---

Sources: Adapted from American Speech-Language-Hearing Association. (n.d.). Hearing loss. Retrieved from https://www.asha.org/public/hearing/Hearing-Loss/; Clarin, G. P. (2015). Auditory neuropathy spectrum disorder. In *A Resource guide for early hearing detection and intervention* (pp. 8-1–8-8). Logan: Utah State University, National Center for Hearing Assessment and Management. Retrieved from http://infanthearing.org/ehdi-ebook/2015_ebook/8-Chapter8AuditoryNeuropathy2015.pdf

---

or her eye level (Costello, 2011); provide tactile guidance under the hand, forearm, or elbow to encourage tactile awareness (Miles & Riggio, 1999); and use acoustic highlighting, which makes sounds or words longer than normal or uses a singsong way of speaking (Chen, 2014a).

Additional conditions that result in impaired hearing and comprehension include auditory neuropathy spectrum disorder (ANSD) and auditory processing disorder (APD) (see Sidebar 7.2). ANSD ranges from mild to profound and occurs in about 13.4 percent of children with sensorineural hearing loss (Clarin, 2015). ANSD is present when sound enters the inner ear, but the transmission of signals from the inner ear to the brain is impaired. ANSD is also suspected when a child does not understand speech clearly, and the degree of hearing loss does not fully explain the child's poor speech perception.

To better understand ANSD, one might consider the analogy of trying to use a cell phone when the signal is inconsistently received or interrupted. The causes of ANSD are not clear, but the risk factors in infants include high bilirubin levels, low oxygen levels (anoxia), infections, and genetic factors (Morlet, 2010). Co-occurring conditions with CVI and deafblindness, including premature birth and an inadequate supply of oxygen to the unborn baby, are all high-risk factors for ANSD (Roman-Lantzy, 2018; Xoinis, Weirather, Mavoori, Shaha, & Iwamoto, 2007). In APD, the individual is unable to hear well when competing speech or background noise is present. While a person with normal hearing can "tune out" extraneous noise, individuals with APD are unable to do so.

Diagnosing ANSD or APD in children who have CVI is highly complex and requires thorough and ongoing assessment by highly trained personnel, along with information from the child's family and others who are familiar with the child's typical responses to speech and competing environmental noise (Morlet, 2010). Prior to conducting the CVI Range, practitioners should be aware of audiological or language disorders that may affect the child's ability to detect and interpret both visual and auditory stimuli in complex environments.

Early Identification, Referral, and Assessment

There is a need for improved vision screening of children who are identified as having hearing loss (Sharma, Ruscetta, & Chi, 2009). Given the frequency of conditions resulting in dual sensory impairment, it is imperative that when one sensory modality is impaired, practitioners and medical personnel investigate whether the other sensory modality has also been evaluated.

Currently, there is a lack of information regarding the combined incidence of CVI and deafness. The Newborn Hearing Screening Program, a national program for early detection and screening of infants with hearing loss, is responsible for identifying hearing loss in thousands of children each year (Alam, Satterfield, Mason, & Deng, 2016).

However, additional vision screening of infants with conditions commonly associated with CVI would facilitate more timely and appropriate service delivery. Since CVI is the leading cause of visual impairment in the United States (Jan et al., 2013; Kong, Fry, Al-Samarraie, Gilbert, & Steinkuller, 2012; Skoczenski & Good, 2004; Swaminathan, 2011), connecting the efforts of the Newborn Hearing Screening Program with the National Deaf-Blind Child Count would improve early detection of the presence of CVI in infants and children who are deafblind.

Interestingly, children who are deafblind may be more likely to be identified as having CVI and receive appropriate assessment and intervention than children who have only hearing loss or only visual impairment. The National Center on Deaf-Blindness, several schools for children who are blind or visually impaired that serve children who are deafblind, and state deafblind projects provide training in CVI and use of the CVI Range. In-depth training on CVI was instituted as early as 2001 at the Maryland, West Virginia, Delaware, Vermont, Massachusetts, Connecticut, Maine, and New Hampshire state deafblind programs. To date, more than 20 programs have conducted formal training in the principles of the CVI Range and associated interventions. These increased training and advocacy efforts have doubled the incidence of children reported as having CVI and deafblindness over the past 15 years. However, there is still a stronger emphasis on the assessment of one sensory modality at a time within the fields of visual impairment and deafness in general.

Special considerations for vision assessment in children who also have hearing loss or deafblindness require an adjustment in traditional assessment methods. A child who is hard of hearing may detect, search for, turn toward, or reach for a sound-producing toy in a different manner than a child with vision loss only (Parker & Ivy, 2014). For example, a child who has CVI and deafblindness may not respond typically to sound by looking in the direction of a sound-producing toy or gazing at the face of a familiar person speaking. Instead, the child may demonstrate very subtle changes such as

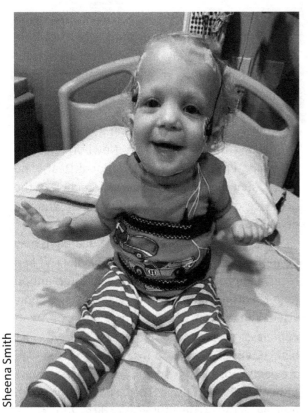

Sheena Smith

The assistance of a familiar caregiver during a medical test or educational assessment can reassure a child who is deafblind and optimize her ability to respond. The caregiver first gains the child's attention and signs, providing encouragement about the process.

sudden cessation of motor activity, changes in breathing or sucking on a bottle, changes in muscle tone, positioning of the head downward as if listening, turning away from the sound source to position the better ear, or fussing when an unfamiliar toy is presented. Children with motor challenges may move their whole body toward the item instead of reaching accurately in the direction of the assessment item (Bruce, Janssen, & Bashinski, 2016). Also, children who are deafblind may become unsettled or agitated when an unfamiliar assessment item is presented, and require reassurance that a familiar person is nearby to interpret immediate changes in the environment by describing what is happening in the assessment environment or identifying assessment materials.

The assistance of a familiar caregiver in the assessment process can optimize the child's ability

to respond by interpreting the child's responses and providing information about the child's preferences as well as successful strategies for communication. Along with parents, a familiar caregiver might be a nurse, day care provider, or an intervener. An intervener is a vital partner on the educational team who provides access to visual and auditory information that the child is unable to gather due to deafblindness. As a trained professional staff member who works one-on-one with a child who is deafblind, the intervener can provide critical connections to other people and the environment and open channels of communication between the child and examiner during the assessment process (Alsop, Blaha, & Kloos, 2000; Alsop et al., 2007). Since interveners must have an understanding of the strategies specific to deafblindness, they can be integral to the process of providing accommodations and modifications during administration of the CVI Range.

Deafblindness and Considerations for Administering the CVI Range

For children who are deafblind, a "one-size-fits-all" approach to assessment and intervention is often ineffective. Their diverse abilities require ongoing collection of evidence with careful consideration of how the child takes in information based on the degree of visual, auditory, and tactile ability and different ways of responding (including verbal, sign, gesture, head turn toward, head turn away, increased muscle tone, decreased muscle tone, cessation of activity, moving toward, or reaching). Too often, educators are not aware of specific assessment and intervention strategies that accommodate the child's type, form, and rate of responding or of strategies to establish a positive interactive style and format for presentation of materials.

Children who are deafblind often have unique learning styles that necessitate ongoing assessment to determine their sensory abilities and preferences, the primary sensory modality or modalities for learning (visual, auditory, tactile, or motor), and how the practitioner should utilize each sensory modality in developing consistent routines and instruction. Using a systematic approach to promote the child's attention within the CVI Range assessment process, the practitioner or parent presents materials in a sequence, starting with presentation of the object by itself, followed by presentation of the object with cues in increasing levels of assistance (Spooner, Browder, & Mims, 2011), as discussed later in more detail.

A child's ability to tolerate competing environmental sounds while visually attending is evaluated in each of the three phases on the CVI Range. Children with combined vision and hearing loss may demonstrate difficulty in key auditory skills such as awareness, discrimination, identification, and comprehension of speech and environmental sounds (Chen, 2014b; Stredler-Brown & Johnson, 2003). For a child who has a hearing impairment, the CVI Range assessment process should include consideration of the child's visual response based on each of the 10 CVI characteristics (Roman-Lantzy, 2018). Hearing impairment or ocular impairment may or may not impact performance on the assessment, depending on the child's learning history, access to sensory supports, type of sensory loss, severity of sensory loss, and use of assistive devices such as eyeglasses, low vision devices, hearing aids, and FM systems. The CVI Range assessment and related intervention strategies are typically not appropriate for a child who has hearing loss and is totally blind, has light perception only, or has severely limited vision as a result of ocular impairment. However, use of the CVI Range is indicated for students who have ocular conditions that are not able to explain the child's functional use of vision.

Practitioners should consider the following skill areas in planning and administration of the CVI Range process for a learner who is deafblind (Ferrell et al., 2014):

- Communication and language
- Tactile exploration and discrimination
- Mobility and motor skills (positioning needs)
- Concept and cognitive development

- Emotional and social interactions
- Hearing and listening skills
- Vision skills

The examiner should be aware of necessary supports through collaboration with the teacher, paraeducator, intervener, or related service providers familiar with the child. Collaboration will determine the appropriate type and position of assessment and instructional materials, an estimate of the child's typical response time, expressive and receptive communication modalities, and supports needed for sensory access, and steps for using assistive listening devices, such as a hearing aid, or language strategies (Bruce & Borders, 2015; Chen, 2014b; Rowland, Chen, Stillman, Mar, & Syler, 2009).

When prompts or cues are used to support the child's looking behavior during the CVI Range assessment, practitioners should present them in the communication mode most appropriate for the child, which could be verbal, visual, or tactile sign language; objects; touch cues; pictures; or augmentative communication devices (Costello, Patak, & Pritchard, 2010). The terms *prompt, cue,* and *signal* are often used interchangeably. For the purposes of this chapter, we use the term cue to indicate any verbal, nonverbal, or visual stimulus that is intended to produce one or more responses. The potential communication methods identified by Chen and Downing (2006) that are applicable to the CVI Range assessment process are provided in Sidebar 7.3.

Preparation for Administering the CVI Range

Practitioners should consider the following information prior to conducting the CVI Range with a child with hearing impairment or deafblindness:

- Parents' report of when vision and/or hearing loss was suspected and/or confirmed
- Medications, medical needs, and presence of additional disabilities that might affect the child's performance,

SIDEBAR 7.3

Communication Options for Children Who Are Deafblind

The following are options that can be used to communicate with children who are deafblind, from simplest to most complex, with examples of each.

Objects

- Whole objects: cup, pacifier, utensil

- Parts of objects: handle of cup or pacifier or part of toy

- Miniature objects: smaller version to represent the real object

- Representational objects: a spoon to represent snack time or a piece of a towel to represent swimming or bathing

Pictures and Symbols

- Photo of identical objects

- Photo of representational object

- Outline drawing of object

- Black-and-white symbol of object

Formal Language

- Sign language and gestures

- Braille

- Spoken word

- Written word

Source: Chen, D., & Downing, J. E. (2006). *Tactile strategies for children who have visual impairments and multiple disabilities: Promoting communication and learning skills.* New York, NY: AFB Press.

including health conditions, motor issues, and social-emotional issues

- The degree and type of ocular visual impairment, including near and distance acuity, visual field deficits, and oculomotor issues

- The degree and type of hearing loss, whether conductive, sensorineural, or mixed, and position on the range from mild to severe

- Comorbidity with other conditions such as APD and ANSD

- Assistive listening devices such as hearing aids, FM systems, sound field systems, and cochlear implants, and

visual devices such as eyeglasses or low vision devices

- Educational history and interventions previously provided, such as services from a teacher of students with visual impairments, or lack thereof

- Knowledge and understanding of the child's biobehavioral states, such as changes in the child's level of alertness, fatigue, subtle motor responses, and breathing (Nelson, van Dijk, McDonnell, & Thompson, 2002)

- Positioning to facilitate head control, sustained visual attention, and motor responses such as use of wheelchair or adaptive seating, tray, slant board, and arm or hand support (Chen, 2014a)

- Environmental influences affecting both assessment and intervention, such as the presence of unfamiliar people and materials, use of proper positioning, room temperature, and relative freedom of movement

- Assessment and intervention routines that build the child's anticipation and understanding of what comes next

Additional Considerations for Administering the CVI Range

Evidenced-based practices identified for children who are deafblind (Bruce, Ferrell, & Luckner, 2016; Bruce, Nelson, Perez, Stutzman, & Barnhill, 2016; Ferrell et al., 2014) that should be used during the CVI Range assessment include the following:

- The educational team
  - uses a collaborative team process to incorporate input for all members and support family participation,
  - includes at least one team member knowledgeable about assessment and instruction for children who are deafblind, and
  - uses methods to promote the child's recognition and understanding of materials and directions, such as sign language; touch cues; object cues; pictures; and salient visual, auditory, and tactile cues.

- Observation takes place in multiple environments with familiar people present and adaptations and accommodations based on the child's functional vision and hearing and learning media needs.

- Appropriate response time is provided for the child to interpret and react to assessment and intervention instructions, such as look toward, reach, turn

head, activate switch, verbally respond, sign, and explore tactilely.

- Salient tactile cues are provided to encourage engagement with and recognition of materials and to promote increased looking behaviors, such as encouraging the child's attention to the surface, shape, and size of the object.

Although research on valid assessment of children who are deafblind is emerging, practitioners should be aware of the etiology of the child's deafblindness when planning assessment and intervention protocols (Silberman, Bruce, & Nelson, 2004). Valid assessment using the CVI Range for a child who is deafblind considers the child's ability to detect incidental changes in the environment and the need for specific supports through use of

Sue Hollis

The teacher is intentionally combining visual, auditory, and tactile supports to promote the student's attention and understanding.

signs or gestures, tactile cues, objects, and the size and position of pictures and books.

The assessment process for a child who is deafblind can be isolating and unpredictable without approaches specifically tailored to the individual child and applied consistently, such as greetings, establishment of joint attention, consistent presentation and location of materials, opportunity for tactile exploration of materials, and affirmation of the child's correct responses in his or her strongest communication modality (Bruce, Janssen, & Bashinski, 2016). As mentioned, incidental information about the people and materials present in the immediate environment must often be brought to the child's attention by providing explanations or cues when assessment materials are withdrawn or moved (Cox & Dykes, 2001; Sacks, 2016).

The communication system or approach is a critical component of the CVI Range assessment process, especially for a child who is deafblind. For many children who are deafblind, a calendar system approach is often used to support and build a child's communication. A calendar system includes representational items that depict the child's daily schedule and provide the child with information about his or her day. The calendar system may consist of actual objects, representational objects or symbols, photographs, written words, or a combination of items, depending on the child's level of understanding and experience. Items are typically presented in an array arranged sequentially by order of the day, either at school, at home, or within the community. As the child's anticipation and learning grows, calendar system items are modified, progressing along a literacy continuum from tangible objects to written words. Calendar systems are often highly individualized to accommodate the visual needs of the child (Blaha, 2001).

During the CVI Range assessment process, the practitioner should note how the child attends to and interacts with each item, based on the 10 CVI characteristics. Does the child seem to prefer some items over others based on color or location in the child's visual field? Does the child accurately reach for each item? Does the child need movement of the item to encourage visual regard? When designing a calendar system for a child with CVI and deafblindness, the practitioner should also consider the 10 CVI characteristics and salient features of each item used in the calendar system. For example, if results from the CVI Range indicate that the child visually attends best to items of a certain color (say, yellow), calendar system items should be marked in the preferred color or have the salient feature of the item adapted with yellow, for example by marking the handle of the child's cup used to represent snack time with yellow tape. If the child requires slight movement of the item to facilitate visual attention, the practitioner might gently move each item used in the calendar system sequence of items and activities. Or, if the child tends to look and look away as he or she reaches for the item in the calendar system, the practitioner might hold the item until the child turns back and looks toward the item again.

The considerations for assessment just mentioned require careful review before initiating the CVI Range. A child with vision and hearing challenges may be perceived as not responding to sensory input or responding incorrectly if adults in the environment are not skilled in observing the child's specific communication strategies and detecting subtle nuances in the child's expressive language and communication (Rowland et al., 2009). One child may need detailed verbal and tactile information about the assessment process and what will happen next. Another child might perform better with limited information and a less interactive approach. When assessment information is used to develop strategic interventions applied consistently across different environments, many children can flourish, achieve independence, and acquire strong sensory skills.

To begin the CVI Range process for a child with hearing impairment or deafblindness, one must first consider using an attentional cue that indicates the child's readiness to learn (Miles & Riggio, 1999). The practitioner might place his or her hands under the child's hands, wait 3–5 seconds, then gently guide the child's hand up to his or her eyes and say, "I have some fun toys to look at." Then the practitioner does something that gains the child's attention. Next, the practitioner systematically presents materials and observes the child's signals, such as changes in tone, breathing, facial expressions, motor movements, gestures, modified gestures or signs, or verbal language and approximations.

The CVI Range assessment process should not be a checklist of yes-or-no responses based solely on the 10 CVI characteristics. Instead, practitioners should note how the child displays signals, behaviors, and responses with regard to each of the 10 CVI characteristics and attend to the child's signals during systematic presentation of assessment procedures. Often, children who are deafblind perceptually "shut down" and deliberately do not attend to stimuli that are not meaningful or are overly stimulating. It is important to establish a rhythm or flow that is predictable and repetitive and promotes the child's responses and interactions (Miles & Riggio, 1999). Instead of presenting materials quickly, with limited time for exploration, the practitioner should encourage the child to interact with and explore materials. If the assessment process is chaotic and unpredictable and involves unfamiliar materials and communication methods, the child may respond negatively or not at all, resulting in an inaccurate picture of the child's true abilities and erroneous results.

Tactile Strategies

For many children who are deafblind, touch or tactile input is often more salient or preferred. Tactile exploration typically involves the child's use of his or her hands, yet they may also use their feet, mouth, or sense of smell to explore materials (Chen, 2014a). Many children who are deafblind also have limited learning repertoires and may perceive that an item is not present if they cannot touch or explore it.

The approach for highlighting salient tactile features often used with children who are deafblind, and which should be considered when administering the CVI Range assessment and intervention to encourage their engagement with the CVI assessment materials, includes the use of hand-under-hand guidance, as identified in Sidebar 7.4.

Although the use of this strategy is effective for many children who are deafblind, further investigation is needed to determine the most effective tactile approaches for children with a wide range of sensory abilities (Chen & Downing, 2006).

It is not unusual for children who are deafblind to attend more to salient tactile and olfactory features of their environment rather than using their residual vision and hearing to inspect and interact with toys and materials. They may repeatedly turn an object over to investigate its surface, size, and shape; examine an object with their mouth or tongue; smell an object; or press an object to the chin to receive tactile sensations through the face or head rather than the hands. As a result, it takes longer for the child to detect materials and tactilely explore them, requiring additional time as a precursor or "warm up" to the assessment process.

Tactile signing has typically been used for children who are deaf and have significant vision loss (Morgan, n.d.). The process involves the child positioning one or both hands on the hands of the person who is signing (Welch, 2016). However, tactile signing can also be useful for children with CVI who have limited visual attention, providing tactile input, encouraging joint attention, and supporting receptive language. For children who tend to look and then look away, a common feature in CVI, and

Catherine Glover

The parent engages her child in close physical contact, providing auditory, visual, and tactile input. For many children who are deafblind, touch or tactile input is often preferred.

SIDEBAR 7.4

An Approach for Using Salient Tactile Features with CVI Assessment Materials

Highlight salient tactile features by first placing the object in the child's hands, allowing time for unguided exploration, and gently guiding tactile exploration of the child's hands over the object's surface, using hand-under-hand guidance, starting from the left of the object toward the right. Note how the child inspects tactile features, using his or her whole hand, palm, fingertips, or isolated fingertips. Access to the item should be provided when the child is looking toward the item. If visual regard does not occur or stops, gently remove the item, wait five seconds, and present the item again. If looking is absent or fleeting, pair presentation of the object with a light source and proceed accordingly. Salient features to consider include the following:

Surface of the Object

- Smooth/bumpy

- Hard/soft

- Pointy edge/corner

- Handle of object

- Switch/activation button

Size of the Object

- Huge

- Big

- Medium

- Little

- Tiny

Shape of the Object

- Round/circle

- Square

- Rectangle

- Diamond

Source: Adapted from Chen, D., & Downing, J. E. (2006). *Tactile strategies for children who have visual impairments and multiple disabilities: Promoting communication and learning skills.* New York, NY: AFB Press.

---

have difficulty sustaining visual attention, tactile sign language can help support attention to language without requiring sustained looking and head positioning.

Sensory Cues

Providing a supportive environment within the CVI Range assessment process, along with systematic presentation of visual, auditory, and tactile cues will assist the practitioner in determining if the child is responding to visual cues only, or if additional auditory and tactile strategies are necessary to facilitate understanding and expectations in the assessment process. The specific cues used in both assessment and intervention should reflect the child's receptive and expressive communication

Michael Williams

The parent provides tactile sign language, and waits for the child's response (left). She follows his lead (right) as they talk about what's going to happen next.

abilities, mainly touch cues, object cues, tangible symbols, gestures, verbal cues, pictures, and manual signs (Chen, 2014a). Sidebar 7.5 describes a variety of tactile strategies and cues that can be used to present materials during the administration of the CVI Range.

During the CVI Range assessment process, it can be difficult to analyze the child's responses to visual items if the child's responses are inconsistent across people, materials, and environments. If the child responds inconsistently, the practitioner should use a systematic progression of cues that facilitates the child's response, such as presentation of a visual stimulus only, and if the child does not respond, a progression of additional cues (visual, auditory, and tactile) to encourage the child's detection of visual materials (Brady & Bashinski, 2008).

During typical visual assessment, auditory cues are often used to elicit visual attention. However, when conducting the CVI Range with a child who has hearing loss, the practitioner should consider use of other sensory modalities to encourage or support visual attention. The child's response to sound should not be a key factor in evaluating visual responding. Given that many children with hearing impairments depend on vision to compensate for hearing loss (through, for example, use of sign language, noticing incidental changes in the environment, or detecting and interpreting facial expressions), practitioners should assess and sup-

port visual responding using other sensory cues (Mafong et al., 2002).

The use of auditory cues in the CVI Range assessment process should involve initial presentation of visual assessment materials without auditory cues and then presentation of auditory cues to reinforce visual responding and engagement. Although the goal of the assessment is to have the child respond to visual cues in isolation in order to obtain a valid measure of their visual ability, children who are deafblind often miss incidental and qualifying information, which in turn requires additional sensory support to facilitate attention and engagement. A potential hierarchy of cues to support visual attention to a target, from least to most assistance includes:

1. Visual presentation only

2. Visual and auditory cue

3. Visual and objects (tactile cue)

4. Visual, objects (tactile), and verbal cues

5. Visual, verbal, and sign language cues

The following steps provide an example of a systematic process for presenting sensory cues during administration of the CVI Range:

1. **Visual stimulus only:** Present visual material (such as a light, brightly colored toy or an environmental or functional object) within 12 inches of the child and wait a predetermined

---

SIDEBAR 7.5

Tactile Strategies for Presentation of Materials during Administration of the CVI Range

- **Hand-under-hand technique:** The adult's hand is placed under the child's hand, gently guiding the child through exploration of and interaction with the object.

- **Hand-over-hand technique:** The adult's hand is placed over the child's hand to support exploration or activation of the object or reaching for the object.

- **Adapted sign:** The form or movement of the signs are modified but relate to the original sign form or natural gesture. Signs are often adapted for children with motor challenges.

- **Tactile signing:** The adult's hands are placed over the child's to receive sign language communication from the child, or under the child's to provide the child with sign language.

- **Key word signing:** Signs and gestures are used to convey simple messages (e.g., using just a noun or a verb).

- **Tactile representation:** A salient tactile feature is used to represent a person, place, or object. Appropriate selection of tactile representations often requires that the adult consider the child's perspective.

- **Touch cue:** Touch is used to provide information (e.g., touching a child's lips to indicate an approaching cup; touching a child's shoulder prior to positioning, touching the side of a child's head to encourage turning toward a toy or light source).

- **Object cue:** An actual object that is used in an activity is used to represent that activity (e.g., a spoon to indicate mealtime, a seatbelt buckle to indicate travel in the car, or a bathing suit to indicate swimming).

Sources: Chen, D., & Downing, J. E. (2006). *Tactile strategies for children who have visual impairments and multiple disabilities: Promoting communication and learning skills.* New York, NY: AFB Press; Downing, J. E., & Chen, D. (2014). Critical transitions: Educating young children in general education preschools. In D. Chen (Ed.), *Essential elements in early intervention: Visual impairment and multiple disabilities* (2nd ed., pp. 463–519). New York, NY: AFB Press.

---

time, up to 30 seconds. Present the object three times. If there is no response, such as looking, reaching toward the object, or change in biobehavioral state, move to the next level cue.

2. **Visual stimulus with verbal cue:** Present visual material within 12 inches and say "look" (or similar verbal cue). Verbal cues should be limited, as the child may focus on interpreting language rather than the task at hand, which is to look. Wait a predetermined

time, up to 30 seconds. Present the object three times. If there is no response, move to the next level cue.

3. **Visual stimulus with tactile cue:** Present visual material within 12 inches and, using hand-under-hand guidance, gently guide the child's hand to the light or toy. Wait a predetermined time, up to 30 seconds. Present the object three times. If there is no response, move to the next level cue.

4. **Visual stimulus with physical/full body contact:** Present visual material within

12 inches while the child is seated in an adult's lap and supported under the upper arm. Wait a predetermined time, up to 30 seconds. Present the object three times. If there is no response, present a different visual item.

The systematic progression of support will depend on the child's visual, auditory, tactile, motor, and communication skills. This format provides practitioners with a structure for presenting materials in a thoughtful manner based on the visual, auditory, and tactile features which best support visual attention for children who are deafblind. Highlighting tactile features during administration of the CVI Range promotes understanding and informs the child about the presence and absence of materials, direction and position of materials, and variable qualities of objects, such as size, surface texture, weight, shape, and temperature (Ferrell et al., 2014).

The following two scenarios provide examples of methods used to support the CVI Range assessment and instruction with students who are deafblind. They underscore the importance of presenting sensory cues in a systematic manner for these children and youths.

Aidan

Aidan is an 18-year-old student who had meningitis at 18 months of age, resulting in significant neurological impairment, cerebral palsy, and bilateral moderate sensorineural hearing loss. He attends a substantially separate classroom in an urban public high school. Educational staff report that Aidan's visual attention to people and materials is inconsistent. He wears cochlear implants, which he received at age 8, and his motor challenges affect his ability to grasp materials. He uses a tactile switch device for expressive communication and to make choices of preferred items. He responds best to simple tactile signs when an adult places his or her hands under Aidan's hands and presents signs slowly and with verbal input. Aidan spends most of his school day in a wheelchair or prone stander,

and he wears a body jacket to support his upper body. His physical limitations require that all materials be brought to his wheelchair and placed under his hands so that he can tactilely experience his world.

Aidan was referred to the school district's teacher of students with visual impairments for an evaluation of his functional vision as part of his transition planning. He had not been receiving vision services for the past five years, as team members believed that his lack of visual response was due to severe intellectual disability.

The teacher of students with visual impairments selected the CVI Range as part of Aidan's functional vision assessment. She began administering the assessment in Aidan's classroom, in a corner away from busy activity. She first presented visual materials, but Aidan did not respond. She then repeated three presentations of visual materials and waited up to 30 seconds, but Aidan did not indicate any response, including looking toward the target or demonstrating changes in breathing, tensing of his hands or arms, extension of his legs, or overt facial expression. Next, the teacher presented a progressive hierarchy of cues, starting first with visual cues, then pairing them with auditory cues, then bringing Aidan's hands gently to the object on his table and providing guidance under the forearm. She noticed that as soon as the assessment item was placed under Aidan's hands, he moved his fingers slightly over the toy and appeared to smile. She continued by presenting a variety of visual items, touching the object to his hands and then bringing each item up into different visual fields (central, right, left, upper, and lower, all within 12 inches from Aidan's face). Each time, the teacher waited 20 to 30 seconds for Aidan to respond. Aidan began to respond to visual items, as demonstrated by his increased smiling and rate of breathing when he detected various lights and illuminated objects.

JoJo

JoJo is 5 years old and lives at home with her grandmother. She has an intellectual disability due to nonaccidental trauma at age 10 months. She is nonverbal, has a severe bilateral sensorineural hearing loss, and has cochlear implants. Her grandmother is concerned that JoJo doesn't consistently orient toward or look at faces. Although medical reports suggest mild optic nerve hypoplasia, these findings don't explain JoJo's lack of visual attention to faces. JoJo detects many sounds in her environment, and she consistently smiles when she hears her grandmother's voice.

Following a discussion with JoJo's grandmother about her concerns and understanding of JoJo's vision, the teacher of students with visual impairments and JoJo's classroom teacher conducted the CVI Range, presenting a variety of assessment tools in each visual field and noting whether JoJo looked in the direction of each item. The classroom teacher had worked directly with JoJo for over two years and she was familiar with subtleties in JoJo's communication. For example, JoJo would often look away when she was fatigued or disinterested. During the assessment, the classroom teacher interacted directly with JoJo while the teacher of students with visual impairments gave directions. After careful presentation of several visual materials and little to no response, the classroom teacher activated a musical toy for 10 to 15 seconds. JoJo smiled immediately and appeared more alert. The classroom teacher then placed the toy in each visual field and simultaneously activated the music. JoJo responded by looking and orienting her eyes in the appropriate direction. The classroom teacher then presented the musical toy in each visual field without activating the music. JoJo still responded consistently and appeared more engaged, anticipating that music was a part of the process.

Models for the CVI Range Assessment with Children Who Are Deafblind

The Division for Early Childhood of the Council for Exceptional Children (2007) recommends that all assessment, regardless of a child's disability, be comprehensive, universally designed, based on

real-world skills, and include ongoing monitoring of the child's development and learning. The principles of universal design for learning (UDL) are especially applicable to the use of the CVI Range with children who are deaf or hard of hearing or deafblind. The three principles of UDL highlight the need for individualized assessment and instruction and can be applied to the assessment process (Center for Applied Special Technology, n.d.; Hartmann, 2011; Hartman & Weismer, 2016; Jackson, 2005):

1. **Multiple means of representation,** using varying levels of complexity, considering a range of perception levels, and including use of visual, auditory, and tactile cues

2. **Multiple means of action and expression,** so that a variety of learning styles and expressive modes are accepted and the child is provided numerous opportunities to make choices and express his or her preferences and abilities

3. **Multiple means of engagement,** based on the child's interests and preferences and including the use of scaffolding supports, additional response time, and repetition

Two different assessment approaches can be used in the CVI Range assessment process for children who are deafblind. The *teacher-directed approach* involves the teacher of students with visual impairments presenting a variety of items in various locations, observing whether the child looks at or in the direction of the item, and directing and controlling all aspects of the assessment session (Sandall, Schwartz, & Joseph, 2001). This approach tends to be used more in clinical settings where time or services are limited.

A second assessment approach, which is often more appropriate for a child who is deafblind, is the *child-guided approach,* which evolved from the work of Dr. Jan van Dijk and his colleagues (van Dijk & Nelson, 1998). Child-guided assessment strategies involve assessing the child in an environment which is comfortable or familiar; using a formative process that guides and monitors the child's interests; following the child's interest and movements and establishing a routine of imitation, turn taking, and reciprocal anticipation; and adapting assessment steps based on the child's interests and emotions. By monitoring and shaping the child's attention and signaling, the adult supports the child's responding to a variety of visual, auditory, and tactile stimuli (MacFarland, 1995; Nelson, van Dijk, Oster, & McDonnell, 2009). The child-guided approach incorporates presentation of a visual stimulus, use of additional wait time, followed by the item's verbal label or sign, and immediate acknowledgment of the child's visual and auditory attention.

Within the child-guided assessment process, *hand-under-hand technique* is used. The adult places his or her hands under the child's and gently guides and follows the child's lead and exploration of play materials (Miles, 2008). The hand-under-hand technique is useful when a child may be resistant to unfamiliar people, toys, and procedures or when a child avoids interactions that are perceived as a "demand situation." The use of touch, physical contact, or hand-under-hand strategies are provided to let the child know the adult is waiting for a response and to gently guide the child's attempts at reaching and manipulation of

toys and materials (Miles & Riggio, 1999). Hand-under-hand strategies may also be helpful in situations in which a child may have significant motor challenges or lack overt looking responses, such as eye widening or head turning, as the adult can feel the child's physical reactions to the presentation of a variety of visual stimuli, such as changes in biobehavioral states, including tensing or movement of the child's hand or fingers.

Overall, the child-guided assessment approach allows for smooth transition from assessment practices to intervention by establishing chains of behavior that are repeated, along with clear signals to help the child anticipate steps of a larger routine or activity (Nelson et al., 2009).

The following two scenarios contrast a teacher-directed approach to conducting a CVI Range assessment with a child-guided approach.

Ms. Roberts, a teacher of students with visual impairments in a large, urban school, is asked to conduct the CVI Range for Jing, who is 6 years old and nonverbal. Jing, who was born at 25 weeks' gestation, has a mild conductive hearing loss due to frequent ear infections and has been assessed by her ophthalmologist as having a visual acuity of 20/200 due to optic atrophy. Jing reaches for toys and materials using her left hand, due to a right hemiparesis.

Michael Williams

Using hand-under-hand technique, the adult places his hands under the child's hands, gently exploring and following the child's lead (left). In this instance, the child begins to direct the adult, communicating through tactile gestures what should happen next (right).

Ms. Roberts plans to conduct the CVI Range in a small assessment room with multiple shelves containing numerous assessment materials and manuals. Jing is seated in a scoop plastic chair at an adult desk. After Ms. Roberts presents a variety of toys and light stimuli in Jing's visual fields (right and left, central, and upper and lower fields), Jing looks to each location and attempts to reach toward items by moving her left hand slightly upward, usually within 5 seconds of presentation. Each time Jing regards various lights and assessment materials, Ms. Roberts removes each item and moves on to the next without comment. Jing is not provided direct access to items following each presentation. About 10 minutes into the session, Jing sweeps several toys off the desk onto the floor and attempts to remove herself from the chair. She vocalizes loudly, appears frustrated, and manually signs "finished" repeatedly. Her classroom teacher comes to the door and escorts Jing back to class.

Compare Jing's experience and responses when Ms. Roberts used a teacher-directed approach to the CVI assessment to the following alternative scenario using a child-guided approach.

Ms. Roberts plans to conduct the CVI Range in a small area of Jing's classroom. Jing is seated in her adapted chair at a small desk in a cubby area where she typically engages in desktop instructional activities. Ms. Roberts presents a variety of toys and light sources in each of Jing's visual fields. As Jing looks to each location and attempts to reach toward items with her left hand, Ms. Roberts encourages Jing to touch and explore each item. Using hand-under-hand guidance with both of Jing's hands, Ms. Roberts rhythmically taps Jing's left hand on each item, while commenting and signing affirmatively, "Jing is looking." Ms. Roberts removes each item slowly, waits for Jing to indicate that she wants another item presented by kicking her feet or smiling, and then presents the item. Jing's engagement with each assess-

ment item is not only permitted but encouraged in an effort to build attention and anticipation and gather assessment information.

Although the teacher-guided approach has the potential to yield findings more quickly when administering the CVI Range, it presents several concerns with regard to gathering valid results. First, communication challenges or difficulties in interactions between the teacher and child may result in underestimating the child's abilities (Nelson et al., 2002). Second, children who are deaf-blind often need tailored supports and additional time to respond to a variety of visual, auditory, and tactile experiences: a warm up to testing or demand situations and exploring materials to gain an understanding about their surroundings and the demands of the task (Ferrell et al., 2014).

An example of a child-guided assessment approach is the diagnostic intervention model (Jannsen, Riksen-Walraven & van Dijk, 2003; MacFarland, 1995). The model offers a systematic approach to assessment in which the examiner arranges the environmental contingencies, establishes joint attention, interprets and supports the child's signals, modifies the interaction as needed, and uses a reciprocal approach to interaction. Originally, this model was intended to facilitate communication, but the approach may be helpful in coaching the child to detect and interpret visual information based on the 10 CVI characteristics. As each CVI characteristic and phase is evaluated, the adult presents, the child responds, and the adult comments and then proceeds with the next presentation, adding additional tactile, sign language, object, or other cues as needed.

As already noted, the CVI Range should be administered in familiar and functional contexts and across multiple settings to be sure that the results are capturing the child's true visual abilities. Once the CVI Range has been completed, repeated assessment probes should be carried out to ensure that the CVI Range findings reflect an accurate picture of the child's visual abilities and learning needs across time and also reflect the child's auditory and tactile needs.

Finally, when the results of the CVI Range are presented to parents and caregivers, they should include clear and concise information, based on the child's skills within each phase and on the 10 CVI characteristics, and targeting areas for future development. Parents should receive detailed information regarding strategies to encourage their child's use of vision, tactile strategies to facilitate engagement with toys and materials, and recommendations for adaptation of materials and communication or calendar system items. Information should include a description of the characteristic, the strategy to support progress, adaptations to support the child's responding, and suggested environments in which the characteristic might be addressed.

Conclusion

The procedures, practices, and recommendations presented in this chapter are intended to make the CVI Range assessment with children who are deafblind more reliable and accurate. To improve access to accurate and valid CVI assessment of children who are deafblind and provide the most effective practice of assessment and intervention planning for this population requires

- screening of infants and children with etiologies or conditions most frequently associated with both CVI and deafblindness;
- in-service training of personnel in the use of the CVI Range, systematic assessment, and instructional strategies; and
- curricula addressing CVI and deafblindness in personnel preparation programs related to the fields of visual impairment, deafness and hearing impairment, deafblindness, and severe or multiple disabilities.

There is a lack of trained personnel in the fields of blindness and visual impairment and deafblindness who are skilled in the use of the CVI Range and evidence-based practices for learners who are

deafblind, such as assessment modifications, material adaptations, and systematic instruction procedures (Parker & Nelson, 2016). Typically, personnel trained in the area of severe or multiple disabilities have skills in observation, assessment, and instruction, while teachers of students with visual impairments, teachers of students who are deaf or hard of hearing, interveners, and deafblind specialists do not (Browder, Wood, Thompson, & Ribuffo, 2014; Ferrell et al., 2014). Although there are several personnel preparation programs in visual impairment and deafness, most programs do not emphasize basic assessment and instructional strategies for this unique population. And, although professionals in the field of visual impairment and deafness are knowledgeable about topics such as eye conditions, assessment of functional vision, assistive listening devices, and environmental acoustics, there is a persistent lack of knowledge in how to teach discrete skills such as promoting consistent use of tactile sign across environments or how to encourage reaching for materials presented in the best visual field. Finally, there is a tendency for these disciplines to attend to or "own" only one sensory disability, as reflected by inadequate training and practicum experiences in the area of deafblindness.

The increased incidence of CVI identified in children who are deafblind over the past 15 years can be attributed to a variety of factors, such as increased research in brain function (Jan, Good, & Hoyt, 2006), increased awareness of service providers regarding risk factors for CVI in the deafblind population, and advanced training of service providers to more accurately assess and identify children who are deafblind. Notably, the increase in the assessment and identification of children with CVI and deafblindness is a direct result of national and statewide efforts to improve competencies of service providers in the use of the CVI Range (such as the New England Consortium for Deafblind CVI Advisor Program, the CVI Mentorship Program in several states, National Center on Deaf-Blindness CVI training provided to Deafblind Projects, and the Perkins-Roman CVI Range Endorsement).

Parents of children who are deafblind with CVI need accurate information about CVI and specific knowledge in how to arrange the home environment to best support their child's vision (Roman-Lantzy, 2018). Frequently, parents are focused on one sensory loss and tend to align with the sensory community that was first identified or the one that is most obvious or most significant. Parents of children who are first diagnosed as deaf or hard of hearing and later have vision loss identified tend to align with the world of deafness as a result of the primary challenges in communication access. For example, parents and caregivers who connect more with the deafness community may misinterpret their child's lack of attention or orientation as resulting from hearing loss issues rather than CVI. It is important to "meet families where they are" and introduce additional CVI and sensory considerations in a respectful and honest manner.

REFERENCES

Alam, S., Satterfield, A., Mason, C. A., & Deng, X. (2016). Progress in standardization of reporting and analysis of data from early hearing detection and intervention (EHDI) programs. *Journal of Early Hearing Detection and Intervention, 1*(2), 2–7.

Alsop, L., Blaha, R., & Kloos, E. (2000). *The intervener in early intervention and educational settings for children and youth with deafblindness.* Monmouth, OR: The National Technical Assistance Consortium for Children and Young Adults Who Are Deaf-Blind.

Alsop, L., Robinson, C., Goehl, K., Lace, J., Belote, M., & Rodriguez-Gil, G. (2007). *Interveners in the classroom: Guidelines for teams working with students who are deafblind.* Logan: Utah State University, SKI-HI Institute.

American Speech-Language-Hearing Association. (2015). Type, degree, and configuration of hearing loss. Retrieved from https://www.asha.org/uploadedFiles/AIS-Hearing-Loss-Types-Degree-Configuration.pdf

American Speech-Language-Hearing Association. (n.d.). Hearing loss. Retrieved from https://www.asha.org/public/hearing/Hearing-Loss

Belote, M., & Maier, J. (2014). Why deaf-blindness and autism can look so much alike. *reSources, 19*(2).

Blaha, R. (2001). *Calendars for students with multiple impairments including deafblindness.* Austin: Texas School for the Blind and Visually Impaired.

Blake, K. D., Hartshorne, T. S., Lawand, C., Dailor, A. N., & Thelin, J. W. (2008). Cranial nerve manifestations in CHARGE syndrome. *American Journal of Medical Genetics Part A, 146A*(5), 585–592.

Brady, N. C., & Bashinski, S. M. (2008). Increasing communication in children with concurrent vision and hearing loss. *Research and Practice for Persons with Severe Disabilities, 33*(1–2), 59–70.

Browder, D. M., Wood, L., Thompson, J., & Ribuffo, C. (2014). *Evidence-based practices for students with severe disabilities* (CEEDAR Document No. IC-3). Gainesville: University of Florida, Collaboration for Effective Educator, Development, Accountability, and Reform Center. Retrieved from http://ceedar.education.ufl.edu/wp-content/uploads/2014/09/IC-3_FINAL_03-03-15.pdf

Bruce, S., Ferrell, K., & Luckner, J. L. (2016, Fall). Guidelines for the administration of educational programs for students who are deaf/hard of hearing, visually impaired, or deafblind. *Journal of the American Academy of Special Education Professionals.* Retrieved from https://files.eric.ed.gov/fulltext/EJ1129776.pdf

Bruce, S. M., & Borders, C. (2015). Communication and language in learners who are deaf and hard of hearing with disabilities: Theories, research, and practice. *American Annals of the Deaf, 160*(4), 368–384.

Bruce, S. M., Janssen, M. J., & Bashinski, S. M. (2016). Individualizing and personalizing communication and literacy instruction for children who are deafblind. *Journal of Deafblind Studies on Communication, 2,* 73–87.

Bruce, S. M., Nelson, C., Perez, A., Stutzman, B., & Barnhill, B. A. (2016). The state of research on communication and literacy in deafblindness. *American Annals of the Deaf, 161*(4), 424–443.

Burkey, J. M. (2015). *The hearing-loss guide: Useful information and advice for patients and families.* New Haven, CT: Yale University Press.

Carvill, S. (2001). Sensory impairments, intellectual disability and psychiatry. *Journal of Intellectual Disability Research, 45*(6), 467–483.

Center for Applied Special Technology. (n.d.). About universal design for learning. Retrieved from http://www.cast.org/udl

Chen, D. (1998). Early identification of infants who are deaf-blind: A systematic approach for early interventionists. *Deaf-Blind Perspectives, 5*(3), 1–6.

Chen, D. (2014a). Promoting early communication and language development. In D. Chen (Ed.), *Essential elements in early intervention: Visual impairment and multiple disabilities* (2nd ed., pp. 395–462). New York, NY: AFB Press.

Chen, D. (2014b). Understanding hearing loss: Implications for early intervention. In D. Chen (Ed.), *Essential elements in early intervention: Visual impairment and multiple disabilities* (2nd ed., pp. 294–340). New York, NY: AFB Press.

Chen, D., & Downing, J. E. (2006). *Tactile strategies for children who have visual impairments and multiple disabilities: Promoting communication and learning skills.* New York, NY: AFB Press.

Clarin, G. P. (2015). Auditory neuropathy spectrum disorder. In *A Resource guide for early hearing detection and intervention* (pp. 8-1–8-8). Logan: Utah State University, National Center for Hearing Assessment and Management. Retrieved from http://infanthearing.org/ehdi-ebook/2015_ebook/8-Chapter8AuditoryNeuropathy2015.pdf

Congenital rubella syndrome: 30 years after the epidemic of the 1960's. (n.d.). *The Free Library.* Retrieved from https://www.thefreelibrary.com/Congenital+rubella+syndrome%3a+30+years+after+the+epidemic+of+the . . . -a017986018

Costello, J. M. (2011, November). *CVI, complex communication needs and AAC: A structure to success.* Presentation at the American Speech-Language-Hearing Association convention, Boston, MA. Retrieved from https://www.asha.org/Events/convention/handouts/2007/0901_Costello_John_M/

Costello, J. M., Patak, L., & Pritchard, J. (2010). Communication vulnerable patients in the pediatric ICU: Enhancing care through augmentative and alternative communication. *Journal of Pediatric Rehabilitation Medicine, 3*(4), 289–301.

Cox, P. R., & Dykes, M. K. (2001). Effective classroom adaptations for students with visual impairments. *TEACHING Exceptional Children, 33*(6), 68–74.

Dammeyer, J. (2014). Symptoms of autism among children with congenital deafblindness. *Journal of Autism and Developmental Disorders, 44*(5), 1095–1102.

Division for Early Childhood of the Council for Exceptional Children. (2007). *Promoting positive outcomes for children with disabilities: Recommendations for curriculum, assessment, and program evaluation.* Missoula, MT: Author. Retrieved from https://www.naeyc.org/sites/default/files/globally-shared/downloads/PDFs/resources/position-statements/PrmtgPositiveOutcomes.pdf

Downing, J. E., & Chen, D. (2014). Critical transitions: Educating young children in general education preschools. In D. Chen (Ed.), *Essential elements in early intervention: Visual impairment and multiple disabilities* (2nd ed., pp. 463–519). New York, NY: AFB Press.

Dunn, W. (2008). Sensory processing: Identifying patterns and support strategies. In K. D. Buron & P. Wolfberg (Eds.), *Learners on the autism spectrum: Preparing highly qualified educators* (pp. 138–159). Shawnee Mission, KS: Autism Asperger Publishing.

Ferrell, K. A., Bruce, S., & Luckner, J. L. (2014). *Evidence-based practices for students with sensory impairments.* Gainesville: University of Florida, Collaboration for Effective Educator, Development, Accountability, and Reform Center. Retrieved from http://ceedar.education.ufl.edu/tools/innovation-configurations/

Garber, M., & Huebner, K. M. (2017). Visual impairment: Terminology, demographics, society. In M. C. Holbrook, T. McCarthy, & C. Kamei-Hannan (Eds.), *Foundations of education: Vol. I. History and theory of teaching children and youths with visual impairments* (3rd ed., pp. 50–72). New York, NY: AFB Press.

Gense, M. H., & Gense, D. J. (2005). *Autism spectrum disorders and visual impairment: Meeting students' learning needs.* New York, NY: AFB Press.

Hartmann, E. (2011). Universal design for learning. *Practice Perspectives: Highlighting Information on Deaf-Blindness, 8,* 1–4. Retrieved from http://www.nationaldb.org/documents/products/udl.pdf

Hartmann, E., & Weismer, P. (2016). Technology implementation and curriculum engagement for children and youth who are deafblind. *American Annals of the Deaf, 161*(4), 462–473.

Hartshorne, T. S., Hefner, M. A., & Davenport, S. L. (2005). Behavior in CHARGE syndrome: Introduction to the special topic. *American Journal of Medical Genetics Part A, 133A*(3), 228–231.

Hatton, D. D. (2014). Advancing the education of students with visual impairments through evidence-based practices. In D. D. Hatton (Ed.), *International review of research in developmental disabilities: Current issues in the education of students with visual impairments: Vol. 46* (pp. 1–22). Waltham, MA: Academic Press.

Hatton, D. D., Schwietz, E., Boyer, B., & Rychwalski, P. (2007). Babies count: The national registry for children with visual impairments, birth to 3 years. *Journal of the American Association for Pediatric Ophthalmology and Strabismus, 11*(4), 351–355.

Individuals with Disabilities Education Improvement Act (IDEA), 20 U.S.C. § 1400 (2004).

Jackson, R. M. (2005). *Curriculum access for students with low-incidence disabilities: The promise of universal design for learning.* Wakefield, MA: National Center on Accessing the General Curriculum. Retrieved from http://sde.ok.gov/sde/sites/ok.gov.sde/files/LowIncidence.pdf

Jan, J. E., Good, W. V., & Hoyt, C. S. (2006). An international classification of neurological visual disorders in children. In E. Dennison & A. H. Lueck (Eds.), *Proceedings of the summit on cerebral/cortical visual impairment: Educational, family, and medical perspectives April 30, 2005* (pp. 61–64). New York, NY: AFB Press.

Jan, J. E., Heaven, R. K. B., Matsuba, C., Langley, M. B., Roman-Lantzy, C., & Anthony, T. L. (2013). Windows into the visual brain: New discoveries about the visual system, its functions, and implications for practitioners. *Journal of Visual Impairment & Blindness, 107*(4), 251–261.

Janssen, M. J., Riksen-Walraven, J. M., & van Dijk, J. P. M. (2003). Toward a diagnostic intervention model for fostering harmonious interactions between deaf-blind children and their educators. *Journal of Visual Impairment & Blindness, 97*(4), 197–214.

Kong, L., Fry, M., Al-Samarraie, M., Gilbert, C., & Steinkuller, P. G. (2012). An update on progress and the changing epidemiology of causes of childhood blindness worldwide. *Journal of the American Association for Pediatric Ophthalmology and Strabismus, 16*(6), 501–507.

MacFarland, S. Z. C. (1995). Teaching strategies of the van Dijk curricular approach. *Journal of Visual Impairment & Blindness, 89*(3), 222–228.

Madell, J. (2013). Educational audiology: From observation to recommendation. *Audiology Online.* Retrieved from https://www.audiologyonline.com/articles/educational-audiology-from-observation-to-11853

Mafong, D. D., Pletcher, S. D., Hoyt, C., & Lalwani, A. K. (2002). Ocular findings in children with congenital sensorineural hearing loss. *Archives of Otolaryngology—Head & Neck Surgery, 128*(11), 1303–1306.

Malloy, P., & Killoran, J. (2007). Children who are deaf-blind. *Practice Perspectives: Highlighting Information on Deaf-Blindness, 2,* 1–4. Retrieved from https://nationaldb.org/library/page/2064

Malloy, P., Stremel Thomas, K., Schalock, M., Davies, S., Purvis, B., & Udell, T. (2009). *Early identification of infants who are deaf-blind.* Monmouth: Western Oregon University, The Research Institute, National Center on Deaf-Blindness. Retrieved from http://documents.nationaldb.org/products/EI-deaf-blind-infants.pdf

McInnes, J. M., & Treffry, J. A. (1982). *Deaf-blind infants and children: A developmental guide.* Toronto, ON: University of Toronto Press.

Miles, B. (2008). *Overview on deaf-blindness.* Monmouth: Western Oregon University, The Research Institute, National Center on Deaf-Blindness. Retrieved from https://nationaldb.org/library/page/1934

Miles, B., & Riggio, M. (Eds.). (1999). *Remarkable conversations: A guide to developing meaningful communication with children and young adults who are deafblind.* Watertown, MA: Perkins School for the Blind.

Morgan, S. (n.d.). Sign language with people who are deaf-blind: Suggestions for tactile and visual modifications. Retrieved from www.deafblind.com/slmorgan.html

Morlet, T. (2010). Auditory neuropathy spectrum disorder and (central) auditory processing disorder. *Deaf-Blind Perspectives, 17*(2), 1–2. Retrieved from http://documents.nationaldb.org/dbp/apr2010.htm#auditory

Moss, K. (2001). Syndromes which often result in combined vision and hearing loss. *See/Hear Newsletter.* Retrieved from http://www.tsbvi.edu/seehear/archive/syndromes.html

Müller, E. (2006). *Deafblind child counts: Issues and challenges.* Alexandria, VA: National Association of State Directors of Special Education. Retrieved from http://nasdse.org/DesktopModules/DNNspot-Store/ProductFiles/25_b77a012d-78ff-40ca-87e7-03bb13784ba4.pdf

National Center on Deaf-Blindness. (n.d.). Why a national child count. Monmouth: Western Oregon University, The Research Institute. Retrieved from https://nationaldb.org/pages/show/why-a-national-child-count

Nelson, C., & Bruce, S. M. (2016). Critical issues in the lives of children and youth who are deaf-blind. *American Annals of the Deaf, 161*(4), 406–411.

Nelson, C., van Dijk, J., McDonnell, A. P., & Thompson, K. (2002). A framework for understanding young children with severe multiple disabilities: The van Dijk approach to assessment. *Research and Practice for Persons with Severe Disabilities, 27*(2), 97–111.

Nelson, C., van Dijk, J., Oster, T., & McDonnell, A. (2009). *Child-guided strategies: The van Dijk approach to assessment for understanding children and youth with sensory impairments and multiple disabilities.* Louisville, KY: American Printing House for the Blind.

New England Consortium for Deafblind Technical Assistance and Training. (n.d.a). Child registration. Retrieved from http://www.nec4db.org/child-registration.html

New England Consortium for Deafblind Technical Assistance and Training. (n.d.b). What is deafblindness? Retrieved from http://www.nec4db.org/what-is-deafblindness-.html

Parker, A. T., & Ivy, S. E. (2014). Communication development of children with visual impairment and deafblindness: A synthesis of intervention research. In D. D. Hatton (Ed.), *International review of research in developmental disabilities: Current issues in the education of students with visual impairments: Vol. 46* (pp. 101–144). Waltham, MA: Academic Press.

Parker, A. T., & Nelson, C. (2016). Toward a comprehensive system of personnel development in deafblind education. *American Annals of the Deaf, 161*(4), 486–501.

Picou, E. M., Ricketts, T. A., & Hornsby, B. W. (2011). Visual cues and listening effort: Individual variability. *Journal of Speech, Language, and Hearing Research, 54*(5), 1416–1430.

Plotkin, S. A. (2006). The history of rubella and rubella vaccination leading to elimination. *Clinical Infectious Diseases, 43*(Supplement 3), S164–S168.

Riggio, M. (1993). Population/demographics: Reaction. In J. W. Reiman & P. A. Johnson (Eds.), *Proceedings of the national symposium on children and youth who are deaf-blind* (pp. 67–72). Monmouth, OR: Teaching Research.

Riggio, M., & McLetchie, B. (Eds.). (2008). *Deafblindness: Educational service guidelines.* Watertown, MA: Perkins School for the Blind.

Roman-Lantzy, C. (2018). *Cortical visual impairment: An approach to assessment and intervention* (2nd ed.). New York, NY: AFB Press.

Rowland, C., Chen, D., Stillman, R., Mar, H., & Syler, L. (2009). *Data summary: Validation of evidence-based assessment strategies to promote achievement in children who are deafblind* (Grant #H324D030001). Portland: Oregon Health & Science University. Retrieved from https://www.ohsu.edu/xd/research/centers-institutes/institute-on-development-and-disability/design-to-learn/completed-projects/upload/Deafblind-Assessment-Summary.pdf

Sacks, S. Z. (2016). Educating students with visual impairments who have multiple disabilities: An overview. In S. Z. Sacks & M. C. Zatta (Eds.), *Keys to educational success: Teaching students with visual impairments and multiple disabilities* (pp. 3–64). New York, NY: AFB Press.

Sandall, S., Schwartz, I., & Joseph, G. (2001). A building blocks model for effective instruction in inclusive early childhood settings. *Young Exceptional Children, 4*(3), 3–9.

Schalock, M. D. (2017a). Child count code sheet. Monmouth: Western Oregon University, The Research Institute, National Center on Deaf-Blindness. Retrieved from https://nationaldb.org/materials/page/1998/11

Schalock, M. D. (2017b). *The 2016 national child count of children and youth who are deaf-blind.* Monmouth: Western Oregon University, The Research Institute, National Center on Deaf-Blindness. Retrieved from https://nationaldb.org/reports/national-child-count-2016

Sharma, A., Ruscetta, M. N., & Chi, D. H. (2009). Ophthalmologic findings in children with sensorineural hearing loss. *Archives of Otolaryngology—Head & Neck Surgery, 135*(2), 119–123.

Silberman, R. K., Bruce, S. M., & Nelson, C. (2004). Children with sensory impairments. In F. P. Orelove, D. Sobsey, & R. K. Silberman (Eds.), *Educating children with multiple disabilities: A collaborative approach* (4th ed., pp. 425–528). Baltimore, MD: Paul H. Brookes.

Skoczenski, A. M., & Good, W. V. (2004). Vernier acuity is selectivity affected in infants and children with cortical visual impairment. *Developmental Medicine & Child Neurology, 46*(8), 526–532.

Smaldino, J. J., & Flexer, C. (2012). *Handbook of acoustic accessibility: Best practices for listening, learning, and literacy in the classroom.* New York, NY: Thieme Medical Publishers.

Spooner, F., Browder, D. M., & Mims, P. J. (2011). Evidenced-based practices. In D. M. Browder & F. Spooner (Eds.), *Teaching students with moderate and severe disabilities* (pp. 92–124). New York, NY: Guilford Press.

Stredler-Brown, A., & Johnson, D. C. (2003). Functional auditory performance indicators: An integrated approach to auditory skill development. Retrieved from http://www.tsbvi.edu/attachments/FunctionalAuditoryPerformanceIndicators.pdf

Swaminathan, M. (2011). Cortical visual impairment in children—A new challenge for the future? *Oman Journal of Ophthalmology, 4*(1), 1–2.

van Dijk, J., & Nelson, C. (1998). History and change in the education of children who are deaf-blind since the rubella epidemic of the 1960s: Influence of methods developed in the Netherlands. *Deaf-Blind Perspectives, 5*(2), 1–5

Vernon, M., Grieve, B. J., & Shaver, K. (1980). Handicapping conditions associated with the congenital rubella syndrome. *American Annals of the Deaf, 125*(8), 993–997.

Welch, T. R. (2016). Communication skills. In S. Z. Sacks & M. C. Zatta (Eds.), *Keys to educational success: Teaching students with visual impairments and multiple disabilities* (pp. 229–259). New York, NY: AFB Press.

Wickremasinghe, A. C., Rogers E. E., Johnson, B. C., Shen, A., Barkovich, A. J., & Marco, E. J. (2013). Children born prematurely have atypical sensory profiles. *Journal of Perinatology, 33*(8), 631–635.

Wiley, S., Parnell, L., & Belhorn, T. (2016). Promoting early identification and intervention for children who are deaf or hard of hearing, children with vision impairment, and children with deafblind conditions. *The Journal of Early Hearing Detection and Intervention, 1*(1), 26–33.

World Health Organization. (2012). *Global data on visual impairments 2010.* Geneva, Switzerland: Author. Retrieved from http://www.who.int/blindness/GLOBALDATAFINALforweb.pdf?ua=1

Wright, P. W. D., & Wright, P. D. (2007). *Wrightslaw: Special education law* (2nd ed.). Hartfield, VA: Harbor House Law Press.

Xoinis, K., Weirather, Y., Mavoori, H., Shaha, S. H., & Iwamoto, L. M. (2007). Extremely low birth weight infants are at high risk for auditory neuropathy. *Journal of Perinatology, 27*(11), 718–723.

Yoshinaga-Itano, C., Sedey, A. L., Coulter, D. K., & Mehl, A. L. (1998). Language of early- and later-identified children with hearing loss. *Pediatrics, 102*(5), 1161–1171.

Index

activities
  addressing, 117, 120*t*, 126–33
  balanced, 97, 108, 114*fig.*, 124, 137–38, 140
  transitioning between, 141
array, complexity of, 100, 104, 115–16, 170*t*, 172
auditory neuropathy spectrum disorder (ANSD), 238–39
auditory processing disorder (APD), 238, 239
auditory scanning, 68, 69, 73, 75
augmentative and alternative communication (AAC)
  approaches, 60–61
  assessments, 73–74
  challenges of, 69–70
  and early intervention, 68
  overview of, 61–63
  recognition of, 65–66
autism spectrum disorder (ASD)
  and facial discrimination, 167
  similarities between CVI and, 168*t*, 236

backlighting, 14, 20, 49, 79, 193
balanced activities, 97, 108, 114*fig.*, 124, 137–38, 140
Bandura, A., 162, 163
Beukelman, D. R., 40–41
blank space, in 'What's the Complexity?' Framework, 117, 122
blind and visually impaired children, history of, 63–64
Bollen, L., 174
braille, 50
branching, 69
Bruner, J. S., 27
Building on Patterns program, 50
Burden, S. K., 213

calendar system, in CVI Range assessment, 244
Candy, R., 213
cane use, 201–2

challenging tasks, 101, 106*t*, 120*t*, 124, 126–32, 136–37
CHARGE syndrome, 229, 236
child-guided CVI Range assessment, 250, 252
cognitive mapping, 186*t*, 194–98
color
  attraction to, as CVI characteristic, 61
  in augmentative and alternative communication (AAC) approaches, 69
  and orientation and mobility training, 205*t*, 207*t*, 209*t*, 214–15
  in Phase III CVI, 16, 18*fig.*
  and salient visual features in literacy, 46–47, 49
  and teaching concept development, 189
  and visual discrimination in literacy, 45, 46
  in 'What's the Complexity?' Framework, 117–22, 136, 143
comfortable tasks, 101, 106*t*, 124
commercial establishments, layouts of, 191–92
comparative language, 28, 29*t*, 30, 32*t*, 36, 191, 200, 208*t*
comparative thought, 30–31, 32*fig.*, 33–34, 36, 44
complex communication needs (CCN), children with, 60–61, 88–89. *See also* Vision Language Learning Communication (VLLC) Framework
  assessment of, 72, 73–74
  augmentative and alternative communication (AAC) approaches to, 61–63
  challenges of, 69–71
  diagnostic categories associated with, 67*t*
  and history of blind or visually impaired children, 63–64
  identification of, 72, 73
  intervention and interprofessional collaboration for, 66–69, 72, 74–88
  prevalence of, 65–66
  unique patterns in, 72–73

concept development, 185–92

conductive hearing loss, 238

context support method, 48, 50

Cortical Visual Impairment (CVI). *See also* CVI
    characteristics; CVI Range; Phase I Cortical
    Visual Impairment; Phase II Cortical Visual
    Impairment; Phase III Cortical Visual
    Impairment; Phases of CVI
    challenges of, 95–97
    early intervention in, 68
    as health and educational crisis, 4
    prevalence of, 64–65
    similarities between autism spectrum disorders
        and, 168*t*, 236
    training and advocacy efforts for, 239

CVI characteristics. *See also* color; distance viewing;
    light; movement; visual complexity; visual fields;
    visual latency; visually guided reach; visual
    novelty; visual reflexes
    and cognitive mapping, 194
    defined, 4
    integrating, in teaching mobility, 198–203
    integrating, in teaching orientation, 185–98
    intersection of social skill competence and, 164,
        170
    orientation and mobility guidelines for, 205–11*t*
    overview of, 61
    in Phase III CVI, 14–15, 16–25
    in specialized approach to literacy, 39

CVI Progress Chart, 4

CVI Range
    and assessing orientation and mobility, 184
    assessment of, 5–8, 10
    assessment with children who are deafblind,
        250–53
    deafblindness and considerations for
        administering, 240–50
    defined, 3
    purpose of, 1

CVI Schedule, 4, 35*fig.*, 36

cytomegalovirus (CMV) infection, 236

deafblindness, 228, 253–54
    communication options for children with, 242
    and considerations for administering CVI Range,
        240–50
    defined, 228–29
    early identification, referral, and assessment of,
        239–40

education in United States, 229
    etiologies and conditions associated with, 234–35*t*
    hearing impairment and CVI, 236–39
    identifying children with CVI and, 230–33
    increase in children with, 229
    learning in children with, 229–30
    medical conditions associated with, 235*t*, 236
    models for CVI Range assessment with children
        with, 250–53
    range of combined vision and hearing loss in,
        232*fig.*
    sensory abilities and challenges in individuals with,
        230

de Jong, T., 174

diagnostic intervention model, 252

direct learning, 31, 33

distance viewing
    difficulty with, as CVI characteristic, 61
    and literacy, 49
    and mediated learning, 36
    and orientation and mobility training, 202–3, 206*t*,
        208*t*, 210*t*, 221–22
    in Phase III CVI, 20–22, 23
    and social skill development, 170*t*, 172–73
    in 'What's the Complexity?' Framework, 104

dorsal stream vision
    defined, 3
    and facial discrimination, 165
    and Phase III CVI, 11, 12–13, 15

Dutton, G. N., 95

Education for All Handicapped Children Act (EHA), 64

ego strength, 176

environment
    and assessing distance-viewing abilities, 172
    and cognitive mapping, 186*t*, 194–98
    detection of hazards in, 200–1
    and map use, 186*t*, 192–94
    and teaching concept development, 190–92
    in 'What's the Complexity?' Framework, 97, 98–100,
        108, 115–16, 126, 127*fig.*, 133, 136, 137–38

Environment Rating Guide, 98, 99*fig.*, 105, 115, 126,
    127*fig.*, 137

extremely complex environment, 100, 120*t*, 137–38

eye gaze, and joint attention, 27

facial discrimination, 164–67

failure, and social skill development, 174–76

Farah, M. J., 164

Farzin, F., 164
Fazzi, E., 212
Feuerstein, Reuven, 31
frustrational tasks, 101, 106*t*, 108, 120*t*, 136, 139–40
functional curriculum, 47, 48*fig.*
functional visual assessment (FVA), 39

Golarai, G., 167
Good, W. V., 213
Grill-Spector, K., 167

hand-under-hand technique, 248, 251
hearing loss and impairment. *See also* deafblindness
 and CVI, 236–39
  rating complexity of environment for those with, 116
  types and configurations of, 238
highly complex environment, 100, 115–16, 120*t*, 133, 140
Hou, C., 164
human guide, 198–99

imitation, 167–70
Individual Complexity Profile, 98, 105, 107–15*fig.*, 124, 125*fig.*, 139
Individuals with Disabilities Education Act (IDEA), 64, 65*fig.*
infants
 comparative thought in, 30
 CVI screening in, 239
 facial discrimination in, 164
 Newborn Hearing Screening Program, 239
 retinopathy of prematurity in, 63
 risk factors for ANSD in, 239

Jan, J. E., 213
Jeffery, L., 164
joint attention, 27, 69

Koppenhaver, D. A., 40

Lahey, J., 174
landmarks, in orientation and mobility training, 204, 205*t*
language experience method, 48, 50
latency. *See* visual latency
Lazonder, A. W., 174
learning media assessment (LMA), 39–40

light
 attraction to, as CVI characteristic, 61
 and literacy, 49
 and mediated learning, 36
 and orientation and mobility training, 206*t*, 208*t*, 210*t*, 219–21
 in Phase III CVI, 18*fig.*, 19–20
 in 'What's the Complexity?' Framework, 98–100, 122
literacy
 and beginning instruction in salient visual features, 46–47
 in children with complex communication needs, 62
 considerations for, for academic and functional curriculum learners, 48*fig.*
 definitions of, 40–41
 foundations for, 44*fig.*
 introducing words, 47–55
 and learning modalities by phase, 40*fig.*
 methods for teaching, 47–50, 51
 prerequisites for, 41–42
 progression of intervention and supports for teaching, 42–43
 sample lesson for teaching, 55–57
 specialized approach to, 39–40
 visual discrimination, recognition, and identification and, 44–46
low-visual-demands task, 101

map use, 186*t*, 192–94. *See also* cognitive mapping
masking, in 'What's the Complexity?' Framework, 117, 122
measles, 64
mediated learning, 31–36
Mehrabian, A., 162
Merabet, Lotfi, 4
minimally complex environment, 98, 115, 124
Mirenda, P., 40–41
mirror neuron system, 169–70
mixed hearing loss, 238
moderately complex environment, 100, 115, 124, 137
movement
 complexity of, 98–100, 115–16
 and literacy, 49
 need for, as CVI characteristic, 61
 and orientation and mobility training, 205*t*, 207*t*, 209*t*, 215–16
 in Phase III CVI, 16–19
 in 'What's the Complexity?' Framework, 122

Mulder, Y. G., 174
multiple disabilities, orientation and mobility considerations for individuals with, 212–13

National Deaf-Blind Child Count, 230–33, 239
neuroplasticity, 138–39
Newborn Hearing Screening Program, 239
nonambulatory individuals, orientation and mobility considerations for, 211–12
Norcia, A. M., 164
novelty. *See* visual novelty
number concepts, 189–90
numerals, dictionary of salient features of, 29*t*
numerosity, 190

ocular blindness, 195
orientation and mobility, 182–83, 225
    assessment of, 184–85
    examples of CVI considerations in, instruction, 213–24
    guidelines for targets, landmarks, and strategies, 204, 205–11*t*
    integrating CVI phases and characteristics in teaching mobility, 198–203
    integrating CVI phases and characteristics in teaching orientation, 185–98
    rationale for providing instruction in, 183–84
    special considerations for, 204–13
Orton-Gillingham method, 48

Parten, Mildred, 171
Perkins-Roman CVI Range Endorsement, 4
Perkins School for the Blind, 4
Phase I Cortical Visual Impairment
    basic mobility techniques for, 198
    benefits of cane use in, 203
    characteristics of, 15
    cognitive mapping in, 195–96
    detection of environmental hazards in, 201
    development of facial recognition in, 165
    guidelines for mobility instruction for, 199*t*
    guidelines for orientation and mobility for, 204–5*t*
    guidelines for orientation instruction for, 186*t*
    interventions in children with CCN and, 75–79
    literacy for those in, 39
    map use in, 192–93
    orientation instruction related to absence of visually guided reach in, 224
    orientation instruction related to attraction to light in, 219–21
    orientation instruction related to color preference in, 214
    orientation instruction related to difficulty with distance viewing in, 221
    orientation instruction related to difficulty with visual complexity in, 218
    orientation instruction related to difficulty with visual novelty in, 222
    orientation instruction related to movement in, 215–16
    orientation instruction related to visual field preferences in, 217
    orientation instruction related to visual latency in, 216
    sample script for teaching children with, 78*fig.*
    teaching concept development in, 188–89
    Vision Language Learning Communication Framework summary and suggestions for, 76–77*t*
Phase II Cortical Visual Impairment
    basic mobility techniques for, 198–200
    benefits of cane use in, 203
    characteristics of, 15
    cognitive mapping in, 196–97
    comparative thought in, 31
    detection of environmental hazards in, 201
    development of facial recognition in, 165
    guidelines for mobility instruction for, 199*t*
    guidelines for orientation and mobility for, 207–9*t*
    guidelines for orientation instruction for, 186*t*
    interventions in children with CCN and, 79–82
    map use in, 193
    orientation instruction related to absence of visually guided reach in, 224
    orientation instruction related to attraction to light in, 221
    orientation instruction related to color preference in, 214
    orientation instruction related to difficulty with distance viewing in, 221–22
    orientation instruction related to difficulty with visual complexity in, 218
    orientation instruction related to difficulty with visual novelty in, 222–23
    orientation instruction related to movement in, 216

orientation instruction related to visual field preferences in, 217
orientation instruction related to visual latency in, 216
sample script for teaching children with, 83*fig.*
teaching concept development in, 189–91
ventral stream vision in, 41
Vision Language Learning Communication Framework summary and suggestions for, 80–81*t*
Phase III Cortical Visual Impairment, 10–12
    basic mobility techniques for, 200
    benefits of cane use in, 203
    challenges of, 13, 22
    challenges to understanding individuals in, 11–12
    characteristics in, 14–25
    cognitive mapping in, 197–98
    detection of environmental hazards in, 201
    guidelines for mobility instruction for, 199*t*
    guidelines for orientation and mobility for, 209–11*t*
    guidelines for orientation instruction for, 186*t*
    interventions for, 25–36
    interventions in children with CCN and, 82–88
    map use in, 193–94
    orientation and mobility assessment in, 185
    orientation instruction related to absence of visually guided reach in, 224
    orientation instruction related to attraction to light in, 221
    orientation instruction related to color preference in, 214–15
    orientation instruction related to difficulty with distance viewing in, 222
    orientation instruction related to difficulty with visual complexity in, 218–19
    orientation instruction related to difficulty with visual novelty in, 223
    orientation instruction related to movement in, 216
    orientation instruction related to visual field preferences in, 217–18
    orientation instruction related to visual latency in, 216–17
    overview of, 12–16
    progressing to, 15–16
    sample script for teaching children with, 87*fig.*
    teaching concept development in, 191–92
    Vision Language Learning Communication Framework summary and suggestions for, 85–86*t*

Phases of CVI. *See also* Phase I Cortical Visual Impairment; Phase II Cortical Visual Impairment; Phase III Cortical Visual Impairment
    defined, 3
    integrating, in teaching mobility, 198–203
    integrating, in teaching orientation, 185–98
    learning modalities by, 40*fig.*
    and two-stream model of visual processing, 12–13
phonetic reading, 47, 49
Pierce, P. L., 40
play, 170–72
positional concepts, 189
power wheelchairs, orientation and mobility considerations for individuals in, 211–12
proprioception, 202
prosopagnosia, 166–67
proximal development, zone of, 173–74

reading. *See* literacy
Reiss, A. L., 167
resilience, 174–78
retinopathy of prematurity (ROP), 63
Rhodes, G., 164
Rizzolatti, G., 169
rubella, 63–64, 229

salient tactile features, in CVI Range assessment, 245, 246
salient visual features
    accessing and interpreting, 25–28
    and comparative thought, 32*fig.*
    and concept development, 187, 188, 189
    dictionary of, of numerals, 29*t*
    instruction in, 28, 46–47
    and literacy, 46–47
    and mediated learning, 36
Scaife, M., 27
schedule, balancing, 97–98
Schedule Recording Form, 98, 105, 117, 119*fig.*, 128–32*fig.*, 133, 137
self-advocacy, 176–78
self-image, 174–78
sensorineural hearing loss (SNHL), 238
sensory cues, in CVI Range assessment, 246–50
sensory input, complexity of, 100, 104, 115–16
shapes, and teaching concept development, 188–89
sight words, 47–53
silence, in 'What's the Complexity?' Framework, 122–23

Single Activity Recording Form, 98, 105, 116–17,
    118*fig.*, 135*fig.*
Skinner, B. F., 162
Skoczenski, A., 213
social learning, 162–64, 167–69
social skill development, 161–62, 178
    adults' role in, 173–78
    and distance viewing, 172–73
    and facial discrimination, 164–67
    guidelines for supporting increased social
        competence, 175*t*
    and imitation, 167–70
    and play, 170–72
    and social learning, 162–64
speech-language therapy, 68, 73
Steelman, J. D., 40
stressful situations, adjusting expectations
        during, 141
subitization, 190
symbols
    in augmentative and alternative communication
        (AAC) approaches, 69
    prerequisites for use of, 41–42

tactile cues and exploration, in CVI Range assessment,
        245–50
tactile signing, 245–46, 248
Tanaka, J. W., 164
tangibles, in 'What's the Complexity?' Framework, 123
targets
    complexity of, 101–4
    in orientation and mobility training, 204, 205*t*
Task Bank, 108, 109–13*fig.*, 124
task complexity. *See also* challenging tasks;
        comfortable tasks; frustrational tasks
    sample interventions for reducing, 121*t*
    during stressful situations, 141
    in 'What's the Complexity?' Framework, 100–5,
        106*t*, 107–15*fig.*, 116, 126–32, 136–40
Task Rating Guide, 98, 101, 102*fig.*, 105, 116, 126, 134*fig.*
teacher-directed CVI Range assessment, 250, 251–52
teachers of students with visual impairments, 4, 10,
        11–12. *See also* mediated learning; 'What's the
        Complexity?' Framework
temporal concepts, 192
trailing, 198, 199
two-dimensional image assessment, 143–44
    Category Summary Sheets, 156, 157–59*fig.*, 160
    and determining instruction and progress, 160

interpreting, 156–60
Response Record forms, 145, 146–55*fig.*, 156
using, 144–56
in 'What's the Complexity?' Framework, 108–15
two-stream model of visual processing, 12–13. *See
        also* dorsal stream vision; ventral stream vision

universal design for learning (UDL), principles of, 250

ventral stream vision
    defined, 3
    in Phase II CVI, 15
    in Phase III CVI, 12–13, 23
    as prerequisite for literacy, 41
Vision Language Learning Communication (VLLC)
        Framework, 60, 71–88
visual breaks, 101, 103, 108, 133
visual complexity. *See also* 'What's the Complexity?'
        Framework
    difficulty with, 61, 95–97
    and literacy, 49
    and mediated learning, 36
    and orientation and mobility training, 202, 205–6*t*,
        207–8*t*, 210*t*, 218–19
    in Phase III CVI, 20–21, 23–25
visual fields
    absent or atypical, as CVI characteristic, 61
    and literacy, 49
    and mediated learning, 36
    and orientation and mobility training, 202, 205*t*,
        207*t*, 209*t*, 217–18
    in Phase III CVI, 19
visual fixation, and literacy, 41
visual identification, 26, 44–46
visual latency
    as CVI characteristic, 61
    and literacy, 49
    and orientation and mobility training, 202, 205*t*,
        207*t*, 209*t*, 216–17
    in Phase III CVI, 18*fig.*, 19
    and social learning and imitation, 170*t*
    in 'What's the Complexity?' Framework, 104–5
visual learning media, 108
visually guided reach
    absence of, as CVI characteristic, 61
    and orientation and mobility training, 206*t*, 209*t*,
        211*t*, 224
visual-motor demands, in 'What's the Complexity?'
        Framework, 104–5

visual motor response
    and literacy, 49
    in Phase III CVI, 18*fig.*, 23
visual novelty
    difficulty with, as CVI characteristic, 61
    and literacy, 49
    and mediated learning, 36
    and orientation and mobility training, 203, 206*t*,
       208*t*, 211*t*, 222–23
    in Phase III CVI, 18*fig.*, 22–23
    and social learning and imitation, 170*t*
    in 'What's the Complexity?' Framework, 98–100,
       104–5
visual recognition, 26, 44–46, 190, 191
visual reflexes
    absent or atypical, as CVI characteristic, 61
    and orientation and mobility training, 206*t*, 208*t*,
       211*t*
    in Phase III CVI, 22

visual schemes, 26, 28, 31, 187
Vygotsky, L. S., 162, 173

'What's the Complexity?' Framework, 94,
      141–42
    additional considerations in, 138–41
    case study for, 94–95, 124–28
    goal of, 96
    introducing, 97–105
    observation stage of, 105, 115–23, 126–38
    preparation stage of, 105–15, 124
    sharing stage of, 105, 123–24, 138
    and taking vision for granted, 95–97
wheelchairs, orientation and mobility
      considerations for individuals in,
      211–12
words, introducing, 47–55

zone of proximal development, 173–74

CPSIA information can be obtained
at www.ICGtesting.com
Printed in the USA
BVHW090019110123
655954BV00006B/57